Following Father Chiniquy

Following Father Chiniquy

Immigration, Religious Schism, and Social Change in Nineteenth-Century Illinois

CAROLINE B. BRETTELL

Southern Illinois University Press • Carbondale

Printed in the United States of America

18 17 16 15 4 3 2 1

Publication of this book has been partially funded by a generous donation from Southern Methodist University.

Cover illustrations: *top*, Reverend Charles Chiniquy (cropped; *Fifty Years in the Church of Rome*, by Charles Chiniquy); *bottom*, French Canadian immigrants, St. Anne, Illinois, circa 1900 (author's collection)

Library of Congress Cataloging-in-Publication Data
Brettell, Caroline.
Following Father Chiniquy : immigration, religious schism, and social change in nineteenth-century Illinois / Caroline B. Brettell.
pages cm
Includes bibliographical references and index.
ISBN 978-0-8093-3416-2 (pbk. : alk. paper)
ISBN 0-8093-3416-X (pbk. : alk. paper)
ISBN 978-0-8093-3417-9 (ebook)
ISBN 0-8093-3417-8 (ebook)
1. Chiniquy, Charles Paschal Telesphore, 1809–1899. 2. Catholic ex-priests—Québec (Province)—Biography. 3. Catholic ex-priests—United States—Biography. 4. Protestant converts—Québec (Province)—Biography. 5. Presbyterian Church in Canada—Clergy—Biography. 6. Canadian Americans—Illinois—History—19th century. 7. Emigration and immigration—Social aspects—Illinois—History—19th century. I. Title.
BX9225.C43B74 2015
282.092—dc23
[B] 2014038828

The paper used in this publication meets the minimum requirements of American National Standard for Information Sciences—Permanence of Paper for Printed Library Materials, ANSI Z39.48-1992. ∞

To the memory of Jean-Henri Merle d'Aubigné,
Blanche Merle d'Aubigné Biéler,
Zoë Browne-Clayton Biéler,
and Jacques Louis Biéler

Contents

Illustrations

Preface

Research topics sometimes emerge in strange ways. Before launching this study of several French Canadian immigrant communities in rural Illinois, I had worked almost exclusively on the history and ethnography of Portugal and on Portuguese immigrant communities in Canada, France, and the United States. The Portuguese people with whom I came into contact repeatedly asked about my Portuguese ancestry—they found my interest in them somewhat curious. I could claim no personal attachment. My involvement with the current study, however, is quite the opposite.

Although I do not consider myself to be of French Canadian heritage, I was born and raised in Montreal. My grandfather, Professor Charles Biéler, brought my grandmother and their five sons from Paris to Canada in 1908 and took a position at the Presbyterian College, then affiliated with McGill University. One of his responsibilities was the teaching of young French Canadian Protestant theologians. In the letter of appointment, the principal of the college, John Scrimger, offered my grandfather a salary of $2,500 per annum,

> with a promise of increase from February 28th, 1909 on the understanding that you should give such service in connection with the French Mission work in Montreal and elsewhere during nine months of the year as may be agreed on without interfering with your college duties. This work cannot well be defined in detail at present and may vary from year to year, the object being to keep you in constant

touch with the evangelical work carried on by our church among French-speaking Roman Catholics for which the students under your charge are being trained.

The tasks assigned to my grandfather were quite appropriate, for both he and my grandmother were descended from French-speaking Protestant Swiss families. Indeed, my grandmother's father was Jean-Henri Merle d'Aubigné, one of the early historians of the Protestant Reformation.[1]

Before my grandparents arrived in Montreal, they received a friendly letter of welcome from Reverend Joseph Morin, a popular and prominent member of Montreal's French Canadian Protestant community. Morin, who greeted his new colleague in person on his arrival in Canada, was married to Rebecca Chiniquy, one of two daughters born to Reverend Charles Chiniquy. Chiniquy was an apostate priest who was responsible for one of the most dramatic and nationally renowned schisms of mid-nineteenth-century America. Although his name can still arouse a reaction in Quebec, he is little known in the United States or in the state of Illinois, where he made his home for just over forty years and where he instigated his schism.

My father, Jacques Louis Biéler, and his four older brothers grew up with the story of Charles Chiniquy. Indeed, on December 18, 1916, my uncle André Biéler, who was serving at the time in World War I, wrote in a letter to his mother that he had "met at the Ruban Bleu an old man who is a great admirer of father Chiniqui. He's an old rector who has a nephew in Montreal. He's sad at having given to someone his last treatise on Chiniqui, and he would like someone to send it to him. I gave him dad's address and I think he'll write to him about that." It is to my father that I owe the initial idea for this study. Earlier in my career, I took a teaching position at the University of Illinois at Urbana-Champaign for a semester. I lived in Chicago, and each week as I drove south on Interstate 57 to the university, I passed the exit to the town of Bourbonnais. A passing reference to this town in a letter home sparked something in my father's memory, and when I was in Montreal on a visit, he placed a book, *Fifty Years in the Church of Rome*, in my hands. This book is Chiniquy's autobiographical account of his years as a Catholic priest and of his eventual confrontation with and battle against Romanism. As I read through the book, the framework for a new research endeavor emerged. Later, with generous support from the Social and Humanities Research Council of Canada and the National Endowment for the Humanities and with a home provided to me at the Family and Community History Center at the Newberry Library, I launched the research for a project I titled "Father Chiniquy and the

French Canadian Settlements in Central Illinois." I am grateful for all these forms of support.

Though incidental to the study, the project involved a kind of coming home for a Canadian living in the United States as an immigrant, a Canadian whose father was himself an immigrant, and a Canadian whose paternal grandmother was descended from a union of two prominent Huguenot families, the Merles of Nîmes, France, and the Aubignés of Geneva, Switzerland. If more personally connected than any of my other research endeavors, before or since, this study of the brave and hardy French Canadians who moved to the Midwest of the United States in the 1840s and 1850s has not represented an unusual intellectual departure for someone whose interest in immigrant populations spans many years.

There is one more way in which the writing of this book represents a coming home. Research for the book brought me into contact with both professional and amateur genealogists, many descended from some of the original French Canadian settlers in Illinois. They attuned me to my own genealogy—not only to the kinship links but also to the "writing genes" I may have inherited. This book is dedicated to the authors in my family: to my great grandfather Jean-Henri Merle d'Aubigné, whose name popped out of a page as I was reading an 1862 issue of the *Presbyterian* as the author of a major history of the Protestant Reformation; to my grandmother Blanche Merle d'Aubigné Biéler, who left for her grandchildren, including the granddaughter she knew for only seven years, a written history of our Huguenot *Famille de Refuge* and for her five sons a treasured handwritten manuscript, *Nos Origines*; and to my mother, Zoë Browne-Clayton Biéler, who, as a professional journalist, taught me not only how to recognize a good story but also, I hope, how to tell it well. Finally, this book is offered in loving memory of my father, Jacques Louis Biéler, whose intellectual curiosity and eternal optimism were and remain a constant source of inspiration.

Acknowledgments

I am indebted to a number of institutions and individuals who have helped over the years in the production of this book. First, I thank the staff members of the following libraries and archives: the Montreal Public Library, the Archives of the Archbishopric of Montreal, the Archives of the Seminary of Quebec, the library of the Presbyterian Historical Society in Philadelphia, and the Illinois State Historical Library. I am grateful to the Iroquois County Genealogical Society, the Kankakee County Historical Museum, the Kankakee County Genealogical Society, the Kankakee Title and Trust Company, the Probate and Circuit Clerk Office of the Kankakee County Courthouse, the Watseka Historical Museum, and the McCormick Theological Seminary at the University of Chicago. Special thanks go to the editors of the *St. Anne Record* and the *Kankakee Daily Journal*. At the Newberry Library, where this project began, I was aided by the staff of the Family and Community History Center, particularly, John Jentz, Janice Reiff, Mary Lynn Dietsche, and Rima Schultz, as well as Paul Gehl. Among other people who were helpful along the way are Aidan McQuillan, Edward Kantowitz, Margaret Bedard, Norma Meier, Donald Deslauriers, Reverend John Stevens, Father John Lane, and Father Donald Lund. There are also numerous others (too many to name) in Kankakee, St. Anne, Beaverville, and L'Érable with whom I had informal conversations. I thank them all. I am extremely grateful to the National Endowment for the Humanities and the Social Science Research Council for supporting this research. I thank collectively my colleagues in the Social Science

History Association, who have, over the years, provided a home for an anthropologist interested in history. Finally, I thank Karl Kageff and other members of the editorial team at Southern Illinois University Press for helping to shepherd this project to fruition.

Following Father Chiniquy

Introduction

"Kankakee County has never conferred citizenship on so picturesque and notable a figure" is the claim made in the January 17, 1899, *Kankakee Daily Gazette* obituary of Charles Chiniquy, a Roman Catholic priest who became a Presbyterian minister. Although the life and legacy of this apostate priest may largely be forgotten today, except by a few extreme antipapist or anti-Catholic groups, at the time of the obituary the characterization of Chiniquy was no exaggeration. In the late 1850s and early 1860s, the eyes of the international Roman Catholic Church and of various Protestant denominations were turned on a few small settlements of French Canadian immigrants in northeast Illinois where Charles Chiniquy had instigated a religious schism. This schism and its impact upon the lives of a group of French Canadian immigrants who settled in Illinois in the early 1850s provide the focus for this book. The scope of the book, however, is broader than the local, regional, or historical. What happened amidst these people reflected larger national tensions and social processes, some of which are still evident in relation to twenty-first-century immigration to the United States. The central religious conflicts of the mid-nineteenth century, a period when nativism was pervasive and the anti-immigrant Know-Nothing Party was at its height, were played out on the prairies of Illinois among a group whose ethnic identity was rooted in Catholicism. The schism resulted in the fragmentation of what had been a culturally homogenous community. Thus, the current volume offers an opportunity to examine, in a microlevel context, a range of important historical and anthropological questions concerning immigration, ethnicity, and religion. Among these are differential processes of "assimilation" and social mobility, changes in household and family structure, the way in which social identities are constructed and reconstructed through time, the role of conflict and boundary making in social life, and the significance of charismatic leadership in processes of social and religious change.

A historical anthropologist and scholar of immigration, I have been trained to think comparatively, looking for both similarities and differences. Although attuned to the particularities of historical events and local ethnographic settings, I also look for commonalities and patterns in social processes. In an effective characterization of historical anthropology, J. D. Peel argues that it is an approach that deals with "a triangle of relations: first, those between ethnohistory (or history as representation) and the past or change-sequence that it represents; second, those between this past and the social forms of the present that are its outcome; and third, those between the present social forms . . . and the representations of the past, or ethnohistory, for whose production the present forms provide the context."[1] This triangle of relations is implicit in my approach to historical anthropology, an approach that explores the presence of the past as much as it explores the past itself and an approach that is rooted in social theory.[2] As anthropologist Lawrence Taylor writes in his own historical study of Dutch immigrants in Long Island, New York, "ethnographies are, at their best, dialogues between the hypotheses and assertions of social theory and the richly complex reality of particular human worlds."[3] It is in this sense that this book is located at the dialogical intersections between anthropology and history, drawing on the perspectives and literatures of both disciplines. This introduction lays out the theoretical framework that is critical to my analysis, beginning with a discussion of the French Canadian immigrant presence in the United States.

French Canadian Immigrants in the United States

When considered in the context of American immigration history more broadly, French Canadian immigrants in the United States are a comparatively understudied population. Yet, this is a population that freely crossed a permeable northern border in significant numbers during the nineteenth and early twentieth centuries, hence offering a parallel with the southern border crossings of more recent times. One historian comments that "of all the ethnic groups that emigrated to New England, the Franco-Americans are among the least known. People are unaware of their numbers as the sixth largest minority of European origin in the United States and 10 percent of American Catholics."[4]

Several important monographic studies were done of the French Canadians who settled in specific New England towns between 1840 and 1920, among them Tamara Hareven's study of the Amoskeag Company in Manchester, New Hampshire; Mark Paul Richard's study of Lewiston, Maine; and William Hartford's study of Holyoke, Massachusetts. Also, broader monographs focus on the New England region as a whole, as well as important collections of essays on the French Canadian experience in the United States.[5] Most recently, historians in Quebec have turned their attention to this topic.[6] And yet, despite this wealth of important scholarship, this migration flow has not been accorded the same attention as that given to the nineteenth- and early twentieth-century migrations of the Irish, Italians, or Jews. One explanation for this absence of attention in the broader literature of immigration, as well as in the public imagination, is the regional concentration of the bulk of French Canadians in New England and their settlement in small towns rather than in the big cities of Boston, New York, and Chicago.[7] Another is the deep historical presence of French-speaking peoples in North America that was associated with early colonization and the development of New France. The nineteenth- and early twentieth-century migrations were part of a much-longer tradition of francophone settlement within a North America that was in flux and in formation prior to the late eighteenth century.

Although less well understood than other ethnic groups in the United States, French Canadians have suffered from a particular characterization embodied in the phrase "the Chinese of the Eastern States." The appellation, used by Carroll D. Wright in an 1881 report to the US Bureau of Statistics of Labor, summed up a late nineteenth-century assessment of this immigrant population as having no interest in the civil and political institutions of the United States or in their educational system.

> They do not come to make a home among us, to dwell with us as citizens and so become a part of us; but their purpose is merely to sojourn a few years as aliens. . . . They are a horde of industrial invaders, not a stream of stable settlers. Voting, with all that it implies, they care nothing about. Rarely does one of them become naturalized. They will not send their children to school if they can help it.[8]

This description, which certainly should resonate with some readers in relation to attitudes about more recent immigrant populations (particularly those from Mexico), was much debated and later clarified and modified by Wright himself.[9] However, Franco-Americans lived for decades with the legacy of a stereotype that became more racist and nativist as it was rewritten by those who quoted Wright out of context. The strongest reaction emerged in response to an article by Robert Dexter in the *World's Work* in 1924 that refers to French Canadian immigrants as "Fifty-Fifty Americans." In the 1920s the Ku Klux Klan moved into the northeastern United States and made the Franco-American Catholics in the state of Maine an object of their derision. As historian Mark Paul Richard observes, "The French language, the Roman Catholic faith, and the formation of ethnic enclaves distinguished French-Canadian descendants in protestant Yankee New England and the Ku Klux Klan took notice."[10]

Several twentieth-century social historical and social scientific studies of the French Canadian immigrant population in the eastern United States, some of them grounded in solid empirical evidence and some not, seem to have carried forward a particular assessment of this ethnic group. The composite image that emerged has been of an inward-looking population dominated by priests, with little interest in education and better housing, with a low degree of both geographical and social mobility, with minimal expectations, an unwillingness to get involved in strikes and other union activities, with low rates of naturalization, and generally with resistance to assimilation.[11] All these attributes were supposedly inherently "French Canadian" and derived in part from early studies of French Canadians in Quebec that also emphasized the absence of any goal of social mobility as a central value in traditional French Canadian culture rather than a more appropriate approach that might emphasize a set of responses to particular social, economic, and political contexts.[12]

Another theme in the scholarship on French Canadians in the United States has been the emphasis on their temporary status. These were migrants whose long-range plans were to return to their country of origin. Dean R. Louder and Eric Waddell, for example, state, "Once in New England, and sometimes in the Midwest, the farmers attempt to recapture their losses in accumulating a small capital, with the aim of reinvesting it in a family farm in Quebec."[13] Hareven describes the back-and-forth movement between Quebec and Manchester, New Hampshire, that linked families in both places into a single social system, a form of what more contemporary scholars might label transnationalism. Historian Bruno Ramirez, focusing on 1900 to 1930, describes the "petits Canadas" (little Canadas) that were part of the "psychic maps of Quebeckers," familiar places to which individuals migrated and remigrated: "This practice of repeat migration did not merely respond to economic need; it also reflected familiarity with the southward path to be pursued."[14] Yves Roby and Yves Frenette use the phrase "birds of passage" to describe these migrants; Richard Sorrell, comparing the French Canadians of the late nineteenth and early twentieth century with Mexican and Puerto Rican migrants of more recent periods, refers to "commuting immigrants."[15] The comparison is apposite because this mobile population considered themselves to be of the American continent and not immigrants to America.[16] As Jean Lamarre observes, "since the beginning of the nineteenth century, many French Canadians had acquired the habit of crossing the border to take advantage of seasonal jobs in the agriculture and forestry sectors in northern New England."[17] Further to this point, it was only in 1930 that the restrictions on immigration that emerged in the 1920s to control the immigration of southern and eastern Europeans were ultimately applied to Canadians. As suggested above, these dimensions of French Canadian migration to the United States, perhaps, offer an important explanation for why their story often remains outside the mainstream story of immigration to America in the late nineteenth and early twentieth centuries.

To some extent, the notions of Fifty-Fifty Americans and of something supposedly inherent in French Canadian national character that resulted in their assessment as the least socially and economically ambitious of all foreign-born populations in the United States can be related to the emphasis that has been placed upon the cultural centrality of *survivance* in scholarship. Wright identifies its importance: "I am inclined to think that whatever prejudice there has been in the public mind against the French Canadians has arisen from the seeming disposition of the French to insist upon preserving a distinct national existence within the Republic."[18] In short, the explanation for the apparently slow social mobility of French Canadians in the eastern United States, by comparison with other immigrant groups, was found in the tenacity with which they held on to their own culture, a tenacity that was ideologically reinforced by the concept of *survivance*, the maintenance of French Canadian ethnic identity.[19] Leon Bouvier speculates that low educational and occupational achievement could, in part, be explained by the fear on the part of Franco-American parents that their children would lose their language, culture, and religion (and, hence, their identity) if they continued in non-French, nonparochial high schools.[20] William F. Hartford observes that in Holyoke, Massachusetts, more than half of the city's school-aged French Canadian youths attended parochial institutions in the 1890s; Richard LeBlanc points to the system of education as a powerful factor in delaying the process of "Americanization" among Franco-Americans, more generally speaking.[21]

Sociologically, the concept of survivance was first introduced by sociologist Mason Wade, although historically its roots are much deeper. Wade points to the parish as the focal point for the maintenance of French Canadian identity and the parish priest as the major guardian and spokesman. Survivance was pursued within the institutional framework of the Roman Catholic Church.[22] From their pulpits, priests thundered sermons about lost faith and lost identity. "Soyons Canadiens veut dire, avant tout, soyons catholiques" (To be Canadian is, above all, to be Catholic) is the phrase in the November 3, 1869, *L'Étendard National* of Worcester, Massachusetts.[23] Gérard Brault describes survivance as part of a nationalist ideology in Quebec. French Canadians were "duty bound to preserve their cultural identity" and expected to "fulfill a sacred mission, namely to preserve Catholicism in America."[24] One Catholic priest issued an explicit warning about what he called the process of "Americanization": "We are Catholics, we wish to live as Catholics, but we desire to be Catholics of the French language. Why, in fact anglicize ourselves, why become 'Yankees' when our French culture, so abundant and so varied, can contribute to the cultural enrichment of the United States?"[25] The French Canadian parish, in another writer's view, "offered to the Canadians the most favorable conditions within which to maintain for a long time their religion and their national language. They are truly at home. They live together, marry one another, become neighbors and property owners. They have their Church and their convent, what else do they need to form Canadian villages in the very heart of the United States?"[26] Roby points to a growing interest in the national parish after 1865 as the "sole institution capable of safeguarding the distinctive characteristics of the French-Canadian nation. . . . They became 'keystones' of survivance, conferring upon it an ostensible sacredness."[27]

For some time this survival strategy worked. In comparison with many other immigrant languages in the United States, use of the French language appears to have survived much longer, in some communities as late as the 1960s. This language persistence was achieved under the auspices of a range of institutions—schools, liberal arts colleges, newspapers, radio stations, and the Roman Catholic Church—and it was shaped by the long-term challenges of Irish Catholicism. By the 1980s, however, some New England Franco-American communities were expressing fear that their language and culture risked being lost forever. Scholars themselves were documenting the decline not only in language but also in the role of parochial schools, some dating it to the mid-twentieth century if not even somewhat earlier and in association with the decline of emigration from Quebec, the Depression, and World War II. Scholars were equally beginning to question the dichotomy that opposed, almost uncompromisingly, survivance and assimilation, emphasizing instead a negotiated identity that drew elements from both—more akin to acculturation than assimilation, perhaps.[28]

Do any of these descriptions of French Canadians in New England apply to those who settled in the Midwest? Did the process by which they became part of the American fabric happen at the same time or earlier? Did it look the same? Clearly, the context was fundamentally different. These immigrants to the Midwest encountered a frontier rather than a Yankee stronghold. They participated in the formation of a culture rather than a struggle against absorption by one that was already formed. Their populations were not constantly renewed as were those in New England. Lamarre notes that although some young men went to Michigan and Wisconsin prior to 1860 to take temporary employment in the logging industry, "the migratory movement to the West before the Civil War was of a permanent and familial nature, centered around the acquisition of land with the intention of maintaining an agricultural way of life."[29] This is a very important difference from the New England migrations. A second is that after the Civil War, these migrations to the American Midwest declined, not only, as Lamarre suggests, because it was no longer an agricultural frontier but also because agriculture in Quebec had itself recovered and new farming opportunities opened up in the Canadian west.

As with the New England migrations, the French Catholic clergy was extensively involved in the settlements in Michigan, Wisconsin, and Illinois. In these concentrated, rural communities, in areas where "society was still in the process of formation," there would be, they thought, an even greater opportunity to preserve religion, language, and nationality than in the cities and factory towns of New England.[30] Lamarre reinforces this point, observing that on the Michigan frontier "the migrants enjoyed considerable latitude or autonomy—their young communities could develop in continuity with their traditional values, without being obliged to integrate into a dominant culture. This situation contributed to the maintenance of their French-speaking, Catholic cultural identity, allowing the French Canadians to put off until later the task of defining themselves in terms of their new social and cultural environment."[31]

But, what about the settlements in northeast Illinois that are the subject of this book? There the power of the Catholic Church was eroded from within soon after the arrival of the first generation of immigrants. What did this mean for their migration experience and for the way in which they formed their communities on the frontier? What did the schism mean for the relationships that they drew between a religious identity and an ethnic identity? How important was religion to preserving an ancestral heritage, as has been argued for the New England Franco-American communities?[32]

Ethnicity, Religion, and Immigrant Identity

In 1974 a six-point definition of "ethnic group" emerged from a conference the Social Science Research Council sponsored. Ethnic groups are social categories "with a past-oriented group identification emphasizing origins; with some conception of cultural and social distinctiveness; which are component units in a broader system of social relations; which are larger than kin or locality groups and transcend face-to-face interaction; which have different meanings both in different social settings and for different individuals; and which are emblematic, having names with meaning for members and analysts."[33] In his discussion of these characteristics of the ethnic group, Harold J. Abramson puzzles quite directly about the question of whether ethnicity inevitably includes a religious dimension. And, conversely, "does the meaning of religion theoretically entail a distinctive ethnic quality?"[34] He further ponders the close relationship between migration and the reformulation (or formulation) of both religious and ethnic boundaries. The schism among the French Canadians in Illinois epitomizes the process of reevaluation of both national and religious commitment that sometimes occurs within migrant populations.

In the disciplines of both anthropology and history, ethnicity emerged in the 1970s and 1980s as an important analytic concept, representing "a shift toward new theoretical and empirical concerns."[35] It has permitted scholars to explore how social groups are formed and changed, how they cohere, where and when they come apart, and the nature of the relationship between individual and collective identities. Studies of ethnicity focus not only on social interaction but also on the symbol systems that are in operation to give meaning to interaction. Ethnicity is, at times, an independent variable that explains phenomena like social mobility, occupational achievement, or political behavior. At other times it is a dependent variable, explained by settlement patterns, shared group experience, or family background.

Several scholars have distinguished theoretically between the "old" or "primordial" ethnicity and the "new" or "optional" ethnicity.[36] The former conceptualization accepts the notion of a culturally homogenous social group and argues that ethnic identity is the result of deep-rooted attachments to group and culture. Ethnicity is a given. If there is change, it is described in relation to the processes of acculturation and assimilation. However, one author suggests, this approach fails to "account for the re-emergence of ethnic consciousness among 'assimilated' groups."[37]

The new or optional ethnicity is more flexible. Those who adopt this approach draw attention to the malleable boundaries of an ethnic group and to "nesting hierarchies of we/they dichotomization. . . . The process of assigning persons to groups is both subjective and objective, carried out by self and other, and depends on what diacritics are used to define membership."[38] In other words, some concept of otherness is important to the "delineation, maintenance, and transformation" of ethnic boundaries. "The content of any group's definition of 'self' is thus determined both structurally in relation to 'other' and culturally in relation to the situation."[39] Research is often directed not to final outcomes but to the changing situations in which groups or individuals find themselves and to which they must adapt. Social historians have used the situational approach to document "the many faces of ethnicity at different places in the country, the variety of circumstances encountered by the groups, and the changes that affected their destiny."[40] They have argued that "ethnicity evolves from a complex dialectic that exists between an immigrant group and the host society but also among the immigrants themselves and among members of the host society."[41] Ethnicity, in short, has a "contingent historical nature."[42] Of particular interest in both historical and anthropological research are situations of social and political confrontations that are "marked" by ethnic negotiation, leading anthropologist Joan Vincent to argue that ethnicity is ultimately an aspect of conflict theory. Sociologist Sandra Wallman concurs: "Differences between groups of people turn into ethnic boundaries only when heated into significance by the identity investments of the other side."[43]

In a comprehensive review of the concept of ethnicity, anthropologist Marcus Banks divides the "new" ethnicity into two approaches: the instrumentalist approach that focuses on ethnicity as a political strategy pursued for pragmatic interests; and the situational approach, emerging from the theoretical work of Fredrik Barth, which emphasizes the fluidity and contingency of ethnic identity that is constructed in specific historical and social contexts.[44] It is important to emphasize, however, that these approaches are not mutually exclusive and that both are analytically useful.

The situational understanding of ethnicity is closely linked to research on the social construction of identity that argues that identity is dynamic, processual, multilayered, and contextual and is formed in interaction. As Zdzislaw Mach argues, "we always define ourselves in relation to others, and the aspects of our identity which are stressed in a given situation depend on these others and their identity."[45] Mach goes on to observe that perceived differences are sharpened in situations of conflict. Anthony Cohen's work on symbolizing boundaries follows a similar line of argument. Drawing on the idea of the segmentary nature of social life, first formulated by anthropologists in their study of African kinship systems, as well as anthropologist James Boon's observation that in all cultures and in all identities, there is a view across the boundary, an inevitable playing of the vis-à-vis. Cohen suggests that people delineate "those boundaries of their social lives which demarcate more powerfully and meaningfully their sense of similarity to and difference from other people."[46] Of course, the paradox here is the tension, apparent in current anthropological theorizing, between ideas of transnationalism, globalization, and unbounded cultures, on the one hand, and reemergent nationalism, ethnicity, and the cultural construction of difference and community, on the other.

Putting aside this paradox for the moment, it is certainly apparent that the approach to ethnicity and identity that argues for fluidity, contextualization, and the view across the boundary (often in situations of conflict) offers a viable alternative to the more typological and categorical approach to the immigrant experience that is implied in concepts such as assimilation, acculturation, or incorporation. It allows us to avoid comparing homogeneity (acculturation/assimilation) with heterogeneity (pluralism) and frees us from the assumption of a single "outgroup" or host society. It is not predicated, as the assimilation model is, on the notion of a final end when people are no longer what they were but incorporated into something else. Finally, the notion that individuals and/or groups have multiple identities that are never fully abandoned (although they may be reinvented) and that are made more or less salient depending on the context or situation can be easily encompassed by this alternative approach. This approach also offers a resolution to Abramson's conundrum about the relationship between religion and ethnicity. Finally, the fluid and boundary-making approach to ethnicity allows us to conceive of people who can consider themselves part of "the other" at one point in time and distinct from it at another point in time. Clearly, the definition of "the other" is itself subject to variation.

Andreas Wimmer observes that Barth's work has directed some of the most recent work on the boundary-making dimensions of ethnicity to focus not on "'the culture' of ethnic group A or B, but rather how the ethnic boundary between A and B was inscribed onto a landscape of continuous cultural transitions."[47] In his own formulation, Wimmer argues that ethnic boundaries are "the result of classificatory struggles and negotiations between actors situated in a social field.... Ethnicity is not primarily conceived as a matter of *relations* between pre-defined fixed groups ... but rather is a process of *constituting* and *re-configuring* groups by defining the boundaries between them."[48] As part of his critique of how ethnicity has been conceptualized in immigration studies, Wimmer suggests several new approaches that involve different units of analysis than the ethnic group. One, he proposes, might build on the "social drama tradition in anthropology" because this approach illustrates "how various principles of classification . . . come into play and are negotiated between actors who pursue a variety of classificatory strategies."[49] In this book I place the social drama at the center of my theoretical framework as a way to engage the fluid, processual, and boundary-making dimensions of religious, ethnic, and other identities.

Social Dramas and Charismatic Leaders

Anthropologist Victor Turner first outlined his concept of social drama both as a unit of time and a unit of analysis in his study of village structure among the Ndembu of central Africa. "The social drama," he relates, "is a limited area of transparency on the otherwise opaque surface of regular, uneventful social life. Through it we are enabled to observe the crucial principles of the social structure in their operation, and their relative dominance at successive points in time."[50] In a number of subsequent writings spanning his career, Turner sharpened and developed the concept as part of what Graham St. John labels his "political anthropology of processualism."[51] Social dramas are situations of intensely lived conflict that emerge within social groups and "activate classificatory oppositions."[52] They involve a public breach of the normal workings of a society, often including a challenge to the extant power structure.

By assembling a large body of comparative research data, Turner determined that social dramas develop along patterned lines and can be broken down into a series of recognized phases. He outlines four: (1) the initial breach of norm-governed social relations when the conflict is made public, (2) the mounting crisis when the breach widens and begins to threaten the peace and harmony of a community, (3) redressive action when attempts are made to achieve formal or informal resolution, and (4) either reintegration, permanent schism, or the emergence of a new crisis. These phases, in Turner's view, constitute the universal processual form (or the narrative structure) of the social drama as an event in which different paradigms come into conflict with one another. Social dramas occur within groups of persons who share values and interests and who have a real or alleged common history. Their main actors are "persons for whom the group which constitutes the field of dramatic action has a high value priority."[53] As the drama is played out, these values and interests are more clearly articulated.

Despite the criticism that has been levied against some aspects of Turner's social drama approach,[54] it remains a useful and compelling analytical framework with which to approach and make sense of the events involving both religion and politics that unfolded in the French Canadian settlements in Illinois. Reverend Charles Chiniquy and a significant number of the immigrants became schismatic. The narrative form of this schism broadly follows what Turner outlines, and a close reading of this form reveals the shifting lines of division between groups striving for power in the context of changing historical circumstances. More generally, in my view, Turner's approach to the understanding of social life, developed over the course of his career, remains intriguing because it encompasses two different models of human interaction that theorists have wrestled with for some time—one rooted in structure, difference, and conflict and the other in antistructure, consensus, and community. These models need not be mutually exclusive, nor do they necessarily imply stasis and preclude change.[55]

Turner's approach has been described as structural processualism, and yet, he argues, particularly in his earliest work, *Schism and Continuity in an African Society*, that social dramas, as moments of conflict, also illuminate tensions within individuals who are equally motivated by egoism and altruism. Chiniquy probably suffered from or thrived on both, and his critics and followers responded differently. But of importance theoretically is consideration of the role of the charismatic leader (and there is no doubt that Chiniquy had charisma) in an event of dramatic social change such as the mid-nineteenth-century schism in Illinois that resulted in so many French Canadians abandoning Roman Catholicism and becoming Protestants.

It is almost an understatement to observe that the literature on charisma and charismatic leadership is by now vast and that the analytical utility of the concepts is hotly debated.[56] The place to begin any discussion of charisma is, of course, with Max Weber, who, as anthropologist Thomas J. Csordas has noted, moved charisma from the realm of theology to that of sociology.[57] Weber argues that charisma should be

> applied to a certain quality of an individual personality by virtue of which he is set apart from ordinary men and treated as endowed with supernatural, superhuman, or at least specifically exceptional powers or qualities. These as such are not accessible to the ordinary person, but are regarded as of divine origin or as exemplary, and on the basis of them the individual concerned is treated as a leader. . . . How the quality in question would be ultimately judged from any ethical, aesthetic, or other such point of view is naturally entirely indifferent for purposes of definition. What is alone important is how the individual is actually regarded by those subject to charismatic authority, by his "followers" or "disciples."[58]

Weber distinguishes among magical charisma, prophetic charisma, and routinized charisma, but he suggests that there is an interplay among these both in and through time.[59] Magical charisma, in his view, is not necessarily connected to leadership or a special vision or mission. Rather, it is limited to the extraordinary personal qualities that some individuals possess. An individual with prophetic charisma, by contrast, has a mission or view of the world, and followers are attached to him because of this vision. Prophetic charisma is the form that has attracted the attention of a majority of scholars. For example, Roy Wallis has suggested that charismatic leaders or those possessed of charisma are "not constrained by the normal conventions of traditional consideration; they seem to draw upon supra-mundane resources in their performance and they convey, by way of divine mandate or enlightenment, a mission to transform the way in which we live. Those possessed of charisma command our allegiance by virtue of that mission and the supra-mundane power or knowledge for which they provide the channel, or of which they are the source."[60]

Weber contrasts the prophet with the priest. The priest can equally have charisma, but it is a function of the social institution of which he is a part. This is routinized charisma and is to be contrasted with the revolutionary charisma of the prophet. The prophet sets himself up in conscious opposition to an established aspect of society and leads with a charismatic authority that conflicts with the legitimate order. Some scholars have refined this distinction to suggest, for example, that a charismatic leader who occupies an institutional office (Weber's priest) may attempt to bring about change by "radicalization from within rather than challenge from without."[61] Weber's view was that the origins of most charismatic movements are in the opposition to or confrontation with existing authorities and that as the movement develops, charismatic leadership frequently changes into authority. He further suggests that over time charismatic authority may become routinized and transformed into legitimate authority. Generally, this occurs when the problem of succession arises or when followers desire permanence and stability. Weber, who actually thought that charismatic authority was short-lived, states that the transformation into a permanent routine structure requires the adaptation of some form of fiscal organization that provides for the needs of the group.

Embedded in the development of Weber's theory, particularly as it relates to personal qualities, is the idea that charisma is validated by the individual's ability to perform exceptional deeds and by the sense of duty of those who follow him and who legitimate his leadership. The charismatic leader, who frequently asks people to join him in a movement for change, must keep working to show people that he continues to have the authority that warrants their support.[62] Thus, it is in times of physical, economic, religious, political, or psychic distress that charismatic leaders are likely to emerge. Robert Tucker has pursued this particular aspect of Weber's discussion: "The key to the charismatic response of the followers to the leader lies in the distress that the followers experience." The charismatic leader is one who "can lead them out of their predicament." Tucker adds that this distress can take varying forms ranging from "the physical and material distress caused by persecution, catastrophes (famine, drought), and extreme economic hardship to such diverse forms of psychic or emotional distress as the feelings of oppression in peoples ruled by foreigners."[63]

Therefore, what is perhaps most crucial in Weber's formulation (although he has been criticized for not emphasizing it enough)[64] is that charisma, rather than being inherent to the individual, is a social relationship constructed in the interaction between leaders and followers. Followers recognize the status and identity of the individual as an inspiring leader. This is the element noted by several scholars of charismatic leadership who find charisma to be a powerful analytical tool in the study of religious and other social movements.[65] For example, Dorothy Willner and Ann Willner define charisma as a leader's capacity to elicit from a following deference, devotion, and awe toward himself as a source of authority. They focus in particular on the strategies, including the use of simile and metaphor in rhetorical speech and the allusions to myth and history, that are used to stimulate this devotion and suggest that whatever the teachings, they must relate to the ultimate concerns of the group.[66] This is precisely the emphasis Csordas pursues in his development of a rhetorical theory that locates charisma in language and performance. Arthur Schweitzer argues that the validity of charisma requires that the self-confidence of the leader and the devotion of the followers interact and reinforce each other. This devotion to followers and the group identities that it generates is central to the arguments of several authors in Jan Willem Stutje's recent edited collection on charismatic leaders past and present.[67] As Stutje observes, "conceptualizing charisma as a relation rather than as a thing helps to overcome some of the difficulties that have plagued the concept of charisma."[68]

Devotion of followers is reinforced by the performance of extraordinary deeds. One author outlines a tripartite approach. The unit of analysis is partly the leader and his personal attributes, partly the followers and their structural position in society, and partly the connection between leader and follower.[69] Similarly, Wallis suggests that although an understanding of "the motivation and drives of the leader require insight into his biography and psychology, the generation and maintenance of a charismatic relationship is crucially a social phenomenon" that emerges in particular situations.[70] Both Benedict Anderson and Hans J. Mol focus on this latter point. Anderson claims that it is necessary to "locate charisma firmly in the perceptions of particular, historically and geographically bounded followings," while Mol observes that charismatic leadership always includes a careful "perception of the times and an identification of the stresses and strains of the nation, group, or community."[71] Mol goes on to suggest that conversion could be expected on the frontier among people searching for new meaning and new identities; charismatic leaders, as catalysts, helped them to find these in a context of rapid change. The connection between charisma and conversion is clearly significant to the case under analysis here.

Those who find the concept of charisma problematic are uncomfortable for diverse reasons. For some, it is ambiguous, imprecise, and has been co-opted too much by popular interests to retain scientific validity. These critics recommend restricting consideration to religious charisma or focusing specifically on the contexts within which it arises. For example, although Bryan R. Wilson does see a historical reality of belief in charismatic leaders who "abrogate and transcend convention, who create discord," and who have an ability to convince others to follow, he rejects applying the term loosely to those who are "are simply colorful or exuberant personalities."[72] Don Handelman is equally concerned about matters of precision and about treating charisma as more than a residual category: "Left over and tossed into the grab bag of the charismatic is the very elemental impact that an individual can have on social order, an impact whose power is not easily traceable to the centrality or centripetality of existing arrangements and order."[73]

For other critics, the concept of charisma lacks explanatory power altogether. Peter Worsley has suggested that rather than being an explanation of behavior, charisma "is a datum, itself an element in sociological analysis—something that (some) people believe." Writing about Melanesian cargo cults, Worsley quite bluntly states that his own perspective derives from Karl Marx "with whose ghost . . . Weber was engaged in a lifelong debate."[74] Clearly, those writing from a Marxist perspective underplay the role and agency of the individual in the march of history and reject, as Worsley has, the subjectivist emphasis on the meanings of actions to the actors themselves. Explanations of social movements, in Worsley's view, must focus on the message—the rights and interests of exploited classes, rather than on the man or the loyalty of the followers to the man.

I disagree with Worsley, or at least I reject the idea that this is an either/or question. I am guided to some extent in my view by the emphasis on bridging structure-oriented and actor-oriented or agentic approaches in social analysis.[75] Sherry Ortner, for example, uses agency to suggest that people can bring about change by exerting power to produce effect. They do so through their "subjective sense of authorization, control, effectiveness in the world," their ability to deal with powerful others.[76] In the case discussed here, the individual agency of a single charismatic leader was vitally important to the story that unfolded, and his actions resonate to this day, including the way that contemporary residents of St. Anne, Illinois, the community at the center of the schism, think about their past.

Following Father Chiniquy

This book, about a religious schism that occurred on the midwestern frontier of the United States in the middle of the nineteenth century, is an anthropological history and, hence, a partial history. Although it tells the story of a particular immigration, it is not a purely chronological monograph. Rather, this case offers the opportunity to explore (think through, think with, and think about) a range of theoretical questions regarding processes of conflict, identity formation, charismatic leadership, religion, the relationship between structure and agency, and the meaning of the past in the present. The book is divided into two parts that evoke different meanings of the phrase "following Father Chiniquy." In the three chapters of part 1, I explore the Chiniquy-led migration to Illinois. Chapter 1 not only sets this migration into the broader context of mid-nineteenth-century French Canadian emigration but also introduces Charles Chiniquy and how he came to lead a migration to Illinois. Chapter 2 takes up the events that ensued after Chiniquy arrived with approximately one thousand families in St. Anne, Illinois. Many of those families followed Chiniquy into religious schism. This chapter draws on the concept of social drama to frame an in-depth analysis of this schism, exploring its processual phases and comparing it to similar events among other immigrants in the American Midwest and, occasionally, elsewhere. It traces the shifting boundaries of identity that were at play in each phase of the schism. Chapter 3 addresses the question of Charles Chiniquy as a charismatic leader. This discussion includes an examination of the autobiographical texts that Chiniquy left behind.

The book takes a different turn in the chapters in part 2. Here the focus is on what followed in the aftermath of schism. Chapter 4 draws on individual-level data from manuscript censuses and other historical sources, as well as the perspectives of family history and historical demography, to explore changes in the community and its population across two generations. The differences that emerged between those members of the French Canadian immigrant population in Illinois who converted to Protestantism and those who remained Catholic are the main subject of this chapter. This chapter also illustrates how processes such as chain, kinship-based, and step migration that are characteristic of population movements in the late twentieth and early twenty-first centuries were equally important in the migration flows in the past. Chapter 5 makes the question of conflict central (in the form of legal disputes), exploring how lines of social differentiation shifted over time. This is equally true of the final chapter in part 2, an analysis of the reemergence of Catholicism in St. Anne, the main town of the French Canadian settlement in northeast Illinois, in relation to the establishment of annual pilgrimage and a series of healing miracles that occurred in the community during the first decade of the twentieth century. This chapter is framed by theories of pilgrimage that have emerged in the anthropological literature as well as by an emphasis on how social relations are enacted in the context of rituals. The conclusion of the book returns to some of the significant empirical and theoretical dimensions of this research, to the question of how distinctive the experience of these French Canadians who settled in Illinois was from those who settled in other regions of the United States, and to some of the enduring legacies of Father Chiniquy and of the schism that he instigated on the Illinois prairie more than 150 years ago.

PART I

"How Could a Man with a Face Like That . . . ?"

CHAPTER 1

From Curé to Colonist: Charles Chiniquy and the French Canadian Emigration to Illinois

Hanging on a wall in the National Gallery of Art in Ottawa, Canada, is Benjamin West's 1771 painting *The Death of General Wolfe.* James Wolfe lies limply at the center of the picture, tended to by three of his military colleagues. At his feet an Indian kneels in a pose that reminds the viewer of Rodin's *The Thinker.* This painting commemorates a famous battle in Canadian history known as the Battle of Quebec. Fought in 1759 on the Plains of Abraham just outside the citadel of Quebec City, it resulted in the defeat of the French army under the command of Louis-Joseph, Marquis de Montcalm by the British forces led by General Wolfe. However, at the height of the conflict, Wolfe was killed.

This battle marked a turning point in the history of Quebec, or New France. Four years later the Treaty of Paris was signed, and New France was passed from French to British control and renamed Canada. Although the Quebec Act of 1774 restored some of the civil laws established under French rule and gave the French-speaking majority greater freedom to practice their religion, the tensions between the two populations were never fully resolved, and in 1791 the British colony of Canada was divided into Lower Canada (or Quebec) and Upper Canada (which came to be known as Ontario). Each region had a legislative council and a legislative assembly. Some harmony was restored, but by the 1820s dissatisfaction was growing about British colonial rule among the French Canadian majority. In 1826 the nationalist Parti Patriote was formed out of the old Parti Canadien and led by Louis-Joseph Papineau. The patriots demanded more control over how revenues were spent in Lower Canada and also sought greater political control over the civil service. The British minority resisted French Canadian demands to centralize power in the popularly elected legislative assembly. By the early 1830s there were electoral riots, and the conflict escalated. A full-scale nationalist insurrection that came to a head in 1837 with a boycott of all British imports to Lower Canada was eventually contained, and several patriots, including Papineau, sought refuge in Vermont.[1]

Beneath the political tensions of this period was a festering economic crisis. Several bad harvest years in the late 1820s initiated a decade of economic misery, if not near-starvation, among the people of the countryside. In addition to inclement weather, crops were plagued by pests.[2] Among those hardest hit were the French-speaking *habitants* of the densely settled Richelieu and Yamaska River valleys, who found themselves unable to pay rents and in jeopardy of losing their farms.[3] Compounding these natural disasters were outmoded agricultural methods that only enhanced soil exhaustion and reduced outputs. The lumber industry, which had partially offset some of the agricultural problems of the late 1820s and 1830s, collapsed by the latter 1840s, a collapse rampant forest fires aggravated in 1845.

These economic crises coincided with a period of significant population increase (by 254 percent between 1784 and 1831) in the province of Quebec. The amount of settled land area, which increased by only 138 percent during this same period, was insufficient to match this population growth, creating a significant number of unpropertied households by 1831.[4] Between 1831 and 1844, the imbalance between population and available land was further aggravated as the marriage rate increased and the birth rate remained high, averaging about 55.0 per 1,000 population between 1821 and 1850.[5]

Thus, in a province where 84 percent of the population was still rural in 1851, the acres of available land were decreasing while the numbers of persons who needed new land to farm were increasing. In some areas along the St. Lawrence River, and particularly in counties near Montreal and Quebec City, farm holdings under eight-and-a-half acres accounted for more than 25 percent of holdings in 1851.[6] Greer observes, "Given the limited supply of land and the requirements of the grain trade, the reproduction and multiplication of farm households could not keep pace with burgeoning population and the result was long-distance emigration and the growth of a landless proletariat."[7] French Canadian emigration to the United States needs to be understood in relation to the demographic and economic hardships of the 1830s and 1840s and to a lesser extent the political unrest of the same period.[8]

The beginning of the nineteenth-century population flow southward from Canada (English- and French-speaking) dates back to the 1820s, but the great surge started during the 1850s and continued through the 1880s. Although there was a sharp decline during the 1890s, migration from Canada picked up again during the early decades of the twentieth century (table 1.1).[9] Between 1840 and 1900, the estimate of net migration of French Canadians to the New England area is approximately 350,000.[10] According to the 1900 census, 810,105 individuals of French Canadian parentage were in the United States, 63 percent of whom lived in New England. Eighty years later it was estimated that five million Americans in the United States were descended from individuals born in Quebec, half of them in New England and one million in the Great Lakes area.[11]

The late nineteenth and early twentieth centuries were the periods of greatest outmigration in numerical terms, but as early as the late 1830s, emigration became a subject of discussion in the Quebec press. In the May 26, 1836, issue of *La Minerve*, the daily departures for Michigan and other parts of the United States were noted: "Not only does emigration from abroad pass across our shores, but the native-born themselves are starting to emigrate from a country which scarcely numbers 500,000 souls, and which still has more than half of its lands uncultivated."[12]

By the late 1840s, the government of Quebec demonstrated its concern with the problem by supporting an investigation under the auspices of the legislative assembly of the province. The motives of the government were clearly ethnopolitical—*survivance* (cultural survival) was a factor in the openly expressed fear that

TABLE 1.1. Canadian immigration to the United States, 1820–1929

Decades	*No. of Immigrants*
1820–29	3,697
1830–39	11,875
1840–49	34,285
1850–59	64,171
1860–69	117,978
1870–79	324,310
1880–89	492,865
1890–99	3,098
1900–1909	123,067
1910–19	708,715
1920–29	945,846

Source: *Historical Statistics of the United States*, Washington, DC: United States Census Bureau, 1949

emigration was detrimental to the continued viability of French Canadians as a people.[13] Critics suggested that emigration was a plot on the part of the British. If the French went south, they argued, the province could be populated with Irish and the colonial status maintained.

In the course of carrying out the investigative charge, the legislative assembly asked local priests in thirteen parishes of the Quebec diocese to respond to a number of survey questions. Among those responding was an individual named Charles Chiniquy, who, at the time of the report, was serving as a *curé* [parish priest]. Chiniquy suggested that as many as seventy thousand French Canadians had departed for the United States in the latter 1840s. While this figure is an early indication of his penchant to exaggerate (the report officially filed a conservative estimate of twenty thousand departures between 1844 and 1848), in his response to the inquiry, Chiniquy clearly established himself as a spokesman for little people, lashing out against *seigneurs* [landowners] who refused to lease out their land at reasonable rates and lamenting the deplorable economic and moral conditions of his countrymen in the United States. To stem the tide of emigration, he argued for the distribution of more crown land to the people and the opening up of lines of communication.

Chiniquy's assessment appeared to corroborate the general conclusion of the legislative committee—that emigration to the United States was a public calamity to be averted at all costs. But to avert it, the causes had to be spelled out more rigorously, and so they were in the 1849 report and in the various provincial newspapers that printed its findings in part or in full. In delineating causes, several segments of the provincial population that were forced to leave their homeland were specified.

1. Workers in Montreal and Quebec City who depart because of the precarious state of commerce and industry, high unemployment, and the more lucrative wages that could be earned in the United States.
2. Workers in the countryside who also lack employment because farmers were increasingly laboring all the land themselves.
3. Workers previously employed as day laborers or raftsmen on the Ottawa River who have been forced to leave because of the depression in the timber industry between 1846 and 1849.
4. The sons of good agricultural families who are unable to find land of their own to cultivate because of the constraints of the seigniorial system. They are heavily influenced by the example of previous migrants.

5. Poor agricultural families who are driven off the land by debts, bad harvests, soil exhaustion, poor agricultural techniques, high rents, and insufficient marketing facilities.
6. Settlers in the new townships who become discouraged by the lack or poor condition of roads and their inability to meet land payments.[14]
7. Peasants of leisure who depart for the same reason as those from the poor families but also because of a general malaise and the visible success of previous migrants.
8. Educated youths who find no careers because of overcrowding, lack of opportunities, and discrimination.[15]

In short, among those who left were young men who were unable to buy, rent, or inherit land for themselves; older farmers who, burdened by debt, were impelled to sell what they had; those who saw less and less appeal in the precarious agricultural way of life; and the artisans who could no longer afford to extend credit to their already heavily indebted farming clientele. Emigration touched the broadest range of the Quebec French-speaking population.

Several of the factors that caused varying categories of individuals to leave Canada for the United States were to continue to stimulate emigration southward for the rest of the nineteenth century and into the twentieth. In the context of American immigration history, it is the migration to the factory towns of New England that is best known, and it is clearly there that the bulk of French Canadian emigrants went. The mid-nineteenth-century migration to Illinois was smaller in numbers and more limited in its duration although it clearly built upon a deeper historical presence dating back to the establishment of seventeenth- and early eighteenth-century settlements, such as Fort St. Louis (1682), Cahokia (1699), and Kaskaskia (1703), as well as the formation of le Pays des Illinois (the Illinois country) or Haute-Louisiane (Upper Louisiana) in 1717 as an administrative and political subdivision of La Nouvelle France, or New France.[16] Despite the smaller numbers of people who went to Illinois, it was this migration that, in the newspapers of the period, preoccupied both officials and clerics in Quebec, probably because of Chiniquy's involvement with it.

Charles Chiniquy's Early History

Charles Telesphore Chiniquy, the eldest of three sons of the notary public Charles Chiniquy and his wife, Marie-Reine Perrault (or Perreault), was born in Kamouraska,

Quebec, in 1809.[17] He was orphaned at twelve, but with the aid of an uncle, Amable Dionne (married to Chiniquy's mother's sister), he was sent to the Nicolet Seminary for his education. When evidence of "immoral behavior" was brought to light (Chiniquy was supposed to have "tempted the virtue" of one of Dionne's daughters), Dionne withdrew his support and refused to have anything more to do with his errant nephew.[18] However, Chiniquy had found advocates within the walls of the seminary and was able to continue with his religious apprenticeship.

In 1833 he was ordained and for the next several years served as curé in various small communities in the province of Quebec before being named as curé of Beauport in 1838 and of Kamouraska in 1842. During the 1840s, Chiniquy became interested in the problem of alcoholism. This interest developed during his years as the chaplain of the Marine Hospital in Quebec City. Though the story may be exaggerated, Chiniquy writes graphically in his autobiography of the autopsy of a drunkard that he had witnessed—a blatant demonstration to him of the pernicious physiological effects of alcohol. His tenure in Beauport, "the very nest of drunkards in Canada," was equally influential.[19] As a result of these experiences, he became a vocal and enthusiastic advocate of total abstinence and during the next several years roamed the province preaching the virtues of temperance. In 1840 he founded a temperance society and quickly, so he claimed, converted more than thirteen hundred of his Beauport parishioners.

His overzealous approach to the problem was not fully endorsed by the Bishop of Quebec, who, according to Chiniquy, once commented that teetotalism was a Protestant affair. The consistently cautious approach to Chiniquy's activities adopted by church authorities is substantiated in the correspondence of Bishop Bourget of Montreal. In one letter to Chiniquy dated October 26, 1848, Bourget suggests that all drinks are not poisonous—"after all, then we could not say mass."[20] At the close of this letter, Bourget demonstrates a clear understanding of certain aspects of Chiniquy's character and warns him to "distrust pride which is so subtle and so dangerous." Chiniquy's ability to enthrall, almost hypnotize, his audience was quite apparent. He was clearly a captivating speaker and was enormously admired. But he was probably also ambitious and egotistical, and the Bishop of Montreal recognized that he needed to be reined in.

In 1844, Chiniquy published his *Manuel des Sociétés de Tempérance* [Manual of Temperance Societies]. The book sold an unprecedented four thousand copies in the first six months. From this point on, his reputation as the Apostle of Temperance was firmly established, and invitations for speaking engagements seemed endless.[21] However, in 1846, as a result of a reported tryst with a woman,

Chiniquy was forced to leave the Diocese of Quebec.[22] After apologizing for his faults in a rather humble letter to the bishop, Chiniquy entered the novitiate of the Oblates of Mary Immaculate at Longeuil, a community across the river from Montreal.[23] He remained for just over a year before returning to his temperance crusade under the auspices of the Bishop of Montreal. During the next several years, Chiniquy claimed to have converted over two hundred thousand individuals to the cause of abstinence.

The newspapers faithfully reported his comings and goings. An April 9, 1849, article in the *Montreal Witness* cites more than eighteen thousand who had made a solemn promise never to take a drop of intoxicating liquor.

> The patriotism and religious preaching of the eloquent missionary M. Chiniquy has been like an electric shock over the whole population. At his voice, every heart has been moved, minds undecided and even adversaries have been conquered. . . . In less than four days, more than 18,000 French Canadians have embraced total abstinence and of all those who have not joined the society there are perhaps not one-tenth who do not applaud with all their hearts the success of this admirable work. . . . Hundreds of his hearers were weeping as he portrayed the evils of intemperance.

While the account may contain an element of journalistic hyperbole, it also suggests the oratorical skills with which Chiniquy was endowed and that were clearly to serve him well throughout his life. No less important was the impact: "When the Chiniquy crusade got underway, imports of alcohol sank to the lowest point in decades. Domestic production also hit bottom as the campaign crested in 1849–50. By 1850, Chiniquy had apparently succeeded in turning a society long known for its *joie-de-vivre* into the most bone-dry temperance stronghold in North America."[24]

Temperance was only one of Chiniquy's causes during this period. In what was to become supreme irony in light of his later career, he took up an equally ardent campaign against the Protestants in the province—whom he referred to as "les Suisses" (the Swiss)—despite the fact that he had gained admiration from them for his opinions on alcoholism. He condemned les Suisses for "hunting bishops and curates, persecuting nuns, and having a false Bible." He called on all Catholic French Canadians to put them out if they appeared on the doorstep with propaganda.[25]

During the next three years, accusations as to Chiniquy's insubordinate, outspoken, and unwise behavior came to the attention of Bishop Bourget. These included his abuse of the prohibition against eating meat on Fridays, his indiscreet comments from the pulpit that were considered offensive to women, and his overly political sermons. The bishop warned him to "watch his language and to use moderation in his predications."[26] As these accusations were accumulating, Chiniquy received an invitation from Bishop Jacques Olivier Van de Velde of Chicago to preach his message of temperance in Chicago. During his trip to Illinois, he was evidently struck by the wealth and vastness of the American Midwest, and an idea began to take shape in his mind.

After his return to Canada, Chiniquy continued his outspoken preaching and, according to some accounts, his philandering.[27] He was soon in trouble again and in October 1851, Bishop Bourget, feeling that he could no longer either protect or tolerate this very independent individualist, signed an interdict that suspended Chiniquy from his duties as a priest. At this time, Van de Velde of Chicago was in Montreal, and Chiniquy asked to be placed in his service. Van de Velde had already appealed to Bourget in writing for French-speaking priests to help him in the formation of a new diocese. He believed that the growing numbers of French Canadians in Illinois needed their own parishes where they could "follow the religious customs of Canada with priests of their own background because they have no confidence in Irish and German priests." He asked for "priests with a zeal and piety that is strong enough to resist the temptations to which priests are exposed in this western part of the United States."[28] Bourget, to satisfy both men, agreed to the request and arranged for Chiniquy's *exeat* from the Diocese of Quebec.[29]

French Canadians in the Kankakee Valley

Soon after his arrival in Chicago in October 1851, Chiniquy proceeded sixty miles south of the city to Bourbonnais, where a small but growing settlement of French Canadian immigrants had established itself along the banks of the Kankakee River (map 1.1). The town derived its name from a French Canadian fur trader Francis Bourbonnais, who had arrived in Illinois as early as 1825. Bourbonnais married a Pottawatomie woman, who had been given 640 acres as a reservation along the Kankakee River.[30]

Noel LeVasseur, a *voyageur* who had, under the auspices of the American Fur Company, set up a trading post among the Pottawatomie Indians, settled at Bourbonnais in 1832.[31] Sometime after 1837, LeVasseur returned to Canada to encourage the emigration of his compatriots to Illinois. Several families came in 1844 and more in 1848 and 1849. A Quebec City solicitor named J. N. Bossé reported to the government that 205 persons had left the parish of Cap St. Ignace for

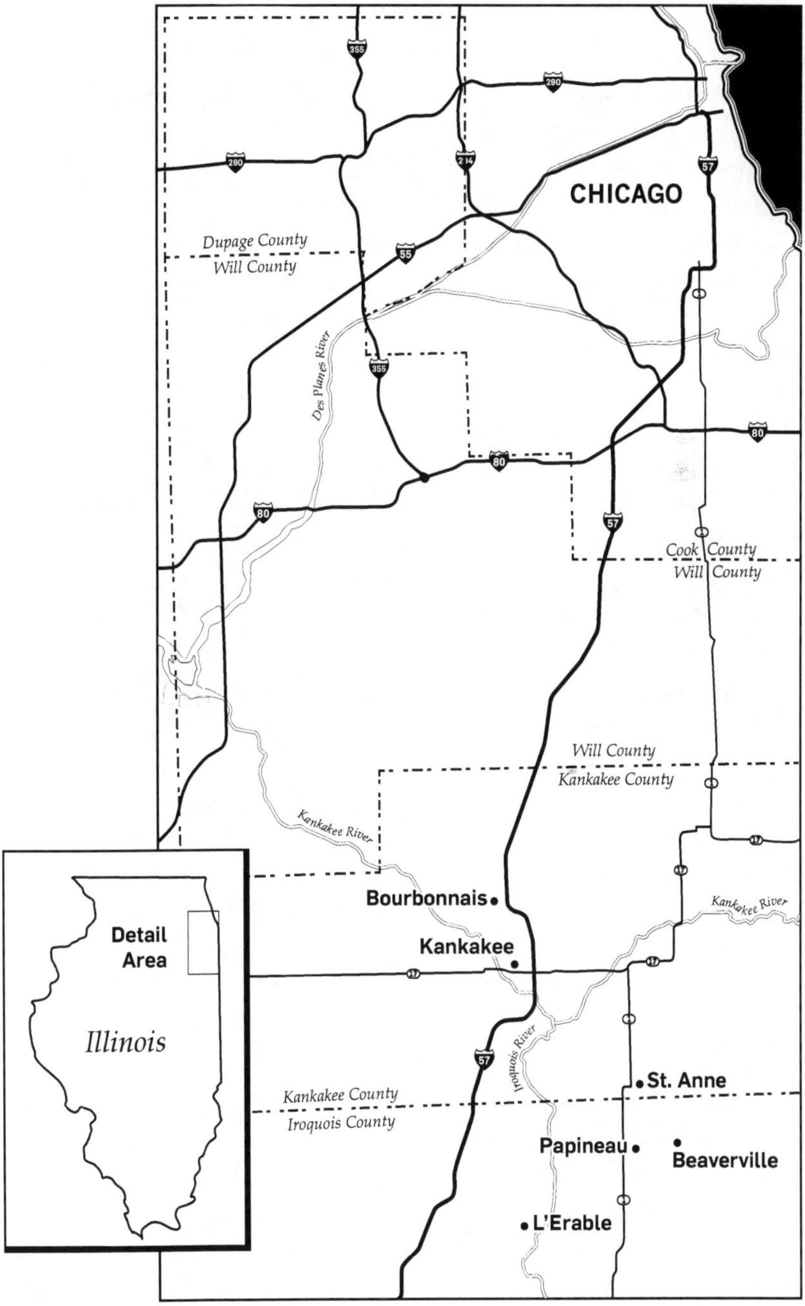

MAP 1.1. Part of northeastern Illinois, including the towns settled by French Canadians. *Map prepared by Jeremy Linden, via Marquand Books.*

Illinois in 1848.[32] These new arrivals settled in Bourbonnais and bought or rented anywhere from fifteen to forty acres to farm, some of it from LeVasseur himself.[33]

In September 1845, Monseigneur William Quarter, first Bishop of Chicago, wrote at the request of several Canadian immigrants in Illinois to Bishop Bourget, requesting a priest to "labor with apostolic zeal for the salvation of the souls of these excellent and deserving Canadians."[34] This was followed by another letter to the bishop from a Scots Canadian resident of Bourbonnais named Peter Spink. This letter, almost ironic in its premonition, reiterated the request for a priest and told the bishop of the fifty or so French Canadian families settled in central Illinois and of the numbers arriving each day.

> It is impossible for you to imagine the loss that our religion suffers in these parts by the lack of a priest who knows the French language. The majority of Catholics are Irish and thus the priests are also. Since they do not know our language, many of us cannot receive the sacred sacraments. . . . It is not necessary to speak to you of the errors of those of our country who come to this country with little or no education in religion and who find themselves in the midst of a Protestant population always ready to insinuate their principles and to find believers among men with little instruction.[35]

In a second letter in March 1846, Spink reminded Bourget that Easter was approaching and still there was no French-speaking priest. Women, in particular, he said, were very little disposed to confessing to priests of a foreign nation, and since his last letter, eleven more families and a number of single men had arrived in the community. The Bishop of Montreal finally responded, and in May 1847 the first resident priest, René Courjeault, arrived. He counted 59 families upon his arrival and 108 by fall. His observations concerning the rapid influx are substantiated by several other commentators, including the Canadian government: "For two years, those from the counties of Bellechasse, l'Islet, and Kamouraska [Canada] have been selling their land to buy new land in the states of the west. They almost all head for Chicago by the canals and the lakes. These new emigrants have kinship connections with those already settled in the environs of Chicago who went there after the troubles."[36] Another observer notes that these first settlers on their return to Canada "offered such colorful tales of the advantages offered by the western prairies that a good number of Canadians did not hesitate to leave to establish themselves in this new promised land."[37] In May 1849 Courjeault was prompted to send a letter to *Mélanges Religieux*, a publication associated with the Catholic Church, to request help for the building of a church at Bourbonnais: "On leaving their country, the majority of emigrants like to place their fortunes under the watchful eye of the religion whose gentle influence they have so many times submitted to in Canada."

In the 1850 population census, 248 families were enumerated in Bourbonnais Township, whose total population was 1,720. Of these, 201 (81 percent) were French Canadians. A handful of other French Canadian families were scattered in other townships of Will and Iroquois Counties. The Canadian-born in Illinois (both French- and English-speaking) in 1850 numbered 10,699, or 1.3 percent of the total population of the state.[38] However, it was Chiniquy's visit in the spring of 1851 and his resolve to organize a group of French Canadian colonists to settle to the south and east of Bourbonnais that gave renewed impetus to this westward migration.

Chiniquy's New Cause

You vant to kno who 'tis I am? You're stranger man, I see;
I don' min tell to you som't'ing concern' de life of me.
My fadder's com from Canadaw long vit Père Chiniquy
Vay in de early fifty year; To lan' of libertee.
An I am born here on de State, an' rose soon high to be
De captaine of de Marguerite, dat sail de Kankakee.[39]

Chiniquy had published a letter about Illinois in several French-language newspapers in Quebec in August 1851. Beginning with the premise that the flow of emigration would not stop until the government of the province initiated certain changes in social and economic conditions, he proposed to turn these French Canadian migrants away from the towns of New England that were the "tombs of all that is dear to a Canadian: his religion, his language, and his nationality" and lead them, instead, to the Midwest. "Nothing," he continued, "is more discouraging than to see with what ease our youths are exposed to the contagion of heresy, impiety, and indifference." He contrasted the miserable conditions he had witnessed among his compatriots on the East Coast with the happiness and prosperity of those living in the Midwest. He recommended that those with the penchant to emigrate, as well as those already in the eastern United States, join him in Illinois, where land was cheap and plentiful and where a "sober and religious man" can thrive. Indeed, his aim was to assemble all emigrants in one place, in new rural French Canadian communities where they could maintain their language and their culture and avoid "the snares of Protestantism." He ended with the following admonition in the August 22, 1851, *Mélanges Religieux*.

> Young man, if you are happy in Canada stay in your country because exile is the greatest evil of all; but if you no longer find a place for yourself along the great river; if, by the negligence of your leaders, you cannot penetrate the forest without risking starvation, or to plough in the mud of the swamps, or to drown yourself in the rivers, if you are squashed under the feet of a tyrant there, then go to Illinois, a land sanctified by your fathers.

Chiniquy himself arrived in Bourbonnais in November 1851 and soon after moved out to the Beaver mission about twelve miles south and east of Bourbonnais with a number of new settlers. In a November 27, 1851, letter to Bishop Bourget, Van de Velde of the Chicago diocese describes Chiniquy's intentions to build a church at Beaver Creek in the spring.[40] This building was, indeed, completed—a forty-foot-square chapel—and in April 1852 Bishop Van de Velde dedicated it to Ste. Anne. Thus, the community of St. Anne, Illinois, was born.

As indicated earlier in this chapter, Chiniquy's interest in French Canadian emigration predated his first trip to Illinois. He had visited some of the communities of his countrymen in New England and the Midwest and reported his findings: "I have traveled as far as Detroit and everywhere I met a large number of Canadians and the majority appeared to be in the most deplorable situation with regard to fortune and morale. Canadians in the United States are generally employed in the vilest of work in manufacture—as carters or day laborers."[41] Clearly, he had changed his tune by 1851 and 1852 when he was enthusiastically extolling the benefits of emigration to the Midwest. The author of the article "Les Illinois et M. Chiniquy" in the September 26, 1851, *l'Avenir* notes the hypocrisy: "If the paradise of the Canadians is no longer in the East where M. Chiniquy placed it last year, can we be assured that next year it will be in the West where he places it today?"

Despite Chiniquy's clearly stated desire to assemble a Catholic community in the Midwest where French Canadians could prosper both materially and morally, the Quebec Catholic Church did not respond to the idea in a wholeheartedly favorable manner. Indeed, during the fall and winter of 1851 and the spring of 1852, the pages of newspapers like *Mélanges Religieux*, *l'Avenir*, and the *Courrier du Canada* were filled with discussions, pro and con, of this westward migration. In a general way, the opposition can be attributed to the overriding sentiment of agrarian nationalism, a sentiment to which Chiniquy in some sense ascribes in his initial appeal. Some of the particular claims Chiniquy made about the possibilities in Illinois were attacked as false advertising. Some simply did not like that he was stimulating further emigration.

To a large extent, the opposition or support followed its particular political and religious predilections of the newspapers. Thus, the Catholic Church mouthpieces *Mélanges Religieux* and *La Minerve* published letters from individual emigrants who clearly regretted their departure. In *Mélanges Religieux* on February 4, 1852, a woman named Denise d'Arché, for example, laments coming to "this unfortunate country where we suffer so many troubles, regrets, miseries, and deprivations of all kinds and above all the bitter absence of religious consolation." She goes on to advise others to think carefully before "hazarding their well-being, their health, their fortunes, and above all their religion." Some who returned to Quebec during the spring of 1852 described the problems they had encountered, happily bidding *adieu* to Bourbonnais, Chiniquy, and Courjeault. In the May 17, 1852, *Le Canadien*, the returned call themselves "duped victims who had been seduced by soft words. . . . For the enchanting and seductive picture that you made of the riches and beauties and advantages to be offered Canadians at Bourbonnais, we sacrificed our lands, our houses, our wealth, our household; to find this terrestrial paradise but where, alas, we found only deception, bitterness, frightful disappointment, misery and deprivation." These writers claim to have seen more misery and poverty in Bourbonnais than they had ever witnessed in Canada.[42] They felt that their decision to return was an act of honor and patriotism and accused Chiniquy of unjustifiably criticizing his own country in order to keep them in Illinois.

Virtually simultaneously, the May 13, 1852, *La Minerve* published a story of four men who had sold everything and, leaving their families behind, went to Bourbonnais. The trip was hard and cost more than thirty *piastres* each. The trip from Chicago to Bourbonnais, which cost an additional fifteen piastres, took two-and-a-half days. The four men found there a harsh climate and a terrain with little wood with which to defend themselves against the rigors of the climate. The prairies were covered with water. "The houses of the village of Bourbonnais," they claim, "are so badly built that they look like our barns rather than our houses." This correspondence is substantiated by a letter from Reverend Isadore Antoine Lebel, a Catholic priest who had served the French Canadian population in Chicago since November 1850. Lebel had received letters of inquiry from French Canadians in Halifax, Kamouraska, Montreal, Rimouski, Ste. Claire, St. Gervais, St. Leon, St. Gilles, and St. Nicolas.

In his letter and with a somewhat patronizing tone, Lebel claims that the Canadian was the one who exploited with the least profit the resources of the Midwest, who lived in the most misery, and who was often the dupe of Yankee tricks because he was the least prepared to emigrate and live among a population "with different usages, different instruction, language and religion." Lebel cites a long list of reasons to explain why they lived less happily: a less healthy climate ("the air is replete with miasma, cholera abounds because of the humidity, water is less good"); more variable temperatures, long cold winters and hot summers, frequent and fatal rain and storms; difficult communications on bad roads and in winters that are long and hard; expensive provisions and clothing; houses that are badly built and heating stoves that are less efficient; churches that are not as nice or as rich and a religion that is "not as pretty, less impressive, and less practiced." Lebel ends his letter with a postscript promising to receive those who come but advising rich and poor to stay at home.[43]

The more neutral *Le Moniteur Canadien*, on the other hand, in April 1852, asks if it was "more nationalistic to encourage potential emigrants to remain in Quebec to serve as the foot soldiers of the ambitious who hope to aggrandize themselves at the expense of the poor *habitants*?" The writer defies anyone to find farmers in Illinois who in a few years have not doubled the value of their land.

In a May 1852 article, a writer to this same newspaper counters the reports that speculators had sent the price of land skyrocketing in the Bourbonnais–St. Anne area and relates that as soon as land office opened in June, land would be available at $1.25 per acre. Much consternation was expressed in the pages of various newspapers over the sums Chiniquy had quoted to be sufficient to start a new life in Illinois—he claimed $200 to $240, while the bishop thought $800 more realistic. Chiniquy responded that his sum was a projection for a young man, not the father of a family.

LeVasseur himself responded to what he considered to be disgraceful and dishonest misrepresentations of the situation in Bourbonnais. His letter, published in the June 17, 1852, *Le Moniteur Canadien*, states that he agrees with what Chiniquy had said about the advantages of Illinois, that his view was based on twenty years of experience, and that while their intention was not to encourage people to emigrate, they did want to share their well-being with others. After accusing both Courjeault (who had by this time left Bourbonnais) and Lebel of stirring up trouble, he concludes by claiming that "the advantages that the farmer will encounter in our prairies are infinitely superior to those that he will pay dearly for in the icy forests of Canada. While some may miss Canada, in Illinois they can be confident of a future for their children."

LeVasseur also responded precisely to various published misrepresentations and particularly to a letter fifty Canadians signed. LeVasseur claims that these individuals had spent a good part of the winter in a drunken stupor (hence, their dislike of the Apostle of Temperance) and the gunshots that they reported upon their departure were "no more than a youthful celebration, on the part of the moral and good-living members of his community, of their departure." As to Lebel's remarks about insalubrity and death, LeVasseur observes that since the beginning of the year there were fifty-five baptisms and only fourteen deaths, among them one adult who drowned and another who suffered from epilepsy, and "The water is good, meat is cheaper; wood is available, autumn is beautiful and the notion of more harsh winters than in Canada is ridiculous."

It is important to pause briefly to consider why there was such a strong negative reaction on the part of Catholic authorities in Canada to this emigration. It clearly arose from a growing fear of a population drain that would undermine their political and social position within the province of Quebec. Later in the century, when it became evident to the church that the habitants were not willing to give up the opportunities available to them through emigration, a new approach that involved the re-creation of parish life on foreign soil was adopted.

Not all clerics were in complete opposition to Chiniquy's scheme. In an April 1852 letter to Bishop Bourget, Bishop Van de Velde describes a visit he had made to St. Anne. The people there, he reports, "are reconciled to their fate and admire the zeal of their pastor whom they esteem and love quite sincerely." Chiniquy himself responded to the attacks, saying it had never been his intention to encourage emigration. He repeats his warning that those at ease in Quebec should not abandon what they had. But for those living in misery, Illinois could offer a new future. He continued to see God's hand in sending so many French and Irish Catholics, to ensure a place for the Catholic Church in the west. He saw himself as part of a larger mission.[44]

Despite all attempts to discourage emigration to the American Midwest, during the three years after Chiniquy's arrival in Illinois, it was estimated that between nine hundred and one thousand families left Quebec and some of the New England states to settle on forty square miles of land in central Illinois with the newly renamed town of St. Anne at its center. In fact, during the decade of the 1850s, emigration to the Midwest (Michigan, Wisconsin, and Minnesota as well) was on a par with that to New England. By 1860, however, emigration to the Midwest had tapered off as New England increasingly became the favored destination.[45]

The New Settlements: St. Anne, St. Mary, Papineau, L'Érable

The prairies of central Illinois to which the French Canadians came in the early 1850s were different from the land in Quebec they had left behind. In the first place, this region remained relatively unsettled, and while a great deal of acreage was already in the hands of speculators, federal government lands were still available at $1.25 per acre.[46] Only about 4 percent of the available acreage in the central counties of Illinois in 1850 was improved in farms.[47] In the mid-1850s, the railroad company listed "over 2,000,000 acres of selected prairie, farming and wood lands . . . in tracts of forty acres and upwards to suit purchasers on long credits and at low interest rates situated on each side of their railroad extending all the way from the extreme north to the south of the state of Illinois."[48] The price of this land varied from $5 to $25 per acre according to its location, quality, and distance from stations and settlements. The credit terms involved low interest and delayed payment of principal. Although the amount of railroad land available for sale had been reduced to 1,400,000 by 1859, at the end of the decade, only 10 percent of the fertile land in the state was as yet under cultivation.[49]

In 1850 ten cities in the state were incorporated, but this in itself was a major change from 1840.[50] During the 1850s, the network of railroads traversing the state was expanded, and Chicago became the transportation hub of the Midwest. The prairie regions of eastern and southern Illinois that had previously been avoided by newcomers because of poor access were progressively settled.[51] Riding the Illinois Central line southward from Chicago in 1855, a traveler named William Ferguson made passing reference to the "old French settlement" at Bourbonnais (despite the fact that the railroad bypassed it). A few years later, a Scot named James Caird also journeyed through this area. After commenting upon the rich, black, loamy soil of the undulating and sparsely settled prairies, he described "passing through a settlement of French Canadians. . . . Each settler has about forty acres and their farms are laid out along parallel roads at right angles to the railway. They exhibit signs of careful cultivation."[52]

Although Bourbonnais was the first community in northeastern Illinois to be settled by French Canadians who ventured to the Midwest in the 1840s, the focal point of Chiniquy's migration effort was to the east and south, in and around an area known as Beaver Creek in Iroquois County. In 1847, a German American named Henry Jacobus came from Decatur City, Indiana, to Beaver Creek and a year later bought 160 acres of government land adjoining what was later platted as the village of St. Anne. He remained there until 1853 when he moved to the adjacent township of Aroma. Much of the land of St. Anne Township continued as prairie and marsh until 1848.

Sometime in 1850 Michel Allain moved from Bourbonnais to Beaver Creek with his wife, their two sons, Ambrose and Antoine, and their families. Michel had purchased a quarter section from George Casseday, a land agent in Danville, who, since 1845, had been acquiring much of the land in the area soon to become part of Kankakee County. On July 21, 1851, Michel Allain deeded this land, 160 acres, to his two sons. In *Fifty Years in the Church of Rome* (1886), Chiniquy describes the two small homes built by the Allain brothers on a hill at Beaver Creek. Although there are indications that several other French Canadian immigrant families moved out to Beaver Creek prior to Chiniquy's arrival, he clearly stimulated the rapid growth of the settlement in 1851 and 1852.[53] By the end of January 1852, forty cabins were built, and by April the first church was finished.

Ste. Anne was organized as a parish of the newly formed Kankakee County in 1853, and in October 1855 a Catholic school for boys was started. St. Anne Township was created in 1857 from parts of Aroma and Momence Townships as thirty sections spanning six miles east to west and five miles north to south.[54] In April that year the first town officers were elected. Three of them were French Canadians—the supervisor, John B. Lemoine; the tax collector, Achilles Chiniquy (Charles Chiniquy's brother); and one of the constables, Camille Betourni. The other constable was an Englishman named W. C. Sutton, and the clerk and justice was a native of Virginia named Lawrence Kibbon.[55]

As increasing numbers of French Canadian immigrants moved into St. Anne Township, it became necessary for some to spill over into adjacent communities in Iroquois County (see map 1.1). To the immediate south, they settled in Papineau. Papineau Township was originally settled by Dutch immigrants who arrived in the 1840s. At that time, the township was called Weygandt after one of the major immigrant families. Life for the earliest residents of Weygandt Township was harsh. Farming was difficult because the soil was sandy. In 1855 half the population, which by this time also included Yankee and German settlers, died in a severe cholera epidemic. As the region was increasingly infiltrated by French Canadians, it was renamed Papineau after the great Quebec nationalist hero of the 1830s.

Among those settling in Papineau were Antoine Lottinville and his family. The Lottinvilles are the source of a famous Illinois French Canadian immigrant story. They were with a group crossing Lake Ontario on the steamer *Atlantic* as it headed for Detroit. The steamer collided and sank. Only 120 survived, including the entire Lottinville family. Having lost everything, they were helped by

LeVasseur, and as one of the first French Canadian farming families in Papineau Township, they thrived.

A sawmill was soon built in Papineau by a settler named Joseph Delude. The first school was opened in 1861, and a Methodist church was built in 1867. The village was finally incorporated in 1874 with Fabian Langdoc as president, C. P. Lottinville as clerk, Joseph Laveaux as treasurer, and Thomas Lottinville, A. P. Shipley, Octave Laplante, Ezra Savoie, and John Massey (Massé) as trustees. A Catholic church was erected in 1872, and attending priests came from nearby parishes of Ste. Marie and Ste. Anne. Eventually, it was demolished and never rebuilt. The majority of Papineau residents, whether Protestant or Catholic, worshipped in the churches of St. Anne Township. In 1885 Immanuel Church was founded by German immigrants and served German speakers until 1916. In 1959 this church was renamed Immanuel United Church of Christ.[56]

Adjacent to Papineau Township was Beaver Township. The southern part of this township, around the community of Donovan, was a Swedish-immigrant stronghold. The northern part had been settled by Norwegians in 1835, but a cholera epidemic in the following year wiped out half the population, and the survivors moved to Wisconsin. The French Canadians moved into the northern part of Beaver Township, founding the village of St. Mary (Ste. Marie) along the border between Beaver and Papineau Townships. The first settlers (with family names like Arseneau, Boudreau, Benoit, Dionne, Fortin, Lafond, and Nourie) arrived in St. Mary in the spring of 1853; Joseph Caillouette built the first house in 1857. The village itself was platted in 1859 on land belonging to Charles Arseneau, who still has numerous descendants in the community. By this time roughly fifty families, who previously had been attended by the L'Érable priest, were worshipping in the church built in the community on twenty acres of land that Arseneau also donated. St. Mary continued to grow. In 1872 the Cincinnati, Lafayette, and Chicago Railroad linked the town to the Chicago markets. The Lambert family owned and operated a bank, a grain elevator, and a lumberyard; in the early 1900s H. L. Lambert started a tile factory that eventually employed twenty-five men.[57] In 1895 six sisters of the Holy Heart of Mary arrived from Paris to direct a parish school that became Holy Family Academy, which opened with sixty pupils. The academy boarded children from the countryside, and the enrollment grew rapidly, necessitating a new building that was completed in 1905, four years before the cornerstone was laid for the new church (fig. 1.1). In that same year, the town of St. Mary was renamed Beaverville.[58] By 1915 three hundred students attended Holy

FIGURE 1.1. St. Mary's Catholic Church, Beaverville, Illinois. *Photo by Caroline B. Brettell.*

Family Academy. The school remained active until 1969, and in the mid-1970s the buildings were razed.

The final village in the area French Canadians settled is L'Érable in 1853 and 1854 as a mission of Maternity Church in Bourbonnais. The name L'Érable (maple) comes from the sugar maple, many of which were planted by the original settlers. Spink, Chiniquy's adversary in a slander lawsuit (discussed in the next chapter), was a resident of L'Érable in the early years. He acquired large tracts of lands that he later sold to newcomers. In 1854 a chapel dedicated to St. John the Baptist was built on land Spink donated, and St. Jean Baptiste Day, a Quebec feast day, was celebrated on the twenty-fourth of June. In 1875 the wood-frame church that still stands was completed (fig. 1.2). In 1857, L'Érable was platted but never incorporated. By the end of the 1850s, the French Canadians in L'Érable and the surrounding acres of Ashkum Township were soon outnumbered by French-speaking immigrants from Belgium. Many descendants of these Belgian families—the Chagelons, Grossaints, Lamottes, Lemenegers, to name a few—still remain in the area.[59]

When Joseph Tassé traveled to the area in the early 1870s, he remarked on the "frenchness" of St. Anne and the other settlements—"the church, the school

FIGURE 1.2. St. John the Baptist Catholic Church, L'Érable, Illinois. *Photo by Caroline B. Brettell.*

and the convent grouped together, the aspect of the houses surrounded by green gardens, the frank hospitality of the *habitants,* the completely Gallic gaiety which characterizes them, the French accents, . . . nowhere else in the United States does one find perhaps a settlement with as much of a truly Canadian cachet."[60] Yet, Tassé makes no mention of an event that had wrenched these communities apart in the late 1850s and that had a profound impact on their way of life.

CHAPTER 2

The Social Drama of a Religious Schism

On November 8, 1853, Bishop Bourget of Montreal opened, perhaps with some trepidation, a letter sent to him by Reverend J. Lemaistre, the pastor he had recently appointed to succeed Charles Chiniquy at the Maternity Church in Bourbonnais, Illinois. Lemaistre relates,

> Chiniquy, after having been the cause of the fire of the old church of Bourbonnais, whether because he had been deplorably entangled with M. Lebel over the issue of Canadian emigration, or for having mixed in the intrigues of the elections, left me nothing but a sort of large shed for a church with more than 1000 piastres of debt. He appropriated all the money that was sent from Canada to rebuild the burned church. During the nine months that he was in Bourbonnais, he exhausted the people with his collections and did nothing to repair the misfortune that came to the parish through the ruin of their church.[1]

Though Chiniquy quickly fled to the neighboring community of St. Anne, gossip about his role in the destruction of the church in Bourbonnais continued for several years.[2] This was but one of a series of incidents in a social drama that played out over a ten-year period but with an impact of much-longer duration. This chapter traces the story of this social drama through its phases of breach, crisis, redressive actions, and ultimate resolution. Throughout, it is possible to identify the subtle and shifting boundary-making mechanisms that became part of the process by which a group of French Canadian migrants, led by their parish priest, began to build their new life in the American Midwest. One also sees, reflected in this localized social drama, broader tensions and conflicts that characterized American society in the 1850s and 1860s. One cannot be understood apart from the other, and both form part of the analysis here.

The Breach: Challenging the Power Structure

One of the earliest Canadians to settle in central Illinois was a man named Peter Spink. Soon after his arrival, Spink began to speculate in real estate, buying large tracts of land, particularly in Iroquois County, to sell to those who followed. He and Chiniquy quickly came into conflict over these matters, and Spink accused Chiniquy of publicly slandering him. According to Spink, Chiniquy had claimed from his pulpit on or about January 10, 1854, "There is one [meaning Spink] among you who perjured himself in front of the Esquire Smith in Spring Creek. It was Esquire Smith that told me in the presence of witnesses." Spink claimed in a February 3, 1855, suit in Kankakee County Circuit Court that it was Chiniquy's intention to ruin and destroy Spink's reputation. On another occasion, according to Spink, Chiniquy accused him of suggesting to the chamberlain in Middleport, Illinois, that he prosecute French Canadians who had cut timber on government land. As a result of this statement, claimed Spink, many of his French Canadian countrymen refused to conduct further transactions with him.[3] Chiniquy hired an Illinois lawyer named Abraham Lincoln and filed a countersuit. (From this time, Chiniquy dates his "close" friendship with Lincoln and later wrote a pamphlet *The Murder of Abraham Lincoln by the Jesuits*.)[4]

Spink asked for a change of venue, believing he could not get a fair trial in Kankakee County; the trial was moved to Champaign County Circuit Court in Urbana, Illinois. Chiniquy supporters traveled from Kankakee County to Urbana to be present at a trial that was receiving significant attention in the Illinois press. At the May 1856 session of the Champaign County Circuit Court, the jury failed to find a verdict in the case, which itself occupied almost the entire four days of circuit business. In a trial that was not without its dirty tricks, the chief witness for the plaintiff was accused of giving false testimony. A postponement until the October session provided Chiniquy with time to publish a plea for support to help him defend his name. The case was eventually settled out of court, each side paying its own expenses and Chiniquy issuing a public retraction. Spink, who accepted the retraction, later moved to Minnesota.

Chiniquy's involvement in the Spink affair strongly displeased the Catholic episcopal hierarchy in Illinois, but the most serious breach, the one that truly challenged the power structure, was that which developed between Chiniquy and Anthony O'Regan, the Irish Bishop of Chicago, who succeeded Jacques Olivier Van de Velde in 1853. The norms called into question were those governing the ownership and administration of church property, delivering the Mass in French instead of Latin, and providing laypeople with access to the Bible. Chiniquy took on both the sacred and secular authority of the Catholic Church.

The church, parsonage, and school in St. Anne had been constructed on property initially owned by Chiniquy. While the people wanted to hold the property in full and allow their pastor free use, "according to the almost universal practice in the United States,"[5] O'Regan, in accordance with the principle of trusteeship, desired Chiniquy to send him titles to all the property. Chiniquy refused.[6] He based his refusal in part upon the troubles that the Chicago French Canadian community was also having with O'Regan, although in this case it is not fully apparent the extent to which Chiniquy himself incited the reactions there.

According to the French Canadians in Chicago, as soon as O'Regan arrived in the city, he was told that the French priest Isadore Antoine Lebel was too popular and that his church was attended not only by his French and Canadian people but also by Irish and German immigrants. As a result, funds were being diverted from the episcopate. O'Regan removed Lebel in 1856, and although he promised the people that they would have another French-speaking priest, he did not send one, telling them that they should accept the priest he chose. Under protest, O'Regan eventually complied but not before making the new priest, Father Lemaistre, promise that he would receive no one but the French in his church. Lemaistre felt that this was an impossible demand and when he did not comply, he, too, was ordered out. What followed were accusations that the bishop had tried to extort funds from Lemaistre before permitting him to stay.

In addition, conflicts had emerged over the church building itself. The first French-speaking immigrants in Chicago worshipped at St. Mary's Cathedral, but as it became increasingly English-speaking, the French speakers sought a new house of worship. In 1850 the parish of St. Louis was formed by Reverend Lebel, and a church was constructed on a leased lot on the east side of Clark Street between Adams and Jackson. In 1858, the bishop decided that the Church of St. Louis would have to be moved because it was on leased land. He had purchased a lot from two Irishmen on Sherman Street. The French Canadian parishioners wanted to buy their own lots at Franklin and Quincy and agreed to a subscription only if the church would remain French-speaking. When the bishop demanded the deeds to these lots, a trustee of St. Louis parish informed him that the deeds would not be secured until the lots were paid in full. For the present, the parish could only pay for one of the lots. The bishop, according to the French Canadians, claimed that he could sell all the church properties in his diocese, pocket the money, and spend it as he pleased.

The bishop took action by moving the church building to the lot he had purchased. He installed an Irish priest. "This is the way," claimed the French Canadians in a published statement, "we have been swindled of our church, of the house of our priest, and of our all, by the tyrant Bishop O'Regan; and when a French priest visits our city he forbids him to address us in our cherished mother tongue. And this is also the way that we French Catholics, as a society, have been blotted out of the books of the living."[7]

O'Regan's version of the story is that the French Canadian parish was in debt. Furthermore, they would not support their priest.

> When I arrived in this Diocese, I found [their priest] building a Church in the midst of the Irish and two good miles from the last Frenchman. I made him come and attend to his own Church. The Church was built on leased ground... and the lease was made to the Bishop so I was responsible for the rent. The congregation would not even pay the old rent, nor support their Priest. This was demanding a remedy. I proposed to buy a lot and move the Church on it; I bought one for the sum of $2050; I offered $1600 of my own money and $300 to transport the Church.... All that was collected after three months was $35.... I went to their Church.... I offered them $1900 of my own money to procure for them a suitable place for their Church.... I promised publicly that they should always have their own Church, and their Priest if it was in my power, if they would only support him decently.[8]

Although it is not fully apparent which version is true (most likely there were fabrications on both sides), the ethnic tensions underlying this conflict are both evident and important. These tensions became equally significant in Chiniquy's battle with O'Regan and reflect a broader discord within the Catholic Church in American society during the nineteenth century.[9] If ethnic differences were eventually subsumed under the major religious denominations, as Will Herberg argued more than fifty years ago, the process of change was by no means smooth. To this the schism in Illinois attests. The language issue, so fundamental to French

Canadian ethnic survival into the present, was at the center of this confrontation in the Midwest.[10] "Each Sunday," claimed the French Canadians of Chicago, "the zealous and generous Irish go to their church to hear the voice of their priest, who speaks in English. The intelligent Germans have their pastors who speak in their language. The French population is now the one that has neither a priest nor a church."[11]

To summarize, in the early stages of the schism in Illinois, the conflict occurred within a religious framework over religious principles and involved a challenge by a local community (as represented by their priest) against a regional religious hierarchy. However, it was couched in linguistic and ethnic terms much as conflicts that were to emerge later in the century in New England pitted the Irish Catholic hierarchy against French Canadians parishes.[12] One such conflict erupted when an Irish priest named McGee was appointed to lead a French Canadian parish in Fall River, Massachusetts, in 1884. His parishioners made life difficult for him, and he left. After another Irish-ancestry appointee also left, the bishop closed the church.[13] On each occasion when these conflicts emerged, "prelates and senior priests of Irish-American origins had put formidable obstacles to the erection of complete Franco-American parishes, invoking the usefulness of the English language and the susceptibilities of American nativists as regards the use of foreign idioms. Each time the French press and the local French petty bourgeoisie had responded with unbounded desire to reach their goals, often using unrestrained language against the religious hierarchy."[14] The conflicts in New England, and there were several, culminated in the Sentinelle Affair, named after a French-language newspaper, *La Sentinelle*, of 1924. Centered in Woonsocket, Rhode Island, the Sentinelle Affair was rooted in a conflict between diocesan authorities and radical French Canadian nationalists over the use of monies that the French Canadians thought belonged to parochial assemblies.[15] When this conflict ended, a distinct Franco-American parish based on ethnicity had disappeared. In the Midwest, the battle was waged three-quarters of a century earlier and had a different short-term outcome, although in the longer term, the results were the same and part of the larger story of Catholicism in America.

What must be kept in mind is that this was also a battle transported from Quebec, where nationalism for the French Canadians was deeply rooted in religious faith and where local parishes were accustomed to a degree of autonomy vis-à-vis the episcopal hierarchy: "In Canada the people took an active part in the government of the parish through the trustee, or *fabrique* system of parish government. Elected by the people, lay trustees, known as *marguilliers* controlled and administered the financial affairs of the parish. Moreover, there was a strong tradition of independence and local control among Canadian parish communities; this endured until the late-nineteenth century."[16] Chiniquy, according to Quebec abbot Nerée Gingras, viewed the conflict as a matter of patriotism, albeit on American rather than Canadian soil.[17] Anthropologist Victor Turner argues that although a dramatic breach may be made by an individual, "he always acts, or believes he acts, on behalf of other parties, whether they are aware of it or not. He sees himself as a representative, not as a lone hand."[18] Such was certainly the case for Chiniquy, and this becomes even more evident as the crisis intensified.

The Crisis Mounts: Suspension and Its Immediate Aftermath

Before the dissension between O'Regan and the Chicago French Canadian community had fully evolved, the bishop had already decided to suspend Chiniquy from his duties in St. Anne. The action came in August 1856. In addition to the differences that he had with this renegade priest, O'Regan was concerned about Chiniquy's inability to get along with his colleagues, Reverends Isadore Antoine Lebel and Louis Cartuyvels.

Having already asked Bishop Bourget for readmission to Canada to preach against emigration, Chiniquy refused to acknowledge the suspension, claiming on one occasion that it was invalid because it was unsigned and on another that it had never even been issued either in writing or verbally. He continued to carry out his priestly duties. By September 1856, O'Regan, robbed of his patience, took the final step—excommunication. The text of his action was published in numerous newspapers in Quebec, including the *Journal de Québec* on October 23, 1856: "The said Mr. Chiniquy, notwithstanding his suspension, has maliciously dared to exercise the functions of the sacred ministry, to preach, administer sacraments and deliver mass and has thus made himself irregular and has formally placed himself in open opposition to the authority of the church and become schismatical."[19] O'Regan cautioned all Catholics against having anything to do with Chiniquy, warning them that any disobedience would mean excommunication for them as well. Once again, Chiniquy was in the limelight.

There was, clearly, some confusion and concern among the French Canadian settlers of Kankakee County. Two residents of St. Anne wrote to Bishop Bourget in Montreal, inquiring whether it was still appropriate to take communion from Chiniquy. Bourget, supporting O'Regan's actions, responded that Chiniquy had no rights as a priest and advised them to go either to priests in Bourbonnais or to pray in their own homes.[20] Other individuals suspended their concerns about theological matters and stood firmly behind Chiniquy. Town supervisor John B. Lemoine told readers in Canada about the sacrifices that Chiniquy had made to build houses and schools and to feed teachers. He pleaded with Chiniquy not to be daunted by the "wolf" in the Chicago episcopate.[21]

As the crisis mounted, frequent letters were exchanged between O'Regan and Bourget. In one dated November 4, 1856, O'Regan requested good Canadian priests, for "without [them], these settlements will never have prosperity nor peace nor religion. . . . For the past their priests have been to them a curse and a calamity. . . . These men were deeply artful and worldly and in general without truth and piety and honesty and morality. . . . Some are even faithless."[22]

Bourget responded to this request by calling upon Chiniquy's longtime friend Isaac Desaulniers to go to Illinois to rescue the renegade priest and his supporters from "the abyss into which they have fallen," to convince them to submit to the "legitimate authority of their adopted bishop."[23] Desaulniers, in the company of Abbé Louis Moise Brassard, traveled first to Chicago and then to St. Anne to meet with Chiniquy. In Chicago the two emissaries received a series of instructions from O'Regan, who, by this time, was extremely wary of Chiniquy. Desaulniers and Brassard were told not to spend more than one night in St. Anne, to caution people and impress on them submission to the bishop if Chiniquy persisted in his wayward acts, to bring Chiniquy to Chicago to sign a paper of submission, that he would submit to the authority of the Catholic Church hierarchy, that would be read to the congregation and published, to tell Chiniquy to withdraw from St. Anne, and to refuse to celebrate Mass in St. Anne until all these conditions were fulfilled.[24]

In November 1856, Chiniquy penned an expression of regret to O'Regan: "To show to the world and to you my Bishop my firm will to live and die a Catholic, I hasten to write to your Lordship that I submit myself to your sentence and I promise never to exercise the Holy Ministry in your diocese without your permission. In consequence I request your lordship to take away the censures you have proferred against me and against those who have communicated with me."[25] Affirming that his actions stemmed from a defense of religion and justice rather than from ambition, Chiniquy made several requests in return: that a fair-minded Canadian bishop be put in charge of the Kankakee valley, that the French Canadian priest Lebel who had been chased out of Chicago by O'Regan be restored, and that he be permitted to remain in St. Anne as a retired priest.[26] It is apparent that one of Chiniquy's overriding concerns through the fall of 1856 was to remain in the area so that he could resolve his lawsuit with Spink: "My lawyers and witnesses are all here and in Iroquois County. The very moment that I am most needed to be here to protect my honor and innocence you order me to go more than 300 miles. Did you ever consider that by so strange a conduct you seem to help Spink against your own priest."[27]

Needless to say, none of this was satisfactory to O'Regan, who wished to see Chiniquy removed from his diocese: "I would prefer that Chiniquy should go away without any retraction rather than give one, and I shall, as soon as he abandons St. Anne and gives security that he will not return, have no objection to remove his censures without any retraction."[28] Disappointed, he wrote to Bishop Bourget complaining that Brassard and Desaulniers were too sympathetic to their friend Chiniquy. In a reply Bourget expressed regret that the submission was not accepted but admitted that O'Regan knew the situation much better than he. He defended Brassard and Desaulniers and claimed that he might have difficulty sending any other Canadian priests out to Illinois.[29] Reading between the lines, one is left to wonder whether Bourget himself was beginning to believe that French Canadian priests, in general, were not being treated fairly by the Irish Bishop of Chicago.

By the end of 1856, the printed communications of both supporters and critics of Chiniquy were becoming more analytical. In a November 30 letter, a female resident of Bourbonnais named Joselle Michaud had the following warning for Bishop Bourget: "My Lord it is a very bad way that your priests that you sent have of saying all kinds of abominations against the private character of Chiniquy. I do not hide from you the fact that my faith has been challenged in hearing certain things that your priests say. They are not true priests of God when they have neither truth on their lips nor charity in their hearts."[30] A writer to the *Morning Chronicle* on December 1, 1856, moved right to the heart of the matter by suggesting that Chiniquy's conduct "has been treated very much as a subject involving questions of Catholicism and Protestantism. So it does in a large sense; for the grand differences between the two religious systems consists in the assertion by the one of the right of private judgment in opposition to the constraint of authority." This writer went on to argue that the rule of obedience should be the main thing for as long as Chiniquy remains a prelate: "But if Father Chiniquy asserts his right to property as a citizen of the United States and in the courts of the United States, it is manifest that he throws off, by that act, the rule of his own establishment. He should leave it or conform." Clearly, this writer viewed the notion of the church belonging to its parishioners as a Protestant idea. Chiniquy, in this writer's view, had to make a choice.

A letter in the December 26, 1856, *l'Avenir* best sums up the prevailing sentiments at the close of the year.

> We would have better understood their precipitation if Canada had been the theater of difficulties; because in Canada, ecclesiastical authorities are regularly constituted, their government is in harmony with civil institutions and the people are kept at a distance, refused privilege, and the right to involve themselves in spiritual affairs. But in the United States where Catholicism is only at its birth, where its institutions are in disharmony not with the Catholic religion but with the government which is absolute, and where each citizen is accustomed, since childhood, by virtue of our good institutions, to consider and respect only individual merit no matter what one's social rank, and to scorn vice and crime in whatever guise. . . . Chiniquy has everything to gain in the sympathy of Americans—and the Bishop all to lose—and it is on this ground that the people of St. Anne support and will continue to support until the end M. Chiniquy.

This writer's final suggestion is that the practices of the Catholic Church should be modified to fit more with the government of the country.

Turner argues that in a social drama, during the phase of mounting crisis, "there is a tendency for the breach to widen and extend until it becomes coextensive with some dominant cleavage in the widest set of relevant social relations to which the conflicting or antagonistic parties belong."[31] It is quite apparent that much-broader national tensions were at play in the local conflict taking place in St. Anne during the latter half of the 1850s. If trusteeship was at the heart of this particular local conflict, it was also at the heart of a national conflict. Americans perceived the hierarchical structure of the Catholic Church as antidemocratic. Fear that the goal of the Catholic Church was to perpetuate on American soil the aristocratic form of government and "popish despotism" common in Europe rallied strong support for the nativist Know-Nothing movement. Although Know-Nothingism was beginning to wane by 1856, there is no doubt that the Chiniquy-inspired schism on the prairies of Illinois emerged from the general sentiments of this short-lived political movement and garnered attention because of it.[32] Northerners who supported the Know-Nothing Party were attracted to its anti-Catholic agenda. Tyler Anbinder comments, "Many in nineteenth-century America believed that Protestantism was responsible for the freedom and prosperity that the nation's inhabitants enjoyed. Conversely, Catholicism seemed hostile to everything they valued. . . . They believed that the unlimited control which the Catholic hierarchy apparently exercised over its followers deprived Catholics of the independence necessary for participation in a republican government."[33]

To summarize, the critical boundary defining opposing sides in the ongoing social drama had altered in a short period of time. Protestantism and Catholicism had met face-to-face. Ideologically, democracy was pitted against authoritarianism. As the schism developed a more political tenor in later phases, this latter opposition became much more prominent. The process of schism had reached a turning point.

Redressive Mechanisms: Appeasement and Arbitration, 1857–58

Although an initial redress had been attempted during the fall of 1856, it failed, and for two more years Chiniquy continued to administer to his French Canadian parishioners as a Catholic priest. In a February 14, 1857, letter, Bishop Bourget wrote that in Canada there was only talk of schism with horror and that people deplored the fact that a man who had done so much good in their own country could "lead their compatriots into ruin in a foreign country."[34]

This letter is addressed to Reverend Isaac Desaulniers, principal of the College of Ste. Hyacinthe. As Bourget's envoy, to help O'Regan win converts back to the Catholic Church, Desaulniers apparently had some success. The majority of French Canadians in Bourbonnais, St. George, St. Mary, and L'Érable adhered to their faith, and others, after momentary abandonment, returned. A January 1, 1857, letter in the *Montreal True Witness* expressed thanks for the interest and charity of Canadian prelates and informed compatriots in Quebec that

> through the labors of those whom you have sent to us we begin to see religion revive amongst us; families at discord again reunite in the bonds of the peace of the Lord and are preparing to enjoy that harmony which so universally obtains in our happy Canada. Already upwards of a hundred persons have drawn nigh into the Sanctuary in order to obtain release from the sentence of excommunication which they had incurred by countenancing the performance of the sacred offices of the Church. . . . The movement taking place amongst us, and around us, assures us that the schism is checked; that it no longer spreads; but that, on the contrary, it is diminishing and that we have every reason to expect that in a few months no traces of it will remain.[35]

By April 1857, Desaulniers was able to report to Bourget that 115 families in St. Mary were against Chiniquy, and to this could be added another dozen who had moved from St. Anne since the previous August and twenty-five Belgian families who remained completely opposed. However, he acknowledged that Chiniquy had as many families supporting him, most of them in St. Anne and some in Kankakee. At a public assembly of Kankakee French Canadian citizens on April 27, 1857, it was resolved that the priests from Canada should see to their business in that country rather than send priests to sow discord among those living in the United States.

Throughout the spring of 1857, the events of the previous year were played out in the Quebec press. Chiniquy wrote extensive letters, frequently quoting himself from earlier communiqués. On two occasions, full-paged exegeses written by an individual signing himself anonymously as "Sacerdos" were published in the pro-Chiniquy newspaper *l'Avenir*. It is quite likely that these were also authored by Chiniquy. The *Chicago Daily Tribune* became a vehicle for reviewing the argument between O'Regan and the French Canadians of Chicago. In one communication, a French Canadian expressed umbrage that Desaulniers had accused his own people of being ignorant and illiterate. Finally, in response to further complaints from O'Regan, who made reference in a letter to self-styled vigilantes in St. Anne who intimidated opponents—"You know not what your Canadian people can do in these states. In their ignorance and prejudice, they stop at nothing, they spare no one"—Bishop Bourget sent a second delegation to Illinois.[36]

Leading this delegation was the Vicar General of Quebec, Alexis Mailloux, a man who assembled, perhaps almost obsessively and in the manner of a modern-day special prosecutor, enormous documentation on the Chiniquy affair.[37] On the eve of their departure for Illinois, Bourget counseled his emissaries to only count on the aid of God, be as wise as a serpent, do not fear to state opposition but with charity, keep cool, be on guard in words and actions, work to bring people back into the church, try to make Canadians understand that they should love their bishop and all the priests and make them also understand that they should not be behind each time in supporting the construction of new churches or the sustenance of their priests, be obedient to the bishop, and meditate each day.[38] A letter of introduction from the Bishop of Chicago, published in the *Courrier du Canada* on May 5, 1857, claims that "these holy men have come deserting home and friends that they may teach you the doctrines of truth and life; and that they may save you from the falsehood and corruptions of an artful schismatic."

One of the first achievements of this new delegation was the June 4 celebration in Bourbonnais of a communal ritual of intensification to reaffirm both Catholic and French Canadian values. The excuse was a dinner to honor Desaulniers—"The Canadian missionary who reduced M. Chiniquy to impotence"—before his departure for Canada, said the June 23, 1857, *Courrier du Canada*. Amid the harmony and gaiety of a banquet attended by close to two thousand people, temperance was observed. Everyone joined in the singing of Canadian songs. Spink, as the "founder of the colony of L'Érable," was among those who spoke. According to the June 30, 1857, *Courrier du Canada*, others who addressed Desaulniers and the audience were Joseph Lottinville of St. Mary, who told the priest that he had "prevented the propagation of false and subversive doctrine," and Alfred Spink, a former student of Desaulniers at the College of Ste. Hyacinthe. A procession with decorated horses and a prominently displayed US flag proceeded through the city streets of Kankakee. The claim was made that a moral coup had been delivered to the schismatics. However, toward the close of the celebrations, at the railroad station where the "Catholic Canadians" had gathered to send Desaulniers off, an effigy was burned by presumed supporters of Chiniquy.

O'Regan continued to warn Mailloux of Chiniquy's treachery: "He will, with his usual artifice, turn it to fatal account against the interests of religion. Chiniquy's plan is to entrap you and take the people away from you by affecting to be their friend. . . . We are not safe with him unless we are most cautious." To his mind there was one simple course for the apostate priest: "he should submit humbly and penitently to the authority of the Church and solicit forgiveness."[39] By this time, July 1857, Mailloux had decided that there was an urgent need for schools staffed by French-speaking priests and asked Bourget to send representatives of the Order of St. Viateurs.

In August 1857, O'Regan had had enough and tendered his resignation. In an August 19 letter to Bourget, he claimed he had been in Chicago for three years and without an hour of peace. Although he departed for Rome, criticisms continued. In a November 6 letter to Mailloux, he reported learning of an incident in Kankakee where he was burned in effigy: "What very wicked wretches these Chiniquy people are. May God bless them and save them all from evil."[40]

By November 1857 new charges were hurled at Mailloux and his assistants not only on the pages of Quebec newspapers but also in the *Chicago Daily Tribune*. They were accused of offering a local Kankakee attorney $3,000 to sue the town of St. Anne and Father Chiniquy. The *Chicago Daily Tribune*, November 25, 1857, asked, "Is it possible that for such a guilty and base use, the clergy of Canada employ the money they pick from our poor and over credulous kinsmen under the name of tithes of the Propagation of Faith?"[41] This is followed by a suggestion that

Mailloux and his associates return to Canada rather than face the consequences of the increasing wrath of the young men of St. Anne.

The battle of words continued into 1858. Chiniquy attempted to sweep the problem under the carpet by convincing O'Regan's temporary replacement, Bishop Clement Smyth of Dubuque, that the submission that he had sent to O'Regan had been accepted. In Mailloux's view, Chiniquy perceived this period of transition as an opportunity to reestablish his reputation with the Catholic hierarchy. Smyth was not to be duped. In an April 23, 1858, letter, Smyth reported having received a communication from "some practical infidel of that place telling me that if I would not restore Chiniquy, if ever I went to St. Anne they would burn me at the stake. . . . After such conduct they have the impudence to send a deputation to me. I hope they will stay home."[42]

During the first half of 1858, the word "Protestant" lingered long on the lips of those involved in or observing the affairs of Chiniquy and the St. Anne community. Mailloux noted that the schismatics neither kneeled nor made the sign of the cross. He commented on a dance attended by several "Chiniquyites" where they "ate meat like true Protestants. When one is schismatic, one is almost half Protestant."[43] Chiniquy himself in a letter to Bourget in March 1858 denied the gossip that the pastor and the people of St. Anne want to cease to be Catholic.

In late July 1858, the new Bishop of Chicago, James Duggan, departed for St. Anne with advice from Mailloux to "remind these Canadians of the manner in which they were instructed and raised in Canada; their pure faith and their glorious submission to their superiors."[44] Clearly, the trip—a final formal effort to end the schism—was not successful. Duggan claimed that he had to call for protection from the sheriff when faced with the menacing threats of Chiniquy supporters. An act of excommunication that stuck (in the sense that it was fully recognized by Chiniquy) came on August 3. Duggan delivered it twice, audibly and forcefully, amidst heckling from the assembled crowd. On the twenty-second of the month, Chiniquy formally severed himself, claiming that the bishop was asking of him "not an act of submission, but of adoration."[45] In explaining his decision to his flock, Chiniquy hesitated to use the word "Protestant," telling them instead that they would become Christian Catholics and use the Word of God as their guide. He stripped the chapel he had built in St. Anne of its cross, removed the statue of the Virgin, and banished the Stations of the Cross.[46]

In this dramatic move, he was followed by roughly 80 percent of his congregation in St. Anne, having convinced them that it was a matter of defending their property from the greedy bishops of Chicago and their traditions from the assimilationist and discriminatory penchant of an essentially Irish Catholic clergy.[47] Within single extended families, there were divisions along religious lines, some having chosen to remain Catholic and others following the apostate whom they continued to address as "Father." For example, among the essentially adult children of one of the early settlers in the region, Jean-Baptiste Regnier, all the daughters remained Catholics while the four sons (two of whom lived in St. Anne, one in Bourbonnais, and one in Papineau) followed Chiniquy into formal schism.

In a letter in several newspapers, including in the May 21 issue of the *Presbyterian*, Chiniquy explained the actions that he and his parishioners had taken.

> The awful abuses and exactions of the Romish Bishop of Chicago against which we have thought necessary as Christians and freemen to oppose.... Thousands and thousands have been induced to study the foundations of the ... infallible authority of the Roman hierarchy and have concluded that the imbecility of the people on one side and the most unblushing imprudence on the other is the only source of that power of the Roman Church which keeps so many millions of souls in the chains of slavery and darkness.

Turner suggests that it is in the redressive phase of a social drama, a phase marked by liminality, that pragmatic techniques and symbolic action reach their fullest expression.[48] Certainly, the Catholic hierarchy attempted to adopt a pragmatic approach in sending envoys of similar cultural background to Illinois. By organizing a series of public rituals, they attempted to draw converts back into the fold. The Chiniquyites responded in kind with their own symbolic actions, including the public burning of an effigy. The language of confrontation escalated to new and more colorful heights as accusations were hurled from one side toward the other and back again. By the end of this period of liminality, the confrontation had reached a point of no return, and the new boundary between those identifying as Roman Catholic and those identifying as something akin to Protestants began to emerge. It was in the next phase, the recognition of schism, that this boundary was formalized.

The Recognition of Schism

Early in 1859, Charles Chiniquy returned to Montreal on a speaking tour, determined to explain and justify to his compatriots the actions that he and his colonists had taken. Prior to his arrival, Bourget issued a pastoral letter denouncing the apostate and warning Bourget's parishioners to stay away from the lecture halls where Chiniquy was scheduled to speak. Letters back to Mailloux in Illinois refer to Chiniquy's "shameless" behavior and to the "ignorant and curious" amid his crowd of supporters.[49] The newspapers reported efforts to keep Chiniquy from speaking, lynch mobs, and threats of assassination. The *Quebec Mercury*, swept up in the controversy, criticized the pro–Catholic Church newspapers *Courrier du Canada* and *Le Canadien* of a failure to censure violence. In a February 15, 1859, *Quebec Mercury* editorial, they responded, "We live under a British government and cherish what in Quebec is a mere fiction: every man's house is his castle. Will the Roman Catholic people of Quebec never learn that liberty of speech and action within the limits of the law is every man's birth right?"

In the same newspaper four days later, the debate was escalated further—clearly, Chiniquy's visit had stirred not only Catholic-Protestant rivalries but also the ethnic rivalries between French and English. Several broader factors were in play here: 1859 was the centennial anniversary of James Wolfe's defeat of the French on the Plains of Abraham in Quebec City, it was eight years before the formation of the Dominion of Canada independent from Britain, and the French and English of the united provinces of Upper and Lower Canada were at odds, and government was virtually impossible. The article "The Liberty of Speech and the Appeal to England" refers to a Quebec city council member named Audette, who had argued that the majority should decide who should be permitted to speak publicly and that the magistrate of the city had no right to protect any person to whom the majority might chance to be hostile. In ironic tones, the *Mercury* accused Audette of suggesting that "individual action and personal freedom have been abolished in Canada . . . and the old French despotism restored." A more general accusation was then made—that the Catholic clergy desired a court of appeals in Canada that they could stock with their own people, thereby assuring that every case involving property or reputation would be decided in their favor. The Chiniquy affair became a rallying point for a Protestant minority in Quebec, protected by a sovereign in England, to assert forthrightly its rights against the French Catholic majority. Although Chiniquy had not yet declared himself a Protestant, he arrived at many of his public appearances surrounded by his former enemies "les Suisses." Asked about his Protestantism, he declared himself (evasively in the minds of some observers) in support of a "liberty of conscience."[50]

In Quebec, many former Chiniquy admirers retracted their support from the Apostle of Temperance. In Illinois, certain uncontrollable events during the springs and summers of 1858 and 1859 operated in Chiniquy's favor to maintain the allegiance of the French Canadians in St. Anne and solidify permanent schism. These events ultimately resulted in the final step of the schismatic movement—the affiliation of his new church with Presbyterianism.

The harvests of 1858 and 1859 were poor. Unseasonable rains, insect infestations, and late-summer frosts resulted in crop failures. For lack of feed, hogs and cattle had to be disposed of, leading later to a shortage of meat. Many of the French Canadian settlers were forced to take out second mortgages on their homes and/or farms or chattel mortgages on their farm animals, farm implements, and other personal belongings. Between January 1858 and December 1859, 102 chattel mortgages issued to French Canadians were recorded in the ledgers of Kankakee County. In some cases, a single individual was involved in several such loans. For example, Francis Xavier Dube, a forty-eight-year-old farmer in St. Anne with eight children and real property valued at $1,300, is listed six times during this period.[51] While Dube appeared to be taking his loans from neighbors and compatriots, others were forced to borrow from loan sharks in Kankakee who charged more exorbitant interest rates.[52]

By the summer of 1859, the difficulties faced by his colonists impelled Chiniquy to launch a speaking tour on the East Coast to solicit funds, food, and clothing for his French Canadian converts. He spoke eloquently in Philadelphia to the Presbyterian community, and they responded.[53] Indeed, during 1859 and 1860, the pages of the major journalistic mouthpiece of the Presbyterian Church in the United States, the *Presbyterian*, were filled with references to the converts in Illinois and their plight.

Chiniquy regaled Protestants on the East Coast with powerful (though perhaps apocryphal or exaggerated) stories of particular families whose new faith had been tested to its limits but who persevered. He accused the Catholics of deliberately bringing him and other French Canadians to court repeatedly in order to put them in economic penury.[54] He warned that if support was not forthcoming, the Catholic Church and its representatives would be all too quick to gloat over the fact that the errant sheep were paying for their sins—that the suffering was the Lord's doing. He argued in the August 6, 1859, *Presbyterian* for the "sympathy and substantial aid of evangelical Christians of every name; and we trust they will not be permitted to be crushed by the perseverance and powerful machinations of that corrupt hierarchy they have renounced."

Chiniquy's accusations did not fall on deaf ears. The Presbyterian Church was one of the earliest to become involved in the nativist and anti-Catholic movements of the first half of the nineteenth century. During the 1830s, readers of the

Presbyterian followed closely the debate between the Reverend John Breckenridge and John Hughes, a Roman Catholic bishop of New York, on the question of whether either the Roman Catholic religion or the Presbyterian religion was "inimical to civil or religious liberty."[55] At the meeting of the Presbyterian General Assembly in 1834, Reverend Philo F. Phelps delivered a speech that "gave to Presbyterianism the impulse that was to make it the leading church in the crusade against Catholicism in coming years."[56] The following year, Lyman Beecher published his *Plea for the West*, in which he argues that the future of the nation would be decided on the western frontier. If theologians did not take an interest in this vast region of the country, Beecher believed that it would fall prey to the antiliberal and antirepublican spirit of Catholicism.

The events in St. Anne, Illinois, offered a response to this "plea for the West." One anonymous reader of the *Presbyterian*, in the July 20, 1859, issue, offered a broader historical context for what had occurred there: "Since the days of the Reformation no fact in the history of the Church of Christ is more worthy of the attention of the Christians than the moral reformation which is occurring in this state of Illinois among the French-Canadian and Belgian Roman Catholics." Indeed, Chiniquy was given the epithet "the second Luther" by a visitor to St. Anne, who, identifying himself only with the initials E. P., wrote a letter to the *New York Commercial Advertiser* that the *Chicago Press and Tribune* reprinted on October 14, 1859. Although certainly not without its own bias, this letter is, nevertheless, a rather heartfelt and revealing description of Chiniquy's charisma (a topic the next chapter takes up) and of the most important aspects of the schismatic movement Chiniquy had instigated.

> Mr. Chiniquy is a short thick-set man, and his head and neck similar in form to H. W. Beecher's, and if you could see and hear him in his own house and among his people, you would think the days of Luther were come again. . . . At three o'clock the bell sounded. There is a large green in front of their building called "Church," and the latter resembles in appearance a high wooden country school house. The American flag was floating in the breeze at one end, and a lady told me that the American flag was their banner outside, and the Bible their banner within the building. It was a Sunday school only in the afternoon; but oh, if you could have seen, as I did, the crowds seated in that large room, old men and young, women and children, all with the Bible in their hands and learning to read in English. . . . They had singing

> several times, using our familiar psalms and hymns in French.... About thirteen hundred were present during morning service, and about a hundred Romanists came out of curiosity. Of these, many were moved to tears and it will be without doubt the means of their conversion.... Mr. C. is one of the most eloquent men I have ever heard. He sways the whole body of his hearers and, though speaking in French, his soul is in his face and gestures.... The people of St. Anne are very poor, and must suffer if they do not have help, but people East are beginning to wake up, and Mr. Chiniquy receives something every week.... I was told that he feeds 25 persons daily at his own house; and the people all love him, and think that all he does is right.... I wish every lady East knew just how it actually was here; they would never regret giving money for the cause. You see, if they lose their hold of the Church here, a Romish priest will come in.... I long to see the day, which Mr. C. says is not two years off, when every French family in this country will have the Bible.

The fate of the schismatic French Canadians in Illinois became a primary rallying point not only in the battle between Catholics and Protestants but also among the various Protestant sects themselves. Representatives of the Episcopalian and Baptist Churches traveled to St. Anne with their own religious tracts in hand. A report simply signed, "A visitor" (it, like several of the other letters cited above, could have been penned by Chiniquy himself), in the *Presbyterian* on October 1, 1859, draws attention to the potential threat that these varying denominational influences might have: "Nothing would be more pleasing to Rome than to have the attentions of these people turned away from the gospel, and fixed upon those things which engender strife. The colony does not need these denominational tracts. Let those who send them give of their money to redeem the church and school property. These poor people need clothing and food and the Bible." Another article, "Sectarianism in St. Anne," concludes, "Those truly converted are but babes needing to be fed with the sincere milk of the word. Yet on one side is an Episcopalian pressing on their minds the claims of episcopacy; on the other are Baptists clamoring about immersion.... At such a sight angels might weep if angels could shed tears."

The Presbyterians congratulated themselves for sending money when others only sent religious tracts and for dispatching an able financier, Reverend Moses Staples, to negotiate in person rather than by letter: "Others wanted to win him over by religious conversion.... We secured him and his congregation by trust deed and mortgage duly registered."[57] Meanwhile, the Episcopalians were also making claims of converting the colony to their faith. Indeed, Staples came into conflict with the representative of the Episcopal faith and accused him of intruding on Presbyterian turf.

These sectarian conflicts persisted into the early 1860s with each denomination claiming the most adherents. Chiniquy tried to stem them by claiming that he and his colony did not yet know enough about the differences between them to embrace one. What they needed, he said in the October 15, 1859, *Presbyterian*, was support so as to avoid becoming "a wilderness on which the Church of Rome will plant her victorious colors." With these words, Chiniquy powerfully evoked the image of a battleground where a serious war was being waged.

His appeals worked. By late November 1859, "$8,000 in cash, 100 boxes, averaging 275 to 300 pounds in weight, 18 barrels weighing about 200 pounds each, 5 large trunks and 2 bales all of them filled with goods of almost every description" had been shipped to Illinois, the December 1, 1859, *Chicago Press and Tribune* reported. When Chiniquy returned from the East Coast at the end of December, he was greeted with cannons and demonstrations. His bodyguard came in from St. Anne to escort him home, according to the January 5, 1860, *Kankakee Gazette*. Though the analogy is loose, Chiniquy can be likened to other millenarian prophets documented in various places at different times. His ability to come through with material goods enhanced his power and social status. The coincidence of religious fervor with charismatic leadership, drought, and famine is not uncommon.

Not everyone responded favorably to Chiniquy's achievements in Philadelphia, New York, and Boston. By the close of 1859, the reality of the famine had itself become a matter of political debate. The *Chicago Daily Times* on December 12, 1859, in "The Kankakee Famine: Politics and Religion" suggests that Chiniquy was sustained by two papers, the *Tribune* of Chicago and the *New York Journal of Commerce*, both of which, according to the *Daily Times*, had a "mission to overthrow the Pope." The *Daily Times* accused the *Tribune* of egging Chiniquy on in the interest of "making capital for the Republican Party. . . . The Catholic Church, its prelates and ministers were denounced as the natural allies of Democracy and slavery, while the pure men who had rallied round Mr. Chiniquy were the evangelized teachers of pure political truth."

The article went on to demonstrate changing voting patterns that had resulted from the schism and the *Tribune*'s involvement in it. Before 1858, the entire vote of French Catholics in Kankakee was cast against the Democrats. Even the Know-Nothing Party had been favored over the Democrats. But the *Daily Times* suggests that as the schism proceeded, the Democratic Party gained more votes from Catholics who were scorned in the *Tribune* pages. As a result, the *Tribune* changed its tune when the issue of famine arose: "How politics do change some men's notions of religious truth."[58]

In the December 1, 1859, *Chicago Tribune*, Chiniquy was now accused of fabricating a famine so that he could raise money to pay off the mortgages that he had secured on his own properties at high interest. Substantiation came in the form of an "eye-witness report" (a phrase that clearly evokes the informed authority of the writer) of a *Tribune* reporter who had traveled to St. Anne: "Father Chiniquy's parishioners are better off than they have ever been . . . enjoying the luxuries of life. Their church buildings are in the hands of Protestants and in no danger of being wrested from them."

> True they are in debt for their land; true they are poor; true, they must study economy to make both ends meet; but the same things are true of half the men in this and every other State; and the pretense that they ought to be singled out as the objects of a special charitable effort is a bold invention of Father Chiniquy himself. We hope to hear no more of this impudent begging, no more of the mistaken and unnecessary gifts of our Eastern friends.

The reporter argues that sums sent from the East Coast would have the negative effect of "confirming the shiftless and lazy habits" prevalent in the colony. No one, the article concludes, was starving: "There are some to whom the distribution of a few of the necessaries of life would not come amiss. . . . But this want could have been easily supplied at a very small expense by an appeal to Kankakee or Chicago." This fact was reiterated by local leaders and businessmen in Kankakee who were concerned about the negative reputation their region was receiving in the press, a reputation that would deter those contemplating settlement in the area. At a local meeting, they resolved to correct the image that was being transmitted and pointed to the natural abundance of the region, including that St. Anne itself was shipping thousands of bushels of grain to market.

> Kankakee County is one of the best in the State. It is quite well timbered and watered, and its soil is unsurpassed by any in the world. It is admirably located, accessible by railroad to the best wheat market in the world. . . . We have an inexhaustible quarry of limestone, water power capable of driving many mills. . . . There never was a better opening for capitalists to invest in manufacturing

> business. . . . Property, owing to the great financial pressure, is very cheap. . . . A great portion of the land is still unimproved. Farms, admirably located, can now be purchased at almost half their real value.[59]

Nevertheless, there was an acknowledgment that St. Anne had been peculiarly afflicted by the loss of crops for three years past. Several churchmen who had visited the region substantiated the claims of suffering. Reverend Daniel Heilig described families subsisting on cornbread and water. Reverend Robert Farris of St. Louis told of Chiniquy impoverishing himself for his people. Reverend John Wilson related that fifty children were kept from school for want of shoes and clothing, and a large number were in school but barefoot.[60]

As to Chiniquy's claims that the ownership of his church was itself in danger, *Tribune* writers quoted from documents dated October 3, 1859, in the county clerk's office that say that the Protestant church in Kankakee was deeded to Reverend Moses Staples, agent and attorney for the Presbyterian General Assembly, O.S., for $1,000 on the conditions that it be known as the "Christian Catholic Church" and that it remain Protestant, keeping itself "wholly and entirely disconnected from the control of the Roman Catholic Church, or any of the Bishops or Priests, and shall remain Protestant, and not connect themselves with any ecclesiastical body of evangelizing Christians, or any church of a sectarian character, without the consent of said General Assembly." The deed stipulates that if these conditions were broken, the Presbyterian General Assembly was to be repaid with 10 percent interest. The chapel in St. Anne was mortgaged to the same parties under the same conditions for $2,000 paid to the trustees of the general assembly. It is more than likely that these deeds, which survive in local archives, help to explain Chiniquy's decision to eventually join the Presbyterian Church wholeheartedly.[61]

In response to such charges, Chiniquy accused his opponents of selling themselves to priests who guaranteed them votes in the next election. The *Tribune* report was dismissed because the writer had only been in St. Anne for an hour, clearly not enough time to develop the authority of a true eyewitness. Chiniquy himself claimed that whenever he had spoken, it was only about St. Anne and not about the entire Kankakee region. "I hope," he wrote in the December 28, 1859, *Kankakee Democrat*, "that there is not a man who will find fault with my having tried to save my people from the cruel sufferings of starvation and nakedness to which they were exposed." Needless to say, locals in Kankakee were most offended by his labeling of them as "infidels," as reported in the January 5, 1860, *Kankakee Gazette*.

Chiniquy was supported by a group of native-born farmers in Aroma Township, adjacent to St. Anne. In a January 25, 1860, letter in the *Kankakee Democrat*, these "Americans in favor of Chiniquy" state,

> He appears to be closely imitating the example of that blessed one who was on the earth over 1800 years ago, by his clothing the naked, feeding the starving and giving drink to the thirsty. . . . We believe with many others that the statements made by Father Chiniquy in regard to the real wants and suffering in Kankakee County to be true. We know that could Father Chiniquy bring money here to loan at six or seven percent per annum it would greatly relieve the present embarrassment of this county in money matters by curtailing the thirty to seventy percent per annum money loaners. Only the rich oppose him.

As with many social dramas related to religious matters that are of more recent date (for example, the PTL Ministry scandal and the conflagration at the Branch Davidian compound in Waco, Texas), it is as difficult to ferret the truth about the situation in Kankakee County in 1857. More impartial newspapers of the period did document problems with both crops and the weather. A general panic that began in 1857 as the boom conditions of the early part of decade subsided created an economic crisis that was then further aggravated by several bad harvest years.[62] Only in 1860 did near-normal conditions return. The evidence from deed and chattel mortgage records of the period substantiates the difficulties that local farmers were having keeping themselves afloat even though the most exorbitant loans referred to by Chiniquy in his orations cannot be substantiated for more than a handful of individuals. The American and Foreign Christian Union, under the leadership of Staples, sent people to St. Anne to assess the situation, and they reported that "amid two hundred families, four-fifths of those who sowed failed to reap a bushel of wheat; the greater portion of the 15,000 bushels of corn gathered was soft and could not be used for grinding; the early frost equally affected buckwheat; the debts amounted to $18,000 secured in trust deeds that would soon be foreclosed and the interest amounted to 9,000 to 10,000 annually," the December 21, 1859, *Kankakee County Democrat* said.[63] Some observers of the time raised their eyebrows at why problems arose only for farmers in St. Anne, but people in the region today claim that it is perfectly possible for crop failures to be extremely localized. If some wondered at the time why only converts appeared to be suffering, Chiniquy himself claimed that the famine had affected Catholics and Christian Catholics,

Americans and French Canadians alike, a fact substantiated by Reverend Baird in his report on the colony.[64] What is evident, however, is that there were those who made religious capital of the issue. An 1859 report of the American and Foreign Christian Union claims that it was the Lord's doing that St. Anne was afflicted: "God always humbles a people before he exalts."[65]

To summarize, once the schism was recognized, it became a cause célèbre among various Protestant denominations who had been watching closely the rapid growth of the Roman Catholic population during the 1850s. Religion became a contested political issue, and among the converts in St. Anne a new political identity, and, hence, a new boundary of difference emerged, layered over the religious divide that resulted from schism.

Stabilization? Joining the Presbyterian Church

According to Reverend R. Baird's account of the schism, Chiniquy reported approximately 695 families in central Illinois had followed him into schism and close to 200 elsewhere.[66] Chiniquy was clearly guilty of exaggeration, a tendency already noted in the discussion of his early history. He may also have been dishonest with funds and generated more conflict than necessary. This was certainly the accusation of Philip Worcester, Kankakee county clerk, in a statement "The Chiniquy Humbug," printed in the January 5, 1860, *Kankakee Gazette.* He called Chiniquy a "pious swindler" and accused him of sowing discord in what had been, prior to his arrival, a peaceful settlement. The metaphor of a battlefield, used frequently by both sides, was certainly appropriate, and events that followed tend to substantiate Worcester's viewpoint.

In the early part of 1860, Chiniquy appeared before the Chicago Presbytery and "gave a lengthy and detailed statement of the measurements which had induced him to renounce popery and to desire connection with the Presbyterian church, and was then carefully examined as to his experimental acquaintance with religion and as to his views of the doctrines of the Holy Scripture and of the sacrament and of Church polity. His responses having proved satisfactory, it was moved and seconded that he be received as an ordained minister."[67] With this action, Chiniquy and his Christian Catholic parishioners embraced Protestantism fully, renaming their church the First Presbyterian Church of St. Anne and entering under the jurisdiction of the Presbytery in Chicago.[68]

Antoine Lottinville, a Catholic resident of Papineau, gave his view of the event in a June 1860 letter to a daughter who had remained in Quebec.

Chiniquy looks constantly for any possible means to gain adherents. To make you laugh and to show you how he plays with the poor ignorants of St. Anne, I will translate here parts of his statement which appeared in an article which I found in the *Kankakee Gazette*.

> My friends, I have a great news to announce to you this day. I have joined the Presbyterian Church and I want you all to join it. It is the richest church in the Union. It has a capital of over $500,000 in the treasury, the interest of which is to support new congregations. There are some amongst you who will ask for a week of reflection; but it is useless. You cannot learn much in a week, and therefore you will not know more then about religion than you know now. . . . It is the best religion in existence. Do take my word and join it immediately. Why would you not take my word? Did not Peter take the word of Christ, when he ordered him to leave his wife, his children, and his boat, etc. and to follow him? Do not refuse me this favor because whenever other churches have given me four dollars apiece, the Presbyterian Church has given us ninety-dollars. One Presbyterian gentleman alone promised me $15,000 for the purpose of building a fine stone college in our town. You need very badly to join a rich church, to get assistance in defending that dreadful lawsuit that will be commenced against you for the purpose of taking our church from us. Besides, I have the promise of some $50,000 to redeem your lands from the hands of your present creditors. Do not leave me in confusion; you know that I have never deceived you as yet; do not let that money slide from you. Try the Presbyterian religion for a year and if you are not satisfied with it, then we will shall try another Church. Now let all those who want to join the Presbyterian Church stand up.[69]

About two-thirds of those who had supported Chiniquy for two years followed his decisions. The remainder joined the newly formed Baptist Church.[70]

Chiniquy expresses the hope, in the February 18, 1860, *Presbyterian*, that his decision would not draw criticism from other denominations "because this would please the Church of Rome which tells people that each Protestant group hates the next." It is evident that Chiniquy feared the fragmentation of his movement as a result of the local proselytizing of Presbyterians, Episcopalians, and Baptists.

He most likely felt that his movement could only be kept together through a firm commitment to one of these Protestant churches. In the same article, Chiniquy also continues his appeals for money by recounting the plight of specific individuals—a half-clothed woman who died of starvation and left three young children in his care, for example. In the spring of 1860, the Chicago Presbytery met in Kankakee, and several members who visited St. Anne pondered the "changes these people must have experienced and how thoroughly they must have yielded up their old prejudices and modes of worship." By the same spring, the economic difficulties of the past two years had all but disappeared, although on April 21, 1860, the *Presbyterian* was still carrying stories about needy colonists.[71]

By June, local and national newspapers were reporting good harvests. Reverend Staples wrote to the *Presbyterian* that there was no more need for money, although clothing for the coming winter would help. In July Chiniquy, supported by funds from the Chicago Presbytery, took his leave of the community to engage in an extended European lecture tour. In what is a clear indication of his powerful abilities with language, Chiniquy quoted from John Milton in a letter in the August 11, 1860, *Presbyterian* just after his departure: "The triple tyrant is trembling on his tottering throne and the children of those whose blood was so often shed are coming down from their mountains to reap in the valleys of Italy the crop which is ripe." Although the process of reintegration was seemingly complete and although Chiniquy had left the scene for a few months, the needs of his "children" continued to preoccupy the Chicago Presbytery for the next several years. New boundary markers began to emerge from within the Presbyterian denomination.

A New Social Drama, 1860–63

By October 1860, "evils in the French Church of St. Anne which the session of the Church now constituted are unable to redress" were brought to the attention of the Chicago Presbytery.[72] Certain elders, including Chiniquy's brother Achilles, were charged with immoralities and the misuse of funds. Achilles, who admitted to an "addiction to the use of profane language," agreed to withdraw from the position of elder. But the damage was done, and in December 1860 approximately 120 parishioners of the First Presbyterian Church of St. Anne petitioned the Chicago Presbytery to be permitted to establish a Second Presbyterian Church under the leadership of Reverend Theodore Monod, who had been serving in Chiniquy's place during his absence. The Presbytery responded by appointing a commission to examine the issue.

Father Chiniquy returned to St Anne late in 1860 and eventually agreed to the separation, though not before attempting to defame Monod. While in London, Chiniquy had written a letter to Fréderic Monod, a distinguished Protestant minister in France and Theodore Monod's father.[73] Fréderic, in turn, contacted the Chicago Presbytery about Chiniquy's letter and its "vague and undefined accusations against his son." He lamented the fact that what was going on in St. Anne was to be hampered by the fault of men and wondered whether Chiniquy's letter was meant to stir further intrigue. He claimed that prior to this attack, Chiniquy had spoken favorably of Theodore and asserted that none of what Chiniquy had put in the letter could possibly be true.

In a response to Fréderic's letter, Chiniquy, by this time back in St. Anne, replied in February 1861 that it had "cost him not a little to tell you those things and that my heart bled and still is bleeding as your own on that account. I hoped that on my arrival in my colony I might have comforted you by writing to you that I had been deceived. But alas the sad truth is that I had not told you half of the reasons that we have, both of us, to weep." He went on to make an allusion to homosexuality and to accuse Theodore, whom he had put in his house to replace him in his absence, of "taking away the confidence of my people."[74]

Fréderic dismissed Chiniquy's letter as calumny. Chiniquy later retracted the charges, and the Chicago Presbytery assured the senior Monod of the "affectionate confidence in which they held his son."[75] With approval from the Chicago Presbytery, the Second Presbyterian Church was formed in February 1861 with Theodore Monod serving as minister until 1865 when he was replaced by Reverend H. E. Lippert, a German who also officiated over the French Presbyterian Church in Kankakee. The first elders were André Chagnon, Philippe Ducharme, Sévere Martin, and Placide Boudreau, and the first deacons were Magloire Desmarteaux and Toussaint Martin. Of these men, only Ducharme was over forty, a Papineau township farmer with $1,000 in real property in 1860 and five children living at home. Sévere Martin, Chagnon, and Desmarteaux were thirty, thirty-one, and thirty five with three, five, and four children, respectively; Martin and Desmarteaux were farmers with real property valued at $600 each, and Chagnon was a joiner with $2,000 worth of real property. Toussaint Martin, a twenty-eight-year-old shoemaker, had three children and $1,000 in real property; Placide Boudreau, eighteen and a teacher, was in 1860 living with his father, Joseph, a forty-one-year-old farmer. Among the schismatics, it appears that those who remained with Chiniquy were on average older than those who stood behind Monod.

The Second Presbyterian Church leased a house from Cyrille Miron at $5 per month to serve as their sanctuary and by November had hired a sexton and agreed every member was to bring in a load of firewood for the winter. Membership continued to increase in the following years until by 1881 eighty-nine families were in the congregation.

Disagreements over church discipline seem to have caused the split with the First Presbyterian Church. Monod had emphasized an orderly spiritual life. A letter signed A. H. in the April 6, 1861, *Presbyterian* claimed that fifty-seven members had been admitted to the new congregation by late March 1861. On his visit to St. Anne, A. H. met several young men and women: "Each of these seemed to understand clearly that in professing Christ before men they were renouncing the sinful pleasures—the pomps and vanities of the world." Many of these illiterate converts, the visitor reported, traced their serious religious awakening to Monod.

If the reprimands and disciplinary actions taken by the Second Church elders and reported in the session minutes are any indication, this serious and pious approach continued during the two and a half decades of existence of the Second Presbyterian Church. For example, in July 1866 it was brought to the attention of the elders that three members had taken part in a ball. They were called on to acknowledge their faults to the whole church. At the same time, O. Brosseau was called before the session to answer charges of not being able to live in harmony with his wife and to have caused a public scandal. By August 8, Brosseau had withdrawn his membership, but Mrs. Brosseau was exhorted "to submit to her husband and to be meek towards him." The following January the same "sister" who had acknowledged her sin in attending balls was again caught in the act and told that she would not be admitted to the Lord's table "until she give satisfactory evidence that she has renounced her worldliness." The most severe action came against Mary Laroche in February 1870. Miss Laroche confessed to the session that she had "attended three promiscuous dances in three places: at Mr. Baptiste Goyette's, a Roman Catholic; at Mr. Antoine Masse's, an Episcopalian; and at Mr. Mose Morin's, an elder of the First Presbyterian Church." The session resolved that

> in view of all the public and private instructions which that sister had received, in view of all the cases of discipline which she had witnessed in the church and in her father's family, and in view of the position of the other churches of St. Anne in reference to the question of dancing, the said Mary Laroche shall be excommunicated . . . unless she should show repentance and confess publicly before the church to have dishonored her profession of Christ.

She did not repent for another year and at that time was readmitted to communion. By November 1871 she was again reported for attending a meeting where there was "promiscuous dancing." Again she repented and was forgiven. Clearly, the members of this church were determined to survive by setting themselves apart and by publicly shaming their members to adhere to the tenets (especially those against dancing and drinking) of their faith.[76]

A second source of dissatisfaction and disagreement that led to the division into two Presbyterian congregations in St. Anne arose from Chiniquy's actions: matters of "common fame," including giving false statistics, and his supposed mismanagement of church funds from the Presbyterian General Assembly to benefit the colony at large. At an April 1861 meeting in Aurora, having heard Chiniquy's explanation of the charges, the presbytery found itself "unable to pronounce any satisfactory judgment. The public rumors are still rife and rather tending to increase than die away. It is therefore the judgment of the committee that neither the name of Reverend Chiniquy can be adequately vindicated if innocent nor the cause of right and the honor of religion be fairly maintained without a formal thorough judicial process."[77]

After a lengthy hearing, extensively reported in the Chicago Presbytery minutes, Chiniquy was exonerated, largely on the basis of reasonable doubt and misunderstanding. For example, to the charge that he had indicated to certain Episcopalians that he favored affiliation with that church, thereby deceiving one party or the other, Chiniquy responded that he "earnestly and sincerely preferred Presbyterianism . . . but failing to convince and satisfy all to go together, in the spirit of enlarged charity, he had sanctioned the wishes of those of his colony who desired to connect themselves with the Episcopal church."[78] To the charge that he had exaggerated statistics on the number of converts, the Presbytery questioned whether such exaggerations were criminal and concluded that "whilst in the course of the evidence certain indiscretions on the part of Mr. Chiniquy in certain instances arising from a want of proper knowledge of Presbyterian usages, and his peculiarly impulsive and sanguine temperament as well as his previous ecclesiastical training were developed, the Presbytery find nothing in evidence to impeach the sincerity of his notions or the integrity of his character."[79] A representative of the committee who visited St. Anne in late July 1861 noted that the great mass of people were adhering to Chiniquy (more than eight hundred communicants) despite the second church and small Baptist and Episcopalian groupings.

The Second Presbyterian Church of St. Anne elders conferred on May 15 on the measures to be taken after Chiniquy's acquittal by the Chicago Presbytery. They decided not to alter their decision to remain as a separate church and recorded their "surprise" at the acquittal, "regarding it as injurious to the interests of truth and righteousness and to the good name of the Presbyterian Church."[80] They also entered a second complaint to the synod against the Chicago Presbytery ruling.

In the fall of 1861, the Chicago Presbytery resolved to cease all connection with the school at St. Anne, "leaving Mr. Chiniquy to manage the educational interests of his people in his own way."[81] However, they also advised Chiniquy to abstain from any interference with the functioning of the French Protestant Church in Kankakee, a warning that emerged from attacks that Chiniquy had made against Moses Staples. The members of the Second Presbyterian Church received this news "with deep sadness," regarding it as "doing further injury not only to the Presbyterian Church but even to the cause of evangelical religion."[82]

By August 1861, Staples had protested in the *Courrier du Canada* about Chiniquy's habit of sending money he had raised to his brother Achilles. People in St. Anne believed that Achilles was dishonest and had used substantial portions of the funds to speculate.[83] Staples declared himself no longer Chiniquy's friend. During the spring of 1862, Chiniquy brought one civil suit against Staples for an accounting of money Chiniquy had entrusted to him and a second suit for slander against Reverend J. B. l'Hote, Staples's successor as pastor of the French Presbyterian Church in Kankakee. This eventually led to the Chicago Presbytery bringing a new inquiry and new charges of "unministerial and unchristian conduct" against Chiniquy himself. He was accused of helping to prevent the payment and collection of some promissory notes the Board of Education of the General Assembly issued to help bring the colonists out of penury (these were managed by Staples and later l'Hote),[84] misrepresenting the facts with regard to a "college" established in St. Anne to train young French Canadians for work as colporteurs, instigating a suit for libel against l'Hote, bearing false witness, and violating the *Book of Discipline*.[85] The nature and purpose of the college, in particular, became the subjects of lengthy discussion in the *Presbyterian* and the various Kankakee papers.[86] During the summer of 1862, the Chicago Presbytery several times summoned Chiniquy before them; all of them were ignored. The relationship between Chiniquy and the Chicago Presbytery deteriorated to such an extent that eventually the only course of action open to the Presbytery was suspension. The charge was contumacy. Chiniquy withdrew his congregation from the Chicago Presbytery but not before accusing them of having more Jesuitism than the Romish church.[87]

In June 1862, the First Presbyterian Church of St. Anne applied for admission to a Canadian Presbytery. The deputation the Synod of the Canada Presbyterian

Church sent to Illinois to investigate concluded that it had seen and heard nothing that "justified withdrawing confidence from Mr. Chiniquy."

> They subjected him to severe scrutiny—they tested his statements by every means in their power; they examined voluminous documents in his possession, which the Presbytery have not yet seen; they found a large and enthusiastic congregation attached to him as their pastor, and resolved to adhere to him; they saw three young men under instruction for the Gospel ministry, and had good evidence presented to them of the fact that at one time upwards of thirty young lads, from 14 to 21 years of age, were desirous to study for the ministry whatever their fitness for this profession might be.[88]

At an assembly, the delegation asked all those who professed to be under Chiniquy's pastoral care in St. Anne to stand up and counted not less than 550 people, mostly adults. A show of hands demonstrated that with one exception they were all in favor of joining the Canadian synod. Although the Canadian synod preferred a reconciliation between Chiniquy and his congregation and the Chicago Presbytery, over the following year it became apparent that such a reconciliation was impossible and that neither side was willing to relent. Sympathetic to his work and in its desire to see it continue, the Synod of the Canada Presbyterian Church voted to admit Chiniquy and his congregation to the Presbytery of London, Ontario, in June 1863.

The Reverend Alexander Kemp, the chairman of the committee the Canadian synod set up to evaluate Chiniquy's application, offered his own assessment of the situation in St. Anne.

> We are not insensible to the defects which may be found in Mr. Chiniquy's character. We know in this part of Canada what a French-Canadian priest is and we are not disposed to set up too high a standard by which to measure any of them who may escape from the demoralizing delusions under which they have been trained. The school is still going on. The students who were preparing for the ministry are scattered—some to war, some to business. The great bulk remain steadfast to Mr. Chiniquy.[89]

Kemp, who found most of the allegations against Chiniquy untenable, believed that it was, in part, Chiniquy's ignorance of the procedures of the Presbyterian Church that misled him. Equally, Kemp felt that "to a brother whose position demanded the maximum of consideration and charity, the Presbytery dealt out the maximum of their severity."[90] Kemp concluded his final report on the Chiniquy affair by lamenting that the Chicago Presbytery, "entrusted with the guidance and preservation of one of the most striking awakenings of the French people that has occurred on this continent, [has caused] a people to be scattered and peeled—a flock breaking up into factions, some of whom, alas, discouraged and perplexed are turning again to the bondage from which they had well nigh escaped."[91] Above all, Chiniquy's success and popularity among the converts won him support from the Canadian synod, and in 1876 he was invited by the newly formed board of French-Canadian Evangelization of the Presbyterian Church in Canada to work among the French Canadian population in the Dominion. This he did for almost five years before returning to full-time residence in St. Anne in 1881 and resumption of his duties as pastor of the First Presbyterian Church.

The Denouement: Reemergence and Reunification

The confrontational aspect of the schism was kept alive in the years following 1863 by occasional events that provided individuals with the opportunity to hurl invectives at one another. In 1866, for example, Lemoine, an early follower of Chiniquy who ultimately remained a Catholic and became a justice of the peace in Kankakee, authored a circular advertising a Catholic charity concert in Kankakee in January 1867. The concert was to raise money to build a church, convent, and some Catholic schools "to protect our dear little Canadians from the incessant attacks of the unhappy Chiniquy. . . . The foxy Chiniquy," he warned, "will not lose this good occasion to vent himself on our bishops and to turn everything into ridicule."[92]

In 1869 claims of a new famine affecting the populations of St. Anne and St. Mary opened old wounds. Kemp made a personal visit to the area to assess the situation and determined that the wheat and corn crops were ruined. Many men, assessing their losses, had moved north with their teams to work on the railway, but they were not paid by the subcontractors. Dysentery and typhoid were rampant. Though substantiated by Stephen Moore, an attorney in Kankakee, in the September 23, 1869, *Kankakee Gazette*, P. Gendron challenged the new-famine claims in the newspaper on October 14. After raising doubt as to Moore's ability to even comment on St. Anne, he said that the failure of wheat was usual in an area not considered ideal for that crop and that both oats and potatoes were in plentiful supply.

> It is true that our corn crop is a partial failure this year, on account of the heavy rains . . . but I do not know that Catholics or even Protestants other than those under the pastoral care of Mr. Chiniquy have fared any better; yet no call has been made for relief by anyone from either of those counties except from Mr. Chiniquy [who has] reinaugurated the wholesale begging system of 1858 and 1859. [This] casts shame and dishonor on this splendid colony. There were no grounds in 1858 and 1859 and there are no grounds today.

Gendron's letter, in turn, provoked vituperative responses, including the claim that he had personally solicited signatures from Chiniquy's enemies. Pierre Laplante, a farmer in Papineau, accused Gendron of promoting discord and hard feelings and categorized him with the "cynics of St. Anne who never fail to discover a swindler in the charitable man, a treacherous plot in any commendable effort to assist the destitute."[93] By November 11, the *Kankakee Gazette* decided to publish no further personal commentaries but only communications that were based on facts. A decade later, the newspaper was clearly no longer game to nourish the local conflicts between Protestant and Catholic French Canadians.

Whether Chiniquy was the source of these occasional references to hard times in St. Anne is uncertain, but, of course, he played his part in fanning the flames of controversy through his preaching and his writing. In 1876 he published *The Priest, The Woman, and the Confessional*, a volume that angered many who considered it straight "filth" but which was read internationally by growing numbers of anticlericals.[94] A decade later, the first of many editions of his autobiography *Fifty Years in the Church of Rome* was published. The confrontational language is apparent from the opening dedication to Colonel Edwin Sherman, who, Chiniquy claims, helped him in his research of the true murderers of the martyred Abraham Lincoln.[95] He also dedicates the book to "Americans! You are sleeping on a volcano and you do not suspect it! You are pressing on your bosom a viper which will bite you to death and you do not know it. Read this book and you will see that Rome is . . . the deadly enemy of your schools, your institutions, your dearly bought rights and liberties."

Chiniquy was absent from St. Anne for lengthy periods. The longest was between 1876 and 1881, when he worked for the board of French-Canadian Evangelization in Montreal. It was this board (known as a committee until 1875) that continued the support of St. Anne. Chiniquy lectured throughout Quebec, where he claimed many converts but also faced violent mobs. In one incident, several hundred British volunteers confronted several hundred French Canadian students.[96] Chiniquy also traveled abroad spreading news of his achievements and his anti-Romanist gospel. In June 1880 the St. Anne congregation requested the French-Canadian Evangelization board to return Chiniquy and gave the promise of a salary of $500 per year. This came at an opportune moment, because Chiniquy was escalating a conflict with the board over the property on which the school in St. Anne was built. Once he conveyed the property to the board, he was allowed to leave Canada. The board and the congregation agreed to a salary of $1,200 per year, each paying half. Chiniquy was requested to "abstain in future from all communications through the press or otherwise reflecting upon the Board or its management."[97]

In 1882 Chiniquy requested and was granted permission to leave for Britain for six months. Reverend M. R. Paradis took over the First Presbyterian Church. In September 1883, Paradis reported on his congregation to the *Presbyterian Record*.

> As we are weak financially, it takes us a pretty long time to do much. . . . Materially, improvements to the church, in the way of platform, ceiling raised, plastering, painting, etc. have been made to the amount of nearly $250. The Ladies' Sewing Circle and the Young People's Society lately started are doing good work. Spiritually, at communion last month twenty-nine persons joined the Church, three of whom were baptized. In the Sabbath school, though the attendance is no larger, the interest has increased greatly and the progress in learning is manifest, especially among young people.[98]

By 1884 Chiniquy was back in Canada again. In June, in a letter to Margaret Lighthall, a member of a prominent Protestant family in Montreal, he mentions having received "bruises and wounds in riots in Quebec."[99] He prepared to return to Illinois.

The residents of St. Anne and nearby Papineau who had "kept their faith" were forced to attend Mass in neighboring St. Mary until 1872 when a new Catholic church was built in St. Anne to replace the building Chiniquy had claimed for his new religion. In an October 17, 1871, letter to Bishop Bourget of Montreal from Father P. Beaudoin, a pastor in Bourbonnais, Bourget was advised that St. Anne required "a prudent man who with this quality could do incalculable good. Chiniquy is not as dangerous as one would believe. He makes more noise abroad than at home."[100] Indeed, the Catholic church leaders in Chicago, fearing that the number of converts to Protestantism, more broadly, would grow, appealed to the Viatorian Order in Quebec to send French-speaking clerics to Illinois to undertake the work of winning the settlers back into the fold. In 1886, as a further attempt to revive Catholicism in the area, a relic of Ste. Anne was sent to Illinois from the shrine of Ste. Anne de Beaupré in Quebec, and a novena and feast of Ste. Anne were established (this feast is the subject of chapter 6).

In 1884, when the *Kankakee County Atlas* was published, little was said about the Presbyterian churches in St. Anne for fear that it might "unnecessarily wound the feelings of others or engender a controversy from which no good could result."[101] The atlas estimates that a significant number of families belonging to the church had sought new homes in the far West.[102] The membership of the First Church was 625 communicants; that of the Second Presbyterian Church was counted at 126.

In the previous year, talks had been initiated to bring the two Presbyterian churches back together. A series of united prayer meetings was organized by the pastors of both churches. Each church worked for four years "mutually helping each other and cultivating kind feelings."[103] The final steps toward reunion were taken in 1887, prompted by Chiniquy's decision to retire as pastor of the First Church on January 1, 1888. The May 9, 1887, session minutes for the Second Church state,

> The union of the two congregations in St. Anne is the most important and chief event in the history of French Protestantism in Illinois since the reformation accomplished among the French Canadians under the admirable and splendid leadership of Father Chiniquy. May it not be proclaimed that the case of these two churches becoming one, thus showing this rare Christian generosity and largeness of views is a glorious example to other divided sections of the church of God who by uniting would not only save the offerings of Christians generally but also save Christianity of petty scandals. . . . Oh that men, Christian men would sacrifice their narrow and peculiar notions and views and realize more deeply the profound service of saying "United we stand and divided we fall."

The processual form of this second social drama is similar to that of the first, but the outcome is different. The breach was made public as conflicts with the Chicago Presbytery emerged. The conflict escalated but was temporarily resolved by the creation of two separate churches and the admission of Chiniquy's church into the Canadian Presbytery. This time, permanent schism was avoided, and, ultimately, the reintegration of the two congregations was achieved.

The reunited church remained under the Presbytery of Chatham until 1892 when it was returned to the Presbytery of Chicago. In that year, ground was broken to build a new church (fig. 2.1). Dedicated in 1893, this structure still stands today,

FIGURE 2.1. First Presbyterian Church, St. Anne, Illinois. *Photo by Caroline B. Brettell.*

although it lost its steeple in a tornado in 1916. Earlier in 1893, Chiniquy, who had resided in St. Anne (when he was not traveling and lecturing) for five years simply as a parishioner, returned to Montreal permanently to live out the remaining years of his life with his wife, Euphémie (he married his former housekeeper in 1863), and his daughters, Emma and Rebecca, who both eventually married Protestant ministers themselves. In a farewell sermon in March 1893, he was still warning his converts to be "on guard against Romanism—the insidious ways of priests and Jesuits are mysterious—beware of sects and divisions."[104]

Chiniquy returned to Illinois in 1895 (by this time he was eighty-six) to attend a meeting of the Chicago Presbytery in River Forest. Although somewhat apprehensive given the troubles in the 1860s, he delivered a three-minute speech. He was an old man, and four years later he died and was buried in Montreal, still refusing the offer of absolution from the Catholic Church (fig. 2.2). A few days before his death, he had called a notary to his room to assist him in the preparation of a "Profession of Faith," which was published in both French- and English-language newspapers in the province. This document explains precisely the reasons why he could never be reconverted to Romanism, among them his continued distrust of auricular confession, what he considered the "idolatrous" worship of the wafer, the shedding of the blood of martyrs, and the problem of priestly celibacy.[105] According to his son-in-law Reverend Joseph Morin, Chiniquy insisted that he never be left alone during the last few weeks of his life. He was afraid that the Roman Catholic Church might somehow claim his repentance and reconversion.

Wars of Words: The Rhetoric of Social Dramas

In his formulation of the social drama, Turner argues that each phase can have its own speech form. In the St. Anne schism, clear rhetorical themes emerge in the recurring use of particular words and in the discourse that characterize the conflict at different stages. It was as the crisis mounted that Chiniquy's own evocation of slavery and servitude, as well as the emphasis on the opposition between authority and submission, on the one hand, and private judgment, on the other, took shape. His position is reflected in some of the published communications of his followers. For example, a series of resolutions was passed in September 1859 on the anniversary of the schism. These resolutions were printed in the *Presbyterian* on September 17, 1859. Attributed to Augustin Faucher, a twenty-two-year-old parishioner in St. Anne, is the proposal that the Lord be thanked "for granting unto us the grace to break the *chains* which the Popes and Bishops of Rome have forged for the *thralldom* and shame of humanity."[106] The name of Francis Duclos, a thirty-three-year-old farmer in Papineau, is attached to a resolution proclaiming the celebration of the day when "we ceased to be slaves of men and became disciples of Christ." The following statement, attributed to Alexis Blanchette, a fifty-four-year-old farmer, raises the theme of freedom in opposition to slavery: "Whereas we have the privilege of living under the protection of the glorious flag of the United States, we desire more than ever to enjoy the rights connected with that privilege, and to regulate our affairs ourselves as Christians and as citizens."[107]

Research on the Know-Nothing Party in the northern United States has emphasized the importance of antislavery politics to the movement.[108] It has also drawn attention to the rhetoric of individual autonomy and liberty associated with antislavery sentiments: "To lose one's autonomy was to become a 'slave.' . . . Few nativists thought they were exaggerating, then, when they denounced Roman

FIGURE 2.2. Charles Chiniquy's grave, Mount Royal Cemetery, Montreal, Canada. *Photo by Caroline B. Brettell.*

Catholicism as 'slavery' which stripped the liberty of the independent vote from Catholics and non-Catholics alike."[109] Chiniquy was, no doubt, influenced by these political debates and the language with which they were vocalized, and this may, in part, explain the use of the terms "servitude" and "slavery" as rhetorical devices in his battle against Romanism.

To this rhetorical theme of slavery, Chiniquy eventually added one that relates directly to the matter of ethnic survival (*survivance*) so dear to the hearts of French Canadians. Chiniquy, it will be recalled, accused O'Regan of blotting the French Canadians out of the book of the living, of denying them their very breath, in a statement from a French Catholic meeting in Chicago in 1856: "The present Bishop of Chicago has breathed his deadly breath on us, he has killed us. . . . Instead of guiding us with the Cross of the meek Jesus he has ruled over us with an iron rod. . . . The French are the only ones whose beautiful language is prohibited and which is not heard from any pulpit in Chicago."[110] Late in life, in an August 12, 1894, letter to the Roman Catholic Bishop of Montreal, Chiniquy uses similar language, this time in the context of Quebec itself, to describe the general oppression of the French Canadian people: "The stern voice of historical truth tells you that a handful of insolent tyrants had taken the notion that the French Canadians were good only to draw their water and cut their wood. More and more every day they were trampling under their feet our most precious and sacred rights. . . . People of French-Canadian descent were like southern slaves, fit only to serve their conquerors."[111]

For its part, the Catholic hierarchy waged its war of words against Chiniquy using the rhetoric of sexual immorality, particularly during the phase when redressive mechanisms were put into place. The goal was to reduce Chiniquy to "impotence," but the method was through allusion to numerous sexual dalliances, that is, that the behavior that supposedly began in Quebec continued in Illinois. In August 1856, Chiniquy's foe Peter Spink in a letter to the Grey sisters in Montreal claims that Chiniquy was guilty of "dishonorable crimes" and was trying to "corrupt" Spink's wife and daughter.[112]

One of the documents solicited by the prosecutorially minded Vicar General of Quebec Alexis Mailloux, whom Bourget had sent to Illinois in the spring of 1857, is a manuscript of recollections from a man named Godofroi Lambert, who had served for a time as an assistant to Chiniquy in St. Anne.[113] The Lambert document is full of innuendos about Chiniquy's sexuality. It purports to record faithfully several occasions when Lambert had witnessed Chiniquy enter the private rooms of women and remain inside for several hours when their husbands were absent. Lambert labeled one woman a "public prostitute" and claimed that Chiniquy stayed with her through an entire winter. Chiniquy's tactic, Spink suggests, was to publicly defame those women who rebuffed him so that they could not be acceptable witnesses. Lambert refers to conversations that the prelate had with him about women and prostitutes and of priests who had been with women. In a verbatim style, Lambert quotes an interchange in which Chiniquy explained why none of the lawyers in Canada were religious—because, so Chiniquy said, according to Lambert, they are always settling the cases of priests. To demonstrate Chiniquy's hypocrisy, Lambert describes that Chiniquy touched the stomach of a woman in Bourbonnais who was pregnant and said, "No puppies of Cartuyvels [the Catholic priest serving that parish] but little Chiniquys." The woman had twins and remained faithful to the schism.[114]

Vicar General Mailloux also claims to have received a declaration from Marie Labrie, who later became Lambert's wife. Labrie, a schoolteacher who lived in Bourbonnais, told of an occasion when she journeyed from Bourbonnais to St. Anne in a carriage alone with Chiniquy. She claimed that he fondled her; he removed her glove, held her hand, and then caressed her. When Labrie told the priest that she feared that what he was doing with her would displease God, he denied it, and when they arrived in St. Anne, he told her to come to see him the next day, and he would confess her. In her testimony, Labrie accused Chiniquy of taking liberties several more times, claiming to be her friend and dispelling any fears of sin. At one point, she recounted, he suggested that relations between girls and priests were not prohibited.

Labrie later moved to St. Anne, and Lambert was urged to marry her. They were left alone until one day, in the schoolroom, she claimed, Chiniquy grabbed her "in a most indecent manner," pressing himself against her, caressing her, and telling her that succumbing would not prohibit her from loving God. On another occasion, Labrie declared, he entered the school, sent the children away, and asked "that they commit the last crime. God gave me strength and I pushed him off."[115] She recounted one more incident, accusing Chiniquy of "uncovering himself indecently." At this point she told her husband, and a little later they moved from St. Anne.

Mailloux added a notation to the copy of this declaration that he kept among his own papers. What has survived, he states, conforms to the original that he destroyed "so as not to save certain details that one cannot read without embarrassment."[116] Whether there ever was "an original" remains uncertain. What is important, however, is that these two items demonstrate not only Mailloux's obsession with Chiniquy but also the tactics that were used to defame him. Indeed, in a June 1858 letter to a Quebec priest, Mailloux states that "nothing is finished except the memoir by Lambert on the intimate life of Chiniquy that you ought not to communicate but to a few friends. . . . As to the notebook, it is for you alone. . . . With all this material we will be able to build an edifice of immorality against the priest of St. Anne."[117]

Chiniquy himself did not shy away from sexual innuendo. After leaving the Catholic Church, in his book *The Priest, the Woman, and the Confessional*, he "documents" all of the sexual immoralities of Catholic priests that he had witnessed during his period as a member of the Church of Rome. Clearly, these references to priestly sexuality are neither unique nor new, and it is impossible to prove one way or another whether what was said about Chiniquy is true. What is more important, however, is to recognize how these accusations were used rhetorically in an attempt to topple Chiniquy just as they are involved today, founded or unfounded, in battles with religious leaders who have gained control of the hearts and minds of large numbers of people.

This chapter presents the narrative history of a schism as a social drama within the lives of a group of French Canadian immigrants who settled in Illinois in the 1850s. Although I have focused with the thoroughness of a historical ethnographer on the details of the specific events in St. Anne, by framing them as a phased process, my aim is to draw attention to the common elements in the development and resolution of social conflicts, more generally, and to the way in which these conflicts generate significant change and define and redefine boundaries of identity.

Although quite specific to a particular time and place, the St. Anne schism manifested in microcosm aspects of the larger battle that was being waged in the middle of the nineteenth century for the religious and political domination of the American frontier. The United States as a whole was coming to terms with an ever-expanding Catholic immigrant population, and the confrontations between Protestantism and Catholicism that had erupted by midcentury were to continue throughout the century.

Yet, if the overriding conflict was institutional, broader principles (Turner calls them "paradigms of social life"), particularly the opposition between authority and liberty, underlie the institutional confrontation. These principles must be viewed not only in the context of the mounting crisis over slavery that itself became the focus of the revivalist movements of the 1850s but also in relation to a process of Americanization whereby a bureaucratic social order was replaced by one that was more democratic and individualistic.[118] Just as the American flag flying at one end of Chiniquy's new "church" symbolized democracy, the Bible in the hands of those who worshipped there represented a religion that was to be based on individual faith and interpretation rather than on hierarchical authority.

The central role of the Bible should not to be underestimated. One Catholic descendant of the early settlers in central Illinois remembered a time in her own life when reading the Bible for oneself was disapproved of and discouraged. Chiniquy opens his own autobiography, *Fifty Years in the Church of Rome*, with a recollection of an incident in his childhood in his Quebec hometown when the priest came to Chiniquy's home to take away the Bible that his father owned and had read to his son. This incident is explored in the next chapter; here I simply note that Chiniquy's own account of it clearly establishes the Bible as a powerful symbol of religious liberty, in particular, and social liberty, more generally. Chiniquy refers to a liberty of conscience rather than full-fledged Protestantism in the early years of his schism. These ideas are reinforced in Chiniquy's obituary on the front page of the February 9, 1899, *Presbyterian Record*: "He is gone but the work is only begun. The Bible, the charter of individual and national liberty, is still but little known among the great body of the French Roman Catholics of Quebec. There is neither demand for it nor supply."

The principles of liberty and authority (republicanism versus papal despotism) were at stake in a range of other religious conflicts or schisms among nineteenth-century Midwestern immigrant populations, whether Protestant or Catholic. In some cases, these schisms were the result of differences brought from the homeland.[119] In others, they erupted anew on American soil as a result of the tensions within a nation and an American Catholicism in the process of formation.[120] Reinhold Niebuhr, in his study of the social sources for denominationalism, states that motivations for schism emerge from the social differences that exist between immigrants and natives, between different ethnic groups, and between different economic groups—all of these characteristics of an increasingly heterogeneous society.[121] Other scholars have suggested that such schisms reflect the struggle within immigrant communities when old identities become obsolete, but new ones have yet to be forged.[122] All of these themes can be identified in the schism that occurred in Illinois in the mid-1850s.[123]

As a result of this schism, new social divisions were created in St. Anne. In Quebec the animosities of Protestants and Catholics were themselves rooted in the rivalry between the English-speaking and the French-speaking populations, each of which was more or less internally unified. In St. Anne, the French Canadian immigrant population itself became internally segmented. The end result was the emergence of three, perhaps four, separate communities where one had existed before—two Presbyterian, one Catholic, and one Baptist.

In Turner's original formulation of the process of social dramas, the individuals at the center are key. Sandombu, a Ndembu man with ambitions to be headman of Mukanza village, challenged the authority of the headman, Kahali, just as the ambitious Chiniquy challenged the authority of Bishop O'Regan. Some of those who have analyzed schismatic movements more generally have suggested that although leaders cannot be considered as the sole cause of schism, they are, nevertheless, important.[124] In his own application of the social-drama model, Daniel A. McFarland refers to the "strategic framing efforts of actors who are embroiled in resistance episodes."[125] There is no doubt that Chiniquy's charismatic personality and oratorical skills contributed not only to the progression of the schism from breach, through crisis and redressive actions, to schism and final resolution but also to the amount of attention that was paid to it at the time. The next chapter takes up the force of this personality.

CHAPTER 3

Charisma, Conversion, and Narrative

Holding a picture of Charles Chiniquy as an older man with kindly eyes and a long, white beard (fig. 3.1), a contemporary resident of St. Anne looked up at me and asked, "How could a man with a face like that have caused such turmoil!?" Few of those who have written about Charles Chiniquy have been able to maintain a neutral stance. The man has either provoked extreme indignation or drawn unqualified praise. His critics called him "the shame of his family, the dishonor of the Catholic Church." His admirers hailed him as a second Martin Luther. His books have been labeled insidious and perfidious.[1] His first biographer, Marcel Trudel (1955), is meticulous in demonstrating all the "lies" contained in Chiniquy's two-volume autobiography, with an air of insistence that itself raises further questions about the meaning of Chiniquy the man in the context of Quebec history.[2] In a more balanced assessment, Canadian historian Pierre Berton comments, "It is not easy to like him, for he was clearly a hypocrite, a liar, a sensualist and an egotist. Yet it is hard not to admire him, for he had courage, charisma, passion and a golden tongue."[3]

Newspaper accounts of the day describe Chiniquy as exceptional, suggesting that he had certain personal qualities that one might understand as charismatic. These are certainly noted in his obituary in the *Presbyterian Record* in 1899: "As an orator, taking that term as power to sway the multitude by speech, it is probably that in his prime he stood unparalleled among Canadians. . . . Men may differ as to his methods of work, but there can be no difference as to the remarkable personality of the man, and men of his stamp usually make their own methods."[4] Equally,

FIGURE 3.1. Reverend Charles Chiniquy. *From Fifty Years in the Church of Rome by Charles Chiniquy.*

Chiniquy had the charisma of his office as a priest, and despite excommunication and conversion, the French Canadian immigrants of St. Anne continued to call him "Father Chiniquy," suggesting a sustained special relationship between him and his followers. He had a vision and a mission, but they were initially to bring about change from within. Only when that appeared impossible did he contemplate an alternative.

Although I find most compelling the argument that the location of charisma is in the relationship between leader and followers, Liah Greenfeld argues that "genuine charisma means the ability to internally generate and externally express extreme excitement, an ability which makes one the object of intense attention. . . . It is this quality which makes it possible for a charismatic person to become a leader."[5] This suggests that an analysis of Charles Chiniquy as a charismatic leader should, perhaps, begin with an examination of his personal characteristics and of aspects of his life story that gave him or that he used to give himself a special aura. For this we must rely to some extent on his writings, primarily his two-volume autobiography, *Fifty Years in the Church of Rome* and *Forty Years in the Church of Christ*. Both were penned toward the end of his life and are in many senses a justification, looking backward, of the events. In essence they are a life story folded within the pages of a polemic against Romanism and the Catholic Church. They may fit loosely into the category of personal religious accounts, such as those anthologized by Jon Alexander, and, certainly, they, like many other accounts, are what Alexander describes as intentional artifacts, written with design and purpose for an audience, in this case an anti-Catholic audience.[6]

One purpose of this chapter is to explore further some of the personal characteristics that shaped Chiniquy's charisma and, hence, address the role of the individual agent in processes of social change. The analysis here occasionally sets Chiniquy into a comparative context by introducing other examples of charismatic leaders who through the force of their personality led people to alter, sometimes radically, their way of life. I am inspired here by Jonathan Z. Smith's observations, in an essay on the Reverend Jim Jones, that understanding only comes if we remove an individual or the events he instigated from the realm of the unique and make it "an instance of something known, of something we have seen before."[7] This is good practice in both comparative history and cultural anthropology.

A second purpose of this chapter is to link charisma and agency with work on narrative in cultural studies, the social sciences, and social science history.[8] Donald Weber states that what is missing from Victor Turner's work is "a recognition of culture as political contestation: the battle over narrative power, the fight over who gets to (re)tell the story and from what position."[9] However, Turner did once suggest that the social drama is "the experiential matrix from which oral and literary narrative have been generated."[10] Other scholars have suggested that narrators create order out of disordered experience, giving unity to the past through their stories about it.[11] J. D. Y. Peel in an effort to integrate narrative with practice theory and its emphasis on human agency, observes that narrative is "the principal means by which agents integrate the temporal flow of their activities."[12] And, writing about the reemergence of narrative analysis in sociology, Patricia Ewick and Susan S. Silbey comment that as people tell stories about themselves, "using sequences of statements connected by both a temporal and a moral ordering, they both constitute and interpret their lives."[13] Chiniquy's autobiographical construction of his two lives, one in the Church of Rome and the other in the Church of Christ, as well as several other writings (including his provocative *The Priest, the Woman, and the Confessional*) can be approached within this framework of narrative analysis. How did Chiniquy use his narratives to construct and represent himself in relation to the events in Illinois? What does he identify as the formative moments in his life, and how did these shape his own moral stance toward what occurred? How is his two-volume autobiography more than a mere chronicle of events? How did it give him power over the (re)telling of the events? What arguments do they contain, and how should those arguments be interpreted? These are some of the central questions addressed in this chapter.

Charles Chiniquy, Charismatic Leader: Shaping a Personality

Immediately, and especially by comparison with other charismatic leaders, one is struck by the formative incident with which Chiniquy begins the first volume of his autobiography, *Fifty Years in the Church of Rome.* Apocryphal or genuine, it is his own representation of the source of his religious calling. The chapter "The Bible and the Priest of Rome" opens with an account of his father's decision to leave theological seminary to study law and become a notary. His father was presented with a French and Latin Bible from one of the superiors upon his departure from the seminary, and Chiniquy claims that it is with this Bible that he was taught to read. He recounts the way the stories of the suffering of Jesus moved him. He also tells of Sabbath days in northern Quebec when weather was bad and the roads impossible to traverse. Neighboring farmers would come to the Chiniquy house in the evenings, and then "my parents used to put me up on a large table in the midst of the assembly, and I delivered to those good people the most beautiful parts of the Old and New Testaments."[14] Similarly, when the family went to church, "the farmers would take me into their calèches at the door of the temple, and request me to give them some chapter of the Gospel. With a most perfect attention they listened to the voice of the child, whom the good Master had chosen to give them the bread which comes from heaven."[15] Chiniquy clearly attributed special gifts to himself, gifts that were manifested early in his life.

He goes on to tell of a day in the spring of 1818 when the priest appeared at the family's door. After the exchange of some pleasant conversation, the priest asked Chiniquy's father, "Is it true that you and your child read the Bible?" Chiniquy's father answered in the affirmative, and then the priest responded,

> Do you not know that you are forbidden by the Holy Council of Trent to read the Bible in French? . . . Do you not know that you cannot allow your child to read

> the Bible? . . . Mr. Chiniquy you have gone through a whole course of theology; you know the duties of a curate; you know it is my painful duty to come here, get the Bible from you and burn it.

Chiniquy describes the anger that rose in his father, who summarily showed the priest the door. Chiniquy concludes his account of the incident: "Thou knowest, O God, that it is to that Bible, read on my mother's knees, I owe, by thy infinite mercy, the knowledge of the truth today."[16]

Giving his flock access to the Bible became, as mentioned in the previous chapter, one of the central principles in Chiniquy's conflict with the Roman Catholic Church. It became a symbol of freedom and independence of thought, ideas that Chiniquy viewed as central to the new country to which he had emigrated and ideas that were central to much nineteenth-century anti-Catholic literature.[17] Later in his biography, in the chapter that deals with his seminary education, Chiniquy picks up this theme again: "Among the forbidden books of the college I found a splendid Bible. It seemed to be of the same edition as the one whose perusal had made hours pass away so pleasantly when I was at home with my mother. . . . I read its divine pages until the scholars returned." He later admits to one of his teachers that he read the Holy Book, questioning why it is forbidden and records his memory of the response.

> My dear Mr. Chiniquy, your answer and your arguments have a force that frightens me, and if I had no other but my own personal ideas to disprove them, I acknowledge I do not know how I would do it. But I have something better than my own weak thoughts. I have the thoughts of the Church, and of our Holy Father the Pope. They forbid us to put the Bible in the hands of our students. This should suffice to put an end to your troubles. To obey his legitimate superiors in all things and everywhere, is the rule a Christian scholar like you should follow.[18]

Once in Illinois Chiniquy recounts a meeting in Chicago of all the priests in the diocese. Again he claims he was confronted about his desire to put the Holy Book in the hands of his people, this time by Bishop O'Regan. In Chiniquy's words, O'Regan said to him,

> Mr. Chiniquy, I hear very strange and damaging things about you, from every quarter. But the worst of all is, that you are a secret Protestant emissary; that, instead of preaching the true doctrines of our holy church, about the immaculate

> conception, purgatory, the respect and obedience due to their superiors by the people, auricular confession, etc., etc., you spend a part of your time in distributing Bibles and New Testaments among your emigrants: I want to know from your own lips, if this be true or not.

He reports being chastised by O'Regan, who called him "a disguised Protestant, since the very day you were ordained a priest."[19]

The Bible reappears once more in Chiniquy's account of his discussions with the Presbyterian Church. "Admitted into the Presbyterian Church with the Bible Alone in My Hand," chapter 18 of *Forty Years in the Church of Christ* describes the trip that he and a delegation from St. Anne made to Chicago in 1860. They were received and examined by the Chicago Presbytery: "They unanimously consented to receive us into the great Presbyterian family and offered their Westminster Confession of Faith for us to adopt, and thus declare ourselves faithful children of the Presbyterian Church. They were, however, not prepared for the disappointment they were to meet when I respectfully requested them to withdraw that book and to put the Bible in its place, as the only standard of our faith and life." When told that this was impossible and that rules could not be changed, Chiniquy recorded his reply.

> Mr. Moderator, please do not forget that you have here to deal with babes in the faith. You must bear with children when they request you to give them the food which you are not accustomed to give to full-grown people. We do not come here to teach you any lesson, we want to be taught by you. However, we respectfully ask you to allow us to give you the reasons why we want the Holy Bible to be the only key which will open to us the gates of that Church of Christ. . . . When we ask you to grant us the honour and privilege to become Presbyterians, it is not in a narrow, sectarian sense of the word, it is the large, broad sense of Christianity. . . . Allow me to tell you that after reading many of the books published by the most learned men of your different denominations, we have come to the conclusion that your differences are more in appearance than reality.

Invoking a passage from chapter 15 of the Gospel of St. John—"I am the vine, ye are the branches"—Chiniquy went on to describe the various Protestant denominations as branches on the vine of Christianity and concluded,

> Evidently there are some varieties of views between the many different denominations which form the Church of Christ. But so long as Jesus and Jesus alone, the

> Son of God and the Saviour of the world, is their only hope, their only refuge, their only life, and His Gospel their only rule of faith, we want to press them all to our hearts as our brethren on earth, and our co-citizens in heaven. This is the reason that . . . we ask you as a favour to allow us to lay our hands on the Bible as the only door through which we wish to enter the grand and noble Presbyterian Church.

Chiniquy does not record the response, but he does say that a delegation from the Chicago Presbytery traveled to St. Anne and received the multitudes "as newborn children of the great Presbyterian family."[20] The metaphor of rebirth, fundamental to conversion, is significant.

Chiniquy suggests that one additional incident beyond the conversation between his father and the local priest in Quebec that occurred in his youth was formative to his distrust of the practices of the Roman Catholic Church and eventually the spur to his separation and conversion. In other words, in his own narrative he constructs his behavior and the formation of his beliefs as systematic rather than spontaneous, as something that emerged from a half a lifetime of living within the Church of Rome. The second incident occurred after his father's death in 1821, when Chiniquy was twelve years old. The priest again appeared at the family's house: "He had the reputation of being rich, and as we were poor and unhappy since my father's death my first thought was that he had come to comfort and to help us. I could see that my mother had the same hopes. She welcomed him as an angel from heaven." But Chiniquy tells of a conversation that turned quickly to the question of the Bible and of what the family owed for the services rendered for the funeral. Chiniquy's mother had no money, but the priest was insistent, and eventually he took the family cow in payment, much to the dismay of Chiniquy's mother, who told her son, "If you ever become a priest, I ask of you never to be so hard-hearted towards poor widows as are the priests of today."[21] This incident places the Roman Catholic Church, through its agent the local priest, in the role of oppressor.

In addition to the distrust that these incidents generated (or justified post facto), Chiniquy recounts yet another formative experience that shaped his spirituality and sense of mission. He relates in chapter 32 of *Fifty Years* about a typhoid-fever epidemic that ran rampant in Quebec during the spring of 1837 and to which he eventually succumbed.

> For nine days, I suffered the most horrible torture in my brains and the very marrow of my bones, from the fever, which so devoured my flesh, as to seemingly leave but the skin. . . . On the ninth day . . . the last sacraments were administered to me,

> and I prepared myself to die, as taught by the Church of Rome. . . . Now and then, in the paroxysms of the fever, I used to see awful visions. . . . On the thirteenth night as the doctors were retiring, they whispered . . . "he is dead, or if not, he has only a few minutes to live. He is already cold and breathless."[22]

Chiniquy then tells of his prayers to SS. Anne and Philomene.[23]

> I added to my former prayer the solemn promise to have a painting of the two saints put in St. Anne's church, to proclaim to the end of the world their great power in heaven if they would obtain my cure and restore my health. Strange to say! The last words of my prayer were scarcely uttered when I saw above my head St. Anne and St. Philomene, sitting in the midst of a great light, on a beautiful golden cloud. St. Anne was very old and grave, but St. Philomene was very young and beautiful. Both were looking at me with great kindness. . . . St. Philomene had such an expression of superhuman love and kindness, that I felt myself drawn to her by a magnetic power when she said distinctly: You will be cured! And the vision disappeared. . . . At the disappearance of the two saints, I felt as though an electric shock went through my whole frame; the pains were gone, the tongue was untied, the nerves were restored to their natural and easy power.[24]

Chiniquy was cured, but he had also been divinely called.[25]

> The next morning the news of my miraculous cure spread through the whole city with the rapidity of lightning, for besides a good number of the first citizens of Quebec who were related to me by blood I had not less than 1,800 penitents who loved and respected me as their spiritual father.[26]

Godofroi Lambert's manuscript (housed in the archives of the Seminary of Quebec) lambasting Chiniquy contains several references to this story and other miracles that Chiniquy claimed to have experienced or performed (sometimes in connection with his temperance work) when he was preaching. Clearly, they are what lent him an aura of the superhuman that became a foundation of his charisma for the people of St. Anne, who, even in the words of his critics, thought he was a saint. They are, in a sense, the stories that most had to be challenged and delegitimized in order to undermine Chiniquy's power and leadership.

The comparisons can be made between the stories Chiniquy told about himself and those of other charismatic spiritual leaders, for example, Jim Jones, who also lost his father at a young age and felt adrift in the world. Jones told a reporter in 1953 that at the age of seven, he started to preach the gospel to the people who needed it the most, which gained him a reputation as a child evangelist with a gift for oratory.[27] In addition to preaching for adults, Jones carried out make-believe church services for neighborhood children. He, too, recounted a terrible bout with illness that sent him into a feverish coma during which time he experienced a revelation.[28]

A second example can be found in the Hebrew poet Chaim Nachman Bialik, who, according to scholar David Aberbach, identified "the death of his father when he was six years old and his separation from his mother soon after as a pivotal crisis of his life, motivating his creativity and his public role."[29] Bialik, too, spoke of early and formative religious experiences in the local Pentecostal church to which a neighbor took him. Other charismatic leaders who lost family members—a father, a mother, siblings—at early and formative ages include Adolf Hitler, Ben Gurion, Jiddu Krishnamurti, Abraham Lincoln, and Maximilien Robespierre.[30] There were those who, like Chiniquy, claimed to have had intense visions.

> While in California in 1922, Krishnamurti was transformed by an overwhelming spiritual experience. For several consecutive days, amid excruciating pain in his head and spine, he had visions and hallucinations of the so-called higher beings. He emerged from this trance-like state in ecstasy: "The fountain of Truth has been revealed to me and the darkness has been dispersed. . . . I have drunk at the fountain of Joy and eternal Beauty. I am God-intoxicated."[31]

Aberbach suggests that those among these men who left accounts of their lives have tended to deal rather cursorily with their personal biography prior to the moment that they hit the public stage. By contrast, Jon Alexander suggests that many of those who left accounts of personal faith and of the transitions that led to their calling as a leader have recorded miraculous moments, frequently linked to some sort of visitation.

In other instances in Chiniquy's writings, he points to moments of spiritual awakening. He characterizes the origins of his temperance movement in precisely this way. In "My First Lesson on Temperance," chapter 28 of *Fifty Years*, he describes his work in a Marine Hospital where, through scientific education and exposure to autopsy, he learned of the bodily ravages of alcohol. He also recounts an incident where a young mother, in a drunken stupor, fell while carrying her child. The child died, and with drama Chiniquy describes (but does not explain how) the mother's death—"she fell a corpse on the floor. Torrents of blood were flowing from her mouth on her dead child, which she was pressing to her bosom even after her death." That night,

> I saw the calm, beautiful and cherished form of my dear mother standing by me, holding by the hand the late murderess, still covered with the blood of her child . . . and she said, with power and authority which engraved every one of her words on my soul . . . Go all over Canada; tell every father of a family never to put any intoxicating drink before his children. Tell all the mothers never to take a drop of those cursed wines and drinks. Tell the whole people of Canada never to touch nor look at the poisoned cup.[32]

Chiniquy had experienced his second calling. In chapter 34, "The Hand of God in the Establishment of the Temperance Society in Beauport and Vicinity," he discusses his efforts to launch a reform movement. Although opposed by his bishop, who argued, according to Chiniquy, that "temperance societies are a Protestant scheme" and that he should "preach against drunkenness, but let the respectable people who are not drunkards alone," Chiniquy wrote to Father Matthew of Ireland. With Father Matthew's encouragement, he pursued a course that he considered "the only plank of salvation not only of my dear people of Beauport, but of all Canada." He held a three-day revival of sorts to convert his parishioners to temperance. When news of his success spread, he tells of being accused of heretical practice by the Catholic hierarchy—shunned by his fellow priests but praised by the Protestants of Quebec. Although Chiniquy may have exaggerated the negative stance of the Catholic Church to his activities, he was clearly locating the seeds of his opposition to the teachings of the Church in his activities to spread temperance. Significant, chapter 37 of *Fifty Years* records the visit of a Protestant stranger (whom Chiniquy names John Dougall, editor of the *Montreal Witness* and the *New York Witness*) who praises him for his work, and Chiniquy admits, "I was forced to acknowledge that these Protestants, whom my church had taught me . . . to anathematize and curse as damned slaves and followers of Satan were, in their principles of morality, higher above us than the heavens are above the earth."[33] He caps his own success by telling, in chapter 38, of the Column of Temperance that was erected by the people of Beauport, on a spot halfway between Quebec and Montmorency Falls.

The important point about his activities is that they represented a clear mission to which he drew followers as he moved around Quebec preaching abstinence from alcohol and converting people to the "religion" of temperance with messianic zeal.

In the eyes of French Canadians, he became a saint, and "paintings of him similar to the iconography of saints, particularly the popular St. Louis de Gonzague, were produced and circulated."[34] Chiniquy's temperance work built his reputation such that when he announced his decision to lead an emigration to Illinois, he was both heard and followed. This was his new mission.

Chiniquy recognized that some of his aura derived from the office of priest itself. In *Fifty Years* he describes his ordination into the priesthood. Several times he refers to the superhuman honors, dignities, and powers that had been conferred on him, including the power to convert a wafer into the body, blood, and divinity of Christ, and "The dignity which I had just received was above all the dignities and the thrones of this world."[35] But in short order, reflecting on the charisma of office, he engages in a sharp critique of the idea of transubstantiation, labeling it idolatry. This led him to a condemnation of other norms and practices of the Roman Catholic Church, particularly, priestly celibacy and confession.[36]

From the point of view of the French Canadian *habitants* themselves, those who gave him support during his first mission, the war against alcoholism, and his second, the battle against Roman Catholic hierarchy, two other seemingly contradictory aspects of the social and cultural context of Chiniquy's formation as a Catholic priest in Quebec during the first half of the nineteenth century should be remembered. These offer important evidence of a conflict-ridden cultural environment that probably nurtured the support of charismatic individuals who championed the causes of the people.

First, differences with the Catholic Church had historical precedent in Quebec. Philippe Garigue observes that over half of the eight hundred letters of Bishop Briand after the Conquest of 1760 are letters of blame, reproaches, interdictions, and excommunications. Many were addressed to laypersons who had refused to obey their priests or even their bishop over such matters as the building of a church or the paying of tithes. Garigue states, "The history of practically every rural parish along the shores of the St. Lawrence shows at least one such rebellion against ecclesiastical authority."[37] The area surrounding the town of Trois Rivières was particularly noted for its opposition to clerics, and in one community the conflict ended in schism with a number of French Canadians joining Protestant churches rather than to accept the bishop's ruling over the location of a church.[38] Furthermore, prior to 1840 local clerics were scarce and often poorly educated; the result was numerous cases of insubordination. In an article on clerical life in Quebec during the nineteenth century, one author relates: "The defection of five Catholic priests to Protestantism between 1835 and 1856 (the most famous case being that of Chiniquy), cannot be explained only by the intense propaganda of Protestants of that period. The spirit of independence and the deficiencies of clerical formation are without doubt connected to this phenomenon."[39]

The second factor emerges from this last point. After 1840, precisely the time when Chiniquy's temperance movement was taking off, French Canadian clerics, guided by the powerful and energetic Bishop Ignatius Bourget (later a Chiniquy nemesis), began to reassert their dominance of collective life, a position that had eroded somewhat in the early part of the nineteenth century.[40] However, Chiniquy had already been formed in a more antihierarchical era when local priests had a good deal of autonomy, and giving up this freedom to connect directly with the people was perhaps impossible for him to do.

Whatever unique qualities (including his oratorical skills, for which he won prizes at the Nicolet Seminary) Chiniquy possessed that contributed to his charisma were shaped by the cultural context, or "cultural structuration," of his formation as a priest.[41] Chiniquy himself was an agent in this process through the way that he remembered and constructed the critical moments of his formation and his divine calling. He projected an image of himself as a social reformer, a patriot, and, ultimately, as a rebel against hierarchy, with a goal to overthrow the institutional order and be guided strictly by the word of the Gospel. These images and this message were what attracted followers to his causes.

Leader and Followers: Immigration, Marginality, Hardship

Those who have written about charisma have argued that rather than emphasize a charismatic personality, we should focus on how followers perceive and respond to a leader: "It is not what the leader is but what people see the leader as that counts in generating the charismatic relationship."[42] What factors evoke such perceptions and responses on the part of a population? To answer this question, some scholars have pointed in particular to the fact that during periods characterized by economic instability, social unrest, political instability, and family disorganization, people tend to gravitate to groups led by powerful and authoritative charismatic leaders.[43]

The first issue to address is the experience of immigration itself. Clearly, this is a jarring process of displacement that often disrupts family life, distancing fathers from wives and children or wrenching nuclear families from larger extended families with whom they are used to interacting on a daily basis. It also wrenches families from their communities. Such situations of liminality are ripe for the emergence of charismatic leaders.

In the historical literature, we can find some comparative examples. Gordon Stewart describes a case of emigrants from the New England colonies to Nova Scotia in the latter eighteenth century who were experiencing not only a crisis of loyalty and identity but also near starvation conditions after settling in an isolated community. In their midst appeared an itinerant preacher named Henry Alline, who saw himself as messenger sent by God, and his followers saw his authority as derived from supernatural powers. Stewart notes that as with all charismatic leaders, Alline's success depended more on the message he delivered than on a messiah-like style: "He dealt with the awkward predicament of northern Yankees in wartime Nova Scotia," insisting on "complete condemnation of the American cause." As with Chiniquy, Alline's leadership created divisions while trying to encourage unity: "His very success generated a determined and organized opposition as anti-revivalist groups were mobilized to undermine his influence."[44] Stewart offers this as support for the argument that charisma does not necessarily produce integration or that it produces it in more complex ways, at a supralocal rather than a local level.

Elizabeth Mathias and Angelamaria Varesano describe a community of first- and second-generation Italian migrant workers living in upper New York State in the 1920s and 1930s who felt marginalized by the more settled German Catholics in the region. Not only were they deprived economically during times that became tougher and tougher but they were also deprived religiously in a Catholic Church dominated by another ethnic group that had a different conception of what constituted proper religious behavior. Into this situation of disorientation and disorder came a charismatic leader named Father Jesu, who worked to revitalize their community and their personal and cultural esteem. Mathias and Varesano state, "The Italians were not presented with a new religious system or charter: instead, their original religious system was returned to them."[45] To help resolve their economic distress, he left money in the local grocery and clothing store so that the poor could come for what they needed at no cost to them.

The work of Father Jesu was already well-known among the Italians of Philadelphia, where he was known as a "folk saint who had the reputation of kindness and selflessness and love toward his followers and who was reputed to have the miraculous powers of healing. . . . Our informants have indicated to us that his appearance and his remarkable behavior could only have meant one thing, that Father Jesu was Christ returned to earth to minister to them in their time of crisis." Mathias and Varesano describe the behavior of Father Jesu as metaphoric and suggest that it is this behavior that "resulted in a major response from his followers. . . . When Father Jesu first appeared among the Italian immigrant workers of Migrantville, he was dressed in rustic robes and sandals. He walked through the fields in which the immigrants were working carrying a lamb in his arms and a staff in his hands: he was bare headed, and had long flowing hair and a beard. He walked among them preaching the Gospel and calling them to the Lord's salvation."[46] Alline and Father Jesu offer examples of religious leaders who showed up among already established populations of immigrants. Perhaps what enhances Chiniquy's role is that he actually led his emigration out of Quebec and to the "Promised Land" of Illinois. He emphasized the analogy with Moses, just as Father Jesu cultivated his connection with the divinity of Christ.

But Chiniquy plays this analogy most forcefully in relation to the famine (discussed in the previous chapter) that hit the settlers in St. Anne quite hard. The new Promised Land was Protestantism, a region of "light, intelligence, liberty and true charity."[47] Continuing the use of metaphor, something that has been identified as extremely important to charismatic leadership, Chiniquy then likens himself to Caleb and Joshua, who went out to explore the Promised Land.

> But my joy was not less, when, after the several weeks spent among the new brothers and sisters I had found in Philadelphia and the New England states, I was coming back to my dear but so tried people of Illinois, loaded with the fruits I had gathered on the way. . . . Surely the $56,000 I was carrying were not less precious than the branch cut down with the cluster of grapes which Joshua and Caleb brought to the Israelites in the wilderness.[48]

Ruth Ann Willner emphasizes the way in which President Franklin D. Roosevelt's extensive rhetorical use of the Bible enhanced his charismatic status.[49] Chiniquy did the same in his written work and, evidently, also in his speeches. Not only did he want his followers to have access to the Holy Book but he also wanted them to live it, and he, as their savior, would make this possible.

Chiniquy had performed a miracle by securing monetary donations from the larger Protestant community (in *Forty Years* he labels it manna from heaven), and for this he deepened the loyalty of his followers to him. Max Weber argues that the divine mission of the charismatic leader must be reinforced by his success in bringing well-being to followers: "If they do not fare well, he obviously is not the god-sent master."[50] Chiniquy's description of the bounty that was sent to Illinois reads a bit like the list of goods that participants in Melanesian cargo cults expected: "Before the end of the year, all the mortgages, to the amount of $56,000 were paid. Two hundred barrels of flour had been distributed, with as many bushels of potatoes, and thousands of pounds of meat necessary to make the people forget the terrible calamities which had struck them. Besides that one hundred and fifty large boxes of good clothing had been set to be distributed."[51] In the December 8, 1859, *Kankakee Gazette*, an article on the conversion in St. Anne observes, somewhat cynically, that the people were "willing to exchange their birthright for a mess of potatoes or their religion for an old suit of clothes." Chiniquy himself viewed the famine as serendipity. Had it not occurred, he suggested, his colonists would probably not have been introduced to Protestantism.

The significance of this famine is better understood when placed into a comparative context. Perhaps the best example is the case of Padre Cícero Romão Batista, a charismatic religious leader with exceptional oratorical skills, who spawned a popular religious movement that flourished in the impoverished hinterlands of northeastern Brazil between 1889 and 1934. Padre Cícero presided over a miracle in the backland village of Joaseiro on March 1, 1889. As the religious movement that emerged from this miracle grew, Padre Cícero was excommunicated and denounced as subversive by the Roman Catholic hierarchy, but he became a folk hero to the rural masses.

Significant to the comparison I am drawing here is the fact that this miracle and the movement associated with it developed at a time when the bishop was attempting to "Romanize" Brazilian Catholicism by imposing a stricter doctrinal and moral order and obedience to hierarchy. In addition, at precisely the time that Padre Cícero began his ministry in Joaseiro, the northeast of Brazil was suffering through a devastating drought. Padre Cícero became the deliverer.

> When in 1877 [Padre Cícero] sent many drought victims who had fled to the Valley from the surrounding *sertão* [hinterlands, often the deep interior of Brazil] to the unclaimed lands atop the Araripe Mountains and there obliged them to plant manioc to relieve their hunger, the grateful survivors later attributed their felicity to the priest whom they believed was holy. During the drought of 1888, a similar but admittedly more dramatic episode took place which confirmed for the credulous their own conviction in Padre Cícero's sanctity. . . . As the year 1889 unfolded the drought of the "two-eights" (i.e. 1888) retrenched into the Valley. The people plaintively reverted to prayer to seek divine relief, while the Valley priests led them with renewed fervor. . . . One factor, however, was new: the presence of Maria de Araújo, a twenty-eight year old laundress, single, a native of Joaseiro, and a *beata* [a very devout woman] in the household of Padre Cícero. . . . On 1

> March 1889 . . . Maria de Araújo . . . was among the first to receive communion. Suddenly she fell to the ground and the immaculate white host which she had moments before received became red with blood.

This miracle was repeated for two months. The fervor increased, and in 1892 the Bishop of Ceará, Dom Joaquím, fearing schism and the creation of a "church within the church" suspended Padre Cícero from preaching, hearing confessions, and counseling the faithful. This did not settle the matter. The miracles were discredited, and the bishop asked members of the diocese to ignore them. But significant financial support from prominent regional figures was extended to the dissidents, Padre Cícero's followers, and by 1893 the people of Joaseiro refused to recognize Dom Joaquím's authority. He was, in turn, discredited. Just as Chiniquy made references to O'Regan being in trouble with Rome and having fathered illegitimate children, so, too, in Brazil abusive stories about Dom Joaquím circulated. He, too, was accused of fathering illegitimate children. Such stories illustrated and rationalized the people's defiance of the ecclesiastical hierarchy. In contrast, the people transformed Padre Cícero into a great miracle worker and the arbiter of their souls. "'The ordinary people of Joaseiro are always like that,' remarked Msgr. Alexandrino despondently, '[they] don't recognize any authority except that of Padre Cícero, our Pope.'" There were similar descriptions of the responses among the French Canadians in Illinois. As in Illinois, where Bishop O'Regan went to preach to the French Canadians of their obligations to the Catholic Church, so, too, in Brazil, did Dom Joaquím travel to Joaseiro to tell the people of that community about their obligations to their bishop. Like O'Regan, Dom Joaquím was shouted down by a populace that stood behind their charismatic leader. Dom Joaquím was quoted later as saying that the people of Joaseiro believe neither in the pope, bishop, nor any other ecclesiastical authority. How like O'Regan was Dom Joaquím's statement: "This ignorant mob, composed of criminals and men of every ilk are capable of anything."[52]

Both Padre Cícero and Father Chiniquy issued a challenge to the status quo, and just as has been suggested for charismatic leaders, in general, by such acts they placed themselves in "a potent position with respect to the formation of an image of heroism."[53] They also carried out deeds that removed their followers from intolerable conditions. This, too, enhanced their respective positions as charismatic leaders. Both men eventually routinized their leadership but in different ways. Padre Cícero followed a secular path by becoming one of the most important political chiefs in the history of the Brazilian northeast: "His movement, once religious, became eminently political, and a mainstay of the conservative political forces."[54] Chiniquy followed a path of religious routinization by becoming a minister in the Presbyterian Church.

Max Weber argues that an important motive for routinization, beyond the problem of transferring leadership to a successor who is not blessed with the characteristics of a charismatic personality, is the desire for some sort of security. Part of this security derives from putting a movement on a more solid economic basis so that the needs of the administration are no longer met by "booty, contributions, gifts, and hospitality."[55] This is precisely what Chiniquy did as he took the steps toward formal alliance of his church with the Presbyterian Church. He noted that although he had changed the name of his church to the Christian Catholic Church, everyone, even Protestants, continued for some time to refer to it as the Church of Chiniquy.[56] This caused him concern, and, thus, he sought to situate his movement within something bigger, less personalistic, and more stable. His approach closely approximates the changes that Roy Wallis describes whereby a leader directs the process of routinization and, as a result, controls and uses institutionalized structures to buttress his own authority rather than to have it constrain him.[57] Chiniquy, as noted in the previous chapter, turned to the world stage, becoming an international spokesperson for Protestantism and anti-Catholicism. Although he had disagreements with his immediate successor in St. Anne leading, as discussed in the previous chapter, to a split in the Presbyterian Church itself, eventually the conflict died down such that the reunited Presbyterian Church of St. Anne could focus on the spiritual well-being of its members. Weber, it should be remembered, emphasizes that material well-being alone was insufficient. Charismatic leaders had to offer their followers a purpose, a vision, a sense of identity.

I draw one further comparison—with Jim Jones, who, inspired by Marcus Garvey's back to Africa movement, led an emigration of the members of the People's Temple, first from Indiana to California and then to Guyana. Writing about Jones, Hans Mol argues that Jones, like the other charismatic leaders discussed here, garnered his followers by genuinely caring about their suffering and their needs.[58] But he also built his following by representing himself to them as the embodiment of Christ who had come to rescue them from their oppression, including the oppression of institutionalized religion. John Hall contends that it was to enhance his image as a prophet that Jones "brought to bear his most elaborate dramaturgical procedures," including faith healing.[59] He moved to the extreme, a charismatic leader who created dependency relations in his followers, required them to turn over the bulk of their financial resources to the temple, and, ultimately, isolated them from the rest of the world.[60]

For his actions Jones drew controversy. Like Chiniquy, he was taken to court numerous times, frequently for libel and slander. He was labeled an anti-Christ by some, self-serving, conceited, if not mad. His religion, his detractors said, was a sham.[61] His sexual appetites were well-known and out of control. Johnson describes that charismatic leaders "seek ways to reinforce their power and to overcome its precariousness." If Chiniquy did this by eventually allying himself with the Presbyterian Church, Jones did it through "organizational growth, . . . seeking an isolated environment, developing an ideology to justify members' total commitment to the group and its cause, and creating rituals to symbolize and reinforce this commitment."[62] The latter, of course, includes the final end, mass ritual suicide. But Jones failed because the community he created was based on escape rather than on building something new.[63]

Padre Cicero, Jones, and Chiniquy share the multifaceted qualities of leadership that are outlined by anthropologist F. G. Bailey, who suggests that leadership is not only "the art of controlling followers" but also that leaders have to have a certain boldness and audacity. Bailey describes three styles of leadership, two of which are relevant here. One is the numinous image, whereby the leader is presented as a miracle worker; a second is the familial image, whereby the leader is represented as a nurturant kinsman.[64] To many of the French Canadians who came to Illinois, Chiniquy was a miracle worker during those first years of hardship, and to many, even as a Protestant minister, he remained their Father Chiniquy.

Finally, the situation in Illinois was one that was ripe for some form of conversion. Much of the literature on conversion suggests that it is a likely occurrence in situations of relative deprivation or where people are confronted with poverty, disease, or other economic and social stresses.[65] It is these same conditions to which we might look to answer Peter Burke's question of whether there are kinds of followers who are particularly susceptible to charismatic leadership.[66] Chiniquy was a catalyst for change among a group of people who, through their decision to migrate to what was at the time the American frontier, were already seeking some sort of change.

Charisma, Life History, and the Narrative Text

Although much here has been said about the narrative aspects of Chiniquy's autobiographical texts—the stories he has told about his life and the events with which he was involved—more can be discussed. I do so partly in response to James

Peacock's call to anthropologists to accord narrative analysis a proper place within social analysis.[67] Although Peacock was referring to the genre of life history, which has both a deep past and an active present in anthropological method and theory, his emphasis is on "what the native places before us; he himself organizes his experience into a form with its own integrity and force." Peacock also observes that life history is a collective public structure, "a narration, shared with an audience, possibly even a congregation or nation."[68]

If an oral life history is organized as it is told and has a public dimension, a written personal narrative is even more labored, organized, and located in the public domain. Often, as Charlotte Linde contends, the written story is organized to defend a particular action.[69] This is certainly the case with Chiniquy's autobiographical narratives, which in the titles themselves focus our attention on conversion from fifty years as a Roman Catholic to forty years as a Protestant.

Ewick and Silbey define a narrative according to three features. First, it relies on some form of selective appropriation of past events and characters; second, the events in the narrative are temporally ordered (with a beginning, a middle, and an end); third, events and characters are related to one another in an overarching structure, often in the context of an opposition or struggle.[70] This framework is useful in looking at the way in which Chiniquy has told his own story, and each of them is explored in turn.

Certainly, Chiniquy is highly selective in what he tells; his narrative is full of omissions such that his own actions emerge in the most positive and favorable light. The earliest such omission is in his account of why he left the Nicolet Seminary. He passes off his problems with his uncle Amable Dionne in one short phrase as "a misunderstanding," adding that much of his time at the Nicolet Seminary was wasted anyway for he "could easily have learned in three or four years what was taught in those seven."[71] The alternative narrative, of course, is that Chiniquy made a pass at one of his female cousins, his uncle Dionne's daughter, and that this was the reason for Dionne's hasty withdrawal of support.

Further omissions surround his account of why he was removed from Beauport, a parish just north of Quebec City, where he had had enormous success in his temperance crusade, to Kamouraska, his birthplace, farther down the St. Lawrence River. In terms of the prestige hierarchy of parishes, this is a clear demotion. In Chiniquy's words, the two bishops in Quebec City, who had summoned him, spent an hour making "strong appeals to my charity for the multitudes [in Kamouraska] who were sunk in the abyss of drunkenness and every vice, and had no one to save them.... My bishops had spoken to me with such kindness! Their paternal and friendly appeals had surely more power over me than orders. Not without many tears; but with true good will, I consented to give up the prospects of peace and comfort which were in store for me in Beauport to plunge myself again into a future of endless trouble and warfare, by going to Kamouraska."[72] He tells of leaving his books behind in Beauport and of some controversy in Kamouraska surrounding his appointment—he claims he was not welcomed by the elderly and infirm curé or the parishioners but that he hastily made peace with the curé. Marcel Trudel says that there was more to this removal than Chiniquy acknowledges—that another scandal was about to break.

Chiniquy went about building up his temperance crusade in the Kamouraska vicinity. In a single chapter he talks not only of these efforts but also of the curious story of a young girl who faked her own drowning and took up a male identity and the role of the servant Joseph to maintain a relationship with a parish priest. When suspicions rose, the priest had Joseph marry the daughter of a poor neighbor, and both lived in his company. Joseph's disguise was ultimately revealed, the shame of the Church was, in Chiniquy's words, exposed, and the girl was sent off to the United States. Chiniquy uses the story to raise more examples of similar "depravities" among his fellow priests, to condemn auricular confession as "a school of perdition for the priest and his female penitents," and to acknowledge his increasing loss of trust in the Church of Rome. "I wished to depart from this deceitful and lost world," he asserts. The chapter ends with his quick removal from Kamouraska to the monastery of the Oblates of Mary Immaculate in Longueuil, near Montreal. This was an order that supported temperance. Trudel and others tell a different story about Chiniquy's departure from Kamouraska: that he had been paying excessive attention to a woman in a neighboring parish. She finally agreed to meet him, but when he arrived, she was not there. Instead, he was confronted by the local curé and, to avoid public scandal, asked to enter the Oblate fathers. If Trudel's account is accurate, it is both curious and significant that in his own narrative, Chiniquy veils the story with his account of the "girl in the garb of a man."[73]

Finally, there is the matter of his departure from the Oblates. The narrative structure is intriguing because in the very middle of the book, Chiniquy precedes his discussion of his period with the Oblates fathers (*Fifty Years*, chapters 42 and 43) with a long digression (*Fifty Years*, chapter 41) that focuses on the story of Cardinal Newman, a British theologian and Episcopalian, who, in 1845, was ordained as a Roman Catholic priest. Chiniquy's narrative approach to his period in Longueuil is to deride the idolatry and folly of monastic life. He claims that his growing disillusion while with the Oblates finally broke "the strongest tie of my affection and respect for that church." He asserts that he left willingly, but correspondence of the time with Bishop Bourget of Montreal suggests that Chiniquy became deeply embroiled with the internal politics of the Oblates and would not obey his superiors. They were, in other words, glad to see him go. Chiniquy denies this version in his written recollection of a conversation with Bourget: "The rumors which seem to trouble your lordship about my supposed expulsion from the oblates do not affect me in the least, for they are without the least foundation. From the first to the last day of my stay in that monastery, all the inmates from the superior to the last one, have overwhelmed me with the most sincere marks of kindness, and even of respect."[74]

At the middle of the first volume of his autobiography, Chiniquy has forthrightly laid the foundation for his own conversion by increasing his reports of disenchantment, by writing about "last straws," and by invoking Cardinal Newman. Indeed, the chapter on Newman is like a narrative turning point that makes everything that follows—emigration, schism, his own conversion to Protestantism—logical and consistent. Molly Patterson and Kristen Renwick Monroe are illuminating here. They suggest that narrative can be distinguished from other modes of organizing experience because it requires agency and suggests how humans move toward goals. Narratives, they continue, are autobiographical accounts "given by the narrator in the present about a protagonist who bears the same name, who existed in the past, and who blends into the present speaker as the story ends. The story explains and justifies why the life went a particular way, not just causally but, at some level morally. The narrator uses the past self to point to and explain the present and the future."[75]

Subsequent chapters in *Fifty Years in the Church of Rome* cover his invitation to Illinois, his interdiction at the hands of Bishop Bourget (after an incident in the confession that he describes as an effort to ruin him), his departure for Illinois, and his own version of all the incidents that ensued once he was in the Midwest, many of which were touched on in chapter 2 of this book. He does not hesitate to make reference to the "intrigues, impostures, and criminal life of the priest in Bourbonnais," to the challenge to his faith in the Church of Rome, and to the "brigandage" of Bishop O'Regan. The first volume ends with a discussion of the formation of the Christian Catholic Church and the "end of the voyage through the desert to the promised land."[76] In the last chapter Chiniquy breezes through his life as a Presbyterian minister. In the second volume of his autobiography, *Forty Years in the Church of Christ*, he returns to this part of his life to elaborate.

Interspersed among chapters that chronicle events up to 1860 are chapters that question immaculate conception and auricular confession as well as one that outlines the challenge of the Roman Catholic Church to the Constitution of the United States. There is another turning point in two chapters that focus on Abraham Lincoln and his assassination at the hand of John Wilkes Booth, "the tool of the priests." Chiniquy, undoubtedly, exaggerated his relationship with Lincoln, tapping into the myths about and admiration for another man to legitimize his own course in life. Just as Lincoln emancipated the slaves, so Chiniquy had emancipated his own people.

In the prefatory note to *Forty Years in the Church of Christ*, Chiniquy's son-in-law Reverend Joseph L. Morin relates that although the volume "abounds in striking incidents and events in the author's wonderful career, [the] book is not designed to be a connected autobiography."[77] And, yet, it continues Chiniquy's story after some revisiting of the early events in his life and several reaffirmations of the centrality of the Bible to his faith and his conversion. He describes his many missionary tours, first in Quebec, where he was confronted with "Romanist mobs" and where he claimed he had a close brush with death at the hands of an assassin. According to Chiniquy, similar mob incidents occurred on subsequent visits to the province, but he was always saved by Providence.

The chapter structurally at this volume's center, "My Re-Baptism," is an account of the ritual confirming his conversion from Romanism to Protestantism: "When I left the Church of Rome I was kindly advised by the Presbytery of Chicago to be re-baptized. But it seemed to me then, as it seemed to Luther, Calvin, Knox, and many others that my baptism in the Church of Rome was validly conferred. And, after having heard my reasons, the Presbytery unanimously resolved to let me go free on that subject."[78] Chiniquy then discusses a series of incidents that weakened his resistance and led him to accept rebaptism. Much of the rest of this volume deals with his global travels as far as Australia to spread the word. At several stopping points, he reports being confronted by groups of Protestant supporters eager to hear him speak and by groups of Roman Catholic detractors determined to prevent him from speaking.

The overarching structure and the central contest in this two-volume autobiography are, of course, the opposition between Roman Catholicism and Protestantism. Chiniquy's narrative uses conventions characteristic of much nineteenth-century anti-Catholic literature. Perhaps the most famous of such books, one that Chiniquy alludes to in chapter 42 of *Fifty Years in the Church of Rome*, was Maria Monk's *Awful Disclosures of the Hotel Dieu Nunnery of Montreal*, published in 1836. This text, also written in an autobiographical mode, appeared after a series of incidents, including the burning of the Ursuline convent in Charleston, Massachusetts, in 1834. At the time people thought that it was a work of propaganda and identified the real writer as Reverend J. J. Slocum. Yet, despite questions about its veracity and despite the fact that Maria died in wanton poverty in a house of ill fame, the book sold three hundred thousand copies. Writing about the Monk book and a number of other similar texts (although not Chiniquy's), Barbara Welter maintains that such works should not simply be dismissed as fanatical but rather examined for the deep concerns that they express about personal liberty. All these books share a set of themes: the distrust of authority, a call for emphasis on individual judgment, a critique of the institution of celibacy, and a condemnation of church control of the Bible.[79]

As mentioned several times already, Chiniquy's texts, the first of which had gone into its fortieth edition by 1891, picked up most of these themes and added others, for example, the excessive wealth of the church that was built on the backs of the poor. The following passage is a typical example.

> The people see that the enormous sums they give you for the souls in purgatory remain at the bottom of your purses. . . . Continue your infamous commerce in prayers, indulgences and medals; build for yourselves with those funds, sumptuous palaces; rear up gigantic cathedrals; robe yourselves in purple and the finest garments; load your tables with delicate viande; knock down those who disturb your repose; and continue to elect in every country the enemies of the people. But mark well what I tell you: the people will soon wake from the profound slumber in which you have kept them.

This was part of a speech that Chiniquy delivered in Canada, and he goes on to make reference to people forced to emigrate because they are left in poverty, and finally he predicts agitation and vengeance: "You will be dragged with violence from your palaces; and your mournful cries will be but the echo of the cries and desolation of your victims. . . . Your reign, the reign of man, will be at an end, and the reign of Christ, the reign of God's Word, shall have begun."[80]

Clearly, as Chiniquy constructed the narrative of his life, he was influenced by the imagined audience he was addressing, by the social context of religion in the latter part of the nineteenth century, and by a host of literary and cultural conventions. Most often he represented things as an opposition between light (the opening chapter of *Forty Years* is titled "A Sketch of My Life before the Dawn of the Saving Light") and dark (the forces of evil that were out to get him). The closing sections of *Forty Years* offer an extensive vindication of his actions and responses to the "dastardly" attacks against him, including efforts to reconvert him toward the end of his life. Posthumously, his final declaration of faith was included in the volume, a statement he made before several witnesses and that was later published in several French and English newspapers in Montreal. This is then followed by the texts of an address delivered at his funeral, a sermon delivered twelve days later, and the resolution of the Presbytery of Montreal on March 14, 1899, that recognized, "The Rev. Charles Chiniquy, D.D., was naturally endowed with talents of an exceptionally high order."[81]

On August 1, 1889, the *Kankakee Gazette* ran an article about an eightieth birthday celebration for Charles Chiniquy. He had been absent from St. Anne but had returned home. The people in St. Anne spoke of the trials they had gone through. They recalled that when Bishop O'Regan came to take their church, Chiniquy had nailed an American flag on the church building with the phrase "Never surrender" painted on. After several speeches, Chiniquy replied in French, "If the love of his people could prolong his life, it would be extended for many years." The newspaper reported that at eighty, Chiniquy "still has the strength of a youth and his eyes are undimmed." In the context of such a celebration, the past was resurrected, and the crux of the conflict was restated. Chiniquy, the charismatic leader, stood firm in his efforts to guide change for his people. O'Regan, a representative of what Mol has called ordinary leadership, had as his goal the coordination and preservation of the Catholic Church as a whole.[82]

Bryan Wilson claims that charisma "both responds to and causes social change," that it "challenges the existing order," and that it "operates to break the existing authority structure" and "lift sanctions on previously proscribed behavior."[83] These elements were all present in the movement Father Chiniquy led that resulted in the conversion from Roman Catholicism to Protestantism of a significant proportion of French Canadian immigrants who came to Illinois in the 1850s. Chiniquy succeeded in carrying these parishioners with him because he helped them to overcome the hardships that confronted them and to adapt to a new country while maintaining a sense of national pride and identity.

But his actions equally inspired distrust, if not hatred, among those who wanted to maintain an old order. Such powerful dichotomies are part of the kind of movement that Chiniquy spearheaded and the kind of person that Chiniquy was. "The crux of the charismatic process," explains Mol, "is emotional stripping and welding, detaching and attaching, desecrating and consecrating."[84] It is, in other words, a process that is full of contradictions. Chiniquy the person was equally full of such contradictions. Perhaps, Bailey is most instructive here when he contends, in *Humbuggery and Manipulation: The Art of Leadership*, that no leader can survive without deceiving others and that "leadership and malefaction everywhere and at all times go hand in hand."[85] While "everywhere" may be too sweeping a statement, in many cases the partnership of these attributes is quite apparent. They, perhaps, best explain the profound disagreements over the interpretation of Chiniquy's life and deeds.

However, the fact that these were French Canadians giving up a religion that was so fundamentally allied to their historical past and sense of peoplehood is equally important to consider and makes the drama of the event and the conversion that much more compelling. Turner has suggested that the tensions at the root of social dramas are never fully eliminated. The schism in St. Anne was a formative event that shaped subsequent events in the history of the community. Part 2 of this book, therefore, explores the impact of the schism on the lives of the French Canadians who had followed Chiniquy to Illinois as well on ensuing generations.

PART 2

"A Settlement with a Truly Canadian Cachet"

CHAPTER 4

From First to Second Generation: Demography, Economy, and Society of the French Canadian Immigrants, 1860–1900

> The village is very pleasantly situated on a slight eminence in the midst of a rich prairie. The number of families in the settlement is about 400. The houses wear an air of neatness and of comfort which at once seems to be entirely incompatible with the stories of suffering and poverty which have been told in connection with this people. . . . Father Chiniquy has a neat stone house with a large fine garden adjoining it [fig. 4.1]. The other houses are mainly of wood. They have a large building the lower story of which is used for a school for girls and the upper story for the church. The latter will accommodate 700 to 800 and it is not uncommon that 1000 are crowded into it. They also have another large building in which the boys are taught and which is intended to be the germ of an educational institution of a high order and which shall fit young men for work of colportage among French-Canadians in our own country and in Canada. . . . Some of them are heavy in debt waiting for crops to come in. The people are strictly temperate. There is not a drinking place in town.[1]

As noted in the part 1 discussion, the schism had run its course by 1860, although the problems with the Chicago Presbytery were yet to emerge. In that year, the population was canvassed for the federal census. This census provides the earliest socioeconomic and demographic portrait of the settlers of St. Anne and the other small communities of French Canadians that were established after Chiniquy's arrival in the Midwest. This chapter explores several characteristics of this population as it matured and changed during the first forty to forty-five years of settlement. I try to

FIGURE 4.1. Chiniquy residence, St. Anne, Illinois. *From Kankakee County Atlas, 1883.*

bring to life the families who emigrated to Illinois and who were impacted by the schism, following them as they established themselves in the American Midwest.

Many aspects of the migration process that are characteristic of immigrants who enter the United States today were also present among those who crossed the border during the early to middle part of the nineteenth century: chain migration, migration based on kinship and social networks, and step migrations from the first place of settlement to other destinations. Like migrants today, the French Canadians who heard Chiniquy's call and left Quebec for Illinois in the middle of the nineteenth century brought aspects of their culture with them. How fast did these cultural practices change, and how did the religious division that developed early in the settlement process as a result of the schism described in part 1 impact these cultural practices? What is the evidence for both persistence over time and further migration among the descendants of the original settlers? How did survivance play out on the plains of Illinois? These are some of the questions this chapter explores.

The discussion in this chapter derives primarily from an analysis of the census manuscript records for 1860, 1880, and 1900 for St. Anne Township in Kankakee County, for Beaverville and Papineau Townships in Iroquois County, and for the part of Ashkum Township that includes L'Érable, also in Iroquois County.[2] All these areas were settled by French Canadians largely after Chiniquy's arrival, although prior to the French Canadians' arrival, significant numbers of Norwegians had settled in the southern part of what would become Beaverville Township, and Yankee, Dutch, and German immigrants had settled in the 1840s in what would become Papineau Township. But, as indicated in chapter 1, half this population died in a severe cholera epidemic in 1855, and French Canadians moved in. Belgian and French immigrants added to the "gallic" character of L'Érable in the late 1850s, and Dutch immigrants settled in the northern part of St. Anne Township around the community of Wichert in the 1890s. While none of these townships were or remained ethnically homogenous, they were predominantly French Canadian, and for my purposes here, it is the individuals of French Canadian birth or heritage who are the focus of attention. In addition to the census manuscripts, data on religious affiliation (not included on the census) and other material on the settler families and their offspring have been obtained from a variety of sources, including parish registers, other parish lists and directories, cemetery records, newspaper articles and obituaries, property and tax records, probate records, and county atlases.

The Settler Generation: Population, Family, and Economy in 1860

By 1860 nearly a quarter of the population of the United States lived in the states of the Old Northwest—Indiana, Illinois, Michigan, Ohio, and Wisconsin. Between 1850 and 1860, Illinois was one of the fastest-growing states in the United States, its population having increased by 101 percent in ten years, largely as a result of in-migration. Foreigners comprised 88 percent of net migration into the Old Northwest during the 1850s.[3] In 1860, 324,643 individuals in the state of Illinois were foreign-born, compared with 110,593 in 1850. In 1850, the 10,699 Canadian-born (French and English) in Illinois were 1.26 percent of the state population and the fourth-largest foreign-born group after the Germans, the Irish, and the English. In 1860 the Canadian-born numbered 20,132 and were 1.18 percent of the total population.[4]

In 1860 approximately a third of the population of Kankakee County (which included St. Anne Township) was foreign-born, while a fifth of the population of Iroquois County (which included Beaverville, Papineau, and Ashkum Townships) was foreign-born. The total population in St. Anne, Beaverville, Papineau (called Weygandt in 1860), and Ashkum Townships in that year was 3,561, and of these, the total number of French Canadian or French Canadian–descent settlers numbered 2,632, or 74 percent of the total (table 4.1).[5] Of these, 52 percent were male, and 48 percent were female; children fourteen years and under were 53 percent of the population; 30 percent were between fifteen and thirty-four; 7 percent were over fifty years of age. Of the individuals fifteen to thirty-four, almost half (49 percent) were married. By sex, 41 percent of the males between fifteen and thirty-four were married and almost 57 percent of the women were.

TABLE 4.1. French Canadian population ($N = 2{,}632$) by age, sex, and marital status for the townships of St. Anne, Beaverville, L'Érable, and Papineau, 1860

	Single		Married			
Age (y)	*No.*	*Percentage*	*No.*	*Percentage*	*Widowed No.*	*Unknown No.*
			Males			
0–4	323	33.5	0	0	0	0
5–9	202	21	0	0	0	0
10–14	200	20	0	0	0	0
15–19	145	15	0	0	0	0
20–24	62	6.4	28	7.4	0	2
25–29	19	2	61	16	0	4
30–34	9	0.9	76	20	0	1
35–39	1	0.1	55	14.5	0	1
40–44	0	0	36	9.5	0	0
45–49	0	0	30	7.9	1	2
50–54	2	0.2	32	8.4	0	1
55–59	0	0	29	7.6	2	0
60+	1	0.1	33	8.7	2	7
Total no.	964		380		5	18
Percentage of total	70.5		27.7		0.3	1.3
			Females			
0–4	271	32.1	0	0	0	0
5–9	225	26.7	0	0	0	0
10–14	178	21.1	0	0	0	0
15–19	117	13.9	25	6.4	0	0
20–24	27	3.2	58	15	0	0
25–29	10	1.2	69	17.8	1	4
30–34	9	1.1	69	17.8	1	0
35–39	3	0.3	46	11.9	2	1
40–44	1	0.1	40	10.3	3	1
45–49	1	0.1	31	8	2	3
50–54	0	0	18	4.7	1	2
55–59	1	0.1	18	4.7	2	0
60+	0	0	13	3.4	5	7
Total no.	843		387		17	18
Percentage of total	66.6		30.6		1.3	1.4

Note: Percentages may not total 100 owing to rounding.
Source: United States Federal Census Manuscripts, Kankakee and Iroquois Counties, 1860

Age at marriage was generally low, especially for women. Of women between fifteen and nineteen, 18 percent were married, and 65 percent of women between twenty and twenty-four were married. While none of the men between fifteen and nineteen were married, 30 percent of those between twenty and twenty-four were married as were 73 percent of those between twenty-five and twenty-nine. Early marriage was a practice brought from Quebec and distinguishes these French Canadian settlers from groups such as the Norwegians of the Upper Midwest where, in 1860–62 the mean age at marriage for men was 26.4 and for women 25.1.[6] Sophie Castonguay offers a good example of a very young bride and of the fact that this pattern of early marriage persisted among some of the offspring of the first generation of immigrants in Illinois. Sophie, born in Ste. Marie de Beaverville in December 1855, married François Boucher, a twenty-four-year-old native of Quebec, on July 21, 1869. She was not even fourteen. For eighteen years the couple lived with her parents on their farm in Papineau Township and then bought their own farm three miles east of St. Anne. In 1903 they moved into town. The couple, who were Catholic, had ten children, two of whom predeceased their parents. François died in 1922 and Sophie four years later, in 1926, at the age of 71.

In general, and as is characteristic of the migrations of other nationality groups to the American Midwest in the nineteenth century,[7] this was primarily a familial migration, and the society that was built was one based on kinship. The familial nature of the migration is reflected not only in the fairly even distribution of men and women in the overall population but also in household structure (table 4.2).[8] In 1860, the majority (64 percent) of French Canadian households was simple nuclear families; 3 percent were extended, equally by the presence of a sibling or sibling-in-law or by a mother or mother-in-law. One household had a father present and another a father-in-law. Another 3 percent were multiple households made up, like the household in which Sophie Castonguay and François Boucher resided, of two or more married couples of different generations living under one roof with their children. Married couples living alone made up 4 percent of the households, and of these more than two-thirds (69 percent) were younger couples where the male head of household was thirty or under. Widows or widowers with children or of single people living alone each were 1 percent of the households.

The remaining 24 percent of households were either those in which the kin relationships could not be easily determined or households that included an unrelated individual. Twenty-seven of these were simple family households with a live-in servant or farm laborer. Six were extended, multiple, or solitary households with servants or resident laborers. Fifteen were probably multiple family households and six most likely extended, but we cannot be fully certain. If these apparently multiple family households were accepted as such, the total proportion of multiple-family households would rise to approximately 7 percent. Thirty-five households remain difficult to classify. These household characteristics, as well as the low age at marriage, are similar to those described for French Canadians who settled in the frontier eastern townships of Quebec in the 1850s, although in Illinois there appears to have been a somewhat greater tendency to form multiple-generation complex households. Scottish settlers in the eastern townships had more nonfamily youths in their households and married at later ages than did their French Canadian counterparts.[9] These differences in age at marriage and household composition become even more pronounced among the children of the first generation of settlers in this region and, in Jack I. Little's view, suggest some fundamental variations in family culture. The same family culture shaped the lives of French Canadian immigrants in Illinois.

Households were generally large in size (table 4.3). Of households headed by French Canadian men in 1860, 61 percent were made up of six or more persons and 18 percent of ten or more individuals. When distinguished by household type

TABLE 4.2. Percentage of male-headed French Canadian households by type, for the townships of St. Anne, Beaverville, L'Érable, and Papineau, 1860, 1880, 1900

Types of household	*1860*	*1880*	*1900*
Simple	63.8	61.0	53.5
Extended	3.0	5.5	6.2
Multiple	3.2	3.2	3.1
Married couple living alone	4.3	12.4	14.6
Widow/er with children	1.1	1.5	2.4
Person living alone	0.8	2.4	1.8
Other*	23.8	13.9	18.4
Total no. of households	370	474	614

*Any simple family that included a servant is classified as other, as are households where family relationships are unclear.

Note: Percentages may not total 100 owing to rounding.

Sources: United States Federal Census Manuscripts, Kankakee and Iroquois Counties, Illinois, 1860, 1880, 1900

(and only for households where kinship relations could be easily determined), 62 percent of simple family households were made up of six or more individuals, and 16 percent of ten or more. Among those simple family households with ten or more individuals, fully 87 percent of the male household heads were over forty years of age. While I reserve a more in-depth discussion of fertility until later in this chapter, the evidence on household size for simple families indicates very high levels of fertility among the first generation of French Canadian settlers on the prairies of northeastern Illinois. This reflects patterns that were generally characteristic of the French Canadians of Quebec at this time. Two-thirds of the extended-family households that could be identified with any degree of assurance had six or more individuals, and the male household heads were fairly equally distributed above and below forty in age. All the multiple-family households in 1860 had more than six individuals coresiding (23 percent had ten or more individuals), and the majority (85 percent) of male household heads were over fifty years old.

The importance of kinship among the first generation of French Canadian settlers in Illinois is manifested in other ways. Although there appears to have been

TABLE 4.3. Percentage of male-headed French Canadian households by size for the townships of St. Anne, Beaverville, L'Érable, and Papineau, 1860, 1880, 1900

Household size	*1860*	*1880*	*1900*
1	0.8	2.4	1.9
2	5.4	13.3	16.4
3	9.2	10.5	15.9
4	10.8	12.2	16.1
5	13.0	12.4	15.3
6	13.0	13.7	10.7
7	11.1	10.8	6.2
8	9.2	9.5	7.0
9	9.7	7.4	5.7
10+	17.8	7.8	4.7
Total no. of households	370	474	614

Source: United States Federal Manuscript Censuses, Kankakee and Iroquois Counties, Illinois, 1860, 1880, 1900

a preference for establishing a separate and independent household after marriage, the offspring who migrated with their parents as young couples or who married in Illinois soon thereafter often settled nearby, within the same town or township, if not in an immediately adjacent residence. This is easiest to trace in the case of sons, who share a last name with their fathers. In St. Anne twenty-eight households in 1860 shared a family name with at least one other household in the same community for a total of sixty-six households, or 18 percent. In most cases this represents a vertical kinship relationship and in some a horizontal link between brothers. For example, in 1860, household 49 on the manuscript census included Joseph Cheffre, a sixty-five-year-old stonemason with his wife, Harriet, fifty-nine, and three sons, Dolphus, twenty, James, eighteen, and Benjamin, fifteen. In household number 51 was a son of Joseph and Harriett, Joseph Jr., thirty-six, and his wife, Sara, and their son, Joseph, three. In household number 52 lived another son of Joseph and Harriett, Antoine, twenty-eight, his wife, Margareth, and their two children, Marie, six, and Joseph, two.[10] According to the *Portrait and Biographical Record of Kankakee County*, Joseph Sr. lived on a farm one mile east of St. Anne that his sons, who migrated to Illinois in 1851, bought for their father and then called for the rest of the family. Joseph Jr. and Antoine were both born in Montreal; the family had lived in Syracuse, New York, in the 1840s and moved back to Canada before their reemigration to Illinois. Both Joseph Jr. and Antoine married in Illinois. On the 1860 agricultural census for St. Anne, four Cheffres, Joseph Sr., Peter, Joseph Jr., and Antoine are listed with adjacent farms of eighty, forty (twenty unimproved), eighty, and eighty (forty unimproved) acres, respectively. By the 1890s, Antoine, who had five sons and two daughters, resided in the village of St. Anne and owned 150 acres of land three miles south in Papineau Township, Iroquois County; Joseph Jr., who was married three times, farmed 320 acres in Kankakee and Iroquois Counties. Of Peter, who did not appear on the 1860 population census for St. Anne or any of the adjacent communities, little else is known. All the Cheffres became Presbyterians and Republicans, and Antoine, who had a prosperous business as a stonemason, cut the stones for the Presbyterian Church.

In other cases, it appears that several brothers migrated to Illinois at the same time or on the tail of one another and settled together in St. Anne or in one of the neighboring communities. The Regnier brothers, who remained only briefly in the St. Anne area before moving on to Kansas in the 1870s, offer a good example. Jean Baptiste and Angelique Roi Regnier married in Quebec in 1812 and had at least seventeen children, though not all of them survived to adulthood. In 1847 the family migrated to Illinois when Jean was sixty-two and Angelique a decade younger.[11] Six of their children (Isaac, Joseph, who was already married, David, also married, Florence, Abmintha, and Philomene) appear to have emigrated at the same time. The other children followed: a daughter Emilie; the youngest son, Jeremie, who was married in Bourbonnais in 1854; the eldest son, Julien, who arrived with his own family in 1855 or 1856. In addition, several nephews also migrated to the Kankakee County region. According to a descendant, the Regnier family was split apart by the Chiniquy schism. All the daughters (two of whom married Senesac brothers) remained Catholic, and four sons—Julien, Joseph, David, and Jeremie—converted to Protestantism.[12]

Joseph and Jeremie were residents of St. Anne by 1860. Joseph had sixty acres of improved property and twenty acres of unimproved land, worth $1,200. Jeremie owned twenty acres of improved land and twenty of unimproved, worth $300. By 1870 Joseph had lost his first wife, remarried, and had three young children living with him. The value of his real property had increased to $2,000, though he farmed only forty improved acres. He seems to have acquired more livestock. Jeremie added forty acres to his property (increasing the value to $2,000) and six children to his household. The remaining two brothers, David and Julien, lived in Bourbonnais and Papineau, respectively, though in Julien's case, he only appears on the Papineau census in 1880. The parents of these four prospering Regniers also converted to Protestantism, although it is unclear exactly when. In the 1870s Joseph and David moved to Kansas. Julien and Jeremie followed later, as did the parents. By 1883 Isaac had migrated to Minnesota with his family.[13] These two families, the Cheffres and the Regniers, are typical and show how strong the networks of kinship were among large farming families who migrated to northeastern Illinois. These two families also hint at important differences associated with religion, a topic this chapter returns to later.

The majority of the families who settled in St. Anne or the nearby settlements came directly from Canada. In addition to some examples above, Josephine Langellier Laplante offers another. Josephine, born in Quebec in January 1839, migrated with her family to Illinois in 1852, the year of Chiniquy's arrival. She took her communion the following year in the Catholic Church, but "two years later, she, with the whole parish, under the leadership of Father Chiniquy embraced the Presbyterian faith and remained a faithful member throughout the persecutions which followed throughout her life," according to her obituary in the November 20, 1919, *St Anne Record*. In 1865 Josephine Langellier married Philip Laplante, who had been in the Union army, and they had seven children, four of whom survived her death in 1919. Josephine lived in Illinois until 1881 and then moved to Kansas.

A second example is provided by Henriette Martin St. Pierre. Born in St. Leon, Quebec, on June 7, 1816, she married Zephrian St. Pierre in 1833. Henriette and Zephrian migrated to Illinois in 1848 with their five children and settled in Bourbonnais. In 1857 the family moved to Iroquois County, one and a half miles south of St. Anne and in 1860 were a household that included nine children ranging in age from a few months to twenty-one years. The family had become Protestant, and according to Henriette's obituary, she read and studied the Bible faithfully. Henriette, who eventually gave birth to twelve children, lost her husband in 1864 and was left to raise her children on her own. One son, Mose, enlisted in the army at fifteen, telling the army that he was sixteen. He was one of many men from these communities who fought on the Union side during the Civil War. Mose returned to marry and settle in St. Anne. In 1900, at age eighty-two, Henriette was living in St. Anne in the household of her son David, his wife, Mattie, and their children. In 1911, five years after Henriette's death, David and Mattie, who were seventy-four and sixty-seven, respectively, celebrated their fiftieth wedding anniversary. On this occasion, the newlyweds were toasted by a family member, who, when he was about to get married, went to Kankakee on horseback to obtain the license. "When my father-in-law was married," David related, "he went on the train but thought it too long to wait for the train to return so he walked back; when I was married I went in an automobile; now when my little daughter marries, I hope my son-in-law will go for his license in an airship." Immediately after they were married, David and Mattie lived in an old log cabin on Mederic Ducharme's farm. They moved to Loda, Illinois, so that David could take a job in a barrel-making factory. Having saved some money, they returned to St. Anne and bought farmland that they later sold to the Pommier family. David and Mattie moved to Sibley, Illinois, and then to Milford, where they ran a hotel for a year before moving back to St. Anne. During this time, Mattie gave birth to ten children, but three girls and three boys died in infancy. Of the four remaining daughters, three were married and living in St. Anne.[14]

Despite the predominance of direct migration from Quebec, there were also some cases of step migration, that is, of families who had spent some time on the East Coast of the United States before responding to Chiniquy's call and moving to the Midwestern lands of opportunity.[15] The Cheffre family described earlier offers one example. Another example is provided by Francis Mirion, a thirty-three-year-old joiner, and his wife, Marie, twenty-seven. They had a son born in Canada in 1852, two sons born in Michigan in 1855 and 1856, and a son born in Illinois in 1859.

How did this first generation of French Canadians immigrants fare in acquiring land to farm? In 1849 over fourteen million acres of land in Illinois were still in the hands of the federal government. Six years later it was all in private hands. Paul Gates estimates that half of this land, available at $1.25 an acre, was purchased by speculators and then resold or placed under tenancy.[16] In 1850 the Illinois Central Railroad received approximately two and a half million acres of farming and woodlands from the government that it offered for sale in forty-acre tracts and upwards under long-term credit and low interest arrangements. Prices varied from $5 to $25 per acre according to the location and quality of the tract. The railroad claimed that two to two and a half acres of this land could be turned over per day by a team of horses or two yoke of oxen. In addition to these federal land grants and railroad tracts, between 1855 and 1859 Kankakee and Iroquois Counties put swamp land grants (much of which had to be tiled and drained before it could be farmed) onto the market for between 75 cents and $20 per acre.[17] A plat map of northeastern Iroquois County for 1860 shows the extent of the holdings in the hands of the railroad, but of equal interest is the land in the hands of Peter Spink, Charles Chiniquy's nemesis in the 1855 suit for slander. There may well have been something to Chiniquy's complaint about Spink's speculative activities at the expense of the French Canadian settlers, particularly those who moved into the area around L'Érable.

In 1860, 76 percent of the French Canadian male heads of household in the four townships analyzed reported their occupation as farmer. Another 7 percent, of whom three-quarters were under forty, called themselves farm laborers. Skilled craftsmen, such as masons, carpenters, blacksmiths, joiners, shoemakers, wagon makers, and butchers, made up 10 percent; 2 percent was in low white-collar occupations, such as merchant, clerk, and innkeeper; and 2 percent was in high white-collar occupations, such as priest/minister, attorney, and physician. One man listed himself as a laundry man, and the remainder had no occupation listed.[18]

As noted for other historical studies of rural communities in the Midwest, there is a discrepancy between those who reported themselves as farmers on the population census and the individuals listed as property owners on the agricultural census. The conclusion drawn, and it is probably equally valid in the French Canadian case, is that many of these farmers were actually tenant farmers. Tenancy was the surest way for farmers to be assured of a crop during the first year of settlement no matter what their financial status.[19] While some newcomers spent a short time in tenancy, others were tenants all their lives. Residents of St. Anne can still recall their parents tenant farming, sometimes from grandparents but more commonly from absentee owners who had large farms.

In 1860, 255 of 302 (84 percent) French Canadian male heads of household who appeared on the agricultural census could be linked to the population census for the same township.[20] Among those who listed themselves as farmers on the 1860 population census, 36 percent had real property assessed at under $100; 17 percent $100 and $500; and 24 percent between $500 and $1000, leaving 23 percent with real property valued at over $1000. As would be expected, farmer heads of households who were under thirty-five had less real property (42 percent of those with property assessed under $100 were under thirty-five), whereas older farmers had more (82 percent of those with property assessed over $1000 were over thirty-five). Of laborers, 72 percent had real property assessed at under $100 compared with 33 percent of skilled craftsmen, and 14 percent of low white-collar workers.

Of the farmers, 7 percent had personal property valued at under $50; another 7 percent between $50 and $99; 63 percent between$100 and $149; and 22 percent at more than $150. More than half the laborers (52 percent) had personal property valued at under $50; 32 percent between $50 and $99. As one would expect, 67 percent of skilled craftsmen had personal property valued at over $100, with low white-collar workers at 86 percent and high white-collar at 80 percent. The wealth distribution for the overall population of French Canadian male heads of household in the four townships in 1860 based on the agricultural census is provided in table 4.4. The figures for real property are not extremely discrepant with those from the population census, while those for personal property show somewhat greater variation with more individuals classified in the lowest tier ($0–99).

The majority of French Canadians who settled in this area farmed from forty to eighty acres, though some had more acreage and a few somewhat less. The mean of improved acres was fifty-four and the mode forty. For unimproved acres the mean was fifteen and the mode zero, and of total acreage the mean was sixty-nine and the mode forty. Chiniquy owned eighty acres of improved farmland. The frequency distribution of acres owned in 1860 for those listed on the agricultural census is in table 4.5.

A more detailed and precise picture of the composition of personal and real wealth can be gained by looking at the probated estates for the period. For example, Toussaint Raymond, one of the more established farmers, died in 1863 leaving no will but with real estate valued at $1,500 and personal property at $500. He was survived by his widow, one daughter, and four sons. His real property included one section of eighty acres and another of forty acres. His chattel property included a bay mare, a gray mare, two bay horses, a black colt, a suckling colt, a cow, a heifer and calf, three hogs/pigs, four sheep, three geese, fifty hens, a double wagon, a reaper and plow, three harrows, three beds, one stove and pipe, a bureau, one lot

TABLE 4.4. Wealth distribution of the French Canadian population for the townships of St. Anne, Beaverville, L'Érable, and Papineau, 1860

Real property		*Personal property*	
Assessed value ($)	*Percentage*	*Assessed value ($)*	*Percentage*
0–99	39	0–19	7
100–199	2	20–29	4
200–299	4	40–59	7
300–399	5	60–79	3
400–499	7	80–99	1
500–999	22	100–149	58
1,000–1,499	20	150–199	19
1,500+	1	200+	0

Note: Percentages may not total 100 owing to rounding.
Source: United States Federal Agricultural Census, Kankakee and Iroquois Counties, 1860

of crockery and one of tinware, a lamp, a table, a clock, a chair, one pork barrel, twelve bushels of wheat, twenty of corn, twenty of flour, one grindstone, one shaving knife, a chest, a spin wheel, one empty barrel, and a few other farm items. Claims on the estate included two notes, one for $12 and one for $4 and what was owed to a laborer for seven months of work, to another for blacksmith's work, and for bills for wine and notions.

TABLE 4.5. Percentage of farming population ($N = 302$) by acreage owned for the townships of St. Anne, Beaverville, L'Érable, and Papineau, 1860

Acreage	*Improved*	*Unimproved*	*Improved + Unimproved*
0–39	21	85	5
40	39	5	44
41–79	17	6	7
80	15	0	28
81–99	1	1	1
100–199	6	3	12
200+	1	0	2

Note: Columns of numbers may not total 100 owing to rounding.
Source: United States Federal Agricultural Census, Kankakee and Iroquois Counties, 1860

Despite the famine years of the late 1850s, the first-generation French Canadian settlers in Illinois were doing as well in land acquisition as the German immigrants who settled in Missouri who, in 1850, averaged forty improved acres and the Norwegians who settled in the Upper Midwest who averaged 33.5 acres in 1850.[21] For all three groups, this was about the extent of acreage that could be farmed with family labor or, if need be, with an extra hand or two. What is distinctive about the French Canadian settlement, by comparison with the transplanted villages that characterized the rural Midwestern immigrants of German, Norwegian, or Swedish extraction, is that it was largely instigated and organized by a single man, Charles Chiniquy. In several villages and towns in the province of Quebec, as well as in New England, families heard Chiniquy's call, and while not necessarily from the same community of origin, they came to Illinois with a shared French Canadian culture and identity.

The Next Generation: Rooted and Uprooted

By 1880 the generation of children who arrived in Illinois at a young age or who were born there in the period immediately succeeding settlement had or were reaching maturity. The 1880 census data indicate that the total number of French Canadian or French Canadian–descent individuals in the four townships increased only slightly (by forty-one) from 1860 (table 4.6). The number of children under the age of fourteen declined to 46 percent of the total population of French Canadians living in these four townships. The proportion of young adults between ages fifteen and thirty-four had remained stable (at 30 percent), and the proportion of these who were married had declined but only slightly (from 49 percent to 46 percent). The proportion of the population between twenty and thirty-four that was married declined by 5 percent for both men and women—from 64 percent to 59 percent for men and from 79 percent to 74 percent for women. Furthermore, the proportion of women in the age cohort between fifteen and nineteen who were married declined from 18 percent to 12 percent. These are not dramatic changes, but they do indicate a gradual shift in marriage patterns as measured by the age at marriage.

This was a relatively stable population, reinforcing the idea that the migration to these communities in Illinois occurred during a few decades in the middle of the nineteenth century. They were not constantly reinvigorated as were many of the French Canadian communities in New England during a migration that lasted from the middle of the nineteenth century into the twentieth century. Some individuals arrived in Illinois into the 1860s, but they were few in number and

TABLE 4.6. French Canadian population ($N = 2,673$) by age, sex, and marital status for the townships of St. Anne, Beaverville, L'Érable, and Papineau, 1880

	Single		*Married*			
Age (y)	*No.*	*Percentage*	*No.*	*Percentage*	*Widowed No.*	*Divorced No.*
			Males			
0–4	213	25	0	0	0	0
5–9	205	24	0	0	0	0
10–14	187	21.9	0	0	0	0
15–19	135	15.8	3	0.6	0	0
20–24	74	8.7	41	8.9	0	0
25–29	18	2.1	47	10.1	1	0
30–34	10	1.2	65	14.1	1	0
35–39	3	0.3	63	13.6	3	0
40–44	1	0.1	56	12.1	0	0
45–49	5	0.6	42	9.1	1	0
50–54	2	0.2	45	9.7	1	0
55–59	0		29	6.3	1	0
60+	0		71	15.4	16	0
Total no.	853		462		24	
Percentage of total	63.7		34.5		1.8	
			Females			
0–4	227	27.6	0	0	0	0
5–9	210	25.6	0	0	0	0
10–14	189	23	0	0	0	0
15–19	119	14.5	17	3.6	0	0
20–24	42	5.1	67	14.3	0	2
25–29	15	1.8	61	13.1	3	0
30–34	6	0.7	68	14.6	1	0
35–39	4	0.5	79	16.9	1	1
40–44	6	0.7	31	6.6	3	0
45–49	2	0.2	30	6.4	4	0
50–54	1	0.1	44	9.4	6	0
55–59	0	0	26	5.6	4	1
60+	0	0	44	9.4	20	0
Total no.	821		467		42	4
Percentage of total	61.5		35		3.1	0.3

Note: Percentages may not total 100 owing to rounding.
Source: United States Federal Census Manuscripts, Kankakee and Iroquois Counties, 1860

generally had kinship contacts there already. The natural increase was also offset by the departure of some members of the second generation to places farther to the west, particularly to Clay and Cloud Counties in Kansas, where in the 1870s, 160-acre plots of land were made available by the US government under the terms of the Homestead Act. A $10 filing fee was the only capital outlay required to obtain this acreage.[22]

The Kansas migration stream, which began in the late 1860s and gathered momentum in the 1870s, was aided by numerous letters and notices published in the *Kankakee Gazette*. Some of these simply described the best way to travel, while others addressed the quality of the soil, the price of land, and the laws of inheritance that were favorable to widows. Mostly, they were fair assessments that advised people to consider carefully before they made the move: "Now, to all those who have means to get a good team, some money to put in stock, able to furnish provisions or live until they can raise a crop, but not able to buy a farm in Illinois, I say come to Kansas. Those who have good homes with all the comforts of life in Illinois, I would advise to stay there and enjoy them."[23] High land values that made the cost of ownership prohibitive, the competition for rentable land, low wages, low farm-product prices, incipient mechanization, and the loss of equity from foreclosures are some of the push factors that stimulated this migration stream, while cheap land farther west was the most powerful pull factor. To these should be added the yearning to move and the desire to work for oneself: "By the end of the decade [1870s] the western fever had created a furor among the farmers of central Illinois. Gone to Kansas was already a familiar story."[24] Although the majority who had picked up stakes remained in their new home, some became discouraged by drought and insect infestations (there were severe grasshopper plagues in the early 1870s) and returned to Illinois.

One of the earliest to depart for Kansas was Antoine Allain Jr., a son of one of the original St. Anne settlers. Another who departed was Jacques Boucher, born in Nicolet, Quebec, in 1827 and married in the village of Ste. Monique, Nicolet County, in 1850. His bride, Alphosine Beaubien, was born in 1835. With his wife and their sons. Alphonse, Joseph, and Maurice, Jacques migrated to Illinois in 1855 and settled in St. Mary (Beaverville). Ten children were born in Illinois, and in 1873 the family moved to Cloud County, Kansas, where two more children were born. In 1879 Jacques became a US citizen at Concordia, Kansas. Alphosine died in Cloud County in 1898; he died in Rooks County, Kansas, in 1912.

Another example is provided by several of the children of Alexis Blanchette. In 1860 Blanchette was fifty-five and a well-established farmer in St. Anne

Township with real property valued at $1,000 and personal property at $300. He and his forty-six-year-old wife, Leocade, both of whom had followed Chiniquy into Protestantism, had nine children living with them ranging in age from two to twenty-two. In 1870 Blanchette was a widower; five of his children remained in the household, three daughters and two sons. Sometime in 1870 he married Matilda Paradis, and in either 1871 or 1872 he died. In 1877 when probate on his estate was filed, his heirs, including his widow, were listed. The majority of his children, according to these probate records, had migrated west to Kansas, leaving in the 1860s and early 1870s.

New impetus was given to the movement westward in 1878 when the railroad reached Clyde County, Kansas. "So many people are going to Kansas utterly oblivious of the trials and dangers that surround them there," the *Kankakee Gazette* reported. The French Canadian–descent settlers moved onto homesteads that American farmers had abandoned and established communities in Aurora, Clyde, Shirley, St. Joseph, and Concordia, Kansas. Close-knit family and parish life prevailed in these settlements as they had in the Illinois, and ties to the sending communities remained strong.[25] Several from Bourbonnais, Kankakee, and St. Anne made the trip. Although the majority of French Canadians in Kansas were Catholics (indeed, the exodus from L'Érable was significant), there was also a small colony of Protestants who built a Presbyterian church two miles south and a half mile west of St. Joseph, Kansas. The *Kankakee Gazette* of March 4, 1884, notes that Chiniquy had returned from a visit to Kansas and in July of that year, and Reverend Chavez of the Baptist Church of St. Anne departed for a two-month visit to Kansas. As late as the 1880s, families were still departing. "Many are having the 'Kansas Fever.' Whether it will affect them seriously we will state later," the *Kankakee Gazette* reported on February 17, 1887. But by this time most of the farmland in Kansas had been distributed, and the out-migration from Illinois to this particular region began to dwindle. According to geographer Aidan McQuillan, those who survived hardship were ultimately extremely prosperous: "By 1915, they had built up good-sized farms and were producing large quantities of wheat for a booming wartime market. They had become successful commercial farmers, and in matters of farming they were indistinguishable from their American neighbors."[26] Yet, despite this successful economic assimilation, they maintained aspects of their French Canadian identity, and as in Illinois, the French language did not disappear until the 1920s. Today, family names in the telephone directories of Clay and Cloud Counties resemble those in Kankakee and Iroquois Counties.

In 1880 the household structure among those who remained in the four Illinois settlements differed little from 1860 (see table 4.2). Simple family households were still predominant, although the proportion of households made up of couples living alone had increased from 4 percent of the total to 12 percent. Again, this is an indication of an aging population, where the household cycle had progressed but where the full cycle had not yet been reached. Households were also generally smaller in size. Of households headed by French Canadian men, 49 percent were made up of six or more persons in 1880 compared with 61 percent in 1860. The most dramatic decline was in the proportion of households composed of ten or more individuals (see table 4.3). These declines are also a function of the household cycle and the migrations farther westward, but changes in fertility patterns (addressed later in the chapter) also have some importance.

When distinguished by household type (and only for households where kinship relations could be easily determined), 50 percent of simple family households headed by French Canadian males were made up of six or more individuals, a decline of 12 percent from 1860; 6 percent of ten or more, a decline of 10 percent from 1860. Among those nuclear households with ten or more individuals, 68 percent of the male household heads were over forty years of age. Fourteen percent of the households (as compared with 24 percent in 1860) were either those in which the kinship relationships could not be easily determined or households that included an unrelated individual. In the majority of cases, these were simple family households with a live-in servant or farm laborer.

As the children of the first generation of immigrants grew to maturity and married, one factor that can be examined is the extent of exogamy or endogamy within the ethnic group. Exogamy, intermarriage with individuals of other ethnic groups, is taken as an indicator of assimilation or what Milton Gordon has labeled more precisely as marital assimilation.[27] Data on the ethnic background of spouses comes from both the census manuscripts and from extant parish registers for the Catholic churches in the region.

The surviving parish register for the late 1850s through the 1870s for St. John the Baptist Church in L'Érable (where Catholics from other townships were also married) indicates that during the early years, the settlers and their maturing offspring were marrying among themselves despite the presence of Yankees and other immigrants in the region. In this register, 109 marriages are recorded for the 1860s. Seventy-eight of these clearly are marriages between two individuals of French Canadian heritage, nine are marriages between French Canadians and immigrants of other French-speaking countries (Belgium and France), ten more are marriages where one of the partners was French Canadian and the other a non–French-speaking immigrant or native-born American. The remaining twelve marriages are between two individuals of other nationalities. Thus, 80 percent of marriages recorded in the L'Érable register of 1860 through 1869 that involved at least one individual of French Canadian birth are marriages where both spouses were of French Canadian birth.

The St. Anne marriage register for the Catholic Church begins in 1872. Between 1872 and 1879, seventy-eight marriages were recorded. Of these, forty-five were marriages where at least one of the spouses was of French Canadian birth or descent and a resident of St. Anne. In 84 percent of these marriages, both bride and groom were of French Canadian background. This pattern continues into the ensuing decades. Between 1880 and 1889, of the eighty-eight marriages recorded, fifty-three involved at least one French Canadian–descent spouse residing in St. Anne. Of these, 87 percent were between individuals who were both of French Canadian background. Similarly, between 1890 and 1899, of the seventy-six marriages recorded, sixty-two involved at least one spouse of French Canadian descent who was a resident of St. Anne, and 84 percent of these involved two individuals of French Canadian descent. The Catholic spouses of other backgrounds tended to be of Irish or German descent, and in a few cases, conversions from Protestantism were recorded.

The data from the census for 1870 for all four townships tend to support the trends suggested in the analysis of parish registers and, of course, include converts to Protestantism, as well as Catholics. Where identified, 86 percent of male French Canadian heads of household between fifteen and thirty-nine years old had French Canadian wives. Table 4.7 breaks this data on intermarriage down by five-year birth cohorts of French Canadian male heads of household. The comparable data for the 1880 census are contained in table 4.8 and show that a decade later there was still a high degree of ethnic and community endogamy with fully 94 percent of the French Canadian–descent men marrying French Canadian–descent women who were born either in Quebec or in Illinois and presumably in one of the four communities or in nearby Kankakee and Bourbonnais.

Such patterns were not, however, unique to the French Canadians. For example, G. Alexander Ross finds similar patterns of group endogamy among German immigrants in Michigan between 1850 and 1880, and Sonya Salamon notes the persistence of high degrees of endogamy well into the twentieth century.[28] Of eighty-one married couples surveyed in a German immigrant community in east central Illinois in 1977, 72 percent were Germans married to Germans. Concentrated

TABLE 4.7. Birthplace of wives of French Canadian male heads of household, by birth cohort of males, 15–39 years old, for the townships of St. Anne, Beaverville, L'Érable, and Papineau, 1870

Age (y) Cohort	*Quebec*	*Midwest**	*East Coast†*	*France*	*Ireland*
15–19 (*N* = 2)	2	0	0	0	0
20–24 (*N* = 29)	21	7	0	1	0
25–29 (*N* = 59)	51	8	0	0	0
30–34 (*N* = 50)	47	2	0	0	1
35–39 (*N* = 50)	45	2	2	1	0
Total no.	166	19	5	2	1
Total percentage	86	9.8	2.6	1	0.5

* Illinois, Indiana, and Michigan
† Connecticut, Maine, Massachusetts, New Hampshire, New Jersey, New York, Pennsylvania, Rhode Island, and Vermont
Note: Percentages may not total 100 owing to rounding.
Source: United States Federal Manuscript Census, Kankakee and Iroquois Counties, 1870

rural settlements have a good deal to do with these marriage patterns, although the French Canadians have been one of the most highly endogamous of all immigrant populations who came to the United States. One Catholic St. Anne resident in his seventies, who was interviewed during the course of this research, commented that intermarriage was rare until his generation, but what was "worse" was to marry outside one's religion. Another of similar age but a Protestant recalled that when one of her father's sisters dated a Catholic, her parents "had a fit."

What is particularly distinct about the Illinois French Canadian settlements is that layered over ethnic-group endogamy was religious endogamy. During these early years, converts to Protestantism tended to marry other Protestants, and Catholics other Catholics. Between 1872 and 1885, 147 marriages were recorded in the register for the newly formed Catholic Church of St. Anne. Only two of these marriages involved a dispensation for "mixed religion" so that bride and groom, both of French Canadian descent, could marry.

TABLE 4.8. Birthplace of wives of French Canadian male heads of household, by birth cohort of males, 15–39 years old, for the townships of St. Anne, Beaverville, L'Érable, and Papineau, 1880

Age (y) Cohort	*Quebec*	*Illinois/ FC*	*Midwest**	*East Coast†*	*France*	*Other‡*
15–19 (*N* = 3)		3				
20–24 (*N* = 41)	4	35	1		1	
25–29 (*N* = 47)	17	28	1	1		
30–34 (*N* = 65)	39	22	2	2		
35–39 (*N* = 63)	48	10	1	2	1	1
Total no.	108	98	5	5	2	1
Total percentage	49	45	2	2	1	

* Indiana and Michigan.
† Connecticut, Maine, New Hampshire, New Jersey, New York, Massachusetts, Pennsylvania, Rhode Island, and Vermont.
Source: United States Federal Manuscript Census, Kankakee and Iroquois Counties, 1880

Among the couples who married in St. Anne in the years just prior to 1880 were Ambrose Allain and Leonie Faucher. Ambrose was the first white child born in St. Anne, on April 18, 1852, "seeing the light of day in a house on a lot where the Catholic Church is now located,"[29] and he lived his entire life in St. Anne with the exception of fourteen years working on a farm in Pembroke Township. Leonie was the daughter of August Faucher, who was born in La Malbaie, Quebec, in 1817 and married in 1840. August arrived in St. Anne in 1852 with his family, lived there his entire life, and died at age ninety-eight at the home of his son-in-law and daughter. Ambrose and Leonie, who were both Protestant, married in 1878 when she was eighteen, and in 1928 they celebrated their golden wedding anniversary. They had eleven children, six of whom were alive at the time of Ambrose's death in 1935. Two sons lived in St. Anne, one in Chicago, one in Columbia, Missouri, one in Gridley, California, and a daughter in Watseka, Illinois. At the time of his death, Ambrose had three sisters who were living, one in St. Anne, one in

Kankakee, and one in Chicago. Of his six living brothers, two lived in St. Anne, two in Kankakee, one in Arkansas, and one in Duluth, Minnesota. Ambrose and Leonie offer a good example of an endogamous marriage and of long-term settlement in St. Anne that persisted for at least a third of the family into the next generation.

Another aspect of marriages during the first twenty-five years of this colony is the overlapping kinship links. In several cases two sisters married two brothers, while in a few others a form of levirate (marrying a dead brother's wife) or sororate (marrying a dead wife's sister) marriage seems to have been in operation. For example, Mitchell Chayer, a Catholic, who was born in Canada in 1831 and arrived in St. Anne in 1856, married Rose Goyette. After her death he married her sister Mary. James Cheffer (or Cheffre), a Presbyterian, who was born in Syracuse, New York, in 1842 and emigrated to Illinois in 1852 with his parents and siblings, married Agnes Lepage in 1868 and had one daughter. Agnes died in 1879, and in 1881 James married his sister-in-law Delina Lepage. In March 1894 Joseph Vezina and Zilda Vezina were married in the Catholic church with a dispensation of the first degree of affinity because Zilda, who was born Zilda Bourgeois, had previously married Joseph's brother Charles in January 1880. This practice seems to have survived into the twentieth century in a few cases. For example, Frank Chayer, a Presbyterian born in 1875 married the widow of his deceased brother in 1905. After the turn of the century, there were still some Catholic marriages celebrated with dispensations for affinity or for the second and third degree of consanguinity, and in one case a couple had to be remarried several years after the first marriage because an unknown relationship of consanguinity had arisen.

These overlapping marriage patterns, where two (or even three) siblings from one sibling group marry two (or three) siblings from another sibling group or where sisters are exchanged, were quite characteristic of families in rural Quebec as well as among French Canadians who migrated to Manitoba.[30] They are also patterns that persisted in these places into the twentieth century. Nicole Lamaire documents similar matrimonial exchanges in a French village in Newfoundland in the mid-twentieth century.[31] In Quebec, there were special terms for the children of such unions—*cousins frérot*, or brotherly cousins. Highly localized endogamy, as well as marriage practices of sibling and sister exchange, were dimensions of the social patterns in French Canadian parishes.[32] Family and community activities brought groups of young people and groups of siblings together, and this was the context in which potential mates were identified and courted. Thus, despite the migrations westward and a network of kin that eventually extended from Canada to California with a concentration in Kansas and Minnesota, the French

Canadian settlements in Illinois were also, and somewhat paradoxically, insular, and the family culture brought from Quebec endured into the second generation.

Even among those who married and remained in one of the Illinois communities, the powerful ties of kinship are apparent in the continued practice of close residence. The Collette family of L'Érable offers a good example. Louis Collette and his wife, Flavie, arrived in Illinois sometime in the 1850s. In 1860, when both were thirty-seven, they were in a household with six children ranging in age from two to fifteen. In 1870 their son Louis, twenty-four, was married and living in an adjacent house with his wife, Julie, and their baby daughter. Another son, David, twenty-one, was also married, but his wife, Emily, and their baby daughter had moved into Louis and Flavie's home and were living there with Louis and Flavie's five other children ranging in age from nine to twenty. By 1880 five separate households were next door to one another: household 75, Louis Sr. and Flavie, both fifty-one years old; household 76, Nicholas, twenty, and his wife, Eleanor, sixteen; household 77, Peter Collette, twenty-nine, his wife, Delia, twenty-eight, and five children ranging in age from two to eight; household 78, Charles Collette, twenty-seven, his wife, Eva, twenty-seven, and two young children; and household 79, Louis Jr. and Julia, six children ranging in age from a few months to ten years. All the Collette male heads of household were listed as farmers on the population census, but only Louis Sr. and Louis Jr. appeared on the 1880 agricultural census, the former with 220 improved acres worth $4,000 and the latter with 46 improved acres worth $800.

In 1880, 65 percent of the French Canadian male heads of household in the four townships analyzed reported their occupation as farmer. This represents a decline of 11 percent from 1860. Another 11 percent, slightly more than half of whom were under forty, called themselves farm laborers. This represents an increase of 4 percent from 1860. Six percent were skilled craftsmen; 3 percent were unskilled workers. Two percent were in low white-collar occupations, such as merchant, clerk or innkeeper; and 1 percent was in high white-collar occupations such as priest or minister, attorney, or physician. The remaining individuals were listed with other occupations, no occupation, or as retirees. These were still primarily farming communities, although the increase in the proportion of agricultural laborers is further evidence that it was harder to secure a farm in 1880 than it had been two decades earlier.

In 1880 tenant farmers operated a little more than 31 percent of the farms in Illinois, and in central Illinois twenty-five counties had tenancy rates of 35 percent.[33] The tenancy rates among the French Canadians in the four townships near Kankakee varied, with the highest level in L'Érable (32 percent) and lower levels in Papineau (21 percent), St. Anne (18 percent), and St. Mary/Beaverville (14 percent). Conversely, 82 percent of the farmers in St. Anne and Beaverville were owners, with the remaining 4 percent in Beaverville as straight renters. In L'Érable, 62 percent were owners, and 6 percent were renters; in Papineau, 77 percent were owners, and 2 percent were renters. These rates of ownership are somewhat lower than the 95 percent rate of ownership for German farmers in Stearns County, Minnesota, in 1880, which Stephen John Gross argues is evidence of a high degree of egalitarianism among that immigrant group.[34]

Just under half of French Canadian or French Canadian–descent farmers in the four townships were still cultivating farms of eighty acres or less compared with 92 percent in 1860 (table 4.9). However, the amount of acreage that remained unimproved had declined to an insignificant level. This trend toward larger farm units has been noted for the general farming population of east-central Illinois during the final three decades of the nineteenth century.[35] With time, in short, the French Canadian settlers who owned farms had achieved some economic success, and differences in wealth were beginning to emerge. This success was reflected in the assessed cash value of farm property. For 13 percent this value was under $1,000; another 57 percent had an assessment between $1,000 and $2,999; and 29 percent were assessed above $3,000.

County atlas maps for the period show the distribution of these farms in the four townships in Kankakee and Iroquois Counties. The bulk of the farmland immediately surrounding the town of St. Anne was in the hands of French Canadians, and some of these individuals owned more than a quarter section (160 acres), sometimes in plots that were not adjacent. The same is true of Papineau Township,

TABLE 4.9. Percentage of farming population ($N = 313$) by acreage owned for the townships of St. Anne, Beaverville, L'Érable, and Papineau, 1880

Acreage	*Improved*	*Unimproved*
0–40	18	98
41–80	31	1
81–100	17	0
101–199	25	0
200+	9	0

Source: United States Federal Agricultural Census, Kankakee and Iroquois Counties, 1880

although some of the properties close to the town were in non–French Canadian hands, no doubt a reflection of the fact that this settlement was already in existence when the French Canadians arrived. The map for the land surrounding the settlement of L'Érable shows the greater presence of Belgian and French immigrants by comparison with the other townships under study, although French Canadian immigrants possessed significant and extensive pieces of property in this area, as well. In this township, the Iroquois River was a dividing line; land to the west of it was available to the French, Belgians, and French Canadians when they moved into the area in the 1850s, while land to the east had already been claimed by other settlers and speculators. Similarly, not as much land was available in the more eastern township of Beaver, and the French Canadians settled primarily around the community of St. Mary, an area indicated on an 1860 map of Iroquois County with the words "Canadian settlement." Further, in Beaver Township, a few families (Arseneau, Boudreau, Frigon, Lareau, Nourie) predominated in land ownership.

A tax list for St. Anne for 1875 provides some information on personal property for the French Canadian households in that community. For 25 percent of households, the total taxable personal property was under $50; for an additional 17 percent it was between $50 and $99; 17 percent fell between $100 and $149; 12 percent between $150 and $199. Sixteen percent had wealth assessed between $200 and $299, 8 percent between $300 and $399, and 2 percent between $400 and $499. Two households were in the $500 to $599 category, and two more between $600 and $699, and one household between $700 and $799. In addition, five businesses were assessed, two of which, Bastien and Co. and C. F. Blain and Co., had personal assets above $2,000. Among the items taxed were 135 horses and mules, $11,255; 469 cows (with most individuals owning one or two but a few with herds of ten or twenty), $8,135; 203 hogs, $400; 101 wagons and carriages, $1,367. The total value of agricultural tools was a little more than $1,300 and of household furniture $2,228. Clocks and sewing machines were listed separately, and fifty-four dogs were counted. A few individuals had gaming tables, and a few had pianos or organs.

Undoubtedly, as a legacy of the events surrounding the schism in the late 1850s, the economic well-being of the French Canadians in the communities east of Kankakee continued to be a point of controversy. A September 16, 1869, article of the *Kankakee Gazette* reports destitution in St. Anne. Reverend Alexander Kemp, who was involved in the merger of the First Presbyterian Church with the Canadian Presbytery, had made a personal investigation of the conditions of the French families in St. Mary and St. Anne and called for relief for the "industrious, virtuous, and pious French-Canadians, most of whom are Presbyterians."

He claimed to have visited 162 families, including 1,186 adults and 861 children. About 200, he reported, are able to work, and they provide support for the rest. He reported losses in the wheat crop and also observed that some men had gone to work on the railway but had been left unpaid by subcontractors. Another story about the poverty in St. Anne appeared again in the *Kankakee Gazette* on July 28, 1881, with the headline "Devastation Dire." The article describes the people of St. Anne as being on the point of starvation and once more in need of philanthropy. The source for this story is not made clear, but on August 4, 1881, in a story, "Citizens of St. Anne Indignantly Deny Published Reports of Their Condition," Napoleon Bastien, owner of a general store in St. Anne, who was serving as mayor of the town in the 1880s, was quoted as saying that the first article had grossly misrepresented the crops and that the yield was the best in ten years. He failed to see the purpose of the lies and concluded by suggesting that "it seems to be chronic with someone to publish through this broad land every few years that the people of St. Anne are starving. They are not." Laborers, he said, were earning a $1.50 to $2 a day, and farmers were unable to find the hands they needed for their fields. At a town meeting in St. Anne, residents voted to censure and condemn the article as malicious and false. They claimed that the town was more prosperous than it had been for years, and they resented "the continued attempts to represent the people of St. Anne as beggars." This was followed by yet another article toward the end of the month that ran with the headline "St. Anne Prosperity."[36] It listed various improvements, including the completion of two brick store buildings, Chagnon and Soucie and the Gros Brothers, the opening of a shoe store owned by Felix Mason, and an addition to the post office. During the fall, this effort to counter the negative portrait of St. Anne, with stories about barn dances, construction projects, and people's travels to visit family and friends far afield, continued. In the fall of 1884 the newspaper reported that the corn crop would be the best in years, but this was followed by a report in the spring that made reference to the harsh winter that had just ended. In 1886, mechanization had arrived—the hum of a threshing machine was heard for the first time.

St. Anne was changing in other ways, to some extent the result of the building of the railway through the community in the early 1870s. In that same decade the town was incorporated, wooden sidewalks were laid, and a water system was completed. In the summer of 1885 it was reported that the town had forty-one business establishments, five general stores, six dealers in agricultural implements, two drugstores, one exclusive boot and shoe store, three millinery shops, two saloons, one hardware store, one harness store, one creamery, two grocers, four grain dealers, one lumberyard, three coal dealers, one newspaper and printing shop, one grist mill, three hay dealers, five blacksmiths, two wagon and repair shops, and two first-class hotels. All these, as the *Kankakee Gazette* reported on August 27, 1885, were doing an annual business of $300,000 and drew customers from neighboring towns. However, there were some tensions between these small-business proprietors and the farmers whom they served that revolved primarily around matters of credit. The *Kankakee Gazette* on February 21, 1889, reports that the merchants of St. Anne

> buy goods to be paid for in 30 or 60 days and our substantial farmers come in and buy these goods on a year time or even longer without interest and if merchants charge him a shade more than he thinks right he goes to the city where, by the way, he always pays cash. If that farmer was asked to wait a year for his pay for a bunch of cattle he would be struck dumb with astonishment; if the merchant could always get his money he could sell at less profit. The credit system is detrimental to the whole community and we hope to see it soon done away with in St. Anne.

In addition to this variety of business endeavors in St. Anne by the 1880s, there was also diversity in religion—another legacy of the schism of a quarter century earlier. The community by this time had five churches: Catholic, First Presbyterian, Second Presbyterian, Baptist, and Seventh Day Adventists. Since the days of the schism, men of both Catholic and Protestant backgrounds had served as the town supervisor of St. Anne, and, occasionally, there were individuals of non–French Canadian heritage who served as town supervisor.

The Protestant and Catholic populations were different in some ways, one of them being in property ownership. Seventy-four percent of St. Anne farmers listed on the 1880 census could be identified as either Protestant or Catholic.[37] While 23 percent of the Protestant male heads of household had eighty acres or less of improved agricultural land and of these 6.5 percent had forty acres or less, 41 percent of the Catholics had eighty acres or less, and 3.1 percent forty or less. While 29 percent of Protestants had over two hundred acres of improved farm acreage, only 12.5 percent of the Catholics did. These differences are equally reflected in the cash value of farms. While 53 percent of Catholics were assessed at under $2,000, the comparable proportion for Protestants was 34 percent. While 12.5 percent of Catholics had farms valued at over $4,000, the comparable figure for Protestants was 19 percent. Although the figures for St. Anne for 1860 are not easily comparable, there is an intriguing difference. In that year, 56 percent of Protestants had forty acres or less of improved agricultural land and 92 percent had eighty acres or less. For Catholics the comparable figures were 40 percent with forty acres or less and 93 percent with eighty acres or less. For 63 percent of the Protestants, the cash value of land (improved and unimproved acres) was under $1,000 while only 40 percent of the Catholics had evaluations under $1,000. It appears that in St. Anne the Protestant converts not only were doing better economically than they had been in 1860 but also doing better on average than the Catholic residents of St. Anne. However, the bulk of French Canadians residing in the other communities (Papineau, Beaverville, and L'Érable) remained Catholic, and, despite the higher tenancy rates in these other communities, there were also some large and prosperous landowners.

Social historians of nineteenth-century immigrants in rural America have argued that these populations generally did as well as the native-born rural populations and better than their ethnic counterparts who went to the cities. The French Canadians who settled in rural Illinois appear to have been doing better than those went to work in the mill towns of New England. In Biddeford, Maine, not one French Canadian in 1860 was listed as having any real estate or personal property of value, and only sixteen owned real estate or had a personal estate in 1870. In 1870, 492 French Canadian males were listed: 249 factory operatives, 71 laborers, 41 railroad men, 27 brick makers, 18 shoemakers, and 2 machinists, and the rest had a variety of occupations. In 1880, of 1197 male workers, 639 were factory operatives, and 132 were laborers, and only 41 had personal or real estate listed. [38] In general, these French Canadian immigrants were poor when they arrived, and they remained poor. The French Canadian working class of Holyoke, Massachusetts, developed a family economy strategy for survival based on the labor of several members, including children. By 1900 only a handful had moved into the textile overseer role.[39]

Historians of rural immigrants have also described communities that into the second generation tended to remain with their own kind, marrying within their group, building their own ethnic churches, and forming their own associations and institutions, including schools that often educated in the native language (fig. 4.2). While I return later in this chapter to the question of language as it pertains to the French Canadians who settled in northeastern Illinois, it seems that these populations were not unlike their German and Scandinavian counterparts who also settled in Midwest at roughly the same time. When these French Canadians decided to move farther west, it was not primarily out of wanderlust but in search of better farming opportunities for themselves and their families. This, too, was similar to the motivations behind the further displacement of Norwegian immigrants who settled initially in Wisconsin.[40] In both cases, contacts between these new frontier settlements and the parent communities to the east were maintained.

FIGURE 4.2. French Canadian immigrants, St. Anne, Illinois, circa 1900. *Author's collection.*

A New Generation: Population and Community Life

In March 1893, soon after the dedication of the new Presbyterian church, Charles Chiniquy preached a farewell sermon. "He was leaving for the last time," the session minutes read, "and forever a people whom he greatly loved, for whom he had done so much, among whom he had ministered for nearly fifty years. . . . He seemed to be conscious of the solemnity of the moment he had reached in his life."[41] Six years later, Chiniquy died in Montreal, but the communities he had been so instrumental in establishing were firmly rooted in the soil of Illinois.

In 1900 the total French Canadian population in the four townships was 3,116, an increase of 443 individuals from 1880 (table 4.10). Children under the age of fourteen comprised only 40 percent of the total population, a decline of 10 percent from the 1860 proportion. However, the proportion of young adults between fifteen and thirty-four had increased slightly to 32 percent, and 45 percent of these men and women were married. In 1900, an only slightly larger proportion of men between twenty and thirty-four were married than in 1880, 61 percent, as opposed to 59 percent in 1880. Among the women the proportion remained approximately the same, 73 percent compared to 74 percent. Only 11 percent of the females between 15 and 19 were married, and they represented 3 percent of the population of married women in 1900. These proportions are similar to those for French Canadians nationwide. On the 1910 census, 8 percent of French Canadians between fifteen and nineteen were married; 46 percent of those between twenty and twenty-four; 73 percent of those between twenty-five and twenty-nine; and

TABLE 4.10. French Canadian population (N = 3,116) by age, sex, and marital status for the townships of St. Anne, Beaverville, L'Érable, and Papineau, 1900

	Single		*Married*			
Age (y)	*No.*	*Percentage*	*No.*	*Percentage*	*Widowed No.*	*Divorced No.*
			Males			
0–4	216	23.0	0	0	0	0
5–9	214	22.8	0	0	0	0
10–14	204	21.8	0	0	0	0
15–19	140	14.9	1	0.2	0	0
20–24	87	9.3	36	6.1	0	0
25–29	34	3.6	73	12.3	0	0
30–34	11	1.2	97	16.4	0	1
35–39	10	1.1	78	13.2	3	0
40–44	3	0.3	65	10.9	3	0
45–49	3	0.3	46	7.8	2	1
50–54	4	0.4	53	8.9	2	1
55–59	3	0.3	40	6.8	3	1
60+	8	0.8	103	17.4	16	1
Total no.	937		592		29	5
Total percentage	59.9		37.9		1.8	0.3
			Females			
0–4	211	24.4	0	0	0	0
5–9	206	23.9	0	0	0	0
10–14	187	21.7	0	0	0	0
15–19	151	17.5	19	3.1	0	0
20–24	54	6.2	74	12.2	2	0
25–29	27	3.1	97	16.0	1	1
30–34	9	1.0	96	15.8	3	0
35–39	6	0.7	74	12.2	0	0
40–44	3	0.3	49	8.1	5	0
45–49	3	0.3	53	8.7	4	1
50–54	1	0.1	39	6.4	12	0
55–59	1	0.1	50	8.2	8	0
60+	4	0.5	56	9.2	46	0
Total no.	863		607		81	2
Total percentage	55.5		39.1		5.2	0.1

Note: Percentages may not total 100 owing to rounding.
Source: United States Federal Census Manuscripts, Kankakee and Iroquois Counties, 1900

94 percent of those between forty-five and fifty-four.[42] Oral historical evidence suggests that early marriage persisted for several more decades. For example, one female St. Anne resident born in 1915 reported quitting school after the eighth grade to help her mother out at home and was married at seventeen. "Education was not as important in those days as it is now," she said. Her sister also married early.

Overall, whereas in 1860 the ratio of children under fifteen to young married adults between fifteen and thirty-four was 3.2 to 1, in 1900 it was 2.8 to 1, suggesting some decline in overall fertility that I return to shortly. Another major change in the composition of the populations of French Canadians living in these townships of central Illinois during the forty years between 1860 and 1900 was in the proportion of the population over fifty. In 1860, this population represented 7 percent of the total population; in 1880 they made up 12 percent; and in 1900, 14 percent.

The data on the structure and size of households reflect to some extent the aging of the French Canadian population in these townships over the course of five decades (see tables 4.2 and 4.3). In 1900, 6 percent of the households headed by French Canadian or French Canadian–descent males were extended, largely by the presence of a widowed parent and to a lesser extent by the presence of unmarried siblings of the head of household. Almost 15 percent were households of married couples living alone (as compared with 4 percent in 1860), and it is quite apparent that many of these were "empty nest" households. These empty nests explain in large part the decline in the proportion of simple-family households from 61 percent in 1880 to 53 percent in 1900. Concomitantly, of course, the average size of households declined. In 1900 only 34 percent of households were composed of six or more persons compared with almost twice that amount in 1860. The largest decline over four decades was in households of ten or more persons.

Of the French Canadian male heads of household in the four townships in 1900, 45 percent reported their occupation as farmer, a decline of 20 percent from 1880. This change reflected national trends. Whereas farming used 60 percent of the labor force in 1860, it used less than 40 percent by 1900.[43] Another 9 percent of the French Canadian male heads of household in the four townships were listed as farm laborers, and railroad laborers comprised 1 percent (nine individuals). Skilled craftsmen, such as masons, carpenters, painters, cabinetmakers, blacksmiths, tinsmiths, shoemakers, butchers, and bakers, made up 6 percent. Low white-collar occupations, such as merchant, saloon or innkeeper, barber, salesman, teamster, and horse/livery man, were 7 percent, and another 2 percent were in high white-collar occupations, such as priest or minister, attorney, physician, and teacher. One man was a laundry man, nineteen (2.5 percent) were listed as landlords or in real estate, two were in stock raising, and three were grain dealers. The remaining individuals (17 percent) had no occupation listed or were in a range of other occupations (9 percent). The population in 1900 was more diversified in terms of occupation. Low white-collar workers had increased by 5 percent, and some individuals were clearly living off the property they owned. Many of the characteristics of established small-town rural life that were already apparent in the 1880s were further solidified by 1900, although the future of the area was a more pressing concern as it became apparent that fewer and fewer were living off the land.

In St. Anne this solidification is exemplified not only by the rebuilding of the central business district after a devastating fire in 1888 but also by the opening of the First National Bank in 1899 as a state bank and then as a national bank in 1900 (fig. 4.3). The population in the township, of all nationality backgrounds, had grown from 1,158 in 1880 to 1,870 in 1900, and the population in the village of St. Anne proper had increased from 412 in 1880 to 1,000 in 1900. In 1906 the U.S. Wheel and Rim Company, which employed about a hundred people, was opened. In a January 12 editorial, the *St. Anne Record* suggests that the town was entering one of the greatest epoch in its history. Families were moving to town and building large residences, new businesses, such as the Tristate Post and Fence Company, were launched, and old businesses like the brick and tile factory, originally founded in the mid-1880s, were expanding. "It may be that St. Anne will yet be known as one of the chief manufacturing towns of Illinois," the editorial writer proclaims with supreme optimism.[44] However, at the same time this editorial writer observes that on the moral side "a great deal of improvement is needed. . . . But people want to be left alone. They want their freedom to do as they please. If they want to keep their place of business open on Sunday, none must interfere. If they want to gamble in their stores, keep still." This was an issue that the newspaper had dwelled upon the previous year as well, making an allusion to the troubles of the past in the process: "A younger generation is growing up in this town that seems to take delight in everything that is mean, low, and disreputable. And this is a sure way, if unchecked, of filling our prisons and poor houses and insane asylums. We do not want some of St. Anne's history repeated. But to prevent it something must be done. The moral side of the town must be attended to as well as the business side."[45] Some of these moral issues were rooted in temperance debates that I return to in a subsequent chapter, but it is tantalizing to see that the past still resonated in the lives of turn-of-the-century St. Anne.

Real property values were provided for only a portion of the heads of household who appeared on the 1900 census (41 percent, or 307 of 739 male heads of

FIGURE 4.3. Guertin Store, interior, St. Anne, Illinois, circa 1900. *Author's collection.*

household). Of these, 50 percent had assets under \$500, 24 percent between \$500 and \$999, 17 percent between \$1,000 and \$1,999, 8 percent between \$2,000 and \$4,999, and 1 percent above \$5,000. Only 21 percent of the French Canadian–descent male heads of household had personal property assessed at \$1,000 and higher. Of these, 61 percent fell within the \$1,000 to \$1,999 range, 21 percent between \$2,000 and \$2,999, and 7 percent at over \$5,000.

A comparison of county atlases for the turn of the century with those from the early 1880s reveals that much of the land originally acquired by the settler generation remained in their hands or in that of their heirs. These maps also indicate that the majority of French Canadian or French Canadian–descent farmers had quarter sections of 160 acres. A few had more, and some had less. Efforts were made to maintain adjacent plots of land, but sometimes farmers had eighty-acre sections in different parts of one or more townships.

Indeed, by the turn of the century, greater differences in personal wealth began to emerge. After the February 16, 1906, edition of the *St. Anne Record* listed St. Anne, Papineau, and Beaverville taxpayers who paid over \$100, the newspaper followed with an editorial on February 23 drawing attention to the scarcity of residents in the medium range of assets in these communities. Of the thirty-five listed for St. Anne, twenty-five were French Canadian–descent individuals and one was a partnership, Archambault and Delacourt (father-in-law and son-in-law ran a hotel in St. Anne). The remainder were businesses, the First National Bank, Cornish Lumber Company, and St. Anne Light and Water, or individuals of other ethnic backgrounds, including Edward Pallissard, who was born in France. Joseph Nourie Sr. was listed for Papineau, and Moses St. Pierre was for Beaverville. On this list were some of the biggest landowners, and the majority were men of the first generation of immigrants and who came as young children or young adults. For those whose religion could be identified, the list was equally divided between Catholics and Protestants.

One individual on the list was Moise Baron. Born in Trois Rivières, Quebec, in 1836, Baron migrated to United States with his family in 1844, settling first in Aurora, Illinois, then in Manteno, and eventually in Papineau. He moved to the town of St. Anne in 1899. At age twenty-three, he married Philomene Lebeau, and they had thirteen children, all of whom survived. Both he and his wife were Catholic. At the time of his death in October 1908, three of his children were living in St. Anne, five in Papineau, two in Beaverville, one in Chicago, one in Fowler, Indiana, one in Kankakee, one in Tulsa, and one in Crescent City. At his death, Moise's estate was valued at $100,000, $70,000 in real property and the rest in cash and personal property. His second wife, whom he had married in 1900, was to receive an annuity of $400 per year for the rest of her life. The remainder of the estate was to be divided equally among his children, each of whom had already received large gifts prior to his death.[46] Baron had built up his wealth, but the size of his family meant dispersal in the next generation.

Stephen (Etienne) Raymond offers a second example of a well-established Catholic farmer who amassed wealth during the early years of settlement but divided it fairly equally at his death. Born in Montreal in 1817, Raymond migrated to Illinois in 1843, ahead of the Chiniquy migration. He moved to St. Anne in 1853, and although he followed Chiniquy into schism, he converted back to Catholicism sometime in the 1870s. At least one of his sons, however, remained a Protestant. Raymond's first wife, Ellen Fortin (whom he had married in 1848), died in 1852, and in 1855 he married Angeline Dumond, and together they had eight children. Beginning with an initial purchase of sixty acres in 1853, he accumulated more than 620 acres in St. Anne, Aroma, and Papineau Townships over his working life. In 1907, four years before his death, he divided his property, valued at $90,000, among his five surviving children, all of whom were living in St. Anne.[47]

These cases of inheritance merit close examination since it was during the last decade of the nineteenth century and the first two decades of the twentieth century that many of the first generation of settlers died and passed on the property they had acquired. Historians have argued that the relationship between Midwestern rural immigrants and their land was an important factor in the maintenance of cultural continuity with the past and family and community persistence.[48] They, as well as social scientists who have studied more contemporary communities in the American Midwest, have noted variations by ethnic group in how land was transferred from one generation to the next—partibly or impartibly, by sale, premortem, postmortem, testate, intestate—and the implications of these differing transfer strategies for kinship relations.[49]

As is evidenced in the cases described above, the French Canadians seem to have pursued a variety of strategies, distributing property both before and after death, but there was generally an effort to provide equally for all offspring. If the portions were unequal, it was generally because one child had provided some special service, for example, attending to elderly parents. Legators could equally specify sons or daughters as heirs to their farms. Their decisions were sometimes influenced by which children were still living close by. If all their heirs had left the area, a different strategy had to be followed. For example, Desire Castonguay died in 1906 leaving *several* lots in block 8 of Chiniquy's addition to St. Anne valued at $1,000. No chattel property, notes, or accounts are mentioned. The heirs listed are Joseph and Vitale Castonguay of Omega, Oklahoma; Charles Castonguay of Kingfisher, Oklahoma; Marie Flewelling of Crawford, Oklahoma; and Clara Flewelling of Scottsville, Kansas. Indicating that all of his children had received their share as they became of maturity and that they were living in Oklahoma and Kansas, he stated that they were not entitled to any of his property in Illinois. Desire left everything to his wife, Melina. Melina was his second wife, whom he had married in 1891 two years after the death of his first wife, and the mother of all his children.[50]

Those without farmland also took some care with the assets they bequeathed. Joseph Mombleau, a Catholic, born in 1843 in Quebec, migrated to Illinois in 1848. In 1850 he moved to St. Anne. He married Delima Fortier, and they had ten children, seven of whom (including two daughters who were nuns in Chicago) were still living when he died in 1928. Widowed in 1886, in 1890 he married Delima Berard, who was born in Quebec in 1853, raised in Bourbonnais, and arrived in St. Anne in 1886 to keep house for her brother Father Z. P. Berard. Joseph and Delima had two children, one of whom, Berard Mombleau, pastor of St. John the Baptist Church in Chicago, survived Joseph. Joseph, who worked in harness making for more than fifty years, accumulated assets that were primarily stocks and cash worth just under $6,000 and urban real estate. He left his real and personal property to two of his sons, one of them Reverend Berard. After the expenses were paid, he asked that his son Edward receive $500, an amount he deemed sufficient because of advancements he had made to him in his lifetime. He also asked that the children of his deceased son, Moses, be given $500 to be divided equally among them and gave $1,000 to Reverend Berard and anything the reverend wanted from the estate of his mother, Delima Berard, because he was the only son of his parents' marriage, his father's other children being from his first marriage. Joseph ends by observing that for reasons he deemed sufficient, he made no provision for his daughter Leonie Drolet.

These records of inheritance, although scattered and unsystematic, do suggest some characteristics of persistence among this group of French Canadians in Illinois. This is a question that has interested social historians, although, generally, the emphasis is persistence within a single generation between one census period and the next one or two. Kathleen Neils Conzen, however, carries her observations across generations to encompass the question of inheritance. She observes that 73 percent of the German farm families in Stearns County, Minnesota, who were counted in the 1860s were still there after twenty years and 54 percent of the second cohort after twenty-five years.

> In 1880, 55 percent of all the landowners had been in the township less than a decade. By 1895, 37 percent of landowners had arrived sometime during the previous fifteen years. Ten years later, only 15 percent of the landowners had arrived sometime during the previous decade. . . . By 1905, almost half of the pioneer German families of the late 1850s and 1860s had successfully established one or more children on local farms, while another sixth were still farming themselves. Two-thirds of the Irish families had similar success in setting up their children on local farms.[51]

This was not the case, she notes, for the original Yankee settlers, none of whom had passed on their land to their children.

Social historians have often emphasized the greater "community orientation" of European immigrants by comparison with Yankees as an explanation for persistence. Some scholars have suggested that the French Canadian family is characterized by "a strong sense of grouping and integration superimposed on an extensive pattern of migration."[52] Among the French Canadians in Illinois, these almost contradictory characteristics are manifested in community and group endogamy and transfer of property to the next generation, on the one hand, and the movement westward to Kansas among those who grew to adulthood during the first quarter century of the history of these townships, on the other. These contradictions are even more apparent when we look at the later generations. The best evidence comes from an analysis of the obituaries in the *St. Anne Record* between 1906 and 1941. Between 1906 and 1919, 249 offspring are mentioned by place of residence in the obituaries of parents who died during these years. Where there are obituaries of both a husband and a wife, only one was analyzed. While not a perfect measure, it does give some indication of both the persistence and dispersal of second and third generations. Of these 249, somewhat more than a third (38 percent) continued to reside in St. Anne, and an additional 9 percent resided in one of the three other parishes (Beaverville, Papineau, or L'Érable). An additional 24 percent resided in neighboring towns, primarily Kankakee. Thus, 71 percent of these offspring remained in the area and evidently in close contact with one another. Eleven percent lived in Chicago or other towns in northern Illinois, 2 percent in a neighboring state (primarily Indiana), and 1 percent in Canada.

The remaining 15 percent of offspring mentioned on the obituaries for these first two decades of the twentieth century were in other states of the United States, including Kansas, Minnesota, California, Iowa, the Dakotas, Oklahoma, Idaho, Wyoming, and Nebraska. After the turn of the century, the Southwest and the Far West represented the new frontier. The February 4, 1910, *St. Anne Record* reports the purchase of land in Texas by some St. Anne natives, and references are made to the sister of one resident who was living in New Mexico, to another individual who was moving to Arkansas, and of one leaving for Oklahoma. Despite this continued dispersal, family members still looked eastward to the parent communities. In that same year of 1910, in the middle of winter when there were fewer demands on farmers, the Cheffer (Cheffre) and St. Peter (St. Pierre) families held a family reunion in Kankakee that honored those who were now living in Iowa. Forty relatives attended.[53]

Between 1920 and 1941, 518 offspring were listed in the obituaries of French Canadian–descent residents of St. Anne who died during those years. Thirty-four percent of these continued to reside in St. Anne and an additional 5 percent in the neighboring parishes. Twenty-five percent were in neighboring towns, again especially Kankakee, 15 percent in Chicago and northern Illinois, 5 percent in neighboring states, and 16 percent in other states—the largest numbers in Kansas, California, Minnesota, and Michigan.

Almost a century after the original immigration to Illinois, a significant proportion to the descendants of the first settlers were still living in the region but not necessarily in the same communities where population was relatively stable. It was impossible to set up on the farm all the offspring of what were still relatively large families, albeit not as large as they had been in the 1850s and 1860s. Persistence and dispersal are equally characteristic of this immigrant population, and by comparison with the somewhat later immigrants who settled in New England, there was probably greater dispersal. A farm economy could not absorb offspring the way that a factory economy could at that time. Just over a century later, on the plat maps for the early 1980s, the trends of persistence and change are apparent. Close to the town of St. Anne we see farms that have remained in the hands of descendants of original settlers— Benjamin, Bonvallet, Dube, Lottinville, Pallissard, Soucie—as well as the emergence of a large farm in the Cote family. But we also see significant inroads into the northern sections of St. Anne Township by descendants of the Dutch immigrants in Kankakee County. A similar situation appears to have emerged in Papineau and Beaverville Townships, although the acreage left in the hands of the descendants of French Canadian settlers is generally greater. Neither of these townships experienced the massive aggregation of acreage represented by the Cote farms in St. Anne. These two townships, somewhat more isolated and with smaller central towns, have remained more rural. The Belgians and French Canadians in L'Érable also seem to have remained more rooted in the region across the generations. It, too, is remote and largely a farming community.

Survivance and La Revanche des Berceaux: Religion and Fertility

Dere's six children in our fam'lee, Dey's mosly girls an' boys,
Toinettte an' me was t'ankful sure, for all de happy joys;
Dere's Pierre, an' little Rosalie, Antoine, Marie an' Jeanne,
An' Paul he's now soon twelf year, mos' close to be a man;
I's lof all of la petite famille, De garçon mak' me proud,
I haf' gr'ad spirature, for all dat little crod;
My Pierre shall be wan doctor mans, Rosalie will teach school;
Antoine an' Jeanne shall ron de farm, Maria som' man will rule;
An' Paul shall be a curé sure, Ill haf' heem educate,
I work it all out in my head, Oh, I am moch elate.[54]

Whatever aspect of French Canadian immigrant behavior studied, most authors make reference to the concept of *survivance*—the emphasis on survival as an ethnic group that is reflected to this day in the motto on license plates in the province of Quebec—"*Je me souviens*" (I remember). Three fundamental aspects of survivance emerged in a British-ruled Quebec, the preservation of language, customs, and faith. Custom was rooted in the parish and the family. The parish was the vessel of patriotism and of ethnic pride. In the equally "threatening" environment of the eastern United States, the church played a major role in efforts to retain ethnic distinctiveness among French Canadian immigrants. As one New England newspaper puts it, "To be Canadian is above all to be Catholic."[55] And to be Catholic was to reproduce. High fertility, which began during the French regime and continued under English rule, was the means by which the French Canadians waged the "*revanche des berceaux*" (literally, the revenge of the cradles), their "battle" against minority status in Quebec. It was the by-product not only of Catholicism but also of the exigencies of life in rural Quebec.[56] And, yet, some scholars have argued that among the French Canadian immigrants in New England mill towns of nineteenth-century America, families remained large because working-age children were important to the immigrant French Canadian family economy.[57] Several other studies have supported the assessment that the French Canadians in the eastern United States were, with the Irish, the most prolific immigrant group.[58] In 1910, the US Census Bureau provided nationwide comparative statistics on children born to white women of foreign birth. French Canadians averaged 7.38 compared with 7.42 for Poles, 5.79 for Germans, and 5.31 for Scandinavians.

Both the strong bonds of the French Canadian family and the high birth rate have been described as deterrents to the social mobility of members of this particular immigrant population. In comparisons with a number of other white ethnic groups, second- and third-generation French Canadians (or Franco-Americans) have demonstrated among the lowest median levels of school years attended and the lowest median incomes.[59] High fertility and minimal upward mobility prolonged, according to some scholars, the acquisition of middle-class norms, including that of small families.[60] One study further observes that the French Canadians in New England have been second only to the Chinese in the number of years of US residence prior to naturalization.[61] In Biddeford, Maine, in 1950 the Franco-Americans were second from the bottom after the Mexican Americans in terms of median income.[62] Ninety percent still reported French as their mother tongue in the 1970 census. This, too, has been taken as an indication of a slower rate of "assimilation" that may also have contributed to sustained high fertility levels.

It is in this regard that the demographic changes that occurred among the population in the French Canadian settlements in rural northeastern Illinois become particularly interesting to examine. The Chiniquy-inspired schism divided the community and created two subpopulations, one Catholic and one Protestant.

Did differences in fertility emerge, and how quickly, between these two groups that share the same history, cultural background of language and "custom," and residential communities and yet prayed in different churches? Furthermore, how different, overall, is this population of French Canadian immigrants from the more extensively studied French Canadian immigrants who settled in the urban mill towns of nineteenth-century New England?

A number of measures of fertility can be generated from an analysis of census data. In 1860, the average number of children per household for households with at least one child was 4.2. In 1880, it had dropped to 3.9 and by 1900 to 3.3. There was also a decline in the proportion of households with six or more children from 29 percent in 1860 to 17 percent in 1900. Although some of the difference in both of these measures may be due to changes in the number of adult children over fifteen still living with their parents, they do suggest, for the population as a whole, a decline in fertility.

A more common measure of fertility that avoids the problem of changes in the mobility and independence of older children is the child-woman ratio. Although there is some disagreement about the age groupings to be used, I have chosen to calculate this measure as the number of children aged under five per thousand women aged fifteen through forty-nine. I have included the younger age group (15–19) simply because in 1860 an appreciable number of French Canadian women were married at that age and, therefore, exposed to risk. However, since trends in age at marriage also appear to have changed during the latter half of the nineteenth century among the French Canadian immigrants in Illinois, an aggregate child-woman ratio for women between twenty and forty-nine is also included. The figures in table 4.11 are compiled on the basis of children under five per household, and only those women who could be positively identified as currently married French Canadian spouses of heads of households were analyzed. This table indicates a definite decline in the fertility for all age groups between 1860 and 1900, although some of the decline may be due to the effects of declining infant mortality—a factor that I am not able to estimate with the sources at hand. However, in comparison with child-woman ratios for other immigrant groups, some of which are calculated for children under fifteen, it is evident that the fertility levels of the first and second generations of this French Canadian immigrant population were high and in keeping with fertility rates in the province of Quebec. Looking at the 1880 data, in particular, the figures are higher than gross regional and national figures—.75 in the United States as a whole; .50 in the northeast; .91 in the west north central; 1.04 in the south central.[63]

TABLE 4.11. Child/woman ratios* by overall population and by age for the townships of St. Anne, Beaverville, L'Érable, and Papineau, 1860, 1880, 1900

	1860			*1880*			*1900*		
Age (y)	*Women*	*Children*	*C/W*	*Women*	*Children*	*C/W*	*Women*	*Children*	*C/W*
15–19	17	12	0.706	16	7	0.437	17	5	0.294
20–24	46	73	1.587	59	75	1.271	69	73	1.058
25–29	61	111	1.820	58	95	1.638	88	122	1.386
30–34	68	116	1.706	66	102	1.545	88	91	1.034
35–39	44	66	1.500	79	107	1.354	70	83	1.186
40–44	38	36	0.947	31	27	0.871	46	33	0.717
45–49	30	20	0.667	30	18	0.600	52	10	0.192
Total, 15–49	304	434	1.428	339	431	1.271	430	417	0.970
Total, 20–49	287	422	1.470	323	424	1.313	413	412	0.997

* The child/woman ratio (C/W) is derived by dividing the total number of children born to women in a particular age category by the number of women in that age category.

Source: United States Federal Manuscript Census, Kankakee and Iroquois Counties, 1860, 1880, 1900

Table 4.12 presents the child-woman ratios for subsets of identifiable Protestants and Catholics in 1860, 1880, and 1900. Although the number of women in some of the age-group cells is small, I have provided this breakdown as well as the aggregate ratios for all women between fifteen and forty-nine and twenty and forty-nine. The figures for 1900 do demonstrate a significant difference according to religious affiliation. Protestant women of French Canadian heritage were having fewer children than their Catholic counterparts, although both groups of women were having fewer children in 1900 than were their mothers in the 1870s. Furthermore, if these ratios are standardized against one another to control for the differences in the age distribution of each subpopulation, the difference between the Catholic and the Protestant populations remains.

The data for 1860 is somewhat puzzling since we would not really expect any difference between the two religious groups so soon after the schism. Furthermore, it is the ratio for those who were Protestants in 1860 that is higher and appreciably so. While this may be due to sample error, two other possible explanations might illuminate this difference, one demographic and the other economic. If we compare the age composition of the women under consideration, we find that

TABLE 4.12. Child/woman ratios* by religious affiliation for the townships of St. Anne, Beaverville, L'Érable, and Papineau, 1860, 1880, 1900

	1860			*1880*			*1900*		
Age (y)	*Women*	*Children*	*C/W*	*Women*	*Children*	*C/W*	*Women*	*Children*	*C/W*
Protestants									
15–19	4	3	0.75	0	0	0	3	0	0
20–24	8	15	1.875	6	10	1.666	15	19	1.267
25–29	15	30	2.000	12	19	1.583	28	31	1.107
30–34	18	34	1.888	11	18	1.636	24	12	0.500
35–39	17	25	1.470	20	19	0.950	15	17	1.133
40–44	11	8	0.727	8	2	0.250	18	8	0.444
45–49	7	7	1.000	10	10	1.000	17	3	0.176
Total 15–49	80	122	1.525	67	78	1.164	120	90	0.750
Total 20–49	76	119	1.565	67	78	1.164	117	90	0.769
Standardized									
15–49			2.505			1.570			1.238
20–49			2.329			1.570			1.238
Catholics									
15–19	4	2	0.500	6	1	0.166	2	1	0.500
20–24	9	10	1.111	13	18	1.385	18	16	0.889
25–29	10	16	1.600	16	34	2.125	27	38	1.407
30–34	17	31	1.823	25	35	1.400	28	34	1.214
35–39	8	11	1.375	26	50	1.923	33	42	1.273
40–44	8	8	1.000	7	9	1.286	17	21	1.235
45–49	11	5	0.454	9	4	0.444	22	2	0.009
Total 15–49	67	83	1.238	102	151	1.480	147	154	1.048
Total 20–49	63	82	1.285	96	150	1.562	145	153	1.055
Standardized									
15–49			1.806			3.009			2.203
20–49			1.629			2.999			2.144

* The child/woman ratio (C/W) is derived by dividing the total number of children born to women in a particular age category by the number of women in that age category.

Sources: United States Federal Manuscript Census, Kankakee and Iroquois Counties, 1860, 1880, 1900; parish records, cemetery records, county atlases for the four townships

56 percent of the Protestant women were under thirty-five as compared with 60 percent of the Catholic women. Thus, a demographic explanation according to the age composition of the respective religious populations does not prove adequate since a smaller proportion (and not appreciably so) of the Protestant women are in the younger and more fertile age category.

An economic explanation emerges from oral historical material about the schism and from some documentary evidence that lends concrete confirmation to certain aspects of the oral historical interpretation. In 1858 and 1859, as indicated in chapter 2, St. Anne and the neighboring communities were hit by early frosts, unseasonable rains, and insect infestations that resulted in two successive years of poor harvests. A large proportion of the population experienced severe economic hardship. Chiniquy, as noted in an earlier chapter, seized the moment and organized a speaking tour to the East Coast to solicit funds, food, and clothing for his starving French Canadian converts, who had abandoned Catholicism but who had not yet become full-fledged Presbyterians. The community explanation for the demographic success of the schism is that many followed Chiniquy because he had the financial aid they needed during this period of severe hardship. It is clearly plausible that the poorer families and the families that suffered most during these two years of crop failures were the larger families with more small children. Thus, the child/woman ratios of the converts (the Protestants) in 1860 are higher than those of the nonconverts (the Catholics).

When we examine the data on wealth and property in 1860, another difference between the two groups emerges. Those who remained Catholic were somewhat better off than those who converted to Protestantism. Twenty-four percent of the Protestant heads of households had real property valued at $1,000 or more, compared with 37 percent of the Catholics. Thirty-seven percent of the Protestants had real property valued at under $100 compared with 21 percent of the Catholics. Roughly the same proportion of Protestants and Catholics had six or more children (of all ages) living at home (33.7 percent and 33.6 percent, respectively), but slightly more Protestant converts in 1860 (37 percent) had between three and five children than did Catholics (35 percent). The age composition of the male heads of household in the two populations may explain, at least in part, these wealth differences. Protestants males in 1860 were generally younger—52 percent were under thirty-five, and 25 percent were over fifty. Among the identifiable Catholic males in 1860, 45 percent were under thirty-five, and 31 percent were over fifty.

The 1900 census provides yet another measure of fertility. In this year, women were asked two questions related to their fertility: the number of children they had ever had and the number of children still surviving. Table 4.13 tabulates the data for all currently married women over age forty-five in 1900 by reported number of children ever had and religious affiliation. Table 4.14 tabulates the data for all currently married women under age forty-five by number of years at risk, number of children ever had, and religious affiliation.

For both the over forty-five and the under forty-five categories, there appears to be a difference between Catholic women and Protestant women, with the latter group consistently reporting fewer children ever had. The mean number of children ever had for the overall population is 4.8; for the Catholic subpopulation, it is 6.2, and for the Protestant subpopulation, 4.2. Among women over forty-five, 74 percent of the Catholic women had seven or more children compared with 50 percent of the Protestant women. In the under forty-five category, 29 percent of the Catholic women reported seven or more children compared with 7 percent of the Protestant women. Although the numbers in the cells are small, table 4.14 also suggests that both Catholic and Protestant women had rather similar fertility rates during the first five years of marriage but that beyond five years, Protestant women began to reduce their fertility. The r^2 when number of children ever had is regressed against years at risk is .32 for the overall population, .30 for the Catholic subpopulation, and .31 for the Protestant subpopulation. This indicates that something other than length of time exposed to the risk of bearing children has affected differences in number of children ever had in the population as a whole and in the subpopulations.

Age at marriage does appear to have had some influence on these differences. For the women over age forty-five in 1900 whose ages at marriage could be calculated, 42 percent of the Catholic women were married under age nineteen compared with 32 percent of the Protestant women. For the women under age forty-five in 1900, the corresponding proportions were 59 percent of the Catholic women compared with 45 percent of the Protestant women. However, by the age of twenty-five, there is little difference in these two populations. Among the women over forty-five, 74 percent of the Catholic women had married by age twenty-five and 70 percent of the Protestant women. Among the women under age forty-five in 1900, 91 percent of the Catholic women and 90 percent of the Protestant women had married before reaching their twenty-fifth birthday. In other words, the data suggest that varying attitudes toward marriage among the Catholics and the Protestants may have been as important as varying attitudes toward birth control or family limitation in influencing fertility levels.

Finally, although there are some differences between the two religious subpopulations according to husband's occupation (for example, 52 percent of the

TABLE 4.13. Percentages of reported children ever had by married women over 45, by age and religious affiliation for the townships of St. Anne, Beaverville, L'Érable, and Papineau, 1900

Age (y) of women	*No. of children ever had* 0–3	4–6	7–10	11+	*Total no.*
			No religion determined		
45–49	21	14	36	29	14
50–54	27	27	18	27	11
55–59	36	27	27	9	11
60+	33	22	22	22	18
Total no.	16	12	14	12	54
Percentage of total	30	22	26	22	100
			Catholics		
45–49	18	9	32	41	22
50–54	12.5	12.5	50	25	16
55–59	26	13	43	17	23
60+	0	11	22	67	18
Total no.	12	9	39	29	79
Percentage of total	15	11	37	37	100
			Protestants		
45–49	33	13	27	27	15
50–54	40	30	30	0	10
55–59	27	27	33	13	15
60+	21	14	29	36	14
Total no.	16	11	16	11	54
Percentage of total	30	20	30	20	100

Note: "Total percentage" numbers represent column totals divided by the total number of women in each religion category. Some row percentages may not total 100 owing to rounding.

Sources: United States Federal Manuscript Censuses, Kankakee and Iroquois Counties, 1860, 1880, 1900; parish records, cemetery records, county atlases for the four townships

TABLE 4.14. Percentages of reported children ever had by married women under 45, by years at risk and religious affiliation for the townships of St. Anne, Beaverville, L'Érable, and Papineau, 1900

	No. of children ever had				
Years at risk	*0–3*	*4–6*	*7–10*	*11+*	*Total no.*
			No religion determined		
0–4	98	2	0	0	40
5–9	69	31	0	0	32
10–14	43	40	17	0	35
15–19	33	22	44	0	18
20–24	50	20	20	10	10
25–29	33	33	33	0	6
Total no.	89	33	18	1	141
Percentage of total	63	23	13	1	100
			Catholics		
0–4	94	6	0	0	16
5–9	77	23	0	0	22
10–14	22	67	11	0	27
15–19	10	31	52	7	29
20–24	30	20	35	15	20
25–29	0	33	0	67	6
30–34	33	0	33	33	3
Total no.	48	39	26	10	123
Percentage of total	39	32	21	8	100
			Protestants		
0–4	94	6	0	0	17
5–9	88	12	0	0	26
10–14	48	48	4	0	25
15–19	60	33	7	0	15
20–24	14	29	29	29	7
25–29	20	80	0	0	5
30–34	0	67	33	0	3
Total no.	62	29	5	2	98
Percentage of total	63	30	5	2	100

Note: To the extent possible, second marriages, which would underestimate the number of years at risk (a calculation based on age at the census and the number of years married), were eliminated. However, it is not clear how rigorous census takers were in recording second marriages. Percentage totals may not equal 100 owing to rounding.

Source: United States Federal Manuscript Census, Kankakee and Iroquois Counties, 1860, 1880, 1900; parish and cemetery records, county atlases, obituaries for four townships

Catholic male heads of household called themselves farmers compared with 43 percent of the Protestants), within occupational categories the religious variable still appears to affect fertility. Thus, the wives of 70 percent of Catholic farmers had four or more children compared with 40 percent of Protestant farmers.

Throughout rural America, fertility levels were higher during the nineteenth century than they were in Western Europe.[64] For the French Canadian immigrant population in northeastern Illinois, they were particularly high, a result to a large extent of low ages at marriage. Yet, as the century drew to its close, this population also experienced a decline in fertility. A similar decline among East Coast French Canadians and a consistently smaller family size emerged among American French Canadian families by comparison with their Quebec counterparts, with the difference becoming greater over time. "Furthermore," scholar Leon Bouvier observes, "the lingering tendency for French Canadians in Canada to occasionally produce large families is not apparent among the Americans of the same ethnic stock."[65] In another article, Bouvier argues that with the exception of the first generation marrying in the United States between 1850 and 1874, American-married French Canadians were spacing their children at wider intervals than their Canadian-married counterparts, and more dramatic changes occurred in American marriages than in Canadian marriages over the course of the nineteenth and twentieth centuries.[66]

Although this decline in New England has been linked to urban living and mixing with non-Catholics, the Illinois data suggest that simply being outside Quebec and away from some of the strongest pressures for ethnic survival through reproduction may have been just as important. Indeed, the data on the French Canadians in Illinois tend to support those historical demographers who have documented fertility decline in both urban *and* rural areas during the latter half of the nineteenth century.[67] Yasukichi Yasuba and other demographic and economic historians maintain that this decline in rural areas can be linked to the decreasing availability of land.[68] It is certainly the case that when the French Canadians arrived in the Midwest in the late 1840s and early 1850s, Illinois was still a frontier. But the next generation had to look farther west to find their frontier, and those who remained in the Midwest were faced with the dilemma of not being able to leave sustainable acreage to each child if they had large families. Certainly, the property divisions that ensued at the death of larger landholders, such as those described earlier in this chapter, are indicative of the problem that arises with large numbers of heirs. That the overall decline was slow—those who married in the period between 1860 and 1880 were still having sizeable families, although not as large as their parents—was undoubtedly partly related to the existence of agricultural frontiers farther west. Migration has often offered a safety valve for population pressure. By the late nineteenth century, however, this was no longer the case, although movement into cities like Chicago was clearly an option exercised.

However, economics do not tell the entire story.[69] Thus, what is most interesting about the French Canadian population in Illinois is that the decline in fertility manifested itself differently according to the religious affiliation of the subpopulations that emerged as a result of the schism in the late 1850s. These differences tend to support conclusions drawn many decades ago by Douglas G. Marshall in a study of several ethnic populations in rural Minnesota. Nationality, he concludes, is a factor explaining differential fertility decline, but religion is a much more important factor.[70] Similar differences between Protestant and Catholic populations have been revealed among the German immigrant population in Fredericksburg, Texas.[71] The significance of religion in marital fertility decline has been emphasized in the summary analysis of the Princeton European fertility project.[72] Thus, historical data in both America and Europe lend corroboration to differentials that are equally noted by demographers studying twentieth-century fertility patterns among diverse religious groups in the United States.[73] But, what does this religious variable really entail? A clue was offered earlier in the obituary of Henriette St. Pierre, a Protestant and a faithful reader of her Bible. This woman's individual relationship with God and with the Holy Book, unmediated by the male priest, is at the root of a more autonomous set of social values that characterize Protestantism. This individualism and the spiritual equality for women that it implies could extend into decisions about fertility and family life, as has been suggested by J. William Leasure in his analysis of interstate variations in the fertility transition between 1800 and 1860 and also by Daniel Scott Smith in an essay on "early" fertility decline in America.[74] Henriette became a Protestant toward the end of her childbearing, but her grandchildren were raised fully in the Protestant faith. Alternatively, it is also possible to argue that the Catholic priests who came to serve these communities, and particularly St. Anne, in the 1870s knew that the reinvigoration of that religion in the heart of a community divided by schism depended not only on reconversion, which did occur for a small number, but also reproduction. As mentioned above, this was a survival strategy already deeply embedded in French Canadian culture. While it might not explain fertility differentials according to religious affiliation in other parts of the United States and among other ethnic groups, it appears to have been quite powerful in explaining what was going on among these Illinois French Canadian settlers.

Certainly, it is at the foundation for the revival of Catholicism in St. Anne, in particular, that revolved around the emergence of the feast of Ste. Anne. I treat this topic in a later chapter.

Survivance and La Français: Language and Identity

Dis language Anglaise dat dey spe'k,
On State of Illinois,
Is hard for Frenchmen heem to lern,
It give me moch annoy.[75]

Language, specifically the French language, has been fundamental to French Canadian survival. In Quebec, speaking French was one important marker of French Canadian ethnic identity and provided a barrier against absorption within the politically, though not numerically, dominant English and Protestant community of the province. It is no wonder that language became the focus of the new ethnic nationalism that emerged in Quebec with the Quiet Revolution beginning in the 1960s and culminating in Bill 101.[76] In the US immigrant context, the disappearance of language has been used as a measure of assimilation, while its survival has often been read (more so recently in relation to debates about bilingual education or state-level bills to make English the official language of the United States) as an act of resistance to becoming American.

Among the so-called Franco-Americans of New England, especially those who lived in heavily settled communities, such as Woonsockett, Rhode Island, Lewiston, Maine, or Lowell, Massachusetts, the French language survived well into the twentieth century. In the central business district of Lewiston, Maine, 50 percent of the conversations were in French as late as the 1950s, and in Burlington, Vermont, masses in St. Joseph's Catholic Church were held in French until the 1940s.[77] A range of other institutions—religious schools, benevolent societies, newspapers—also served to perpetuate the linguistic foundation of distinctiveness and identity. Noting the remarkable persistence of French language use across five generations in Lewiston, Maine, one author dates the process of assimilation to the 1960s, a time when the French-language newspaper ceased publication, parochial school attendance declined, and intermarriage increased.[78] The survival of French for so long among this particular immigrant population has been taken as yet another indicator of the different path they walked by comparison with Italians, Jews, or a host of other immigrant populations who arrived in the United States in the latter decades of the nineteenth century.

The people who settled in St. Anne and the other communities in northeastern Illinois in the 1850s did not speak much English, and the majority could not read and write. Sixty percent of the male heads of household in 1860 were recorded for the census as being illiterate, while only 2 percent were recorded as literate. In the remaining cases (38 percent), there was no response or no indication. The comparable figures for women were 37 percent, 2 percent, and 61 percent. By 1900, 74 percent of the male heads of household as reported in the census could both read and write English, and 26 percent could do neither or only one. A slightly larger proportion, 89 percent, reported being able to speak English, while 11 percent could not.[79] The poorest English-language capabilities, as one would expect, were concentrated in the older age groups. This was equally true for women.

Daily life during the early years of settlement was in French, and even within oral historical memory, old-timers recalled that people would shout out greetings in French in public; if there was no response, they knew someone was a stranger. The *Kankakee Gazette* reports that French was used at political rallies in the strongly Republican St. Anne in the 1870s.[80] Politics were closely fused with religion because the French Canadian Catholics in other communities, including Kankakee, were, like immigrant Catholics of other national origins, largely Democrats.

Chiniquy, who participated actively in the political gatherings in St. Anne, in the September 11, 1873, *Kankakee Gazette* confirmed the extensive use of French: "St. Anne is probably the only place in the U.S. where the pure French is the only language spoken by almost everyone. . . . There are not more than five or six families who are not entirely French." French was the language of all religious services in this community until 1885, when the Presbyterian Church of St. Anne began a regular English-language service. French-language Bible classes were still in operation at the Presbyterian Church during the first decade of the twentieth century. Reverend Pierre Beauchamp, who served this community from 1906 to 1917, was the last minister to preach in French. From 1917 all the services were delivered in English, and the ministers were of other than French extraction. The change was partially impelled by newcomers to the town who were attracted by growing industry. Economic change brought great population diversity, and the Presbyterian Church responded by slowly eliminating the French language from weekly services.

By comparison, the Catholic Church of St. Anne was slower to convert to English, an indication of the significance of language to religious and by extension ethnic identity for this particular community and of how important a French Canadian priest was to the maintenance of this identity.[81] The Catholic church had French Canadian–descent pastors until 1948, although some evidence suggests that after 1932 all weekly masses were celebrated in English. English was first used in the Catholic Church of St. Anne in 1905 (twenty years after its initiation in the Protestant church) when it was decided that the Mass on the first Sunday of each month should be celebrated in that language. In 1908 alternate communion services were in English. It is important not only to stress again the differences between the Protestant and Catholic communities but also to note that the enduring use of the French language in these communities is similar to the persistence of the German language into the 1950s among rural German immigrants elsewhere in the Midwest.[82] Old-timers in St. Anne in the 1950s could still speak French, but by the 1980s there were few who could speak it, although several elderly people recollected using it as a child.

Within French Canadian immigrant communities, the other institution, beside the Church, that became the fulcrum for the preservation of language and identity was the school.[83] Chiniquy took an early interest in the education of the children of the French Canadian settlers. He maintained this interest and emphasis even after the schism, primarily to promote literacy. Literacy, which was the foundation for an independent reading and understanding of the Bible, was a way to differentiate Protestantism from Catholicism.[84]

The first schooling in St. Anne took place in private homes, and in 1856 a schoolhouse was built under Chiniquy's encouragement. The first teacher, Francis Bechand, was engaged for fifteen months in 1857–58 at an annual salary of $283.83. The school board minutes for August 25, 1862, record a visit to the school where eighty-five children, thirty-nine of them girls, were in attendance: "After a full examination . . . we found in general the children were little advanced in learning and that three-quarters of them were without books and in consequence unmanageable." It was noted that parents were unwilling to furnish the books, and a decision was taken to levy a 1 percent tax to keep the school open and to hire an additional teacher. In October 1868, Gustave Demers boasted in the *Kankakee Gazette* of the success of schooling in St. Anne: "Last Friday, I witnessed a scene to be long remembered by the people of St. Anne. It vindicates the efforts, the motives, and doings of Reverend C. Chiniquy before the Christian public about his school. Five young men who studied in the Savior's College were about to leave for a higher school, Knox in Canada."[85]

The new schoolhouse building burned in 1869, an incident that undoubtedly prompted another investigation of the educational facilities in the townships east of Kankakee, including St. Anne and Aroma. Among the findings of this investigation, published in the November 29, 1869, *Kankakee Gazette*, were that the conditions were generally poor: some schools were without blackboards, and others had no writing desks. The district school in that year united with Chiniquy's school, and together they educated 200 pupils with an average attendance of 140 pupils. The report praised the efforts of Chiniquy's school to educate children in a language that was not their own. A few months earlier, the newspaper had published a letter to the superintendent, ostensibly written by pupils in the school (although it does appear to have the hand of Chiniquy in it).

> You see before you the children of people lately emigrated from Canada. French is our natural language and we respectfully request you to remember this circumstance during the hour of our examination. . . . The difficulties of learning a foreign language which we have never heard our parents speak are very great and the necessity of learning it does necessarily retard the progress we could make. . . . But the desire to become the worthy citizens of this grand Republic, the country of our adoption, has stimulated us to great efforts. It is not necessary for us to tell you that it is to our Pastor Father Chiniquy that we owe in great part . . . the success and prosperity of the school.[86]

The new school erected in St. Anne in 1871 quickly became too small, and beginning in 1879 and continuing until 1887, the first floor of the Presbyterian Church was used free of charge with the overflow in the basement of the Baptist church. The resolution of the school board at that time mentioned the free use of the church facility for the public school "providing said Presbyterian organization be allowed to use a part of the said room for the teaching of the French language, and providing also that said French department shall be under the control of the directors of the public school, but the French teacher to be paid by the said Presbyterian organization." Placide Boudreau, who had come to St. Anne with his parents in 1855, studied at McCormick Theological Seminary, and married into the Changnon family of St. Anne, became the French teacher. He was succeeded by Reverend Christophe Lafontaine, who had studied at the Seminary of Quebec, arrived in St. Anne in 1864, and, under Chiniquy's influence, had converted to Protestantism. Lafontaine stopped teaching in 1888 and entered the mercantile business in St. Anne.

Although a new four-room school building was recommended in 1887 and built on land offered by Chiniquy, it was also about this time that the teaching of French ceased and a two-year high school program was launched. In 1893, one girl graduated from this program. In 1901, the year that the high school program was extended to four years, the school in St. Anne had sixty-eight boys and sixty-seven girls enrolled in grades 1 through 6, seventeen boys and seventeen girls in grades 7 and 8, and twelve boys and fifteen girls in the upper school, for a total of 196.[87] This represents a small portion of the total number of children eligible for school, if we look at the 1900 census figures for children between the ages of five and fourteen (see table 4.10), and these are only the children of French Canadian descent. Although there, clearly, were children in the parochial school and in the rural schools scattered throughout the countryside, these figures still suggest that many children, even in 1900, were getting no more than the basics of education. In 1905 yet another school, this time with eight rooms, two halls, and a basement library with six hundred volumes was built. In 1914 one boy and three girls, two of whom were from French Canadian families, graduated from high school. The following year there were eleven graduates. Older residents of St. Anne in the 1980s mentioned leaving school after the eighth grade so that they could begin work on the farm or in the farm household. One man who was raised in Beaverville said that instead of riding on horseback for eight miles to attend the high school in Donovan, he quit: "Those who had relatives in town sometimes sent their children to stay with them. If the school was only a mile or so away, you could walk. But you only continued in school if it was economically possible."[88]

One elderly female informant, a Protestant, who was born in Beaverville in 1891, said that although her mother, who had attended Chiniquy's school, did not speak English well, the real reason they spoke French at home was out of respect for her grandparents. It was only once she attended school that she began to acquire English, and she only remained in school through the eighth grade because she was needed at home. "When my grandparents died," she said, "there was less need to use French and I no longer remember any of it." Another resident of St. Anne, who was in grade school in the 1920s, spoke of having to walk an hour each way to school because he lived with his parents on a farm. He also stated that his first exposure to English was at school since the language at home, and the only language of his grandparents, was French. Emphasizing that many farm families were not that well off (he was one of eight children), he recalled that when his parents could not pay the nuns, who were the teachers, with cash, they paid with chickens. His education was in the Catholic parochial school system.

In St. Anne, Roman Catholic parochial education was disrupted as the schism escalated and was not resumed until 1873 under the guidance of the new Catholic priest, Michel Letellier. The St. Anne Academy finally opened in 1884 staffed by the Sisters of Notre Dame from Montreal. A high school program was started in 1891, although the number of graduates was small. This program was discontinued in 1929. In 1920 the building burned, and immediately plans were developed for a new academy. There were 217 subscribers for the building of the new St. Anne Academy, and among them they donated $16,159.27, with contributions ranging from as little as $5 to as large as $500. Some companies, such as the Alexander Lumber, St. Anne Mercantile, Baron and Dumais, Sutton Undertaking, and St. Anne Brick and Tile, made contributions, as did the Catholic Ladies Guild with $500. But the bulk came from private citizens, and the majority was of French Canadian descent living in the area but also as far away as Missoula, Montana. This academy, like the Holy Family Academy in Beaverville, which was opened at the turn of the century and closed in 1969, was an institutional bastion of Catholic education in the region and, undoubtedly, contributed to the preservation of French language and French Canadian identity in the area into the twentieth century.

A third institution that can have a similar impact on the retention of language and ethnic identity is the newspaper. There were French-language newspapers in the Kankakee valley, the most notable being the *Journal de l'Illinois*, which began publication in Kankakee as an anticlerical mouthpiece at the height of the Chiniquy schism. Indeed, newspapers developed their own political positions and, in the case of ethnic newspapers, in particular, offer some insight to the process of political incorporation of an immigrant population. The French Canadians in Kankakee County were either Democratic or Republican, depending on their religion, Catholic or Protestant. In a letter to the *Kankakee Gazette* published on September 10, 1868, George Letourneau (who arrived in Illinois in 1847 at fourteen, was in the California gold rush, and became clerk of the circuit court in 1872, sheriff in 1882, Kankakee mayor in 1891, and state senator in 1892) made reference to the French paper, saying that although he was a Republican, "the committee have not yet determined on [the newspaper's] political character if any." But the center of French-language publications eventually shifted to Chicago, and the *Journal de l'Illinois*, which ceased publication after seven years, was revived in that city as the Republican *Courrier de l'Ouest*.[89]

In July 1868 a Franco-American Association was created with Achilles Chiniquy as president, and it called for the foundation of a French paper and the formation of French clubs in each settlement in the Kankakee region. There is no evidence that these goals were met although there are references to the club-sponsored celebrations of St. Jean Baptiste Day, a provincial holiday in Quebec, in the late

1860s and early 1870s. Patriotic observance of this day among French Canadian Catholics in the area persisted into the early decades of the twentieth century.

The first local newspaper in St. Anne, the *Weekly Blade*, began publication in 1884 and included some notices in the French language. The *Blade*, which supported the Democratic Party in a largely Republican town, was succeeded by the *Register* and it, in turn, by the *Enterprise*. The *St. Anne Record* first appeared in 1890 as an English-language newspaper and was published throughout the twentieth century. Clearly, the newspapers were not as important as the schools and the churches, and, ultimately, all these institutions divided as they united because they were built on religious differences as much as on linguistic similarity.

This chapter chronicles demographic, economic, and social change among the French Canadian population in Illinois over the course of two generations. It has also highlighted important differences in the two religious communities, Protestant and Catholic, that emerged as a result of the Chiniquy-led schism of the 1850s. The changes that occurred and that can be broadly read as a process of incorporation progressed much faster in Illinois than among the French Canadians who emigrated to and settled in New England. The communities in Illinois were not constantly replenished as were those on the East Coast. And while some individuals did travel back to Quebec, this, too, was much less frequent. The Illinois communities themselves became "mother" communities for emigration farther westward by many individuals of the second generation. Others moved to Chicago. In 1919 Leon Bonvallet in a letter to the *St. Anne Record* describes his efforts to form an organization to be known as the St. Anne Society, which would be made up of all those residents of Chicago and its suburbs who formerly lived in St. Anne. Approximately sixty people gathered in Washington Park for the first meeting of the society, and they planned a reunion for the following year, as well.

The immigrants in Illinois were not only geographically mobile, they were also socially mobile. They solidified their ownership of land and in many cases were able to pass along substantial holdings to those members of the second generation who stayed in the communities. As time passed, increasing proportions of the population that remained in the original Illinois settlements moved out of farming, especially in the main township of St. Anne. The January 1915 souvenir edition of the *St. Anne Record* includes a full page of pictures of the prominent businessmen in the community, the majority of them descendants of the original settlers, with names like Allain, Allard, Baron, Bonvallet, Brouillette, Dumais, Lebeau, Martin, Robillard, St. Pierre, and Trudeau. It was in this same year that the local newspaper, in an editorial, rejected the concept of the hyphenated American, including, one presumes, the phrase "Franco-American": "Anyone who lives in this country is either a citizen or not a citizen. If foreign born but not naturalized he is not an American, but if he has taken out his papers he is a citizen. Why then not speak of oneself as an American and abstain from using any prefix."[90]

Yet, despite these signs of "assimilation" in the form of geographic, social, and economic mobility, as well as demographic change, the past was not forgotten. On July 16, 1909, marking the fiftieth anniversary of the schism, St. Anne celebrated Chiniquy Days. Among the speakers was Chiniquy's son-in-law Joseph Morin, who had come from Quebec. In 1932, both the Presbyterian church and the Catholic church celebrated homecomings that became the occasion for family reunions that brought people from short and great distances. The Catholic church prepared a dinner "à la cuisine canadienne française" [French Canadian style]. In 1936 the Presbyterian church observed a founder's day, recalling and honoring the memory of Charles Chiniquy and the pioneer settlers. And in 1950 the entire community of St. Anne marked its centennial.

The concept of assimilation implies a straight-line and uniform process of change and, hence, does not adequately capture the idea that change can operate at a different pace in different aspects of life. Nor does it capture the idea that individuals operate with multiple identities that are fluid both in time and across time. Different dimensions of a person's identity can come to the foreground in one situation and be suppressed in another, thus allowing for the "remembrance of things past" alluded to at the end of the preceding paragraph. The next two chapters explore the fluidity of identities that came to characterize the French Canadian settlements in Illinois, first, in relation to other conflicts, major and minor, that were part of the history of St. Anne in the aftermath of the schism; and, second, in relation to the development of an event that has become the focus of what sociologist Herbert Gans refers to as symbolic ethnicity and what I would call symbolic identity.[91]

CHAPTER 5

Disputes and Social Boundaries

The May 4, 1871, issue of the *Kankakee Gazette* reports that of the sixty-five cases in the chancery docket, twenty-three were disposed of, among them the long-standing suit of Charles Chiniquy against the Catholic bishop of Chicago. The piece of property in dispute, that upon which Chiniquy had built his church, was put in Chiniquy's possession, the court ruling that the title of the bishop was void. This is one of many court actions brought by or against Chiniquy while he lived in St. Anne, Illinois, beginning with the slander lawsuit discussed in an earlier chapter in which he was ably defended by Abraham Lincoln. But as far as suits went, Chiniquy was not alone. During the first fifty years of settlement, many other residents of St. Anne were involved in court actions to resolve a wide variety of disputes.

Anthropologists, as part of broader investigation of cross-cultural variations in law and social control, have explored the pervasiveness and meaning of disputes as a form of conflict, as well as the informal and formal mechanisms that exist in a variety of cross-cultural contexts to manage and resolve these disputes.[1] Anthropologists have also addressed the way that disputes and the mechanisms of dispute resolution express and mediate social relationships between individuals or groups of people. Elisabeth Colson suggests that disputes "are aired in circumstances that have much in common with religious rituals, which also mobilize social units"; Sally Engle Merry contends that "the focus on dispute processes is attentive to social interactions and to the way the social world is revealed in moments of fight." Even property claims, Merry argues, are ways of talking about how people behave and the obligations they have to one another.[2]

While shame, ridicule, song duels, and arbitration are some of the mechanisms of resolution identified by anthropologists studying simpler societies, in more complex societies, people generally take their disputes to court. Americans ask the courts to resolve conflicts with their neighbors, as well as those within their families. They also turn to the courts to handle what anthropologist Laura Nader has called the "little injustices" that are served on them by businesses and other institutions, organizations, and individuals of their society. Merry argues that in the United States, "recourse to the courts is rooted in such deep-seated cultural traditions of American society as individualism, equality, faith in the law, and the search for freedom from the control of neighbors and local leaders, traditions noted by Tocqueville early in the nineteenth century."[3]

Some scholars of American history have studied the processes of dispute resolution that engaged the people of the past and have attempted to trace the shift from the more face-to-face procedures of small communities to the increasing use of the judicial system. William E. Nelson, for example, relates that in the cohesive and insular towns of Plymouth County, Massachusetts, in the eighteenth century, disputes were settled internally. However, once these communities came under the influence of the social divisions of the outside world, including those of politics and religion, the systems for internal resolution collapsed.[4] Norma Basch points to the nineteenth century as the period when the concept of contract and, undoubtedly, suits for breach of contract were raised to unprecedented heights.[5] But, as Merry suggests, the dearth of studies on this topic makes it difficult to understand fully the causes of the increase in the extent of interpersonal disputing taking place in the courts as the nineteenth century unfolded.[6] Was it a result of the process of urbanization and of the simultaneous decline in the power of the institutions of family, church, and community as mechanisms of social control? Was it a result of a change in values, a shift from what David Engel labels personal-responsibility individualism to rights-oriented individualism?[7] If we had good comparative work, in the complex societies of Europe, for example, would Americans look as litigious as they are commonly thought to be?[8]

If more general historical studies are few and far between, so, too, are studies of how first- and second-generation immigrants used the judicial system to help them solve their problems and settle differences. This seems somewhat odd since such interaction between immigrants and the courts might be invoked as an indicator of the process of assimilation, or "Americanization," or at least the adoption of some aspects of American identity and cultural values. One study is Lucy E. Salyer's analysis of how Chinese immigrants arriving in California went to court to protest and resist the Chinese Exclusion Acts of the latter nineteenth century. But this is a very specific investigation of challenges to immigration policy rather than of little local injustices or the resolution of personal differences.[9]

This chapter takes up some of these issues. Drawing on circuit-court records for Kankakee County, I discuss dispute and conflict among the French Canadian immigrants (and their descendants) of St. Anne, a community founded, so to speak, in contentious behavior, a challenge to authority, and the assertion of rights. The chapter is framed by two disputes that involved the entire town, both of which can be read for what they tell us about collective community identity and definitions of insiders and outsiders. One took place in the 1860s and 1870s, the other a century later. Between these frames is a focus on myriad personal complaints filed with the courts. Theoretically, I take the position that such complaints are an inevitable part of social life. They are localized social dramas that mark boundaries and, hence, reveal fundamental aspects of social relations, including the process by which social identities are formed and reformed. They show us what unites and divides a population. They show us how a population of immigrant newcomers progressively became part of American society.

Big Business and Small-Town Folk and the Railroad

As demonstrated in chapter 4, by the 1870s the French Canadian immigrants in St. Anne were firmly settled in their new homeland. The divisions the schism created twenty years earlier had not fully disappeared, Chiniquy was still very active both locally and nationally, and French was still the predominant language of daily interaction in the community. It was at this time that the railroad completed its line through St. Anne, bringing benefit but also new controversy. During the phase of development and expansion, communities in the Midwest and West wanted the railroad to run through their town at any cost, but

> once the roads were in operation, dominant public opinion seemed to shift from docility to distrust. Railroads created markets, made towns bloom in the wilderness, lured farmers into planting particular crops, drew settlers from one place to another. People invested their lives and their futures in the towns and markets that grew up along the lines. The railroads became enemies then, not only because of iniquity but also because they seemed to hold the power of life and death over those who lived along the way. To the Midwestern farmer, monopoly meant the railroad[,] and the farmers, who had mortgaged themselves to buy railroads [for their communities], felt that they had created a Frankenstein monster in their midst.[10]

St. Anne's relationship with the railroad was particularly controversial, more so than in other townships in the region and the legacy, perhaps, of the culture of opposition to external authority that had developed as a result of the earlier struggles against church hierarchy.

On April 13, 1876, the *Kankakee Gazette* reported considerable excitement in St. Anne caused by the burning of $30,000 in bonds that had been issued by the town in favor of the Chicago, Danville, and Vincennes Railroad (later the Chicago and Eastern Illinois). This railroad company had received a state charter in 1865 to build a line from southern Illinois to Chicago. Since the company had no land-grant property to sell to generate capital, its board developed a plan whereby those townships that would benefit from the line would share in its cost. The townships raised the funds by holding a referendum in each community. If the referendum was approved, the township sold bonds to raise the cash needed at interest not to exceed 10 percent with the sum due upon completion of the railroad.

In St. Anne the vote, held in June 1869, was 112 in favor and 75 against, and the community pledged $30,000 after securing an agreement from the railroad company to build the road 160 rods, a half mile, closer to the town than originally planned and the station opposite Martin Street. Bonds for this amount, to be paid in eight installments, were issued. Those on the losing side accused those who were in favor of the bonds of having profited financially. They felt not only that the election was illegal but also that the community would never be able to pay. They went to court to escape the indebtedness that the bonds entailed. Years of legal maneuvering followed with some townspeople filing complaints in a lawsuit against the board of village supervisors. St. Anne resident Stephen Raymond filed a plea of trespass on the case in 1871 against Achilles Chiniquy and other board members, claiming they had "wrongfully and injuriously contrived and intended to deceive, circumvent, defraud and injure" him, telling him that if he gave a right of way to the railroad, he would be paid $300. He claimed that they acted fraudulently and unlawfully in this regard.[11] A similar suit for $600 in damages was filed by Stephen Jouberne the following year against Achilles Chiniquy, J. E. Young, Moses Chartrier, and the Chicago, Danville, and Vincennes Railroad. Jouberne, who owned and cultivated a piece of land valued at $5,000 in St. Anne Township, claimed that the defendants wanted a portion of it to be given over to the railroad and told him that the railroad would pay $160. He deeded over this strip, and the railroad was built, but he had received no payment. The defendants were found not guilty, although the judge claimed that Chiniquy and Chartrier could be found guilty apart from the others of fraudulent interest.[12]

The bonds themselves were impounded and placed in the custody of the county circuit clerk in Kankakee. In 1874 the Chicago, Danville, and Vincennes Railroad Company filed a "trespass on the case," a suit for damages, for $100,000 against the town of St. Anne for its refusal to pay.[13] By the time the case was scheduled for hearing in 1876, the railroad had already been in operation for several years. A few days before the court date, the township supervisor, Joseph Guertin Sr., sent Constable Frank Coyer to Kankakee to see if he could get the bonds. The circuit clerk displayed them, and Coyer snatched them, ran out, and brought them to the supervisor and the town clerk, Lucien Paradis, who burned them in the town hall in the presence of a number of citizens who supported the action. One individual who opposed the town's actions was hung in effigy from a pole opposite the town hall.

The townspeople had decided that since the railroad was already built and unlikely to move, they would rather not pay the $30,000. Although several town-board members were arrested (Guertin fled to Canada), there were no prosecutions. The battle over St. Anne's obligations was taken to the circuit court of the United States in Chicago and settled twelve years later when the court ruled the debt invalid in the absence of the bonds. The *Kankakee Gazette* of March 29, 1888, claims that

> the town of St. Anne has again won a decisive victory in successfully defending against the suit brought by the Chicago, Danville and Vincennes Railroad for $100,000. Reverend Chiniquy was part of the delegation that went to Chicago and upon his return on the 10:30 train, he was greeted by 200 people with torchlights, and a band. Father Chiniquy gave an address and synopsis of the suit and at 11:30 all went home rejoicing over the great victory.

The Chicago, Danville, and Vincennes Railroad, struggling for years against insolvency, eventually failed.

Throughout this period and into the early part of the twentieth century, individuals acted on their own as well as in concert in their conflict with the railroads. Numerous citizens in the community brought suits against various railroad companies that used the tracks; these cases were mostly for damages to their farm property that were generally the result of sparks from passing trains starting fires or for animals that passing trains harmed or killed. One animal case is that of Julian Beaupre, who in 1871 sued the Chicago, Danville, and Vincennes Railroad for $130 to compensate him for three hogs that a train killed. He settled for $35.[14] Another is that of Joseph Guertin, by that time back from Canada, who sued the Cleveland and Cincinnati Railroad in 1880 for $105 because the company's train struck and killed six of his calves and crippled two and for $50 in damages for want of a fence. He won $145.[15] In 1882 Joseph Soucie sought $490 from the Cincinnati, Indianapolis, St. Louis, and Chicago Railroad. He claimed that in August 1881 the railroad, responsible for keeping a plot between the railroad track and his hedge free of all dead grass, dry weeds, and other combustible material, had failed to do so, and a train running through set fire to a strip of railroad land that eventually destroyed a portion of the plaintiff's farm property in St. Anne Township. This case was dismissed at the plaintiff's costs.[16] One of the more serious suits was brought in 1901 against the Cleveland, Cincinnati, and St. Louis Railroad for $5,000 via the executor Louis Giroux for the estate of David Giroux. The claim was that David Giroux, who was going, with care, over a railroad crossing with obstructed views was struck and killed by a train that was speeding and did not ring its bell. Giroux left a widow, three children, and grandchildren without support. The settlement was not evident in the documents.[17]

St. Anne residents also sued the railroads or their contractors when wages were unpaid for work completed. But equally the railroad sued individuals when they failed to fulfill a contract. In 1884, for example, the Chicago and Eastern sued Joseph Guertin over an agreement he had made to build a coal shed on his property to service the trains. Guertin had done nothing. Two other suits, in 1873 and 1874, involving Chiniquy and railroad officials also dealt with breach of contract. In both cases the jury found for the plaintiff, Chiniquy, and assessed damages. In one case, the defendant claimed that he could not get justice in the local court.[18]

To the people of St. Anne, the railroad represented the wealthy urban power structure that was increasingly making demands on and challenging the viability of life in the small rural towns of America. Internal divisions were evident in the initial bond election, between wealthier landowners and local businessmen, who wanted to see their town prosper through the advent of the railroad, on the one hand, and poorer farmers and laborers, who feared the level of taxation, on the other. Ultimately, however, the fight united the people of St. Anne in their struggle against a common enemy outside the community. Elsewhere in rural America, the conflicts were between different entities—between farmers and factories in the Northeast, between commercial agriculture and yeoman farmers in the South—but the power imbalance was always present.[19]

In St. Anne, by the turn of the century, this rural-urban opposition was represented by a series of articles in the *St. Anne Record* encouraging people to support their local businesses rather than take the train to Kankakee and Chicago to do their shopping. These businesses were being threatened by bigger and more commercially successful enterprises outside the community. An editorial on November 30, 1939, took up similar issues, this time encouraging St. Anne residents to buy at home rather than through mail-order catalogues. Despite these pleas, the process of decline continued. In the *Kankakee Daily Journal* of January 24, 1984, St. Anne is listed as one of the towns eligible for urban-development grants, which were designed for distressed towns to attract new industries.

Local Injustices

Although the dispute with the railroad galvanized a large segment of the community to work together against an external threat, the majority of legal disputes that characterized life among the French Canadians who had settled in St. Anne could be characterized as local injustices that brought members of the community in confrontation with one another. Many of these revolved around property and inheritance; others involved breaches of contract and personal injury. Still others were conflicts between family members that could not be resolved in the private sphere. At the center of this last category of dispute were issues of morality—forms of behavior that were considered acceptable or unacceptable in small-town America. I discuss each of these forms of local injustice in turn.

Land Is Critical: Disputes over Property

Until well into the twentieth century, the greatest asset for the majority of French Canadians residing in northeastern Illinois was land. Disputes over real property were, therefore, common. Some of these disputes originated in unclear titles to real estate, the result of thousands of transactions that occurred as the west was settled and resettled during a period when registration systems were crude. Equally important were the complex mortgage deals that were made to help farmers stay afloat. The mortgage was the primary mechanism of credit and finance, used to raise money to expand agricultural property, to buy farm machinery, or to cover personal expenses. Land, the major asset against which mortgages were secured, sometimes was sold without the seller advising the buyer of some encumbrance that was still on it from sometime in the past. In St. Anne, many of the suits over title and encumbrances, even those after the turn of the century, date back to the original period of settlement and often involve one of the Chiniquy brothers (Charles or Achilles) or the Allain family, all of whom had acquired land early.

Generally, these were disputes between "insiders"—those who were or had been members of the St. Anne community at one time.

For example, in 1904, Ulysses Cote, who had become a major property owner in the area by the early twentieth century, filed a case against the unknown heirs of J. B. Belanger over a piece of property in St. Anne Township. On May 31, 1857, Belanger had sold the land to and given the deed to Charles Chiniquy, who had owned the property for more than thirty years. The land in question had been identified incorrectly by the scribe who drafted the deed. In 1896 Augustin Cote, Ulysses's father, purchased the farm from Chiniquy and lived there for five years before moving into town. Ulysses claimed that in 1903 he had received title to land by deed from his father, a staunch member of the Presbyterian Church, who was married by Chiniquy to Eudolie Rassico in 1865. Because of the cloud on matters of ownership, Cote complained that the land had depreciated in value, and potential purchasers were timid to buy it. Belanger had died more than thirty years ago, his heirs were not residents of the state of Illinois, and their whereabouts were unknown. The case file lists the names of other possible heirs believed to be residing in Concordia, Kansas, Wisconsin, and Indiana. In the final judgment, the court found no rights in favor of the defendants, and by this judgment, the title was cleared.[20]

In 1905, the court heard the case of Willie Boudreau et al. versus Joseph Boudreau et al. John Boudreau, a resident of St. Anne had died testate on December 29, 1901. In his will he left all his personal property and the use and possession of all real estate to his widow, Philomene, during the time she remained a widow. If she remarried, she forfeited her rights. To his children, Joseph, Willie, Josephine, Zella, Dollie, and Alice, he left all his real estate to be divided after his wife's death or at her remarriage. The real estate consisted of eighty acres in St. Anne Township. His wife did remarry a man named Olivier Grandmont. At the time of the court case, the property was rented to Emile Boudreau as a tenant. The abstract on the property revealed an unreleased trust deed from Joseph Boudreau and Pauline Boudreau, his wife, to Charles Chiniquy, use of Moses Staples, dated February 9, 1860. It had been paid, but there was a cloud. The court was informed that the plaintiffs had no information on whether Staples was alive or dead or who his heirs were. Chiniquy's heirs, Euphemie and Emma Delagneau and Rebecca Morin, were living in Canada and had no title and interest. This matter had to be cleared before partition or sale could occur. Presumably, this is what the court did.[21]

Sometimes, claims were filed because transfers were not properly executed or were revoked in some way. In 1885, in Alexis Rivard versus Celestin Blain, a forty-acre piece of land in St. Anne Township was the center of the dispute. Rivard claimed he had owned it in 1880, but he had sold it by quit claim to Celestin Blain ("That is French for Charles," the sheriff claimed in the courtroom when someone said they thought the name was Charles). In 1879 and 1880, the land was leased to a tenant named Xavier Fortier, who was expected to give half of the corn he produced to Rivard. Fortier claimed he had taken Rivard's share of the corn, twenty-six bushels, to Blain because Blain told him to deliver it to him because it belonged to him. Rivard was claiming that at the time of the harvest, the land still belonged to him. Fortier, with the help of a translator, explained that he had left this farm and at the time of the case was residing at about two miles distant. He claimed that Blain worked the land himself. The court was then told that a Mr. Sprimont bought the land from Blain. In his defense, Blain introduced a trust deed of 1876 for the property. An attorney testified that this property was foreclosed in July 1879 because Rivard did not pay either the taxes or the mortgage installment. The case, which is additionally interesting because of its reference to continued use of the French language, was settled for the plaintiff.[22]

Improper or inexact transfers of property often brought family members into conflict. In 1875 Ambrose Allain filed a complaint against his father, Mitchell Allain, who, Ambrose said, had deeded to him some land in return for caring for him. In 1869 his father left St. Anne for Nebraska, where he asked his son-in-law Alphonse Boudreau to care for him in return for the deed to the same piece of land. Ambrose accused his father of childishness and of going to Nebraska under the influence of alcohol. The father claimed that he left because Ambrose was not supporting him and that indeed in 1872 he had made out a quit-claim deed to Alphonse for the property. He further claimed that he had lived with his daughter and son-in-law for six years and was supported by them entirely. Ambrose rejoined that his father had left voluntarily and had refused "to receive the bounty of the complainant which had heretofore been given." There was no indication of how this suit was settled, but, clearly, it reveals the fragility of familial relationships in the face of property disputes as well as how property could be used by the elderly to assure their care in old age.[23]

Familial disputes over property were often closely tied to matters of inheritance, particularly in situations where individuals died intestate. Nelida Bechard, eighteen years old and a resident of Chippewa Falls, Wisconsin, filed a case against Joseph Bechard, Isaac Giasson Jr., and others in 1892 over real estate in St. Anne Township that her father, Joseph Bechard, purchased from the Illinois Central Railroad in 1877. Joseph Bechard died intestate in 1878, leaving his widow,

Vitaline Dube Bechard, with three children and no guardian. In 1880 Vitaline remarried, and the family moved to Wisconsin. They held onto the property in St. Anne Township and received rent on it until 1882 when Vitaline's father and brother, pretending to act as her agents, sold the land to Giasson for $300. Giasson was to pay the taxes and interest on the $300 to them each year, but he did not. Giasson attempted to sell the land to pay taxes, making no account to Vitaline or her children and depriving them of their rights to the land. A letter, written in French by a St. Anne individual who was clearly representing the interests of Vitaline and her daughter, was included with the docket. The writer was asking for confirmation that no payments were made so that a process to nullify the contract that Vitaline's father had made as well as allow the land to be sold for taxes could be brought to the court. In this letter the writer observes that Giasson "does not have a big reputation among the people here; many complain about him." The eventual outcome was nullification of the 1882 sale.[24]

The courts made every attempt to resolve these familial disputes, some of which were complex and stemmed from families themselves failing to stipulate adequately and clearly a process for property transfer. In 1885, in Stephen Boudreau et al. versus Stanislas Beaupre, a fifty-five-year-old woman named Mary Lariviere, wife of F. X. Lariviere, appeared before the court to claim that in 1850 she was married to Stephen Boudreau, and this marriage ended when he died in 1875. There were two children, Stephen Boudreau and Mary Beaupre. Mary Beaupre had died but left an heir, her son, Stanislas, who was twelve years old. Stephen Sr. had died intestate, leaving land in St. Anne Township. Although no dower was assigned, Mary said she lived on the land until she remarried in 1881, moved into her husband's house in St. Anne, and let her son, Stephen, live on the land with no definite agreement. He was expected to pay the taxes, some of the debts, and what rent he could. Stephen wanted full ownership of the land and in court was claiming that in addition to the obligations of debt and taxes, he had improved the land with a wire fence, a twenty-foot corncrib, a hog fence, and a covered stable. Those acting for Stanislas said that the improvements were already in place, that Stephen had torn them down and rebuilt, and that what he had done was worth no more than $50. In the outcome of this case, Stephen paid his nephew, Stanislas, and his mother, Mary Lariviere, an unspecified sum of money, and a partition occurred. One can assume that Stephen then stayed on the farm while his mother and nephew continued to live in town.[25]

Occasionally, property claims also include petty theft. In 1875 John Collins accused Ambrose Allain Sr., Ambrose Allain Jr., and Charles Allain of removing hay from a barn at Collins switch. Collins was suing for $50. The court found for him after hearing the evidence, awarding $6.80 in damages and $16.70 in costs. The defendants vowed to appeal.[26] In 1885 Moses St. Peter sued Samuel Chartier over a threshing machine valued at $50 that he said Chartier wrongfully took. The case was settled for the return of the machine and payment of court costs.[27] Perhaps, the most trivial property claim, one that demonstrates the extent to which people wanted the courts to settle their personal conflicts, was that brought by David Coyer against Louis Ducharme of the firm of George Ducharme and son. Coyer accused Ducharme of taking a spelling book, "such as that used by school children in the St. Anne public school with the name of Elyme Coyer written in it and a date of September 5, 1894 and valued at 40 cents." The court found for the plaintiff and made the defendant pay him five cents.[28]

Contracts, Debts, and Bodily Harm

The people of St. Anne also brought to the court disputes for nonpayment of debt.[29] Such disputes frequently involve different layers of local and/or extralocal society. The boundaries (and social cleavages) in these cases drawn according to systems of social stratification that distinguished property owners from tenants, businessmen from farmers, retailers from wholesalers, and the like. Farmers bought items on credit from local merchants, and when the farmers did not pay their bills on time, local merchants could not pay their suppliers. Suppliers or those from whom local merchants borrowed money to meet their obligations eventually sued for these debts.

In 1874 Alfred Roy brought a complaint against Alfred Bastien for $20.75 of meat not yet paid for. Roy said, "Bastien has departed from the state with the intention of having his effects removed and that Bastien conceals himself so that the process cannot be served and that he is about to fraudulently conceal, assign, or dispose of his property so as to hinder or delay creditors."[30] In 1895 and 1896 Chagnon and Soucie, a general store in St. Anne, was sued twice, one a $984.38 promissory note at 7 percent interest John Ferns held and the other a $200 promissory note with a forty-day payback agreement with the law firm Granger and Davidson.[31] Joseph Guertin, who also owned a general store, was brought to court on several occasions by various plaintiffs for nonpayment on goods delivered to him. In 1885, for example, the plaintiff was Sprague Warner and Company of Chicago for $300 on items Guertin had ordered. In 1887 the plaintiff was Brooks Brothers of Chicago, which was seeking payment on an order of boots and shoes.

Such suits were also brought by one individual against another for money borrowed and never paid back. Several of these date to the late 1850s and early

1860s when, as previous chapters note, times were particularly tough. Many of these suits were brought against Chiniquy himself, for example, the claim of John Parent for $308.50 (a $270 note with 10 percent interest to be repaid in thirty days) that was filed in 1858, that of Antoine Idrac, filed in the same year, for $53 at 10 percent interest, or that of Peter Schutters for an unpaid note dated March 23, 1862 for $187.25 with 10 percent interest to be paid within sixty days.[32] In one case, also in 1858, Chiniquy was a defendant in an attempt by Michael Morin to settle a debt from John Belanger and John Belanger Jr. for $434.46. Morin claimed to the court that the Belangers had no property but that he believed Chiniquy to be indebted to them or had money belonging to them. Morin wanted to garnish his debt from Chiniquy.[33]

Finally, even Chiniquy's attorney filed a complaint against him in 1860 for unpaid bills on the "work and labor, care, diligence, and attendance" in "prosecuting and defending diverse suits of laws in diverse courts of this state." This case was dismissed for full settlement, and Chiniquy paid the costs.[34]

Two complaints were filed against Moise Langellier, one by Andrew Demers for the nonpayment of $269 borrowed in 1859 at 10 interest, and another by R. N. Murray for $300 borrowed in 1862.[35] The Demers case includes several letters from the Iroquois County sheriff stating that the defendant had the money to pay. In 1858 Paulin Pallissard filed against Oliver Bastien for $78 that Bastien had borrowed in February of that year. In the same year George and Theo Bowen sued Stephen and Cyprien Boudreau, who had signed the notes with marks, for $81.75 and damages of $26 on a three-month loan made in July 1858 and not paid. The estate of William Dougherty sued Desire Castongue of Beaverville in 1859 for $300 on a promissory note Castongue signed on September 26, 1857, agreeing to pay Michael Morin $200 at 10 percent per year.[36]

Complaints were also filed when some service was rendered that went uncompensated or when some agreement was not honored or was contracted under suspicious or fraudulent conditions. In 1866 Frank Legris brought Octave Gauthier to court for recovery of a three-year-old gray horse worth about $150 of which he claimed he was defrauded. A number of residents of St. Anne were called as witnesses, and the jury found the horse to be the property of the plaintiff. In the following year, Peter Bonvallet and Jules Henri were in court over an eviction. Bonvallet owned a two-story dwelling in St. Anne and had allowed Henri to live there with his family as a hired hand to Bonvallet for two months. The term had expired, and Bonvallet was entitled to possession. Henri refused to leave. Henri said in the circuit court that in St. Anne he could not receive a fair and impartial trial before justice

Achilles Chiniquy because the justice "is so prejudiced against me." Henri asked for a change of venue. Two witnesses who were residents in the neighborhood of Bonvallet's house testified that the rental value on the property was $3 a month or $36 a year. The judgment was in favor of Bonvallet to recover $7 in court costs.[37]

When notes, which in some sense worked like cash, were passed from one party to another as part of the settlement of a debt or sale, the cases became even more complex. In 1885 Charles Savoie sued Francis Coyer, Peter Brosseau, and Stephen Ungron. The case involved a team of horses bought for $150. Sometime early in 1882, Coyer, by 1885 living in Indiana, was "greatly embarrassed" because he needed money and borrowed $100 from Savoie at 8 percent annual interest. Savoie extended the loan period at the end of the first year. Coyer said that he sold Brosseau and Ungron a horse and that they were to pay off the debt to Savoie as part of this sale. This had apparently not occurred. The jury found for the plaintiff and assessed the damages at $141.27.[38]

Another complex case, filed in 1890, involved the sale of some horses and brought a number of witnesses from St. Anne to the Kankakee County Courthouse. Fred Lebeau, the plaintiff, known as one of the best horsemen in the state, was born in Iroquois County in 1864 to Israel Lebeau and Philomene Tatro, who came to the St. Anne area in 1854 and converted to Presbyterianism with Chiniquy. Fred stayed on his parents' farm until he moved to St. Anne at twenty. In 1888 he formed a partnership with J. D. Bishop, who was in 1890 the defendant, to deal in horses. Bishop also traded in grain, lumber, hay, and coal in partnership with his brother but ultimately became insolvent and faced with the loss of his property. Lebeau then claimed that Bishop had made some sort of transfer of the partnership property, worth $2,140 in notes and $1,100 in bank accounts and liabilities of $1,900, to his father-in-law, Thomas Lottinville, from a wealthy Catholic family, without his knowledge. Lebeau told the court that he wanted to pay up but was fearful of Bishop's judgments. Lebeau said he could not read or write, so he would not know anything of the contents of the papers of transfer if they existed and did not authorize any transfer. One of the witnesses, Nazaire Bertrand, a blacksmith in St. Anne, who, when he heard that Bishop had sold out, approached Lottinville about money Bishop owed Bertrand for shoeing horses. Lottinville, Bertrand said, told him to charge Bishop and Lebeau. Another witness was George Soucie, a merchant in St. Anne for fifteen years, who testified that Bishop had asked him if he wanted to buy the horses in question and that he would give him a good price. The plaintiff's father, Israel, a farmer for thirty-six years and who could not read or write, said that he had only heard about the bill of sale from Lottinville: "If it was good it was good, but I never knew or understood what had been done." Bishop denied that he was insolvent or indebted and said that Lebeau was present for the sale of the horses and made no complaint. Another witness, Levi Martin, said that he heard Bishop ask Lebeau if the note Lottinville signed for the goods and things he bought would be satisfactory security and that Lebeau had said he would investigate. Peter Lamoreaux of Chicago said Milton Lamoreaux on May 25, 1890, sold some imported French draft horses to Bishop and Lebeau for $775 for $200 in cash and the remainder in notes. In August he went to St. Anne for the balance, and Lebeau said he had disposed of the assets of the firm and did not have enough to pay the debts. Lamoreaux said he accepted $316. In his suit, Lebeau was asking for an injunction against Bishop and Lottinville to stop them from interfering with the property so that he could settle the matter. The outcome of this case is not clear, but it illustrates the complexity of business dealings by some members of the community.[39]

Personal-injury cases between local entrepreneurs, on the one hand, and town government or other residents, on the other, reveal further lines of division and difference within the community. In 1888 Lionel Becs and Joseph Sewell sued town officials Moses Chartrier, Louis Duclos, and Frank Wilkins. Becs and Sewell, who were in the creamery business in St. Anne, had water rights from a well near their establishment. They said the officials "unjustly intending to injure and prejudice [them] and to deprive them of water, cut, dug and made a hole in the ground nearby and broke and severed a pipe carrying their water stopping it from flowing into the pump." In another case, in 1894, Joseph Sprimont claimed that highway commissioners Moses Baron, Charles Shriep, B. N. Powley, and Legere Martin, in control of a public highway across Beaver Creek in Papineau, were not maintaining it in safe repair and condition. In addition, Martin should have kept in good repair his barbed-wire fence around his land next to the highway, because Sprimont's horses became entangled in the wires and tripped. Their flesh was lacerated, and they were rendered of no value. He was seeking $200 in damages.[40]

One of the more complicated suits, for $5,000, was brought against Joseph Guertin in 1881 by Mary and Severin Caron. Guertin owned a general store, where, the Carons claimed, Guertin sold a pistol to their son Albert, who was under twenty-one, a minor. He loaded the pistol, it discharged and killed him, "depriving [the parents] of his services." The parents were poor farmers, spoke little English, did not know much about legal proceedings, and were poorly qualified to manage a lawsuit. For $10 they hired a justice to represent them and were required to find witnesses to prove the sale of the pistol since the defendant kept no register of the weapons he sold. Guertin brought other witnesses, one a boy who said he was playing with Albert with a toy pistol that belonged to Albert's brother Alvin. Mary Caron was home and knew he was shooting it off. He forced a cartridge into it. Another witness, Nelson Delibac, also said he saw Albert shooting a toy pistol, the cartridges came from a Mr. Grosse and Albert had cut them down to put them in the pistol. This witness also claimed he heard Mary Caron say "she did not expect to get anything out of Mr. Guertin but she wanted to make him spend all the money she could." What lay behind this statement, suggestive of animosity between a poor family and a rather well-to-do entrepreneur in the community, we do not know for sure, but Guertin won.[41]

The Personal Is Judicial: Family, Morality, and Murder

The courts in the past as in the present are occasionally called in to settle personal family matters or to make some pronouncement on matters of morality. These cases also illustrate social cleavages as well as core values held by the community, and in several of them, various members of the community were brought in to testify for or against their neighbors. Certainly, one of the issues at the root of familial problems was alcohol, a matter that, in the early twentieth century, became the subject of intense debate, dividing the community into "wet" and "dry" camps. Indeed, on a few occasions the state had filed cases against some French Canadian residents for selling liquor without a license.[42] But more commonly, it was individuals who brought personal matters involving alcohol to the attention of the court. In 1873, for example, Rosalie Coyer sued John B. Allie of St. Anne for $2,000 because he sold Joseph Coyer, her husband, whisky on August 15, 1873, and at other times. Allie, she claimed, caused her husband's intoxication, and her husband became greatly debilitated and so physically and mentally incapacitated he could not work, had lost money, and was discharged from the Chicago and Danville Railroad. She said she and their children were dependent upon him for support. Allie said he had not sold or given alcohol to Coyer, and "Coyer did not become drunk and incapacitated from attending to his usual business and was not discharged from a lucrative position by reason of being drunk and that said Joseph Coyer did not make $50 a month and that said Rosalie was not then dependent on said Joseph Coyer for this support and for the support of her infant children." On March 6, 1874, Mrs. Coyer withdrew the suit when Allie agreed to pay her $15.[43]

In another case, filed in 1876, the town of St. Anne through its officials sued a family named Goyette. Two matters were at issue, one involving Louis Goyette, who was accused of alcoholism, an impaired mind, and the inability to handle his own affairs, and the second about Goyette's brother and his family that the community of St. Anne was supporting. Several promissory notes for a variety of liabilities against Goyette were introduced into evidence, and several community members testified. Hubert Lepage, a relative by marriage to Louis Goyette's daughter, stated he had known Goyette for several years, and "Louis has been an excessive drinker of strong intoxicating liquor for the last 2 or 3 years and it [is his] belief that the excessive use of such liquors has so impaired his mind that he is unfit and incapacitated from doing any business whatsoever." Goyette owned property valued at from $5,000 to $6,000, and there was a danger of him spending his estate and he and his family would be broke, resulting in the St. Anne community having to support them. Indeed, in 1875, in another case of the people versus Louis Goyette, an injunction was sought because Goyette had sold lands and personal property illegally, some of it to his brother Antoine. Goyette said, according to his wife, Marie, that "he would dispose of all his property as he pleased and thereby prevent his affiant from getting any of it." Given these circumstances and Goyette's history of court proceedings, a conservatorship to manage his affairs was granted in January 1876.[44]

Introduced into evidence relating to this case was a letter written by Joseph Guertin that related the circumstances of Louis Goyette's poor relations, his brother and family, to the town supervisor and ex officio overseer of the town poor. This paper declares

> that there is now residing in said town a man by the name of John Goyette who has a family consisting of a wife and seven children, allowing the oldest a girl being above the age of sixteen. Six of said children are girls and all are living without means of subsistence or means of earning a livelihood. All are paupers and unable to earn a livelihood from unavoidable causes. John Goyette is unable to earn a livelihood on account of a bodily infirmity, the loss of sight of his eyes. Said Goyette or the members of the family are not paupers by reason of intemperance or other bad conduct upon their part but their pauperism is wholly unavoidable by them. Goyette has no children able to support him or his wife or parents or sister able to support him but has a brother by the name of Louis and a brother of the half-blood by the name of Antoine, one of said brothers residing in St. Anne and other in Papineau. Louis and Antoine are able to support said John Goyette and his family. They have been informed of the destitute and impoverished condition of said John Goyette and his family but they refused to support him. They are now dependent upon the community for food and almost destitute of proper clothing.

In February 1872, the St. Anne supervisor asked for a court order requiring Louis Goyette and Antoine Goyette to support their brother John and his family, but it had been dismissed. In January 1878 a jury found Louis reformed from use of intoxicating drinks and restored to reason and a fit person to have control of his property. Clearly, this case represents well the conflicts between family and community, as represented by state-based institutions, over the issue of responsibility for those who are poor.[45]

Alcohol seems to have been at the root of several petitions for divorce, one as early as 1868 when Zoe Bouchard, a member of the small Baptist congregation in St. Anne, sued David Bouchard for divorce.[46] Zoe claimed that she had been living with David for twenty-five years, but during the previous two, he had deserted her and the family, failing to provide for them. He is, she claimed, "an actual and habitual drunkard and remains sober only when he is without money." She said he beat and abused her and threatened her life and that she would be in danger as long as she remained his wife. The couple had six children, fourteen, sixteen, nineteen, twenty-one, twenty-three, and twenty-four, who had helped their father to acquire wealth. Several witnesses testified to his drunkenness, and another claimed that David Bouchard was totally insolvent, working as a day laborer and drinking his money as fast as he earned it. The court dissolved the marriage.

More such cases appeared toward the end of the century, all of them among members of the Protestant community of St. Anne. Despite a growing antidivorce sentiment after the Civil War, the divorce rate in America rose dramatically from 1.2 divorces per 1,000 marriages in 1860 to 2.2 in 1880, 4.0 in 1900, and 7.7 in 1920. Elaine Tyler May puts it in somewhat different terms, telling us that while the population increased by 300 percent between 1867 and 1929, the number of marriages rose by 400 percent and the number of divorces by 2,000 percent. Approximately 1 in 6 marriages was terminated in court by the end of the 1920s.[47] The Midwest, particularly the state of Indiana, and the West had particularly high rates of divorce, but Illinois was also known for its rather liberal divorce laws.[48] The primary grounds for divorce were adultery (generally, on the part of the woman), desertion, and cruelty. Some of the French Canadians in Illinois pursued these grounds in their petitions to dissolve their marriages. For example, in 1898 Caroline Betourne filed for divorce from her husband, Amedee Betourne, a resident of Lyon City, Minnesota, who, after twenty-one years of marriage abandoned her and their two children, ages six and twelve, running off clandestinely in the company of a concubine, Emma Rakestraw. Caroline said that since 1894 Amedee had "given himself up to adulterous and licentious practice, carnal connections with Jennie Cheffer and with other women. . . . Before his departure, he told her and his mother he was going to open a saloon in Kankakee and had them sign a mortgage and trust deed. Then he took the money and ran away, always wasting money with lascivious behavior." In the absence of Amedee, who was found at fault for not appearing in court, Caroline was awarded ownership of a piece of property in Manteno Township, just north of St. Anne Township. Her marriage was dissolved, and she was awarded full custody of her children.[49]

Another divorce petition was filed in the following year by Addie Belanger, a Presbyterian. Addie claimed that she had married Treffley Belanger in 1890 and lived with him until 1899 when she left him. She and Treffley had a child named Mattie born in 1895. For the past four years, "Treffley has given himself up to strong drink and for upwards of the last 2 years he has been drunk all the time when he could get money to buy liquor and has been an habitual drunkard," she said. When drunk, "he has choked me and threatened to cut me up with a butcher knife and has locked me and our child out of the house and kept me out all night during cold weather and has utterly failed to furnish sufficient food for me and our child. In colder parts of the winter, he neglected and refused to buy coal." Treffley responded that his wife had left him without cause. He denied drinking and that he "requested and commanded her not to be associated with a certain lewd woman of bad repute but she continued." He locked her out, he said, against this woman, insisting that she could come in but not the other woman. He claimed he had provided coal although he is poor and had never used harsh words except when he remonstrated her against the lewd woman. He insisted that his wife "by the life she is leading and the vicious and depraved associations she is consorting with is unfit to have care and control of their child." This case remained open until 1902 when Treffley returned to court to say that his wife had left Illinois and that his daughter was undoubtedly with her and that she had never returned. A divorce was granted.[50]

In 1905 the court heard the divorce and request for support of Helen Bouchard versus William Bouchard. Extreme accusations were made on both sides. William, a Baptist, seventy-two years old, who could not read or write, had no way of earning a livelihood but was worth about $4,000 and could only gain income by selling land. He was unable to support himself and depended on the charity of friends and relatives. Shortly after he married Helen in 1903, she began to abuse and mistreat him, making his life miserable.

> On or about May 6 1903 she did in a vicious manner grab and take hold of his private parts and pulled him out of bed causing him extreme pain and suffering;

> then on June 6, 1903 she grabbed and laid hold of him in an ugly and surly manner, viciously threw him on edge of bed and bore down on his head and neck; and another time (on or about the 1st of November 1903) she threatened to pull his guts out and he was scared and frightened and left his home in the possession of Helen and went to stay with relatives.

Helen, forty-seven years old, in feeble health, without property, and unable to make her own living, claimed that she was "true, chaste, and dutiful and that he was cruel and struck, pinched, choked and assaulted her; he used abusive language, neglected to furnish and provide her with clothing and furniture." She said that he left her on June 13, 1903, and returned on September 12 and during that time had not supplied her with the necessities of life. He left again in November. She stated that he was worth about $4,200. He claimed that the only way he could comply with the $160 per month that she wanted for support was to mortgage the house, but she refuses to go along with that. The court found Helen guilty of extreme and repeated cruelty toward William and that he was justified in leaving home. But William was ordered to pay Helen $340 in alimony within thirty days in addition to court fees.[51]

Nor was St. Anne without cases that included charges of more serious physical harm. A. E. Diamond sued Celestin Blain in 1867 for assault. Diamond told the court that Blain had "beat, bruised, and evil treated him; pushed, dragged, and pulled him about and kicked him and ruined a pair of trousers and a shirt." Blain, in his defense, said that Diamond had assaulted him at the house of his wife, Mary Diamond, "and with drunkenness and violence raised a sugar bowl to strike and would have struck an infant child and would have destroyed furniture and at request of his Diamond's wife he took away the sugar bowl and removed the plaintiff from the home." The court heard about the difficulties between husband and wife, and when Mary agreed to pay her husband $1,200, he agreed to dismiss the suit.[52]

Some disputes involved sexual morality. In 1871 John B. Boule accused August Lottinville of surreptitiously abducting, persuading, inducing, taking, and carrying away a minor child, Georgina Boule, with force and arms on November 14. Boule was asking for $400. The outcome of this case is uncertain, but in January 1872 Henry Lottinville, twenty-two and a brother of August, married Georgina Boule, and they went on to have seven children.[53]

In 1874 Victorine Hines sued Achilles Chiniquy for slander when he called her a whore. She claimed that her material witness, Napoleon Chiniquy, could not appear because he was a sailor on the Great Lakes and did not remain in one place long enough to give a deposition. Without his testimony, her case could not go to trial because he could prove that the defendant, Achilles Chiniquy, said she was a famous public character, a whore, long before she married. Achilles came before the court to claim that Victorine had no property, could not be liable for damages, and could not pay the costs of a suit. Moses Morin and Frank Wilson then appeared and stated that they agreed to pay all the costs that might be adjudged against Victorine. Two years later a formal plea for damages of $2,000 was filed. Willemine Morin and Mary Lafrançois were witnesses for Victorine. The court registered that

> whereas the plaintiff now is and always has been a chaste and virtuous and honorable woman and hath been accounted esteemed and reputed as such among her neighbors as well as of good reputation and fame by all other people and hath all her lifetime continued chaste and unsuspected of the atrocious crimes of adultery or fornication or any such enormous crimes, nevertheless the defendant has continued maliciously and wickedly to injure and defame her good name and reputation and to bring her into disgrace and infamy and to subject her to the penalties and punishment provided by law in such case to wit on January 15, 1874 in a certain discourse in which he charged adultery and thereby intending to charge the plaintiff with having been guilty of the crime of adultery and then and there intending that said citizens who then and there heard of said charge should so understand—that he did utter these false, scandalous, and malicious and defamatory words and that she gets her living by the seat of her ass (meaning by whoring), that she is a whore (meaning she keeps a whore house), that she is a strumpet, a lewd women, meaning to charge her with adultery and keeping a brothel. She claimed she had fallen into disgrace with people with whom she was in great esteem.[54]

There is no indication of the final outcome in this case.

Other crimes were also occasionally committed by members of this community. In April 17, 1879, Louis Coyette and Maxime Belgard were indicted for forgery. In 1896, arson was the focus of a case of the people versus Stanislas Gagne, accused of setting fire to buildings with the intent to burn them. The buildings in question were owned by Amelia Blain. There was no evidence that she authorized the fire. It was suggested to the court that Gagne was of unsound mind.[55] Gambling was occasionally an issue. Peter Marlaire was fined $200 for playing cards with money in 1906. Accusations of theft were brought before the courts from time to time. As early as the 1860s, Charles Chiniquy brought a woman named Roxana Crown, who was his housekeeper, to court. He accused her of stealing a gold watch. In return Crown sued Chiniquy for $5,000 and slander in 1864. Her court record states

> whereas the plaintiff is a good, true, honest, just, and faithful citizen of the state of Illinois and as such hath always behaved and conducted herself and until the committing of the several grievances by the defendant had never been suspected to be guilty of theft or any other such crime accuses Chiniquy of wickedly and maliciously intending to injure her and bring her into public scandal, infamy and disgrace by causing it to be believed that she was guilty of theft.

Chiniquy observed that she could have her trunks broken open and should, therefore, give herself up: "I know it was a temptation and your first offense. I don't blame you. I love you and would forgive you a thousand watches if you will give it up. . . . Tomorrow morning you will come and I will settle with you and pay you off for you can't stay any longer with the suspicion resting upon you." Noting that he had missed several things from his house during the summer, he suggested that Crown put the watch at the foot of his secretary.[56]

But perhaps the most dramatic criminal case in the history of St. Anne, one that remains unsolved and one that continues to remind the residents of the significance of the name of Chiniquy, was the murders of Emile Chiniquy and his wife in their beds in the middle of the night, in the early morning hours of October 19, 1898.

> In all the history of St. Anne, it has never been so stirred and shocked as this morning. . . . The little village, which is a pretty hamlet, has had many sensations in its time. The Chiniquy imbroglio in which the opposing forces of hostile religious demonstrations battled for supremacy; the mysterious burning of the Catholic church; the atmosphere of romance and adventure which the presence of the famous agitator Father Chiniquy created; the frequent visitations of burglars from outside; the annual pilgrimages of hosts of religious devotees—all these have invested the little town with a strong and lively interest from time to time; but no event has ever shook the place from center to circumference and reached out until it affected the surrounding countryside as the mysterious murder of the two well-known citizens.[57]

Emile, son of Louis Chiniquy, the youngest brother of Charles, came to St. Anne with his parents in 1867 and married Victorine Bourgeois. They had four children.

Emile farmed for a time, and then, turning the farming over to his oldest son, he opened a meat market in town in the 1890s. He became a prosperous merchant, and the family lived comfortably.

The bodies of Emile and Victorine were brutally mangled and their skulls crushed, presumably with meat cleavers that were missing after the crime. Blood was all over the bedroom, where they were found by their youngest son, whose screams immediately brought his elder brothers, Adolph and Emile, and the housekeeper, Lizzie Marcotte.[58] The detectives determined that Mrs. Chiniquy, whose body was lying near the door, was trying to get out of the room and alert her three sons when she was cut down. The detectives also conjectured that she was killed because she awoke and recognized the assailant who was after her husband.[59] Among the evidence is a broken kitchen window pane, a knee imprint in the window box beneath it, and a bloody towel in the kitchen that the assailant probably used after the deed was done to clean his hands.[60]

According to the newspaper account, "a Negro man" named Ringo was arrested, but he provided a solid alibi, and no charges were ever brought against anyone whether for lack of evidence or because of some reluctance on the part of authorities. A committee of local jurors the county coroner appointed interviewed a number of witnesses, one of whom mentioned insurance policies that husband and wife carried on each other for $1,000 and $2,000, respectively, a fact that cast suspicion on someone in the household. Among the rumors that circulated in town was one suggesting a jealous husband of a woman with whom Emile had had an affair took revenge. "There is an intimation that Mr. Chiniquy was of a sensual nature," one newspaper reported, adding that reports conflicted about the state of disarray of the bedroom where the crime had occurred. Another report mentioned a problem with a man in Kankakee who owed Emile money on a bill and when he was forced to pay, threatened to get even. Others in the community thought that one of the sons was the culprit. The *Kankakee Gazette* of Wednesday, October 19, 1898, reports that the son told a neighbor, Tennis Beaupre, that his mother and father had killed themselves during the night. The jury concluded that the crime was premeditated rather than the result of a botched robbery, although the mattress at the scene of the crime, according to one report, had been pulled up and curled over as if someone was looking for money beneath it.

The youngest son, Oscar, eventually went to live with his sister, Laura, and her husband, Gaspar Marceau, and they eventually moved to California. Another son, Emile, attended St. Viateurs Seminary in Bourbonnais and drowned in the Kankakee River three years later at the age of fourteen. The probated estate revealed numerous debts and outstanding bills. Both real and personal property were sold to pay these debts as well as the cost of the inquest and the funeral. The real estate included several lots in the third range of Allain's subdivision to St. Anne and others in Kankakee, as well as 120 acres of agricultural property in sections 29 and 32 of St. Anne Township. At the settlement in December 1899, each of the two older children received $659.64, and L. Drolet, as guardian for Emile and Oscar, received $1,319.29. The crime was never solved, and the house where it took place stood empty until John Soucie bought it.

The legacy of Charles Chiniquy, the suggestions of sexual impropriety, and the evidence of rifts between wealthy merchants and those who were poor and indebted to them makes this case interesting as a metaphor for discord and tension that characterized St. Anne and, undoubtedly, other small towns in America during the latter nineteenth century. And, the hint that a black man—an outsider—might have been responsible presaged yet another social cleavage that did not erupt with full force for another sixty years.

Black and White: Racial Tensions in St. Anne High School

If the conflict with the railroad served as the marker of the identity of the people of St. Anne as rural farmers in the 1860s and 1870s, one hundred years later a different aspect of identity as "white" came into play. In the 1960s local newspapers reported racial tension and conflict at St. Anne High School. Blacks had moved into Pembroke Township, adjacent to St. Anne, during the Civil War, but the population remained small until the Depression. At that time, many black families who had lost their jobs in Chicago expressed a desire to return to the land and gathered in Pembroke Township, in some cases lured by unscrupulous land dealers.[61]

In the *St Anne Record* of August 17, 1939, an article with the headline "Chicago Negroes Open New Town East of St. Anne" tells of Leesville, set up under the leadership of Mr. Lee as part of a "back-to-the-soil" movement. "We know that farm life is better because we are producing the things we need. Farming also produces a progressive mind, free from arrogance, selfishness, and individualism. It tends to bind mankind together with love, peace and harmony: We the settlers of Leesville want to create better American Negro citizens." Among the first to buy forty acres at $12.50 per acre were Henry Scott and his friend John Simmons. Between 1935 and 1936, approximately forty more black families settled in the area. These numbers increased after World War II and included several veterans and their families.[62]

There were problems in providing schools. Between the 1860s and 1959, the educational needs of black and white children in Pembroke Township had been met in scattered one-room schoolhouses. Beginning in the 1960s, the Pembroke children were bused to St. Anne, a community that was 99 percent white, as compared with Pembroke, which was 99 percent black. The number of local black children was supplemented by the children of black families in Chicago who were sent to relatives in Pembroke Township to keep them out of trouble. Discontented with what was happening, those parents in St. Anne who could afford it began to pull their children out of the public school and send them to private schools in Kankakee. Even Protestant parents were sending their children to parochial schools. As a result of these actions and the fact that the birth rate in St. Anne was declining, the student body of St. Anne High School became 80 percent black within a few years. Ninety percent of the staff and school board members were white. This rather unusual situation laid the basis for conflict.

By the late 1960s, the school had become overcrowded; hostilities were intensified both within and without its walls. The tensions culminated in violence. Students refused to go to classes, and the classes were, therefore, dismissed early. Subsequently, children were locked in the schoolrooms, and armed guards were around the facility. This situation continued for several years. The National Association for the Advancement of Colored People (NAACP) was called in and charged that the school followed discriminatory and segregationist practices. The NAACP argued that blacks never played certain school team positions, that the homecoming queen had never been black, and that there were never any ballot boxes in Pembroke Township.[63]

On December 9, 1975, the school was closed by the Illinois Office of Education because the building was deteriorating to the point where it did not meet national safety standards. Twice, voters in St. Anne turned down a referendum to build a new school. The *Kankakee Journal* reported on December 10 that the "problem-plagued" school of St. Anne represented a situation unique in the history of Illinois. There was no other school like it in the state—a school with a predominantly black student body and a predominantly white board and staff. One black board member claimed that the school was run in a racist manner. A white student commented in the pages of the newspaper that she was in the minority and for this reason would never be elected student council president or homecoming queen.

Early in 1976, the pastors of churches in both townships assembled to sponsor a prayer meeting to heal the communities. Jesse Jackson visited the community to join in the efforts to alleviate the tension and violence and promote open discussion and problem solving. Although the conflict eventually died down, the poverty level of the school endured into the 1980s. Large numbers of students fell into the indigent category, and over 60 percent of them were on the free lunch program. The school was put on a probationary list for a time.

Racial identification or whiteness is no longer an aspect of self that is prominently manipulated by the residents of St. Anne as it was in the 1960s and 1970s. However, at the time it was clearly the predominant social category by which the residents of St. Anne defined their identity vis-à-vis an "other." The concept of whiteness has an interesting history in relation to US immigration history, because many European immigrants when they first came to the United States were often constructed as other than white and over time became white.[64] The epithet attached to the French Canadians as the "Chinese of the Eastern United States" falls into a similar category of racist exclusion. Although this phrase was not a part of the Illinois experience, the process by which those of different national origins became white, hence putting aside even further their affiliation to a particular culture in order to distance themselves from other oppressed populations, is worth consideration. Those who theorize about whiteness suggest that whites do not necessarily think of themselves as a race unless they are filling out a form or in certain situations when they are surrounded by those who are not white. This latter dimension is what happened in St. Anne in the 1960s, resulting in the emergence of a white identity and a period of complex race relations in the history of the community.

In an exhaustive study of the business of trial courts in Chippewa County, Wisconsin, between 1855 and 1954, Francis W. Laurent found that contract obligations and real-property actions were the most numerous civil actions—that is, conflicts of economic interest.[65] The highest proportion of contract actions focused on alleged defaults on promises to pay money. In times of depression, real-property actions generally involved mortgage foreclosures; in times of prosperity, actions focused on title. Domestic-relations disputes centered on divorce, and in more than half of the tort actions, bodily injury or negligence was at issue. Stephen Daniels documents a steady increase in the percentage of divorce-related matters between 1870 and 1960 in his study of legal cases in two rural counties of Illinois.[66] If the research of Laurent and Daniels offers two points of comparison in a relatively understudied area of nineteenth-century social history, it appears that the kinds of disputes that occurred among the population of French Canadians in St. Anne were no different from those that occupied populations elsewhere in the Midwest during the late nineteenth and early twentieth centuries. Such disputes were part of a larger pattern of conflict that historian Jon Gjerde has argued was common within local communities in the rural Midwest during the nineteenth century "because the boundaries between communities were often strictly defended."[67]

Among the French Canadian immigrants in Illinois, the disputes and conflicts were both inner-directed and outer-directed, the latter perhaps shaped by the first major other-directed conflict, the schism that created a religious divide within the community at the moment of its founding. These forms of conflict are related, and both highlight lines of difference. Ultimately, they tell us something about identity formation and how it changes over time as immigrant communities become part of American society. Identity formation is equally shaped by the larger forces of history—economic, social, political—that affect small-town life. Just as the religious schism took place at a time when religious identity was contested in the national context, the conflict with the railroad took place at a time when agriculture and industry (country and city) were at odds. And St. Anne went through its own experience with racial tensions as that issue exploded on the national scene in the 1960s as part of the process of desegregation that followed the Civil Rights Act of 1964. In these larger conflicts, internal divisions that often occupied daily life were obscured for the sake of broader and more singular aspects of identity that created a different basis for polarization.[68] But these were supplemented by myriad smaller conflicts that invoked both the rights-oriented individualism and the personal-responsibility individualism that have been found in another county of Illinois, Sander, in a more recent period.[69] Like the Dutch immigrants of West Sayville, New York, who are the subject of another historical ethnography,[70] the French Canadians in Illinois were also part of a "community of confrontation," and these confrontations reveal not only fundamental lines of both unity and disunity in social relations but also, as Marc Ross suggests in his analysis of the culture of conflict, central interests and values that emerged in the process of becoming American.[71]

CHAPTER 6

The Miracles of St. Anne: The Historical Origins and Meaning of a Religious Pilgrimage

Drive sixty miles south from Chicago on Highway 1, the old Dixie Highway, cross Highway 17, seven miles east of Kankakee, Illinois, and you will eventually pass through the town of St. Anne. From the north, the first thing that will catch your eye is the spire of the Catholic church topped by an open tower with a copper-green dome (fig. 6.1). On the right at the entrance to the town, a very prominently displayed sign boasts of the fact that this is the locus of the "Original Shrine of Ste. Anne in the United States." Stop to ask someone about the shrine, and he or she will immediately talk about the pilgrims who come each July to observe Ste. Anne's holy day in this community. Given the notoriety of St. Anne, Illinois, in the middle of the nineteenth century as a place where Catholics converted to Protestantism, the sign at the entrance to the town and these references to pilgrimage are both ironic and startling. How and why this shift in reputation occurred are the subjects of this chapter.

Unlike much of the literature on pilgrimage, my emphasis here is less on the pilgrims than on the place: that is, on the historical, political, and cultural context that gave rise to the miracles of Ste. Anne, and on the multiple and changing meanings of the pilgrimage, particularly to local residents.[1] However, even from this perspective, it is possible to engage several of the theoretical debates about pilgrimage that have emerged from the seminal work of Victor Turner and Edith Turner, as well as broader work by anthropologists on miracles, religious festivals, and community celebrations, more generally.[2] Of particular importance is an explanation of how this pilgrimage, as ritual, enacts social relations.

FIGURE 6.1. St. Anne Catholic Church, St. Anne, Illinois. *Photo by Caroline B. Brettell.*

Establishing a Pilgrimage Center

As the schism described in chapter 2 proceeded, those settlers in St. Anne who remained Catholic were forced to travel ten miles to the satellite community of St. Mary (now Beaverville) to worship. Although a small frame chapel was eventually erected in St. Anne by a visiting priest named Reverend Lapointe at his own expense, there was no resident priest in the community. In October 1871 Father Beaudoin of Kankakee asked Bishop Bourget of Montreal for a priest for St. Anne: "It will be necessary for this locality to have a prudent man; with this quality he would do incalculable good. Chiniquy is not as dangerous as one could believe. He makes more noise when he is abroad than when he is at home. He is known and spoken of with scorn, even by Protestants."[3] Bourget must have taken some action. Father Michael Letellier was sent to St. Anne. Among the records in the Catholic church at St. Anne are some undated notations of Father Letellier's activities, evidently written on the eve of or soon after his departure from the community in March 1883.

> I, the undersigned, was named pastor of St. Anne by the Right Reverend Thomas Foley, administrator of the diocese of Chicago. I found in St. Anne an old frame chapel falling to pieces. The whole of the furnishings consisted of one old missal which we used, a very beautiful alb embroidered by Mrs. P. Pallissard, one old chasuble, a beautiful surplice also embroidered by Mrs. Pallissard, and an old chalice of brass with a silver cup and paten. . . . I directed the mission since, and furnished it with everything you see today. . . . I also built the church, paid the $1294, built the barn, the fences, etc. and I leave it with the consent of Archbishop E. A. Fechan, who, after repeated requests on my part, has finally relieved me of the responsibility of this mission, so difficult.[4]

As he indicates, Father Letellier pushed for the construction of a new church. The site chosen—the highest spot in St. Anne—was on land originally owned by Ambrose Allain and Antoine Allain, the two brothers who settled in the area before Charles Chiniquy arrived. The church was completed in 1872, the same year that the Chicago, Danville, and Vincennes Railroad began to serve the newly incorporated village.

> The Catholic citizens of the mission of St. Anne subscribed $4500 in 1872 for their church, and this subscription was in the form of notes payable to the treasurer of a Committee of Trustees (it is inconceivable that anyone imagine the priest to be honest enough to hold the money). The consequence was disastrous for the mission and most of the notes are uncollected and not collectable, the Committee having been dissolved the day of the transfer of the property to the Catholic Bishop of Chicago in March of 1878 which made this mission so impossible in 1880 that his Grace judged it to be necessary to send me all over the diocese to collect wherever the local pastors would allow me to do it.[5]

This text, followed by a list of those who did contribute to Father Letellier's collection efforts, clearly indicates that fifteen to twenty years later, the legacy of schism was still strong and that serving the religious needs of this community was stressful both emotionally and financially.[6] Chiniquy himself was still a resident of

St. Anne, albeit frequently absent on lecture tours, and his church was well established. In 1872 to 1873, according to a report submitted to the Canadian Presbytery, the First Presbyterian Church had 150 family members, 50 single individuals, 210 communicants, 7 elders, 7 other officeholders, 5 Sabbath schoolteachers and 22 in the Sabbath school, 100 students in the regular school, and 150 volumes in the congregation library.

A decade after the new Catholic church was built, a $7,000 debt remained, and Letellier himself had bought the land across from the church for $400 and deeded it to the diocese. Letellier also took it upon himself to reconvert several of those who had abandoned Catholicism. He carefully recorded the names of those who had abjured the schism of Chiniquy since Letellier had been named pastor, among them Chiniquy's own brother Achilles, who had served as a captain in the Civil War and who was a prominent citizen in the community.[7] One of the first marriages performed in the new church, on September 18, 1873, was that of Gabriel Franchère, a merchant from Chicago, and Eugenie Chiniquy, daughter of Louis Chiniquy, Charles Chiniquy's other brother. Other Chiniquys from this branch are listed among those paying pew rents in October 1873.

The efforts of Father Letellier laid the foundation for the restoration of Catholicism in St. Anne. On June 18, 1885, the *Kankakee Gazette* reports, "We noticed last Saturday at 10:30 A.M. 23 teams hitched in front of the Catholic Church, 16 in front of the First Presbyterian Church, 9 in front of the Second Presbyterian Church, and 5 in front of the Baptist Church." Printing these figures in the newspaper offers yet more evidence of how important the religious divisions still were. Further impetus for the reemergence of Catholicism in St. Anne came in 1886 when the priest of Notre Dame Church in Chicago, Father Achilles Bergeron, brought a group of pilgrims by train to St. Anne to celebrate the feast day, July 26, of the patroness of French Canadians. Though the novena in honor of the saint had been celebrated in St. Anne, Illinois, since the founding of the new parish, it was Father Bergeron who made this community into a destination of pilgrimage.

The cult of Ste. Anne has deep historical roots in French Canada. The "origin myth" tells that a group of seventeenth-century Breton sailors, facing shipwreck off the coast of New France, prayed to Ste. Anne for protection, promising to build a chapel in her honor if they were saved.[8] Their lives were spared, and they accordingly erected a tiny shrine close to the shores of the St. Lawrence River twenty miles downstream from Quebec City. The place came to be known as Ste. Anne-de-Beaupré for the beautiful meadow (*beau pré*) where the chapel was located. In 1658, following the miraculous cure of a cripple named Louis Gimont, a new chapel was begun but never completed because of its proximity to the shore. In 1662 a structure of stone and timber was erected on a hill nearby, and there were more miraculous cures. Pilgrims, both French and Christianized Indians, came to worship, and soon the cult was widespread enough to warrant a new building that was finished in 1676 and that served the needs of the faithful for two hundred years.[9] In the late nineteenth century, a new spurt in devotion to Ste. Anne, known as the mother of the afflicted, made it necessary to build another shrine. Completed in 1876, it was, in turn, after a fire in the 1920s replaced by the basilica that still stands today.

The reinvigoration of Ste. Anne-de-Beaupré in the 1870s, which has been attributed to spiritual influences from France and the emergence of railway transportation,[10] laid the basis for the development of a counterpart pilgrimage among the French Canadians of the Midwest. In the years after the first pilgrimage, pastors from the neighboring (though not necessarily French Canadian immigrant) towns began to bring their congregations to St. Anne, Illinois, and slowly the shrine grew in importance. In June 1893 lightning struck the church, and it was virtually destroyed. A new building was completed in the spring of 1894, though decoration of its interior continued for six more years. In the year that the new building was erected, as the result of an appeal from Reverend Father Bourassa of Pullman, Illinois, a relic, the bone of a hand, was sent from Rome to St. Anne, Illinois, via the cardinal of Quebec.[11] This action laid the foundation for a decade of growth that culminated in a series of miracles experienced by pilgrims during the first decade of the twentieth century.

The Miracles at St. Anne, Illinois

Throughout the final years of the 1880s and the 1890s, the local newspaper reported on the increasing numbers of pilgrims who came to St. Anne in mid-July. They were housed in the dormitory of the fourth floor of the St. Anne Academy, a school opened in 1883 by the sisters of Notre Dame. There were vague references to miraculous cures. For example, the August 1, 1889, issue of the *Kankakee Gazette* reports that "an excursion train from Chicago consisting of ten coaches and a baggage car arrived with at least a thousand French Catholics on their yearly pilgrimage to worship at the shrine of St. Anne. They spent the day in singing and prayer. Last year it was said that miracles were performed and that many who came as invalids and cripples went away healed." And in the issue of July 29, 1898: "It is almost annually reported that miraculous cures have been effected in front of the altar. About eight persons variously afflicted were presented at the shrine yesterday but no prominent cures were announced." Although healing miracles were often major themes of pilgrimage in French Canada, particularly among villagers who lived in rural areas remote from urban medicine,[12] it was not until 1904 that a miracle in St. Anne, Illinois, drew more than a passing reference.

A headline of the *Kankakee Journal* on Wednesday, July 24, of that year reads, "A MIRACLE AT ST. ANNE." The story that follows tells of a twenty-two-year-old woman from Calumet, Illinois, named Matilda Cunnea, whose legs had been paralyzed for two years. Having arrived in St. Anne at the beginning of the novena, she assisted in the daily prayers. On the evening of July 24, two days prior to the culmination of the feast, she reportedly turned to a nun and said, "Sister, I feel that I am cured; that I can walk. Assist me, please, to my feet." She rose and began to walk. The story continues: "The father, President of Calumet National Bank, who had bid his daughter goodbye to take the train back to Chicago was recalled and overcome. No cure for her previously had been effected, despite all that medical science can do." That this became the signal miracle of the shrine of St. Anne, Illinois, is evidenced by the fact that Cunnea's wheelchair is kept to this day in a side chapel of the church as a reminder of the event.[13] The site had acquired the "spiritual magnetism" necessary to sustain a pilgrimage center.[14]

Cunnea returned to St. Anne the following year, but that year another pilgrim, a six-year-old girl from Chicago named Lucille Walsh, was the focus of attention as she took the first steps in three years.[15] "Before the eyes of 4000 people," reports the *Kankakee Journal* on July 27, 1905,

> the miracle was wrought. . . . Dear Ste. Anne I have come here to ask you to make me well, lisped the child with a world of confidence in her voice. I want to walk like other girls. Make me well and strong. . . . For a minute she remained with her arms outstretched in supplication and her eyes sparkling. With anticipation she tried to rise to her feet. The weight of the plaster cast which has encased her for two years hampered her, but surely though slowly she stood erect. The mother stood pale and breathlessly expectant, ready to catch her little one. Eventually she walked and the mother dropped to her knees.

The newspaper account goes on, "So far as is known, no one of the several hundred pilgrims from Kankakee witnessed the miracle." This cure is also reported on the front page of the *Chicago Tribune* on July 27, 1905, and notice is made of the pilgrims from St. John the Baptist Church at Fiftieth Street and Peoria who had made the trip south to St. Anne and who brought bottles of holy water back to those unable to participate in the pilgrimage journey.

In 1906, the year that the parish hall was built to accommodate the increasing numbers of pilgrims who came to St. Anne, the "largest attendance (about 5500) ever known in the history of the parish" was recorded.[16] People poured in from every direction, people

> who were not jolly pleasure seekers, but who sought the blessings of the venerable saint and the Almighty. They were a quiet, peaceful and pious assembly who respected the full intent of the occasion. . . . They were worshippers. . . . All the distressed in body and soul, all who have dear ones afflicted in any way had been preparing themselves for the journey hoping to have their supplications answered and the glory of the saint manifested by a miracle.

In that year three more miraculous cures were reported: Barbara Bertoncelo of Cardiff, Illinois, who stood without the aid of crutches after seventeen years; Mrs. A. F. Page of Muskegon, Michigan, who had been an invalid for over a year and who "had been advised by her physicians to go to St. Anne to see what they would do for her"; and Mayme Chaney, also of Muskegon, a cousin of Page, who was "cured of blood poisoning" (fig. 6.2).

By this time the format for the feast day that followed the nine-day novena had been established. A Low Mass occurred at seven or eight in the morning; a High Mass was celebrated at mid-morning with sermons delivered in both French and English; a meal was served in the convent hall at noon; a prayer session was held after lunch, and this was followed by a procession with the sacred relic around the town. At the end of the procession, participants returned to the church for an additional prayer session, and the relic was passed from pilgrim to pilgrim, who touched it with their lips.

In 1907 there were fewer pilgrims from Chicago because the railroad had refused to extend a special rate, but the neighboring towns of Kankakee and Bradley sent a thousand people, and three thousand came from communities farther to the south. The procession that year was a mile long, following a route that took it south on Letellier Street, east on State, north on Fifth, and west on Grant. More miracles were reported. "Miss Pierce of Delphi, Indiana, a seventeen-year-old girl paralyzed for four years, threw away her crutches and walked unaided from the church altar to the convent. The inspiring spectacle aroused a triumphant chorus

FIGURE 6.2. Pillar of crutches left by those healed, St. Anne Catholic Church, St. Anne, Illinois. *Photo by Caroline B. Brettell.*

from a multitude of hopeful worshipers."[17] Others cured were Michael McCormick of Kinsman, Illinois, a boy of eight, who had been crippled since birth; Daisy Lamond of Kankakee, blind for thirty-two years; and eight-year-old boy named George Nerry from Lost Nation, Iowa, who threw away his braces. Among those cured in 1908, when twenty-five hundred pilgrims attended, were twenty-one-year-old Blanche Grabe of Des Moines, Iowa, suffering from hip disease; Joe Searle of Kankakee, twenty-one; Mary Licey, twenty-two, of Carroll, Iowa, suffering from anemia; Monica Lanigas of Illinois, who had been deaf and dumb since birth; and Mrs. J. H. Devinney of Chicago, who was paralyzed.

While attendance in 1909 had dropped and the "number of cures were fewer" in 1910, when two thousand people attended, Mrs. Moses Mercier of Concordia, Kansas, had her hearing restored, and Mrs. Clement Lavoie of St. Anne threw her crutches away and walked in the procession. Both these women were of French Canadian ancestry. In 1911 trainloads from all directions—from Pennsylvania, Nebraska, and Iowa—came to town as

> the fame of the shrine spread. . . . Three times daily the people join in chanting the hymn "The Good Ste. Anne" which was the song of the Canadian *voyageurs* as they explored the lands of New France. Men and women haggard with disease, children unable to stand or so crippled that they had to crawl forward joined the procession. Several of those who declared that they had been aided by their attendance at the pilgrimage in previous years have returned seeking still other benefits while many are coming for the first time. Some claimed to have received benefit but a lady from Springfield, Illinois who is afflicted with a large tumor on the side of her face could not notice that she had received benefit.

In 1911 and again in 1912, those who had been previously cured—Michael McCormick and Matilda Cunnea among them—returned. In 1912 there were no miracles but "many sufferers were aided by divine service and given strength to bear their afflictions."[18]

In 1914 smaller attendance was blamed on the fact that other towns—Bradley, Brighton Park in Chicago—had acquired relics and, in 1915, on threatening weather. Fewer of the physically or mentally afflicted who had sought relief in previous years attended, and a few cures were reported. The people, however, remained unidentified. In 1916 and 1917, undoubtedly due to World War I, there is no report of the feast. In 1918 it was celebrated, but the crowd was not as large as in previous years, and no miracles were reported, but by 1919 the feast seems to have regained some of its past momentum with a larger crowd and a stirring procession. In 1921, two thousand pilgrims reportedly attended, and housing them was difficult because the academy that had been used to accommodate visitors had burned. Residents of the town took pilgrims into their homes. This practice continued the following year, and the town advertised itself as "a peaceful locality and an ideal place for the novena which, as carried on, becomes a spiritual retreat." By 1925 "people of many nationalities joining together in honoring the Good St. Anne" were observed. A similar observation about the diversity of the pilgrim population was made two years later, and novena prayers continued to be led in both French and English. In 1928 the *St. Anne Record* observed that "the town that had seen religious strife for a few years quietly and unexpectedly became a mecca for thousands of worshippers. . . . The devotion has spread and is now popular with Catholics all over the Midwest." Two thousand attended that year, and the procession was "inspiring in its holy attitude and beautiful for its quaintness and simplicity." In these years the newspaper took it upon itself to write of the history of the community and of Ste. Anne-de-Beaupré in order to explain how the devotion was brought down to the village nearly a half century earlier by French Canadian pioneers.[19] There were no references to miracles.

The novena and feast continued through the 1930s, and in 1937 the Golden Jubilee year of the shrine was celebrated in connection with a community homecoming. In 1939 the procession was the largest seen in recent memory, with people marching six abreast. At one time nine buses and five hundred cars were parked, and the sale of religious articles was brisk.[20] A number of invalids suffering from blindness, deafness, and paralysis were in attendance, and one arthritis sufferer reported to a priest that he felt better and could move the fingers of his right hand. The following year more than five thousand pilgrims in seventeen buses and hundreds of cars participated in a novena that had a theme of peace. This number seems to have been sustained during and immediately after World War II. By the 1960s, however, the numbers had dropped to about fifteen hundred. Elsewhere in the Catholic world, a drop in the number of individuals traveling to pilgrimage sites in the 1960s has been linked to changes in the Church that resulted from Vatican II. However, by the 1970s and 1980s, these numbers had risen again.[21]

Celebrating the Feast of Ste. Anne in the 1980s

An article on the front page of the July 11, 1985, *St. Anne Record* announces that the 105th novena in honor of Ste. Anne was scheduled to begin on Thursday, the eighteenth of July and continue until the twenty-sixth. On each day of the novena, there would be both morning and evening prayers with sermons delivered by a missionary priest. On the feast day, Mass would be held at 7, 8, 9, 10, and 11:30 A.M., the last an outdoor Mass. A prayer service of healing and for the sacramental anointing of the sick would occur at 1 P.M., and a High Mass at 2 P.M. would be followed by the procession, "rain or shine." This last phrase was a reference to the fact that the year before, the priest, a relative newcomer to the town, had canceled the procession because of rain. He was sorely criticized, especially since the turnout had been somewhat larger than expected. This was attributed to the fact that in 1983 a television crew had arrived from Chicago to film the feast day and procession, and the priest had apparently received numerous phone calls after the show aired. This publicity and the efforts that the church itself made by circulating intention slips and fliers signed by the pastor of the shrine church stimulated interest in the event.

On the feast day in 1985, as was the custom, breakfast was served by the Holy Name Society from 8 to 10 A.M. and a $4.00 chicken dinner complete with mashed potatoes, green beans, and homemade pie was provided by the Ladies of the Sodality from 10:30 to 1:30. The dinner was served in the parish hall across the street from the church, and immediately next to it a tent had been set up for people who wanted a hot dog or some other light snack. Nearby was another tent that sheltered tables of relics and sacred objects that were for sale. One man observed that in the past, people used to buy more religious objects than they do at present and that it used to be hard to approach the tables. Across the street, adjacent to the church, was a third tent that served as shelter for the 11:30 outdoor Mass. Nearby was the fountain of holy water. Some pilgrims bought and filled bottles with this water, which they then asked one of the priests roaming through the crowd to bless. In the academy building behind this last tent, other priests were taking confession.

One man from St. Anne recalled the days when he drove cartloads of pilgrims arriving on special trains back and forth from the railway station. In 1985, however, nonlocal pilgrims arrived by bus or private automobile. Whereas in the past, pilgrims attended the entire novena, renting rooms from residents of the town, today outsiders come strictly for the feast day. In 1985, there were more women than men in the crowd that grew as the morning progressed, and older people predominated over the young. Various "ethnic Catholics"—Poles, Hispanics, Czechs—were present, many of whom had come as part of an organized excursion sponsored by their own or a local parish church in their community. A Slovak woman from Indiana reported that it was an outing for members of her parish and that this was the first year that her husband, who had recently retired, had accompanied her. They knew nothing about the history of St. Anne. An "anglo" woman from a nearby town said that she had been attending for forty-six years.

Throughout the morning, people milled around, wandered in and out of the side chapel, where the wooden and straw-seated wheelchair of Matilda Cunnea is housed, participated in Mass, purchased gladiolas local farmers brought in, or relaxed in the shade of one of the tents. The dinner was quite popular. One elderly widower from St. Anne, a Protestant, said that he came every year for the hot meal. When pressed further on the presence of non-Catholics at the feast of Ste. Anne, he commented that in the past the Catholic church used to solicit funds from everyone in the community because in some sense the saint's feast day was St. Anne's (i.e., the town's) day. They have stopped soliciting from the Protestants because the Protestants do not solicit from them for their church events. Protestants, according to this informant, never participated in the procession, and they do not today. Many used to sit out on their porches and watch it go by, for it was like a parade. Another Protestant gentleman said that he grew up on a farm and that on the feast day his father used to finish his work early so that he could bring his children to town to watch the procession. He recalled seeing people with big heads who came for the cure. Both men acknowledge that they had heard about the miracles, "but," said one, "who am I to say that they occurred or not." Another lady interjected that the miracles involved people who were not from the area—an intriguing observation to which I will return.

At about 1:30 in the afternoon on the feast day in 1985, an announcement about the special blessings for the "really sick" was made over the loudspeaker system, and people were asked to use their discretion about whether they were really sick or not. This ceremony took place in the church with people approaching the priest at the altar for his blessing. Outside the church, members of the Knights of Columbus had gathered together. They were dressed in their regalia—"to give a little show to the procession," said one. These men, who represent the leaders of the Catholic community in the region, were invited each year by the priest. In 1985 the Knight who was to march at the front in his purple cape was of Irish ancestry, and his wife was of French Canadian descent.

At 2 P.M. the procession started (figs. 6.3 and 6.4). At the head was a group of men carrying the banners of various religious associations, followed by the Ladies of the Sodality, who were joined by some visitors. Then came the Knights of Columbus, as an honor guard, followed by three priests carrying the holy sacrament under a canopy. The mass of pilgrims brought up the rear. Among them were two women in wheelchairs and a few more with walkers or canes. The people, following the lead provided by a voice over a loudspeaker, prayed the rosary and the Lord's Prayer. The procession proceeded on a route south for several blocks, east on a street that was one block north of the Presbyterian church, and eventually north and west back to the Catholic church. One old-timer of St. Anne commented that in the past the route had been longer. Another onlooker, in response to a remark that I made about so many participants, commented, "Everyone needs help once in a while."

FIGURE 6.3. Procession, feast of Ste. Anne, St. Anne, Illinois, circa 1985. *Photo by Caroline B. Brettell.*

After making this circuit around a part of the town, the pilgrims returned to the church for the benediction of the blessed sacrament. Unlike in the past when individuals were more directly engaged in this particular ritual, in 1985 pilgrims stood in the pews and followed the priest at the altar in a series of prayers. Shortly after 3 P.M. the festivities were over. Pilgrims returned to their automobiles, buses, or homes, and the celebration of the feast of Ste. Anne was laid to rest until the following year. When asked about the perpetuation of this event, one Catholic resident commented, "Why should it stop? It is tradition, and many have been healed." When pressed on the extent to which it related to the French Canadian past, he suggested that the connection was very slight.

Based on these observations of the celebration of the feast of Ste. Anne during July 1985, by all indications the ritual practice of this event has become quite standardized. Furthermore, each of the behaviors that Turner and Turner, drawing on the work of the classical scholar Jane Harrison, outline as being associated with sacred objects is present.[22] The first is that of exhibition. In St. Anne the crutches and wheelchair that are associated with the first miracle are permanently on display, and the relic of Ste. Anne continues to be the focal point of the procession and the aftermath ritual of veneration. The second is actions, or what is done. The procession is a dramatic performance for both participants and

FIGURE 6.4. Carrying religious banners, feast of Ste. Anne, St. Anne, Illinois, circa 1985. *Photo by Caroline B. Brettell.*

observers, and its route around the town has symbolic import—a point to which I return shortly. The hourly Mass, the blessing of the sick, and the veneration of the relic are part of an annual ritual routine. The third is instruction. In addition to the instruction in the Masses on the day of the feast, the novena sermons and the booklet that is available in conjunction with them also serve this purpose. All of these behaviors are essential to the successful celebration of the feast. The vociferous objections raised in 1984 after the priest canceled the procession have to be understood in this light.

Midwestern Revivalism: A Question of Historical Context

Although vague references to healing miracles were made during the decade after the first pilgrimage to St. Anne was launched, it was more than fifteen years before a major miracle was thoroughly reported. This raises the question of why the period between 1904 and 1911 or 1912 was one of heightened religious experience if miracles and the response to them are taken as a measure of that experience. Turner and Turner argue that the impact of miracles and the development of pilgrimages to miraculous places can be accelerated or retarded by the intellectual and political climate. This is precisely the approach taken by Donald Kurtz in his analysis of the events surrounding the sixteenth-century miracle of the Virgin of Guadalupe in Mexico: "The miracle of Guadalupe may be understood as an attempt to resolve fundamental contradictions in the changing society of central Mexico, contradictions between Indian society and culture and Spanish society and culture, ecclesiastic authority and civil authority, Erasmian humanism and Aristotelian teleology, paganism and Christianity, justice and injustice."[23] The tensions that Kurtz describes between the Franciscan Juan de Zumaragga and the secular clergy, on the one hand, and between Ecclesiastics and secular political officials, on the other, are similar to those described by Mart Bax in his analysis of the miracles of Medjugorie in late twentieth-century Bosnia as well as in his work on the proliferation of saintly apparitions in the Dutch Brabant during the nineteenth century.[24] In both places, he describes, religious events are the result of factionalism between order clergy and diocesan priests. More broadly, he is suggesting that such religious events and activities must be viewed in the context of competition between or among different religious regimes.

With a somewhat different focus but still one that links religion to broader ideological issues, both Thomas Kselman and Steven Avella and William A. Christian Jr. draw connections between the magnitude of Marian visions and apparitions that occurred both in Europe and America in the late 1940s and early 1950s and during the Cold War. In August 1950, about a hundred thousand Catholics gathered at a farm in Necedah, Wisconsin, not far from US Senator Joseph McCarthy's hometown of Appleton, Wisconsin, to witness a miracle associated with an apparition of the Virgin. Mary delivered warnings about the spread of communism and the need to combat the enemy within. Kselman and Avella point out that Catholics at the time felt that they were more committed to the defense of America against the communist threat than were Protestants. Kselman and Avella also note that tensions between Catholics and Protestants were particularly severe in Necedah. Local Protestants resented the influx of Catholics in the immediate post–World War II period.[25]

While a political explanation that is on the scale of the Conquest of Mexico, the ethnonationalist conflicts in the former Yugoslavia, or the Cold War is clearly not apposite to the case under analysis here, the social and religious context of late nineteenth- and early twentieth-century America should be brought to bear to understand the miracles in St. Anne, Illinois.[26] These miracles occurred in the middle of a period that has been labeled the Third Great Awakening, a period of cultural crisis and spiritual regeneration.[27] Although common throughout the nineteenth century, by the 1870s and 1880s, in association with a general rise in devotionalism, the public discussion of miraculous healing among Protestants and Catholics alike became more intense, and incidents of "faith cures" were increasingly reported.[28] By the turn of the century, revivalism was in full swing. This was era of Billy Sunday, the successor to evangelist Dwight L. Moody. Sunday, an ex–baseball player who was ordained as a Presbyterian minister in 1903, rose to popularity between 1905 and 1920. In April 1907, Sunday was in the vicinity of St. Anne, addressing a meeting in Kankakee. The importance of revivalism to the Protestants of St. Anne is evident in references in the *St. Anne Record* of March 15 and 29, 1907, to a mission in the Presbyterian Church that increased membership in various church societies: "Not to be behind in the procession in the religious sentiments that seem to be sweeping over the country . . . the Protestant ministers and all Christian people of this place are making a united and heroic campaign for Christ, the Church and the home. [This] will lead to a change in the moral and religious life of St. Anne." Such revival meetings continued into the 1910s among both the Presbyterians and the Baptists in the community. On January 18, 1917, the *St. Anne Record* claims that "there has been no religious awakening in St. Anne equal to this one in the past dozen years."

If Protestants throughout America were undergoing a process of rebirth through religion, so, too, were Catholics. The action of blessing the sick became part of myriad Catholic revivals and was the focus for renewed piety. By the end of the century, ritualism was overshadowed by evangelicalism, and miraculous healing became almost a sacramental miracle.[29] The battle for the hearts and minds of midwesterners that had characterized an earlier period of frontier history continued but on a different plane. Yet, it was a battle waged within an increasingly secular environment that influenced both Christian traditions. Indeed, it is worth noting that at precisely this time the people of St. Anne took strong positions on the national debate on temperance. These positions were often coincident with religious identification and with political party affiliation.

The headline of the April 12, 1907, *Kankakee Daily Journal* reads, "Temperance Agitation Stirs Smaller Villages." The article reports that several leading citizens in St. Anne were supporting the dry movement. On May 1 of that year, the saloons in St. Anne were closed for a year, and the town government fell short in its treasury by $1,500. The *Kankakee Daily Journal* relates, "St. Anne is dry, no saloons, no marshal, no lights, no more new sidewalks, one grocery store and one dry goods store and one drug store is all that is needed for St. Anne. Houses and stores are for sale." The *St. Anne Record* of May 13, 1907, reports that the property of Presbyterian minister Placide Boudreau was being used to sell beer: "Reverend

Boudreau will have to explain how he receives rent from property on which liquor is sold." In April of the following year, St. Anne voted to remain dry by one of the narrowest margins in the area—233 to 213. In this context of moral crisis and divisiveness, a participatory and interactive ritual or religious experience, especially among those who believed they were on the side of righteousness, is an effective mechanism of regeneration and unification. Initiation of the feast and, particularly, the healing miracles that ensued revitalized Catholicism in the community. The fact that an open-air Mass has become an integral part of the ritual celebration of the feast day is itself indicative of the perpetuation of an aspect of "revivalist" Catholicism to the present day.[30]

In short, it is within the context of these regenerative and experiential trends in both Protestantism and Catholicism that one explanation for the timing of the miracles in St. Anne and the intensification of the feast can be found. But beyond this historical explanation is the fact that in other contexts, anthropologists have recorded the effectiveness of pilgrimage and other religious festivals and movements in regenerating cultures in distress. For example, Karen Sinclair relates the way in which a pilgrimage to a particular tree imbued with the spiritual power of the ancestors has alleviated the traumatizing dislocation of the Maori, and numerous authors have written about south seas cargo cults or Native American revitalization movements that emerged in situations of intense culture contact with the "white man."[31]

Making Sense of Continuity: A Question of Meaning and Identity

Almost sixty years ago, sociologist William Lloyd Warner defined ritual as any social behavior performed for the sake of expressing a certain meaning or meanings of importance to the group concerned.[32] More recently, Richard Swiderski suggests that "the group" can itself be deconstructed and that feasts (or festivals) can have many "voices" and encompass various symbolic forms. Similarly, Alan Morinis states that a pilgrimage center can house ideals of ethnic identity, regional identity, transnational religious identity, and national identity.[33] The voices and meanings of the feast and pilgrimage of St. Anne have to be explored at two levels—meaning to the group, however it is defined and however it may change with changing historical circumstances; and meaning to the individual who participates in the feast.

At its inception, the feast of Ste. Anne was a vehicle for the expression of French Canadian immigrant identity. Ste. Anne, as the patron saint of Quebec, was a symbol for this identity, and St. Anne, Illinois, was the locus for its expression.

The pilgrimage and the feast, in other words, began in an ethnic realm. Catholicism was important but largely because it was *la foi* (the faith), a fundamental dimension of French Canadians identity. At the time of the first pilgrimage, St. Anne the town was *not* a holy site. No apparition or miracle had as yet occurred to mark the place as one of particular religious focus. Rather, it emerged out of a concerted decision on the part of a French Canadian priest, Father Achilles Bergeron, in Chicago, who believed that St. Anne, Illinois, like Ste. Anne-de-Beaupré in Quebec, should become a pilgrimage center. By contrast with Europe, where the Church hierarchy often had to be convinced about miracles and holy places, in North America ecclesiastical initiative rather than spontaneous miracles or found objects seems to have been at the origin of numerous pilgrimages.[34] Whether Father Bergeron's act of initiation was consciously political is open to debate. Its effect, however, was to reaffirm St. Anne the town as the core of the midwestern French Canadian immigrant diaspora. Indeed, some of those of the second generation who had left the mother community for places farther west, particularly Kansas, began to return "home" at the time of the feast. Feast and homecoming became conflated.[35]

Once the tradition was invented, it was perpetuated, but its survival depended on the flexibility with which various meanings could be ascribed to it and the possibility of transformation from an ethnic shrine to a shrine associated with miraculous cures. While James J. Preston views these as two distinct types of shrines associated with pilgrimage in America, clearly, the experience in St. Anne shows that one can evolve into another.[36] Indeed, there are examples elsewhere in the United States of shrines originally established as a result of devotional acts that became more sacred due to subsequent unusual events or miracles.[37]

By the time of the miracles and in light of the larger historical tensions that have just been mentioned, the Catholic dimension of the feast and pilgrimage had become firmly entrenched as a point of distinction. With a blunt reference to the schismatics of a half century earlier, Reverend E. L. Rivard, a member of the Viatorian order stationed in Bourbonnais, wrote in 1906: "As if in pious reparation for the unfortunate defection of many of the brethren, the French-Canadian Catholics of Chicago and Kankakee have for the last fifteen years made the shrine of 'la bonne Ste. Anne' [the good Ste. Anne] a rallying point, meeting there in large and enthusiastic pilgrimage every year, on the 26th of July."[38] This was an assertion of Catholic revivalism that was important in light of the events that had weakened the faith soon after the community itself was founded. But by this time Catholics of other ethnic backgrounds were journeying to St. Anne. By the 1920s this ethnic mix was particularly noticed and represents an early phase of what Will Herberg describes as the process whereby a land of immigrants became a "triple melting pot" of Protestants, Catholics, and Jews.[39] Those who were miraculously cured were generally outsiders to the community, and their names suggest that some were descendants of other ethnic Catholics. Others were of French Canadian descent, their family names often anglicized by the third generation. Although not central to the analytical approach and argument developed here, it is worth noting that as at a host of other Catholic miraculous sites, those cured at the height of the miracles of St. Anne were primarily women and children. In a discussion of Lourdes and other European miraculous sites, Barbara Pope has suggested that "Catholics who believed in apparitions and miracles could accept the vision of the young, the poor, and the female because they contended these innocents could see what was hidden from the cynical, sophisticated, prideful materialists of the day."[40]

If Rivard's assessment, quoted above, represented a voice of confrontation between Catholicism and Protestantism, other voices referred to a coming together rather than a pulling apart. Anne the saint healed individuals; the celebration of her feast seems to have eventually healed St. Anne the town—or so some people either believed or hoped for. According to the *Kankakee Journal* of July 27, 1904, when the pilgrims arrived in the town, a procession formed for a half mile to the church, with choirs singing the litany of the bonne Ste. Anne: "It was a holiday at St. Anne and those not of the Catholic faith were in holiday attire and viewed the procession from the porches of their pretty homes." By 1910, the July 29 newspaper was writing: "It has come to be here in St. Anne that the 26th of July, commonly known as pilgrimage day, is considered by all as a holiday. All Catholics attending and taking active part in the ceremonies; all Protestants refraining from their usual vocations either in whole or in part and witnessing with devout reverence their sacred ceremonies."

To an ethnic voice and a religious voice was added a total community voice, and this is the one that has persisted into the present. A ritual of one segment of the community was transformed into a ritual for all the community, thereby transcending the contradictions and conflicts that had been forged by the Chiniquy-led schism of the 1850s. In her "Recollections of a Pioneer's Granddaughter," Pauline Chagnon, a native and resident of St. Anne and a Protestant, reminisces:

> [The Novena] was a time of great excitement for us children and I recall going with them (some Catholic relatives) to church and observing all that occurred.[41] It was also a time when people did a great deal of baking and cooking, getting

> ready to feed all these people. And before the Novena some of that congregation went through the town asking help of all the people who were there, so it was really a town project. My mother who canned every vegetable—corn, tomatoes, beans, etc., in two quart cans gave them several of those and that was the general way of doing things. And so, it was not just a Catholic occasion; it was an occasion for the whole town, and it caused a great deal of excitement and entertainment for everyone.[42]

Protestants, in short, had a role in this ritual, a role that revolved around both the provisioning and consuming of the feast-day meal. Such meals are a fundamental feature of festival.[43]

The more marginal but, nevertheless, identifiable role of the Protestants has continued into the present, making them insiders rather than outsiders. Both Protestants and Catholics participate, but the former only partake of the secular feast, while Catholics partake of both the secular and the sacred feast. The Catholic parish hall, where the secular feast is served, is, in the eyes of contemporary residents of St. Anne, the community hall. Although the route of the procession is much shorter today than it was in the past, that it continues to descend south on Letellier Street (named after the first resident pastor of the Catholic church) toward the Presbyterian Church founded by Charles Chiniquy before turning westward can itself be taken as an indication of the community-wide nature of the feast. Processions, through the spatial circuit that they cover, can mobilize a cultural community.[44] Finally, the feast of Ste. Anne has become St. Anne's day, a ritual celebration that keeps the community on the map as a place worth visiting. As indicated at the outset of this chapter, this is precisely how the town advertises itself. When Interstate 57 was built to the east, St. Anne became a detour rather than a town on the major highway south. The feast day is the one time each year when it becomes a destination for outsiders. The media attention that the town occasionally receives has served to reinforce this status as worthy destination. Certainly, the connection between religious events and tourism is one that has been explored by a number of anthropologists looking at pilgrimage centers and fiesta complexes or saint's day celebrations in local communities throughout Catholic Europe and the Americas.[45]

The community that is symbolized by the feast of Ste. Anne has changed over time. This is indicative of the flexibility of the meaning that is inherent in a ritual event of this sort. For individuals who participate in some or all aspects of the feast, meaning is equally flexible and various. Although visitors were more numerous in the past, to this day there are those who come to St. Anne because they believe in the curative powers of the saint and the protective quality of the holy water that can be bottled, blessed, and taken home. Some of these believers are evident—they are the ones in wheelchairs or with crutches or canes who join the procession. Others are less evident because the help they seek and that motivates them to attend successive nights of the novena, to partake of the Masses on the feast day, to walk in the procession, or to venerate the relic is kept private. Some of the pilgrims who come to the community on the twenty-sixth of July are devoted to Ste. Anne as a protector. For another segment of the pilgrim population, the journey to St. Anne is an excursion and a diversion, reinforcing the observed connection between pilgrimage and leisure. A third group of participants are those who view the feast day as a source of sustenance. These are the Protestants, many of them widowers, who come for the meal and the conviviality. The feast of Ste. Anne is like an outdoor picnic in the middle of summer. For a final group—the observers—the procession is a form of entertainment. They admire the lavish costumes of the Knights of Columbus, the vestments of the priests who walk under the canopy and hold the holy relic, the singing, and the prayers. The observers watch the procession as they might watch a parade on the Fourth of July or Thanksgiving weekend.

Victor Turner, in his numerous studies of ritual performances, and Raymond Firth have both argued that public rituals are frequently a key to the social structure and social process of community.[46] Such rituals "recall and present in symbolic form the underlying order that is supposed to guide members of a community in social activity."[47] Inspired by this theoretical approach, many anthropologists have analyzed pilgrimages and other public ritual and religious events as symbolic mechanism through which members of a group display and express their distinctiveness and collective identity.[48] Such events consolidate and reinforce social integration.[49] In an analysis of the Festival of Nations in Rock Creek, Montana, Frederick Errington contends that this event is a public assertion of the resolution of ethnic tensions based on a principle of neighborly relationships.[50] Through this ritual performance, the community not only gains a sense of itself but also of its position in a broader sociohistorical context. Although Errington does not invoke the term, he is suggesting that during this ritual performance, local participants achieve, or at least aspire to create, a kind of "communitas," the term that Turner formulated to describe the sense of intimacy and equality that individuals acquire when undergoing the ritual transition of pilgrimage. This sense of oneness and harmony may be short-lived, and it may deny the realities of both the past and the present, but it is a symbolic presentation of group self.

The concept of communitas has come under careful scrutiny and criticism with several scholars arguing that pilgrimages are arenas for conflict and competition rather than harmony or that "pilgrimage is too varied in content to be analyzed as if there were a single, recurrent, common, manifest factor."[51] In most cases, the emphasis is on the pilgrims themselves—that is, those who have made the sacred journey—rather than on those living or working at the pilgrimage site. Indeed, Turner himself suggests that pilgrimage creates communitas because it is a ritual that occurs away from home. One exception is the work of John Eade, but he, too, questions the relevance of a sense of oneness by describing the nationalistic lines of division among the volunteer helpers (*hospitalliers*) at the international pilgrimage shrine at Lourdes, France.[52] Rather than to reject the concept of communitas, which, after all, Turner and Turner developed as the foundation for a generalizable model of the pilgrimage experience, it would seem more appropriate to ask whether a form of communitas is part of a particular ritual experience and then to address why it is or is not present. Furthermore, following Errington and others who have addressed the meaning of festivals and feast days to local communities, we should explore the local need and desire for a public presentation and representation of harmony and integration. It is in this light that the case of St. Anne, Illinois, is instructive. A healing ritual for individuals ultimately became the healing ritual for the community. It offered a period of time-out-of-time when local residents could achieve a sense of oneness, putting aside the differences that were at the foundation of the creation of their community despite the fact that there is still difference in the roles that are played during the feast. From this perspective, and to part company with Turner, who has said that pilgrimage, as antistructure, cannot be used as a window on culture, I think we can and must *read* the feast of Ste. Anne in St. Anne, Illinois, in its historical and cultural context.

That this sense of oneness is so important to the people of St. Anne is evident in the fact that in the mid-1980s the Presbyterian minister and the Catholic priest began to celebrate ecumenical services for members of the community. They and several residents who were quite cognizant of the history of St. Anne emphasized the special significance that such services held in their community. The salience of divisions that constantly had to be healed and could be healed by a Catholic feast that has become a community festive event is also evident in the occasional newspaper reports of interfaith marriages. One such marriage was given extraordinary coverage in 1984. The bride, Judy Allain, was a Protestant, and the groom,

Ed Beaupre, a Catholic, and the wedding took place inside the Catholic church with the Presbyterian minister as co-officiator. The young people commented that they were taught not to cross religious lines. The newspaper report of this marriage goes on to note that institutions had loosened since the implementation of Vatican II. This event reinforced statements from several residents of St. Anne who knew of interfaith marriages that upset parents who sometimes refused to attend the ceremony.

Members of the community of St. Anne have their own story of the beginnings of this more forthright healing process between Catholics and Protestants, dating it to a particular incident in the 1950s. Prior to that time, the members suggest, Catholics and Protestants often passed each other in the streets and did not speak to one another. Protestants and Catholics formed separate communities. The story is told by a local barber, a Catholic: "One day the Presbyterian minister came into my shop with a long face and complained that he had to put a new floor in his church before carpeting could be laid down. It had to be done quickly because the carpeting was going to be delivered in a few days." The barber, an amateur carpenter, assembled some of his friends, all of them Catholic, and they went over to the Presbyterian church and started to work. The minister saw them there and listened to some of their conversation, which he used during his sermon the following Sunday. The result was a new attitude within the community that began to bring people together. In the 1960s the youth group of the Presbyterian church started occasional meetings with the youth group of the Catholic church. In 1976 the bicentennial booklet *The Saga of St. Anne*, produced by the community as part of the Kankakee County Bicentennial Commission Project, claimed that the project had drawn "the people of St. Anne together from all walks of life and from all religions. They learned to know and like each other much better."[53]

The early history of St. Anne, Illinois, was marked by divisiveness, and the residents of the community have struggled for more than a hundred years to wrestle with this past. Some of this wrestling took place within the realm of ritual. The overall structure of the ritual performance of Ste. Anne's feast day has changed little since the late nineteenth century, and while the attention-getting miracles are now deeply buried in historical, if not folk, memory, the feast itself continues to play an important role in the life of a community. Over time its meaning to the people of St. Anne, collectively or individually, has changed. If initially this ritual event emphasized conflict and difference, ultimately it came to emphasize unity and community identity.

Conclusion

In a *New York Times* op-ed on July 24, 2013, in the midst of the continuing national debate over immigration reform and, particularly, its emphasis on border security, Stephen Kelley, a retired American diplomat and director of the Center for Canadian Studies at Duke University, posed the question of whether a country that cannot deter foreigners from pouring across its borders is in trouble. He then turned to the case of the French Canadians who crossed the northern border of the United States in the late nineteenth and early twentieth centuries to work in the New England textile and shoe mills: "The majority of these job seekers—French-speaking, slow to assimilate, mainly Catholic—entered without visas, work permits, or passports, because during most of this period our land border with Canada was effectively wide open."[1] This writer further observes that the United States survived and absorbed this population, and that at the time, free movement across the border shared with Canada was not defined as a problem. Only in 1926 did this population have to apply for visas to move to the United States permanently; for this population, quotas did not apply just as they did not apply to Mexicans until 1965. And yet, as the introduction to this book points out, the French Canadians in New England experienced discrimination and rejection at the height of their migration just as many Mexican migrants across the country have during much of the twentieth century and into the present.

The comparison between French Canadians and Mexicans in the United States is not unique to this writer. More than forty years ago, in the context of a review of a book about Chicanos in the United States, anthropologist Renato Rosaldo reflects,

> In the late 1950s at Tucson High School, we Chicanos (for even then that is what we called ourselves) sometimes jokingly said we were French Canadians. Probably we were thinking about our language and our distant but distinctive cultural heritage; or perhaps we had in mind the fact that we had come second, and not first, like the Native Americans, and we had collided equally disastrously with the onrushing manifest destiny of capitalism and the protestant ethic.[2]

These two migration flows, one across the northern border of the United States, the other across the southern border, have much in common. As Yves Frenette, Étienne Rivard, and Marc St-Hilaire argue, "francophonie," together with anglophonie and hispanophonie, was "one of the principal elements of the cultural landscape of North America, . . . put in place by the European expansion into the New World."[3] The migrations out of Quebec during the nineteenth century were layered over a much-deeper French-speaking presence in what became the United States. Neither Chicanos nor French Canadians necessarily viewed themselves as immigrants in North America but, rather, more so as founding peoples, arriving after the populations that originally crossed the Bering Straits into the North American continent.[4]

This book has had as its focus an examination and analysis of a group of French Canadians who entered the United States earlier in the nineteenth century than the majority of those who settled in New England; a group that migrated to Illinois in the American Midwest; and a migration that was not constantly renewed and replenished over decades.[5] Further, many of the children of the settler generation—those who grew up in Illinois—picked up stakes and moved farther westward to a new frontier in the state of Kansas. Bruno Ramirez alludes to the tenuous if not ephemeral presence of French Canadians in the Midwest, even by comparison with French Canadians who moved to rural parts of Vermont and Maine at about the same time or earlier who "fundamentally transformed these regions."[6] Fewer in number, and largely self-employed or tenant farmers rather than members of a working-class population living in largely French Canadian enclaves, the French Canadians who migrated to Illinois in the 1850s were not vilified to the same extent as their compatriots in the states of the East Coast. In addition, not only had they migrated to relatively unsettled territory rather than moving in to well-established bastions of Protestantism but also a significant number of them abandoned their Catholic faith and converted to Protestantism. Their schism attracted national attention during a period when anti-Catholic sentiment in the United States was widespread and was supported by a broader national Protestant community.

There are, of course, several ways in which the experiences of those who migrated to Illinois resemble those of their compatriots who settled at a slightly later period in New England. All these migrations were characterized by kin-based links, and family ties persisted across generations, even when children and grandchildren departed for other parts of the United States. Community endogamy endured into the 1880s, and early on, practices common in Quebec, such as that of marrying the sister of one's dead wife or of two brothers marrying two sisters, could be found in the settler population. Many of those who came to Illinois, like those who migrated to Michigan, were step migrants moving out to the Midwest from a first stop somewhere on the East Coast of the United States. Certainly, the French language was important in the early decades of this settlement. Even Chiniquy preached in French in his Presbyterian church, and when the Catholic Church was revived in St. Anne in the 1870s, efforts were made to bring French-language priests to the area. This practice lasted until World War II, suggesting that at least within this segment of the community, efforts at survivance were sustained, in the pulpit if not in the parochial schools. Bringing a relic of Ste. Anne to the community of St. Anne reestablished links with Quebec, and despite the greater distance between Quebec and the American Midwest by comparison with New England, families in Illinois into the second generation retained ties with their home province although they probably traveled back with much less frequency than the French Canadians who settled in New England.

But there are many more ways in which this particular migration of French Canadians to Illinois is distinct from the better-documented nineteenth-century migrations to New England. First, and as pointed out in an earlier chapter, several French Canadian immigrant communities on the East Coast engaged in conflicts with the Irish Catholic hierarchy,[7] but rarely did these conflicts lead to schism and conversion as they did in northeast Illinois. Yves Roby, writing about the Flint Affair of 1884 in Fall River, Massachusetts, describes this event as being of "capital importance" *because until this time, conflicts with Irish priests had been of "slight import."*[8] But the Flint Affair occurred thirty years after the Chiniquy-led schism in Illinois.

The religious change caused by this schism had an important, if sometimes subtle, impact on family and community life and, undoubtedly, laid the foundation for a more outward-looking community by comparison with many of the settlements in New England. Clearly, Charles Chiniquy had a good deal of influence over his converts, at least in the early years, but having quickly severed his connections with the Catholic religious elite, he instigated a different kind of religious institutional climate from that in New England, where populations were very closely bound to the Church, considered it essential for their survival, and did not openly question its leadership.[9] Scholars have suggested that this attachment to church explains the slowness with which French Canadians in New England became involved in labor conflicts.[10] In St. Anne, Illinois, the conflict with big business, in the form of the railroad, came early, as did a host of other interpersonal disputes that marked the sometimes fractured nature of community life as well as the rapidity with which this population embraced the legal system of their country of adoption.

A second important difference is that those who settled in Illinois were able to continue their agricultural way of life, and some successfully built up substantial holdings of land. When they died, they were able to pass on real and moveable property to their children. Here they have more in common with immigrant populations of other national backgrounds (comparisons drawn in this book) and with those French Canadian communities that were established in other parts of the Midwest than with the French Canadians who settled in mill towns of the eastern United States. For example, Michael J. Guignard reports that in Biddeford, Maine, not one French Canadian in 1860 was listed as having any real estate or personal property of value, and only sixteen owned real estate or had a personal estate in 1870. In 1880 just 41 percent had personal or real estate listed. In general, these French Canadian immigrants were poor when they arrived, and they remained poor.[11] Similarly, the French Canadian working class of Holyoke, Massachusetts, developed a family economy strategy for survival based on the labor of several members, including children.[12] By 1900 only a handful had moved into the textile overseer role.

Despite the bad harvest years that Chiniquy capitalized on in his efforts to attract the sympathy (and donations) of the larger Protestant elite, the French Canadians in Illinois, for the most part, became quickly self-sufficient. This self-sufficiency meant that they, like the French Canadians in Michigan, were better able to "integrate into their new environment—socially, politically, and economically."[13] Although the French language survived the first generation in the communities in Illinois, the local newspaper in St. Anne was an English-language newspaper from its inception, and English-language religious services were introduced much earlier than in the French Canadian communities on the East Coast. Although the first generation of French Canadians in Illinois generally intermarried with other French Canadians, these patterns of intra-ethnic marriage were weakened by the second generation. Religious endogamy came to prevail with Catholics marrying Catholics and Protestants marrying Protestants, not infrequently outside the ethnic group. Certainly, the size of families was already decreasing by the second generation, again with some differences between Catholic and Protestant populations. Although religious schools in St. Anne and in Beaverville persisted into the early twentieth century, these schools never had as tight a control over the local populations as those in the more closely knit communities in New England.[14]

So were the French Canadians who settled on the Illinois prairie more rapidly "assimilated" than their compatriots who settled in the mill towns of New England? The assimilation model has certainly provided one way to look at the process of immigrant insertion in the cities of nineteenth- and twentieth-century and now twenty-first-century America.[15] This model fell out of favor after 1960 (largely because it was understood to describe the imposition of mainstream culture on minorities rather than as an ongoing social process), to be subsumed by models of cultural pluralism, multiculturalism, and, most recently, transnationalism. Within the global economy, today's immigrants are said to be operating in social fields that transgress geographic, political, and cultural borders. They maintain their ties to their countries of origin, making "home and host society a single arena of social action."[16] Equally important in research on more contemporary immigrant populations is the argument that the current second generation, in the context of postindustrial economies, will not be as upwardly mobile or as fully incorporated as the second generations of previous waves of immigration. This has resulted in the formulation of the concept of segmented assimilation.[17] This argument, in turn, has led to a reassessment of the assimilation model itself and the thesis that the experiences of immigrants of the past may not be as different from those of the present as they "usually are made out to be."[18] Alba and Nee define (or redefine) assimilation as "the decline, and at its endpoint the disappearance, of an ethnic/racial distinction and the cultural and social differences that express it."[19] This definition, they suggest, does not assume that any group is an ethnic majority or that change occurs only for minority groups. Variations in this process, at least for contemporary immigrants, can be explained by aspects of labor-market insertion, among other things. This is instructive when comparing the French Canadians of New England with those who went to the Midwest and farther west.

It is precisely with this difference that historians of nineteenth-century rural immigrants have wrestled, that is, with the "pace and pervasiveness of the . . . assimilation process" or, conversely, with the survival of ethnic identity among agricultural populations.[20] Historians have pointed to some important variables that influence this process in the rural context. Among these are the primacy of arrival, size and population density of the group, degree of self-segregation, homogeneity (as measured by the closeness of homeland origins and by religious affiliation), and socioeconomic status of a rural immigrant settlement.[21] Kathleen Neils Conzen suggests that "where strong religious belief promoted self-segregation, a settlement could be quite small and still retain its ethnic self-definition; where the community was internally more heterogeneous or more accepting of secular values, it would require greater size or geographic isolation to preserve much cultural distinctiveness."[22]

While relatively homogenous to start with, the French Canadian communities in Illinois, and particularly in St. Anne, became, almost immediately, religiously heterogeneous (through the process of their own internal schism) and slowly more ethnically heterogeneous as settlers of other backgrounds solidified their own presence in the area. Furthermore, these communities were settled by French Canadians from a number of different areas of Quebec as well as by those who came from New England as part of a step-migration process alluded to above. In addition, plat maps from the late twentieth century demonstrate greater persistence in land ownership in the more isolated settlements of Papineau, Beaverville, and L'Érable by comparison with St. Anne. But, ultimately, these are communities characterized by both persistence and dispersal. A farm economy could not absorb offspring the way a factory economy could. Subsequent generations needed to move on, farther westward or into the city.

The problem with the concept of assimilation is that it has implied a straight-line and uniform process of change. Scholars of immigrant groups recognize that change operates at a different pace in different aspects of life. Equally, scholars have recognized that ethnic identity or group identity can be invoked, or constructed, differently in different situations and that identity is itself multifaceted and fluid such that different components of it are made salient in different social and political contexts. It is precisely this approach—how ethnic boundaries are "inscribed onto a landscape of continuous cultural transition" and result from "classificatory struggles and negotiations between actions in a social field"—that I have adopted here.[23] It has informed my discussion of the schism itself, of the disputes, large and small, that characterized the post-settlement history of St. Anne and of the reemergence of Catholicism and the development of the pilgrimage of St. Anne. Based on research in Lewiston, Maine, Mark Paul Richard makes the argument that French Canadians in that community were both loyal and French, both American and French Canadian.[24] In Illinois, the various social dramas that characterize the history of these communities indicate that identities are much more complicated than a simple dichotomy—these immigrants were variously Catholic and

Protestant, rural as opposed to urban, white and not black. Further, at no time did I discover the emergence of a truly Franco-American identity such as that which has been extensively described to characterize the identity of French Canadians who settled in New England. Writing about this identity, from the perspective of the "survivance hard-liners," Roby claims that "the ideal Franco-American was a *bilingual* Catholic-American citizen, one who had assimilated the cultures of both his native and his adopted lands. To preserve this modicum, every effort had to be made to ensure that French kept the status of sole language at church, while retaining predominance at school and for conducting various parochial activities."[25] It is hard to adapt this description to the complexities of life in St. Anne, Illinois, after the schism. There was and is in the Illinois settlements, and especially in St. Anne, a consciousness of French Canadian heritage. But it is a consciousness that is also closely allied with the memory of Charles Chiniquy as the founder of their community.

The famous British social anthropologist E. E. Evans-Pritchard once observed that "we have to distinguish the effects of an event . . . from the part played in the life of a people by the memory of an event, its representation in oral and written tradition."[26] Interesting, but perhaps not unexpected, Charles Chiniquy is both written in and written out of the history of St. Anne. In a glass case on the lawn outside the Presbyterian Church of St. Anne, a piece of stone from the original church building and a fragment from Chiniquy's own house are on display; in the foyer of the church is a bronze bust of Chiniquy. By contrast, in the souvenir-program booklet published when St. Anne celebrated its centennial in 1950, the schism is handled in two sentences on page 17: "From 1852 to 1859 was the period of religious disagreement prevailing in the colony. It is sufficient to say that Father Chiniquy was dismissed from the Catholic Church in 1856 and with him went a considerable number of the parishioners to establish a new church."[27] The centennial celebration included a pageant, opened by governor Adlai Stevenson. This pageant included a series of scenes drawn from St. Anne's history. The earliest scenes depicted an Indian village, a trading post, the arrival of Noel LeVasseur in the region, and the arrival of the Allain brothers in St. Anne. Episode 11, "Dark Days in St. Anne," refer neither to Chiniquy nor the religious rift but to the famine. And if this was the way that the community treated Chiniquy in 1950, it appears that something had changed by 1976. In the book produced to celebrate the bicentennial of the United States, Chiniquy was written back in to local history: "Though he was small of stature, his personality, devotion and influence were exceedingly 'grand.' We salute him as one of the most interesting personalities in the history of St. Anne."[28] But beneath the surface, the controversy surrounding Chiniquy and, hence, the past remains.

In the mid-1980s I delivered a keynote address in Kankakee, Illinois, at a meeting of the Illinois Center for French-Colonial Studies.[29] Among those in the audience were several residents of St. Anne, descendants of the original settlers. Also present was the minister of the Presbyterian church in St. Anne. My lecture dealt with the history of St. Anne, and as I presented my version of it, I avoided some of the more controversial aspects of Chiniquy's biography, mentioning only in passing the accusations of sexual misconduct. However, I did mention his charismatic qualities, the controversies surrounding him during his first decade in Illinois, the heated confrontation with Bishop O'Regan, the eventual schism, the conflicts within the Presbyterian church, Chiniquy's international career, and the "miracles" of St. Anne. I delivered what I thought was a fairly balanced account.

In the question-and-answer period, I was inevitably asked to elaborate on the accusations of sexual misconduct, and I responded by stating what they were and observing that it would be difficult to establish definitively their veracity or falsehood. At another point I was asked about the conversion itself. I emphasized the significance of this change given the roots of French Canadian identity in religion, language, and customs. Prodded by the questioner, a member of the Center for French-Colonial Studies (i.e., not a resident of St. Anne), I emphasized the powers of persuasion that Chiniquy must have had to convince so many to follow him into schism, thus abandoning an important part of their identity—their religion—in the process. I recall hesitating, debating with myself whether to move the discussion to another analytical level—after all, this was a general audience, not an audience of anthropologists. I forged ahead, emphasizing my interest in comparing Chiniquy to other charismatic leaders (as done here in chapter 3) who had influenced people to make dramatic changes in their lives—"like a Martin Luther," I said, making reference to a comparison that was made in Chiniquy's own lifetime, or even, I said, "like a Jim Jones." I heard the gasps from some members of the audience, and after the session was over, a few residents of St. Anne came up to challenge my comment about Jones. I tried to explain further the way in which I was drawing the comparison and thought that I had explained it well.

A few weeks later I received a letter from the minister of the First Presbyterian Church. He enclosed with his letter a newspaper article that reported on my lecture. The headline reads, "Anthropologist Sheds Light on Chiniquy," and set off in bold type in the middle of the first column was the sentence, "As a social scientist and anthropologist, Ms. Brettell says she can't help but compare this dynamic, yet powerful figure of the 1850s to the following Jim Jones had more than a century later." The minister had highlighted several sentences in the article, among them, the bold-type sentence, the phrase "accused of everything from land fraud to adultery" (I did not use the word *adultery*), the sentence "Chiniquy was a troublemaker among his superiors in the Quebec diocese" (I never used the word *troublemaker*), the phrase "often made indecent comments against women and regularly preached overly [doubly highlighted] political sermons" (in my lecture I used precisely these words, but I was quoting from a letter from Bishop Bourget), the phrase "created scandal after scandal" (I did mention several), the word *documented* with reference to the miracles of the early twentieth century (I used the words *reported* and *recorded*, the minister inserted a question mark in the margin), and the paragraph "'He really did possess some commendable traits,' she added, 'especially his desire to educate his parishioners, the majority of whom were illiterate'" (this is probably a direct quote taken from the interchange in the question-and-answer period; in the margin the minister wrote "O.K.").

Although the minister had been in the audience that night and although some items in the newspaper account came from old clippings in the *Kankakee Daily Journal* newspaper files rather than from my lecture, his letter was one of reprimand. He recognized the journalist's mistakes and some of the places where my more careful wording had been turned into historical fact. He acknowledged where "parenthetical conjectures" had been "blown out of proportion," yet he considered this unfortunate. "Presbyterians," he said, "will certainly not like the feeling that their Church here was based on the fanaticism of one who actually confused himself with God, as Jones did, and encouraged mass suicide." Using the newspaper account as his reference, he labeled my characterization of Father Chiniquy "flat and distorted." "Accusations and rumors make good press," he observed, "but they remain just that"—a point I carefully emphasized, though it was clearly not picked up by the newspaper that way. He concluded his letter,

> Certainly he was a rebel, certainly he was a charismatic personality in the sociological sense, certainly he was prone to exaggeration at times. Perhaps he sometimes was guilty of indiscretion or even scandalous behavior. But accurate history must attempt to view him as a human being and in many ways a moral and spiritual leader of his day—to see some reasons for his views and some good in his life. It seems to me unbalanced to seem to believe every charge made against him, and then to tum around and believe without questioning the "documented" healing of the relics of St. Anne.[30]

I was troubled by the letter, not only because this minister had been extremely helpful to me in my research but also because it was apparent that I had clearly offended him and other residents of St. Anne. But as I formulated my response to him, as well as a letter to the editor of the newspaper, I came to realize that the reactions are themselves part of the legacy of Chiniquy in St. Anne and that it is still difficult for people to be neutral about an incident and a man who is part of their history, to be locally constructed in a particular way. Most revealing, perhaps, are the minister's comments about the "documented" miracles as opposed to the undocumented "facts" about Chiniquy's life. The distinction is his, and it signifies that the differences that tore this community apart in the mid-nineteenth century are still there, if more subtle. The past is still present.

Chiniquy's controversial legacy is equally present in Quebec. On April 29, 1972, the French-language newspaper *La Presse* ran a story with the headline "Le Diable et le Bon Dieu" (The Devil and the Heavenly Father). The writer, Jeanne Desrochers, begins her article by remembering that when she was young, the name of Chiniquy was shrouded in mystery and that a young child who was called a "little Chiniquy" was suspected of all sorts of crimes. She relates that a man named Sam Lefebvre told her that when he was young, he only heard the name of Chiniquy referred to with respect and as a symbol of fervor and tenacious faith. Chiniquy, in Lefebvre's upbringing, was an indefatigable servant of truth, a disciple of Christ, who was persecuted and thrown in prison for his convictions. Desrochers acknowledges that she and Lefebvre were raised with different views because she was a Catholic and he was a Protestant and the grandson of an adopted daughter of Father Chiniquy.

By the end of the twentieth century, efforts of a more ecumenical assessment of Chiniquy became apparent. The Saturday, October 16, 1999, *Montreal Gazette* ran a story on page 17 by Harvey Shepherd with the headline "Warming Up to an Old Firebrand." The story reports on a conference, on the one hundredth anniversary of Chiniquy's death, focused on a "cool-headed assessment of the controversial Charles Chiniquy." Cosponsored by the Université de Québec in Montreal and the Presbyterian College (associated with McGill University), the conference was to honor Chiniquy's contributions to both Catholicism and Protestantism. While some acknowledged that there was still reluctance to talk about the man, others wholeheartedly embraced the reforms that he launched. One scholar, Richard Lougheed, a member of the faculty of French-language theological seminary in Montreal, offered the opinion that much of the literature about Chiniquy was mired in polemics. His goal was "to defuse propaganda on both sides which in his view has been too influential in shaping Quebec Catholics' views of French-speaking Protestants."[31] Also involved in the conference were members of the Catholic Christian Rite Community Church, an organization claiming direct descent from Chiniquy's Christian Catholic Church. Also of interest is Jan Noel's analysis of Bishop Bourget's efforts to keep a lid on Chiniquy's sexual misdemeanors—"the full story did not come out . . . until more than a century after his expulsion from the Montreal diocese."[32] This, too, certainly has significance for the late twentieth and twenty-first centuries and the sexual abuses that the Roman Catholic Church currently deals with.

However, despite the efforts embodied in the goals of this ecumenical conference, Chiniquy remains a symbol of powerful anti-Catholic forces in North America and, perhaps, globally given the number of entries (over sixty thousand) that reference Charles Chiniquy on the World Wide Web. This includes links to Chick Publications in Chino, California, a business founded by illustrator and fundamentalist Jack Chick. Chick has reissued Chiniquy's books in paperback editions. The publications list also includes a comic book *The Big Betrayal*, which is "based on one of the greatest Christian classics of all time, *Fifty Years in the Church of Rome*." The publishers note that they have "taken the liberty to update the conversations of the 1800's so as not to confuse the TV-oriented generation. Everything is backed up in Chiniquy's original writings." Chick Publications is responsible for other comic books that purport to tell the "true story" of the converts and for a newspaper called *Battle Cry*, which labels itself as "a Christian publication serving the Bible-believing Protestants of the World" and is full of anti-Catholic slurs.[33]

My own awareness of the existence of Chick Publications and other anti-Catholic movements in the United States was first triggered by a flier that appeared under a windshield wiper of my car in downtown Chicago in the mid-1980s. This flier, published by the Tony and Susan Alamo Christian Foundation, purportedly addresses the pope's secrets and contains a fanatical, vehement, and scurrilous denunciation of the Roman Catholic Church. In it were claims about the role of the Vatican in undermining the liberties of America and even the US Constitution. The flier quotes liberally from the writings of Chiniquy, including the accusation that it was the Jesuits, under Rome's instructions, who assassinated Lincoln. In this flier, the John F. Kennedy's assassination is blamed on Rome and the Jesuits. Indeed, the Vatican, according to this flier, is in control of the Internal Revenue Service, the United Nations, and other, political organizations.[34]

This flier was at the root of several incidents of an anti-Catholic nature that erupted in the United States at the time. In Norfolk, Virginia, statues outside

Catholic churches were defaced in 1984. Church windows in Dayton, Texas, were broken after rumors of a satanic rite spread throughout the community. Tony Alamo, a pop and country singer and former proprietor of a clothing store in Nashville, was at the time the head of a cult headquartered in Alma, Arkansas. His foundation in the 1980s reputedly had assets of roughly $25 million. In 1994 Alamo was imprisoned for tax evasion. Details of this case and other aspects of his life and beliefs can be found in multiple postings on the Internet.

While the reach of the Internet in the early twenty-first century is extensive and global, in the nineteenth century, through his publications, Chiniquy also had global impact. Chiniquy's work *The Priest, the Woman, and the Confessional* was judged at the time of its publication to be one of the most scandalous and immoral books in print, and, yet, it was translated in various languages and reprinted with great frequency. In a chapter in his book *Conflicts in French Society*, historian Theodore Zeldin discusses the confession and how people thought at the time that it compromised women and brought them to depend on priests: "The anticlericals seized on the dubious but vivid polemic of a temperance-preaching Canadian priest, defrocked for immorality, Pere Chiniquy, who denounced confession as 'the cornerstone' of [priests'] stupendous power."[35] The point, of course, is that although the medium (print or the web or Twitter) may be different, the message of distrust of Roman Catholic priests, the pope, and church hierarchy and custom has great consistency. Such is one of the legacies of Charles Chiniquy. And, yet, his actions and their reception seem more understandable in his time, in the latter nineteenth century, than the appropriations of his writings do in the latter twentieth *and* early twenty-first centuries.

Notes

Bibliography

Index

Notes

Abbreviations

AAM	Archdiocese of Montreal, Archives, Catholic Church of Montreal, Canada
AAM-CDF	Chicago Diocese file, Archives, Archdiocese of Montreal, Catholic Church of Montreal, Canada
AAM-RB	Bourget registers, Archives, Archdiocese of Montreal, Catholic Church of Montreal, Canada
ASQ	Archives de Séminaire de Quebec, Quebec City, Canada (numbers are *polygraphie* [various kinds of works] catalog numbers)
CCR	Kankakee County Circuit Clerk, records, Kankakee, Illinois
CPM	Chicago Presbytery, minutes, McCormick Theological Seminary, University of Chicago

Preface

1. See Roney (1996).

Introduction

1. Peel (1995:583).

2. Some have preferred to label the exploration of the "presence of the past" anthropological history rather than historical anthropology. See, for example, Galt (1991); Kemper (1991); Stahl (2001); see also Silverman and Gulliver (1992).

Burke outlines five features of what he calls historical anthropological work that distinguish it from social history.

> Much recent work in social history has attempted to describe general trends on the basis of quantitative evidence; but historical anthropology is deliberately qualitative and concentrates on specific cases. Many works of social history describe the lives of millions of people. Works of historical anthropology, however, are often deliberately microscopic and focus on small communities. . . . Many social historians offer causal explanations of trends over time, explanations which contemporaries would not have understood. . . . By contrast historical anthropologists concentrate on . . . "thick description," in other words the interpretation of social interaction in a given society in terms of that society's own norms and categories. . . . Social history is informed—directly or indirectly—by the theories of Karl Marx and Max Weber. Historical anthropologists tend to be interested in theory, but their "great tradition" runs from Emile Durkheim, through Arnold van Gennep on "rites of passage" and Marcel Mauss on the meaning of gifts, to contemporary figures such as Geertz, Victor Turner and Pierre Bourdieu. (1987:3)

3. Taylor (1983:6).

4. Anctil (1993:41). Anctil was writing in the early 1990s. Given the large numbers of Mexicans now in the United States, this figure of 10 percent is probably no longer accurate. But this does not diminish the point about how much less this group is considered by historians of US immigration, given its numerical size at the end of the twentieth century.

5. See Hareven (1982); Hartford (1990); M. P. Richard (2008). See also Brault (1986); Louder and Waddell (1993, 2008); Quintal (1996); Roby (2004).

6. See Chartier (1991); Frenette et al. (2012); Weil (1989); and Wien et al. (2006). Ramirez (2001) discusses emigration from French Canada to the United States in comparison to that from English Canada, focusing on 1900 to 1930.

7. According to Vicero, "about 75 percent of all French Canadians in New England were located in cities and towns of less than 50,000" (1968:295). In 1900, Fall River, Massachusetts, had 33,000 French Canadians; Lowell, Massachusetts, had 24,800; and Woonsocket, Rhode Island, 17,000. These were the three largest settlements. Vicero states that six other communities in Massachusetts and Maine had between 10,000 and 15,000; ten had between 5,000 and 8,200; and ten others between 3,000 and 4,300 (1968:295). The most rural population was located in Maine, and even there, "only about 45 percent of the first- and second-generation

labor force were reported as farm operators" in 1900 (Vicero [1968:303]; see also Sorrell [1981]). M. P. Richard observes that in 1920 people of French Canadian birth and background comprised roughly half of the residents of Biddeford, Maine (2009:286). Studies of the Franco-Americans in several of these communities are included as chapters in Quintal (1996).

8. Wright (1881:469).

9. Louder, Morissonneau, and Waddell quote the following from an 1889 *New York Times* editorial: "If these Canadians become sufficiently numerous or naturalize in numbers sufficiently large to hold the balance of power in the United States, then they will be a danger for us because they could ask for and receive legislation favorable to their own interests which are different from ours and hostile to the general interest of the country" (1993:5). Substitute the word "Mexicans," and these words would reflect sentiments that some in early twenty-first-century America still hold. See also a brief discussion of this comparison to the Chinese in Roby (2006).

10. M. P. Richard (2009:287).

11. See Abramson (1973); Bouvier (1964, 1981); Dolan (1985); French (1976); Giguère (1982); Kobrin and Goldscheider (1978); LeBlanc (1988); MacKinnon and Parent (2005); Ritter (1970); D. C. Stewart (1995); Thernstrom (1967); Warner (1963). Early, in her analysis of the autobiography of Felix Albert (1982), offers a different point of view, and in one important study of French Canadians in the Midwest, so does McQuillan (1978). See also Hartford (1990) and M. P. Richard (2008). M. P. Richard argues that French Canadians in Lewiston, Maine, chose not only to maintain their language, faith, and French Canadian customs but also to learn English, become citizens, vote, and join in labor protests, celebrate US holidays, and go to war (2008:71). This same author, in his study of the confrontation between the Ku Klux Klan and the French Canadians of Biddeford, Maine, writes expressly against accounts that have "typically portrayed French-Canadian descendants in the northeastern United States as docile or passive, as inordinately dependent upon or controlled by their religious leaders—almost as an ethnic group without agency" (2009:303). See also Roby (2004). Guignard suggests that repatriation agents were important in delaying the naturalization process and commitments to the US communities (1996b:135).

12. See E. Hughes (1943); Miner (1939). See also Louder and Waddell (1993).

13. Louder and Waddell (1983:30).See also Dolan (1985); Anctil (1993); Roby (2004); Roby and Frenette (2012).

14. Hareven 1982; Ramirez (2001:78–79).

15. Roby and Frenette (2012:123); Sorrell (1981:96).

16. I am grateful to the external reviewer of this manuscript for drawing my attention to this point and offering this particular phrasing. Of interest in this regard is Ramirez's 2001 discussion of the "rise of the border" between Canada and the United States in the early part of the twentieth century.

17. Lamarre (2003:15).

18. Wright (1882:12).

19. Parker 1983. See also La Comité Permanent de la Survivance Française en Amérique [The permanent committee of French survival in America] (1945) and Roby (2012).

20. Bouvier 1964.

21. Hartford (1990:137); LeBlanc 1988.

22. Wade 1950. See also Ducharme (1943) and Roby (2012).

23. Quoted in Vicero (1968:362).

24. Brault (1986:7).

25. Quoted in Underwood (1957:213).

26. Hamon (1891:335).

27. Roby (2004:151).

28. Susan Semenak, 1984, For Franco-Americans, It's Now or Never, *Montreal Gazette*, January 9, p. B4; Fox 1995; Roby 1996b; Roby 2004; M. P. Richard 2008.

29. Lamarre (2003:20).

30. Wade (1950:169).

31. Lamarre (2003:80).

32. Roby (2004:3).

33. Outlined in Abramson (1979:7).

34. Abramson (1979:8).

35. R. Cohen (1978:380).

36. See Banks (1996); Eriksen (2002); Faires (1981); Fenton (2003); Gleason (1983); Morowska (1990); Niehaus (1984). Some scholars have argued that these two approaches are not necessarily contradictory (Bun and Kiong 1993). Conzen et al. suggest that the conception of the ethnic group as "an unchanging, primordial solidarity" is ahistorical, but so, too, is the idea that "ethnicity can be invented out of whole cloth" (1992:17).

37. Niehaus (1984:3).

38. R. Cohen (1978:395).

39. Vincent (1974:376).

40. Zunz (1985a:85–86).

41. K. Miller (1990:98).

42. Conzen et al. (1992:17).

43. Vincent 1974; Wallman (1986:230).

44. Banks 1996; Barth 1969.

45. Mach (1993:9). See also Handler (1988); McDonald (1989).

46. Anthony Cohen (1986:1). See also Anthony Cohen (1987); Boon (1982).

47. Wimmer (2009:250). See also Okamoto (2006); Bail (2008).

48. Wimmer (2008b:970); Wimmer (2008a:1027; emphasis in original).

49. Wimmer (2007b:29–30).

50. V. Turner (1957:93).

51. St. John (2008:3).

52. V. Turner (1982:11).

53. Ibid., 64.

54. See Bynum (1992); Rosaldo (1993).

55. Some critics have suggested that Turner's model of the social drama is ahistorical and apolitical (D. Weber 1995:530). While this was certainly a criticism directed against equilibrium models and functionalist approaches that were dominant when Turner first wrote about social dramas, the approach can incorporate historical change as well as political contestation. These are both dimensions of my analysis here. For recent discussion of Turner's approach to cultural performance, in particular, see St. John (2008). For other recent applications of Turner's model of the social drama, see Cottle (2008); Forsey (2006); Fuoss (1995); Hastings (2001); and McFarland (2004). McFarland argues that social dramas are episodes that involve both structure and agency and that some "end in social reproduction while others result in more dramatic social change" (2004:1250).

56. See Potts (2009).

57. Csordas 1997.

58. M. Weber (1947:329).

59. Some theoretical disagreements about charisma derive from a tendency to emphasize one form or the other rather than to explore the interplay. Shils (1965), for example, focuses largely on routinized charisma.

60. Wallis (1982:2).

61. Berger (1963:6).

62. Tucker (1968) insists that charismatic leaders must be part of charismatic movements. Others do not see this connection as universally necessary.

63. Tucker (1968:742ff). See also Burke and Brindarhoff (1981); Lindholm (2002).

64. B. Anderson 1990.

65. See, for example, Barnes (1978); Burke (1992); Lindholm (2002); Stutje (2012a, b); Willner (1984); B. R. Wilson (1975).

66. Willner and Willner (1965:79).

67. Csordas 1997; Schweitzer (1974:153); Stutje 2012a.

68. Stutje (2012b:5).

69. Sanders (1974:182).

70. Wallis (1982b:27).

71. B. Anderson (1990:78) and Mol (1983:42).

72. B. R. Wilson (1975:9). See also Tambiah (1984).

73. Handelman (1985:349).

74. Worsley (1968:xviii, 266).

75. For theoretical discussions of structure and agency, see Giddens (1979). Stutje (2012b) also draws attention to the bias toward structural explanations in the literature on social movements. Issues of leadership and agency are hence omitted from analysis.

76. Ortner (1999:147).

1. From Curé to Colonist: Charles Chiniquy and the French Canadian Emigration to Illinois

1. Papineau remained in exile until 1845 when he was pardoned by Queen Victoria. The 1837 rebellion laid the groundwork for the eventual union of Upper and Lower Canada into the United Province of Canada in 1841.

2. See Ouellet (1980). Greer (1985) disagrees with Ouellet, arguing that economic crisis did not really emerge until the 1830s. Vicero points to the devastation of the potato blight of the early 1840s: "Whereas the potato crop had reached more than 9.9 million bushels in 1831, the effect of the blight was to reduce the harvest by over one half to slightly more than 4.4 million bushels in 1851" (1968:41). For additional discussion of the economic conditions in Quebec in the latter nineteenth century, see Roby (1996a).

3. Vicero 1968.

4. Ouellet 1980. See Greer for a discussion of the *seigneurie*, a system of land ownership established in New France, which he describes "as a species of property vested in an individual (or body), backed by the state, and subject to some government regulation that was limited in scope and only partially enforced" (1985:102).

5. Ouellet (1980:355, 353). See also Henripin (1972).

6. McQuillan 1975, 1990; Vicero 1968.

7. Greer (1985:228). Vicero argues that had Quebec developed a manufacturing industry of any significance by 1850, some of the rural distress might have been alleviated (1968:75).

8. See Roby and Frenette (2012).

9. For further discussion of this early emigration, see Vicero (1968) and Louder and Waddell (2008). See also Lavoie (1972).

10. Vicero 1968. See also Lavoie (1979).

11. Louder and Waddell 1983.

12. Quotations from a French-language newspaper or other French-language source are translated by the author. This includes the majority of the archives that were consulted in Montreal and Quebec City.

13. See Canada (1849). Hayne (1982) suggests that the negative assessment of emigration is prevalent from the 1830s on. By 1870, concern about the depopulation resulting from massive French Canadian emigration led the government of Quebec to engage in a repatriation effort. See further discussion of these dimensions of *survivance* in Roby (2012).

14. Throughout the latter nineteenth century, efforts were made to colonize the townships east of Montreal as an antidote to emigration. See further discussion in Little (2012).

15. Canada 1849.

16. See Havard and Vidal (2003); Vidal (2006, 2012). Vidal observes that in the middle of the eighteenth century, "le Pays des Illinois" area was the most populated region of New France (2012:56). The Pays des Illinois were ceded to the British in 1763, and the area east of the Mississippi River became part of a new British province of Quebec. However, the inhabitants in the area for the most part sided with the Americans during the American Revolution. Napoleon sold the area west of the Mississippi to the United States in 1803. The French language survived in the area into the twentieth century. See Ekberg (2000).

17. Further aspects of Chiniquy's biography are explored in chapter 3. See also Lougheed (2008).

18. Although Chiniquy uses the word *malentendu* (misunderstanding) to describe the breach with his uncle, Dionne's grandson Monseigneur Henri Tétu spells out the "real reason" in his *Histoire de Familles* (1898). Tétu was a prelate, and at the time he was writing, the name of Chiniquy was an anathema to the Catholic Church in Quebec. Sydney F. Smith, a Jesuit, mentions a "moral error" (1908).

19. Chiniquy (1886:335).

20. Bishop Bourget of Montreal to Chiniquy, 10-26-1848, Régistre 5, Archives of the Archdiocese of Montreal, Catholic Church of Montreal, Canada (hereafter referred to as AAM).

21. By 1848 Chiniquy's popularity was so great that a proposal was made for the erection of a metal or marble statue of him with a fountain and a tablet documenting the history of temperance in the Place d'Armes in downtown Montreal. Price (1959) cautions that Chiniquy was certainly not the only cleric of the period concerned with intemperance. On one occasion Chiniquy likened himself to Father Theobald Mathew, an Irish advocate of temperance. For detailed discussion of Chiniquy's temperance crusade set into the context of Quebec history in the mid-nineteenth century, see Noel (1990).

22. He was accused of propositioning a housekeeper while involved in a retreat. The veracity of the accusation, which Chiniquy skirts over in his autobiography, is obviously difficult to substantiate, but it is mentioned in practically every account of his life.

23. The Oblate mission was also devoted to the cause of temperance. A somewhat biased discussion of this phase of Chiniquy's life is contained in Carrière (1955). Chiniquy, of course, recounts his own version in his autobiography.

24. Noel (1990:205).

25. Trudel (1955:118). During this period, communiqués from Chiniquy addressing matters of religion and piety were printed repeatedly in the local newspapers. Beginning in June 1849, he engaged in several months of debate, in the pages of *l'Avenir*, about the relationship of a priest with his people: "The priest, is he not, like you, a child, the servant, the friend of the people. . . . If the people suffer, become poor, does not the priest immediately become a poor slave and unhappy with his people" (6-19-1849, p. 3). The continual dialogue using the print media clearly indicates that Chiniquy had already developed a liking for being at the center of controversy. For further discussion of Chiniquy's engagements with Protestantism, see Laverdure (1987).

26. Bourget to Chiniquy, Régistre 5, 3-3-1849, AAM.

27. A pregnant woman accused him of fathering her child.

28. Van de Velde to Bourget, Régistre 6, 3-4-1850, AAM. Trudel (1955) suggests that Chiniquy forged this letter. While Chiniquy clearly wanted to save his own skin, the request for French-speaking priests, as will be shown, had come from settlers in Illinois as early as 1845.

29. Noel (1990) observes that once Chiniquy was no longer in the picture, the temperance crusade collapsed, and liquor consumption began to rise.

30. C. B. Campbell 1906.

31. Bourbonnais himself may have moved west with the Pottawatomies in 1833 or 1834. LeVasseur's first wife, Watseka, also went west at that time. See C. B. Campbell (1906) for further discussion.

32. Canada (1849:76).

33. See A. Richard (1975) for a history of Bourbonnais. An early French-speaking community in Chicago in the 1830s consisted of a number of mixed bloods and their kinspeople. They went westward with the Indians in the 1840s, and a new wave of immigrants arrived and became associated with St. Mary's Catholic Church, established in 1833. As St. Mary's became Irish and English, the members built a new church for themselves. Controversy over this church erupted concurrently with the controversy in St. Anne, Illinois. The incident is covered in the next chapter.

34. Monseigneur William Quarter to Bishop Bourget, 9-8-1845, Chicago Diocese File, AAM (hereafter referred to as AAM-CDF).

35. Peter Spink to Bishop Bourget, 9-15-1845, AAM-CDF.

36. Canada 1849.

37. Tassé (1874:612).

38. Truesdell 1943.

39. Amsbary 1904.

40. Van de Velde to Bourget, 11-29-1851, AAM-CDF.

41. Canada (1849:82).

42. During the summer of 1851, a severe outbreak of cholera lasted for several years.

43. *La Minerve*, 5-13-1852.

44. Van de Velde to Bourget, 4-23-1852, AAM-CDF; *Le Moniteur Canadien*, 5-27-1852.

45. Vicero (1968:108).

46. Speculators purchased six million of the twelve million acres that the federal government sold in Illinois between 1849 and 1856 (Gates 1931a). Speculators, according to A. Bogue (1963), brought tenancy to the Midwest in the first generation although even in the early period, many were uninterested in seeing the farms worked.

47. M. B. Bogue 1959.

48. Illinois Central Railroad 1856.

49. Gates 1931b; Caird (1859:32).

50. Cole 1919.

51. Gates 1931a, 1945.

52. Ferguson (1856:378); Caird (1859:36). Caird's unremitting praise of Illinois was not well received in Canada, a country he had visited earlier and with which he drew comparisons in his book on prairie farming in America. An article in the *Chicago Press and Tribune*, November 24, 1859, cites several accusations of his "stock-jobbing"—that he was motivated to sing the praises of Illinois because he held stock in the Illinois Central Railroad. One Canadian newspaper published a pamphlet in response to his book *Caird's Slanders on Canada*. The *Tribune* article not only vouches for the honesty and objectivity of Caird but goes on to support his claims with new facts and figures. In addition, the newspaper uses the opportunity to lash back at Canada with its inhospitable climate, gravelly soil, and where "in a single year there were 770 violent deaths. . . . To the Canadians, searching for a new home, trust not to the representations of an unscrupulous press, but come and see."

53. According to the genealogy of the Allain family, two hundred individuals were in the Beaver mission by December 1, 1851, living and working parcels of land acquired from the government or speculators (Allain 1970).

54. I use St. Anne in this book to refer to the township; when reference is made to the Catholic parish, I use Ste. Anne.

55. Anonymous 1883.

56. Iroquois County Historical Society 1985.

57. Ibid.

58. Beaverville Township was organized in 1921 out of the older townships of Papineau and Beaver.

59. Iroquois County Historical Society 1985.

60. Tassé (1874:614).

2. The Social Drama of a Religious Schism

1. Reverend J. Lemaistre to Bishop Bourget of Montreal, 11-8-1853, AAM-CDF.

2. In 1859, in response to a public accusation of the deed made by an Oblate father named Augustus-Albert Brunet, Chiniquy sued for libel. Legal action dragged on until 1861. Reported extensively in the local papers, the suit for $2,500 was settled in Chiniquy's favor, but Brunet, who claimed that he had intended no malice but was simply repeating what he had heard, took the option of a seventeen-year prison term. As things turned out, a group of local French Canadians helped Brunet to escape and return to Canada.

3. *Spink v. Chiniquy* file, Herndon-Weik files. William H. Herndon was Lincoln's last law partner. See also George (1976).

4. Chiniquy's accusations against the Jesuits were taken up by anti-papist/anti-Romanist forces of the day. See Sherman (1893). George (1976) provides the best analysis of Chiniquy's relationship with Lincoln. The trial itself is well-reported in Houde and Klasey (1968) and in Sandburg (1926).

5. *Le Pays*, 10-30-1856.

6. Conflicts over trusteeship were widespread during the nineteenth century (Carey 1978; Stritch 1944). Holt describes the increasing efforts by Catholic clergy, beginning in 1852, to move for ecclesiastical ownership of church property (1973:324). In 1853 the pope sent a special nuncio to the United States to arbitrate disputes, an action that no doubt spurred the growth of anti-Catholic sentiment. Comparable conflicts to the one in St. Anne, Illinois, occurred in Buffalo, New York, and St. Louis, Missouri. Locally, there was a similar incident in Manteno, a settlement north of St. Anne. Examples of rebellion over ecclesiastical authority can also be found in the province of Quebec (Dumont and Rocher 1964; Wallot 1971).

7. Letter to editor, *L'Avenir*, 1-28-1857. I found copies of many of these items in the files of the Archives de Séminaire de Quebec (hereafter referred to as ASQ), 52-40; the numbers in ASQ cites are *polygraphie* catalog numbers. Material on this conflict is in Andreas (1884) and in broadsides Québec newspapers published. These broadsides are among the Mailloux papers at the Seminary of Quebec (ASQ). In the 1860s the French in Chicago established the church of Notre Dame at Congress and Halstead on land Bishop Duggan had given to them. Reverend Joseph Coté served the parish between 1866 and 1884. In 1866 a Society of St. Jean Baptiste was founded. In 1884 the church was moved to Vernon Park and Sibley, and a convent was built adjacent to it. St. Louis became Irish and was burned in 1871. See Paquin (1893).

8. O'Regan letter, October 1856, qtd. in "French Catholics and Bishop O'Regan," *l'Avenir*, 4-15-1857, ASQ, 52-40.

9. See Dolan (1975); Miller and Marzik (1977).

10. Herberg 1955. For a discussion of late twentieth-century ethnic nationalism in Quebec and its association with the preservation of the French language, see Handler (1988).

11. ASQ, 52-40.

12. See Doty (1985); Ducharme (1943); Guignard (1996b); Sorrell (1981).

13. See Roby (1996c).

14. Anctil (1980:208).

15. For further discussion, see Anctil (1980); Brault (1986:70ff); Guignard (1996a); Roby (1996c, 2004).

16. Dolan (1985:178–79). See also Sorrell (1981).

17. Nerée Gingras, n.d., Souvenirs de nos Missions aux Canadiens de l'Illinois de l'Abbé Nerée Gingras [Remembrances of our missions to the Canadians of Illinois of Abbé Nerée Gingras], ASQ 54-1.

18. V. Turner (1974:38).

19. ASQ 50-14a; *Journal de Québec*, 10-23-1856.

20. AAM-CDF; Registers of Bishop Bourget, Archives of the Archdiocese of Montreal, (hereafter referred to as AAM-RB), 10:3-21-1857.

21. *l'Avenir*, 10-30-1856.

22. Bishop O'Regan to Bishop Bourget, 11-4-1856, AAM-CDF.

23. Bishop Bourget to Isaac Desaulniers, 9:2-14-1857, AAM-RB.

24. Instructions from O'Regan to Desaulniers, AAM-CDF.

25. Chiniquy to O'Regan, 11-25-1856, AAM-CDF.

26. Ibid.; ASQ, 50-20d.

27. Ibid. O'Regan wanted Chiniquy to go to Cahokia, an old French Indian settlement on the southwest border of the state just south of St. Louis.

28. O'Regan to Desaulniers, 12-15-1856, AAM-CDF.

29. 10:12-20-1856, AAM-RB.

30. Joselle Michaud to Bourget, 11-30-1856, AAM-CDF.

31. V. Turner (1974:38).

32. For historical analyses of nativism and the Know-Nothing Party, see Anbinder (1992) and Knobel (1996).

33. Anbinder (1992:xiii).

34. Bourget to Isaac Desaulniers, 10:2-14-1857, AAM-RB.

35. One wonders if this is the voice of the people or whether it represents the battle between the leaders of each side, who were making every attempt to convince the reading public that they had the upper hand.

36. O'Regan to Bourget, 2-10-1857, AAM-CDF. O'Regan was referring here to a group of "Chiniquyites" of St. Anne who were organized by Chiniquy's brother Achilles and known as *Les Tondeurs* [the shearers]. A reference to this group was made by Reverend Champeau, one of Bourget's emissaries in Illinois. Organized in the fall of 1856,

> it is said that this company is composed of a dozen men determined to do anything. It seems that a member of this renowned company lost his life in a night foray; the captain of this troop follows closely the potentate of the village, listens attentively to campaign plans and replies always and to each proposition. "Do

not be in pain, Monsieur: We are good for . . ." and the following night a man is fleeced, another beaten, a house broken into, or a building burned, etc. Always the Catholics have to support this punishment. Already no fewer than twenty or twenty-five Catholic families have had to leave the place, sell their properties and seek peace far from Chiniquy. (*Courrier du Canada*, 8-17-1857)

37. The papers of Mailloux, including an almost complete pencil-written manuscript, are in the Archives of the Seminary of Quebec.

38. 10:3-21-1857, AAM-RB.

39. O'Regan to Mailloux, 6-26-1857, ASQ, 50-20.

40. O'Regan to Mailloux, 11-6-1857, ASQ, 50-2f.

41. The English word used in the *Tribune* is "parents." If the letter was in French and was translated or was submitted in a somewhat faulty translation, clearly, the French word *parents* is better translated as "kinsmen "or "relatives" in this context.

42. Smyth to Mailloux, 4-23-1858, ASQ, 50-15.

43. ASQ, 54-3b; ASQ, 50-14.

44. Mailloux to James Duggan, July 1858, ASQ, 50-11s.

45. Chiniquy (1886:790).

46. Chiniquy discusses this in *Fifty Years*. Mailloux later reported that a statue of the Virgin toppled and that the schismatics claimed it had been caused by the wind. Mailloux, who viewed this as impossible, organized a subscription in Bourbonnais to repair it. At the same time, he accused Chiniquy of using the name Christian Catholic so that he could keep the land on which the church was built. ASQ, 54-4.

47. Estimates for supporters and nonsupporters are given in the August 30, 1858, *Courrier du Canada* "Affaires Religieuses des Illinois." All five hundred families in Bourbonnais were reported as Catholics; in Kankakee, twenty-five families backed Chiniquy, and twenty-five were Catholic; in Petite Iles, of the ninety Catholic families, ten were for Chiniquy; similar proportions were true for L'Érable and Ste. Marie.

48. Turner (1974:41).

49. Cydonia to Mailloux, 7-2-1859, ASQ 50-16a; other letters, ASQ, 50-16, 50-16a, 50-16L.

50. *Quebec Mercury*, 2-19-1859.

51. Chattel Mortgages, Kankakee County, Illinois, 18-489.

52. Baird 1860.

53. Calls for greater Christian charity were part of treatises, such as Stephen Colwell's *New Themes for the Protestant Clergy*, published in 1851. Colwell attacked Philadelphians for their neglect of the poor (T. L. Smith 1980). Chiniquy's own account of his efforts during this period is described in *Forty Years in the Church of Christ*.

54. Throughout the years, these suits continued. There are twenty-one suits (excluding two where the Catholic bishop was the plaintiff) listed in the index for the circuit court of Kankakee county where Charles Chiniquy is the defendant. Although some of the dockets are missing, those available for consultation indicate that most were suits for sums of money that Chiniquy owed. One case brought to the court in 1864 was for slander.

55. These letters, which were published alternately in the *Presbyterian* and the *Catholic Herald*, appeared later in book form. See Hughes and Breckenridge (1867). Another extremely popular book, *Romanism at Home* (1847), contains letters written to the Honorable Roger B. Taney by a man who signed himself as Kirwan. Kirwan is the pseudonym used by Reverend Nicholas Murray, an Irish Catholic convert who became moderator of the Presbyterian General Assembly in 1849.

56. Billington (1954:147).

57. Ibid.

58. See Anbinder (1992) for a discussion of the politics of this period about Know-Nothingism. Focusing on a later period, Jensen (1971) clearly demonstrates the way that religion shaped both the issues and rhetoric of Midwestern politics.

59. *Kankakee County Democrat*, 12-21-1859.

60. Staples 1859.

61. Mortgages by the Presbyterian General Assembly, boxes 19-518 and 21-522, Kankakee County Clerk Office. The status of the church in St. Anne was problematic since it was first deeded in March 1852 to Bishop Jacques Olivier Van de Velde by Antoine Allain. As far as the circuit clerk of Kankakee was concerned, the Presbyterians had no guarantees since the deeds to both properties were in question (*Kankakee Gazette*, 1-5-1860). The dispute over the mortgage and deed, the issue at the root of the trusteeship battle, continued for many years. See Circuit Court Records, Kankakee County, Illinois (hereafter referred to as CCR), 62-1473, 62-1549. Finally, in May 1871 the Bishop of Chicago deeded the property to Chiniquy. In return he obtained a piece of land near the village. At some point Chiniquy turned the deed over to the French Board of Evangelization in Montreal. In 1877 the Bishop of Chicago renewed the lawsuit for the property. This suit was

settled in September 1878, and the property was transferred to the board, which in 1892 issued a quit-claim to a reunited First Presbyterian Church.

62. R. H. Anderson 1929.

63. Certainly, the court cases of the period attest to some problem and to the role of the Presbyterian Church, through Chiniquy and others, in trying to help people. In 1873 Antoine Allain brought a suit against Chiniquy and the Board of Education of the Presbyterian Church in the United States (CCR, 42-4389). Allain was claiming that he made an arrangement with Chiniquy in August 1859 to receive $235.55 with a piece of property in St. Anne Township as collateral. This agreement, he said, was made under the following statement of facts.

> At the time aforesaid and previous thereto there had been a failure of crops by reason of extreme wet weather and the complainant, in common with other people in his neighborhood, was in destitute circumstances and required means to assist him and his family to live. Your orator would further show that at this time the said Charles Chiniquy delivered lectures through the United States, England, France, and other European countries against the dangers of the Roman Catholic Church and received large sums of money therefore which . . . he used for the benefit of his colony and people who had lately left the Church of Rome. . . . That Chiniquy made one Moses Staples his agent to disburse his donations among his people and that the said Staples, under the pretense that he wished to guard against being impugned upon by unworthy persons who would make a profession of Protestantism in order to receive aid from the said Reverend Chiniquy required the beneficiaries for assistance to execute a mortgage to a so-called institution known as the Board of the Presbyterian Church of the United States, and that said Staples required your orator to execute and deliver to the so-called Board of Education a mortgage upon the premises above described to become due in five years and bearing 7 percent interest.

64. Baird 1860.

65. Staples 1859.

66. Baird 1860.

67. Reports, Chicago Presbytery, McCormick Theological Seminar, University of Chicago (hereafter referred to as CPM), 1-31-1860.

68. Simultaneously, Reverend J. B. Beaubien, a missionary in Chicago, asked to be received as a member of the Presbytery. A decision was deferred to the April session. Another French Canadian priest, Gustave Demars of Kankakee, was also examined and received in April.

69. Lottinville (1942:45).

70. The Baptist Church in St. Anne was organized in 1858 by the Baptist Home Mission Society with Auger as its pastor. Chiniquy issued a warranty deed to the First Baptist Society of St. Anne on December 10, 1860, and sold the society a town lot for one dollar. A building was erected in 1864. Mission pastors presided until 1882 when Revered Charles Chavez became the first resident minister.

Evidence among the archives of St. James Episcopal Cathedral in Chicago shows that until 1864 Episcopalians also maintained a presence in St. Anne. In his address of that year, the bishop referred to a minister sustained by the American Church Missionary Society. When this society withdrew support, the mission was abandoned. "I receive pathetic letters from these sheep without a shepherd," said the bishop, "but am without any means of supplying their need, and saving them as members of the Church. They must be scattered and the large expenditure ends in utter failure. The responsibility is not ours" (St. James Episcopal Cathedral 1864).

71. On April 7, 1860, the following was reported in the *Presbyterian*, presumably from a correspondence of Chiniquy's to a lady in Philadelphia: "This morning one of my best new converts was turned from his house and has lost his farm for the sum of $30 which he could not pay. His property was worth $300. Saturday next my neighbor who is one of our most respectable farmers will lose his property worth $1500 for the sum of $300." Reverend Baird's report of the same month cites specific sums necessary to remove all debts and relieve extreme poverty (1860). By January of the following year, however, the citizens of the town of St. Anne had taken action to send relief to people in Kansas. Eight hundred bushels of corn were immediately subscribed.

72. CPM, 10-19-1860.

73. SC 1062, Manuscript Collection, Illinois State Historical Library, Springfield, Illinois.

74. Ibid.

75. CPM, 4-10-1861.

76. CPM.

77. CPM, 4-11-1861.

78. CPM, 6-25-1861.

79. Ibid.

80. Minutes, Second Presbyterian Church of St. Anne, 5-15-1861.

81. CPM, 10-22-1861.

82. Minutes, Second Presbyterian Church of St. Anne, 11-5-1861.

83. Not much is known about Achilles Chiniquy except that he did prosper (some thought too rapidly), served in the Civil War (gaining the title of captain), held several local offices in St. Anne, had a number of children, was a notary public, and eventually reconverted and died as a Catholic. In a review of the books during the spring of 1861, no misuse of funds was uncovered.

84. CPM, 4-24-1862. The colonists themselves sent a broadside to local papers outlining their perspective. They accused Reverend Staples of a series of "dastardly deeds" connected with the misappropriation of money and clothing that was sent to relieve the colony. They claimed that he duped illiterate trustees of the First Presbyterian Church of St. Anne to sign a mortgage that was, in fact, a warranty deed. The colonists accused him of transferring notes to a Presbyterian Committee without their knowledge. The broadside, published in the May 29, 1862, *Kankakee Gazette*, was signed by a St. Anne shoemaker named Felix Masson. Opponents, of course, thought Chiniquy penned it. In a letter to the *Kankakee Gazette* published on July 3, 1862, Reverend l'Hote defended Staples's character, claiming that everyone had been in support of what Staples had done for the colony until Chiniquy's return to the United States late in 1860. L'Hote accused Chiniquy of attempting to diffuse the charges against Chiniquy's brother by displacing them on to Staples.

85. CPM, 4-24-1862.

86. Some of the disagreements about the college in St. Anne arose from a linguistic problem in the meaning of "college" in French as opposed to English. Building schools to match those built by the Catholics was an extremely important goal in the Protestant crusade to win the west. See Billington (1938). Chiniquy claimed that he had thirty-six young men studying. Others, including a number of members of the Second Presbyterian Church, the Episcopal Church, and the Baptist Church in St. Anne, begged to differ in an affidavit made in February 1862 before a justice of the peace and published in the *Kankakee Gazette* on March 6, 1862.

87. CPM, 6-18-1862.This action was well covered in the Canadian papers to demonstrate to the Catholics of that country how well their bishops had judged Chiniquy. Chiniquy claimed that his response was primarily economically motivated—that he simply could not afford to transport forty witnesses to Chicago a second time to help him in his defense. He thought that a withdrawal from the Chicago Presbytery would settle both expediently and finally what he viewed as an injustice, given his previous acquittal. Marcel Trudel (1955) argues that Chiniquy supporters were extremely embarrassed by this turn of events. It is true that R. P. Duclos (1913) makes no mention of the incident in his lengthy discussion of Chiniquy.

88. Kemp (1862:1).

89. *Presbyterian*, 3-28-1863.

90. Kemp (1863:5). In this lengthy analysis, Kemp systematically outlines all of the charges brought against Chiniquy and rather convincingly demonstrates their weaknesses and inappropriateness.

91. Ibid., 18.

92. J. B. Lemoine, Circulaire Privée aux Catholiques, Montreal, 12-27-1866, F8967c K2 L555c, Illinois State Historical Library, Springfield.

93. *Kankakee Gazette*, 11-4-1869.

94. Zeldin 1970.

95. The reference here is to Chiniquy's accusations that the Jesuits had plotted the assassination of Lincoln. In a November 10, 1885, letter to Katherine Lighthall, Chiniquy mentions that the "Roman Catholics of Chicago had destroyed the printing plates of his book *Fifty Years* just at the moment when they were beginning the second edition. . . . The Jesuits, feeling incapable of refuting it, burned it, just as their religion and their law burned heretics they could not convert" (C30/F3, Lighthall Papers). Chiniquy claimed he was ruined since he was already in debt for the publication of the first edition. In a letter three months later, he wrote of another fire set to the presses that destroyed the plates for *The Priest, the Woman, and the Confessional*, as well. The first edition of *Fifty Years in the Church of Rome* was printed by the Craig and Barkin Publishing Company in Chicago. A forty-third edition was published in 1886 by Fleming H. Ravell and Company.

Although the Lighthalls were a prominent Protestant family of Montreal, a young Anne Lighthall converted to Catholicism, and in a manuscript about her conversion, she discusses Chiniquy in very negative terms. Her family disowned her after her conversion ("Histoire de Ma Conversion," MS, Lighthall Papers).

96. J. Campbell 1898.

97. Minutes, Board of French-Canadian Evangelization, 5-4-1881, archives, Presbyterian College, McGill University, Montreal.

98. *Presbyterian Record*, 8:230.

99. Chiniquy to Margaret Lighthall, 6-20-1884, C21/F25, Lighthall Papers.

100. Father P. Beaudoin to Bishop Bouget, 10-17-1871, AAM-CDF.

101. Anonymous (1883:21).

102. The reference is to migrations to the region near Concordia, Kansas, by a significant number of the second generation. This migration is discussed in chapter 4.

103. Minutes, Second Presbyterian Church of St. Anne, 5-9-1887.

104. In 1893, Chiniquy's house burned to the ground. A library of forty-five hundred volumes was destroyed together with many personal papers. It is possible that all the records of the First Presbyterian Church between 1863 and 1887 were destroyed at this time. At the time, some church members suspected arson in what was thought by them to be a final attack on the renegade priest. Chiniquy himself referred to threatening letters.

105. A copy of this profession was sent to Archbishop Bruchesi, who, after calling it a series of insults, blasphemies, and sarcasms, returned it. He claimed he could not keep it in the archives of his household (C22/F2, Lighthall Papers). The profession is included as chapter 43 in Chiniquy's book *Forty Years in the Church of Christ.*

106. My emphasis.

107. *Presbyterian*, 9-17-1850.

108. Anbinder 1992; Levine 2001.

109. Knobel (1996:99, 109).

110. ASQ, 52-40.

111. Chiniquy to Bishop Fabre, 8-12-1894, Lighthall Papers.

112. Spink to Soeur Grise, 8-28-1856, AAM-CDF.

113. This manuscript is among the materials on Chiniquy archived at the Seminary of Quebec.

114. Godofroi Lambert, n.d., Memoire de la Vie de Mr. Chiniquy Depuis Son Arrivée dans l'État de L'Illinois Jusqu'à l'Époque [Memoire of the life of Mr. Chiniquy from his arrival in the United States to the present], ASQ 50–7a.

115. ASQ 50-7.

116. ASQ, 50-7A.

117. ASQ, 50-15b. A revealing analysis of Mailloux is in a letter of December 1858 from a man named Felix Lapointe to a Reverend Baillargeon. Lapointe suggests that the Canadian clergy were not well-inspired in their inferences. They were mistaken in the deplorable way in which they fought the battle with the immoral and dangerous weapons.

> Everyone here respects the piety of M. Mailloux, but each knows that his head and his judgment are hardly sane and one is surprised that you have left him for so long at the head of an affair of such great consequence. Did he not write that Chiniquy had only a dozen families behind him and was losing them every day? But in August Bishop Duggan was chased out of St. Anne and Mailloux told us that Chiniquy still had 250–300 families behind him. (ASQ, 50-10B)

118. See T. L. Smith 1980.

119. See Gjerde (1986); Legried and Ward (1982); Munch (1979); Swierenga (1981).

120. Gerber 1982.

121. Niebuhr 1929.

122. Mol 1983.

123. Three decades after the Chiniquy-led schism, a conflict with some similarities emerged among Polish Catholic immigrants in Detroit. There, too, a Catholic priest was at the center of a confrontation over church authority, and the key issues were control of parish assets, lay participation in governance, and the choice of personnel (Tentler 1983).

124. V. Turner 1957; Greenslade (1953:55).

125. McFarland (2004:1250).

3. Charisma, Conversion, and Narrative

1. Tétu 1898; Duclos 1913; Barrett 1958.

2. Laverdure (1987) argues that both Trudel and Sydney Smith, a Jesuit Pamphleteer in London who authored an examination of Chiniquy that was published in 1908, relied on an anonymous document written sixty years after the first Chiniquy scandal that, in turn, had drawn on Henri Tétu's notes. Tétu was the grandson of Chiniquy's uncle.

Until well into the twentieth century, Chiniquy's name was anathema in the province of Quebec (see Berton 1976). Trudel may have been influenced by this climate of opinion. A more balanced approach is found in Lougheed (2008). One should, of course, be skeptical of the verbatim conversations that Chiniquy relates throughout his two volumes—conversations that supposedly occurred thirty or more years prior to publication. These volumes are also riddled with attacks on specific practices of the Catholic Church, auricular confession and priestly celibacy, in particular. These are themes in most anti-Catholic literature. However, I agree with Barbara Welter (1987), who has argued that we should read these for the values they suggest rather than simply dispense with them as fanatical tracts.

3. Berton (1976:138–39).

4. *Presbyterian Record*, 25(2), 2-1-1899, 1.

5. L. Greenfeld (1985:122).

6. Alexander 1983.

7. J. Z. Smith (1982:112).

8. See Maynes (1992); Maynes, Pierce and Laslett (2008); Peel (1995); Sewell (1992); Steinmetz (1992).

9. D. Weber (1995:532).

10. V. Turner (1981:154).

11. Riessman 1993.

12. Peel (1995:582).

13. Ewick and Silbey (1995:198).

14. Chiniquy (1886:10–11).

15. Ibid., 11.

16. Ibid., 12, 13.

17. See Welter (1987).

18. Chiniquy (1886:82, 84).

19. Ibid., 614, 616.

20. Chiniquy (1900:190, 190, 191–92, 193).

21. Chiniquy (1886:43, 47).

22. Ibid., 319–20.

23. In the translated text from which I am drawing these excerpts, these saints are referred to as St. rather than Ste.

24. Chiniquy (1886:321–22).

25. Marcel Trudel cites this incident as one of several stories that the apostate priest was good at composing in his old age (1955:260). No one in the village where it supposedly happened knew about it, according to Trudel. It is not clear on what basis Trudel makes this claim. I take the view that the truth or falsity of this story is less important than its similarity to moments of revelation described by other spiritual leaders who went on to found new movements or to instigate dramatic change.

26. Chiniquy (1886:323).

27. See Hall (1989); Lindholm (1990).

28. Hall 1989.

29. Aberbach (1996:xiv).

30. See the discussion in Aberbach (1996).

31. Aberbach (1996:47).

32. Chiniquy (1886:279).

33. Ibid., 340, 341, 371.

34. Laverdure (1987:41).

35. Chiniquy (1886:163).

36. Laverdure (1987) suggests that this was standard anti-Catholic repertoire

and rhetoric. See, in particular, *Forty Years in the Church of Rome* (132–35), and *The Priest, the Woman, and the Confessional.*

37. Garigue (1964:130).

38. See Demers (1947).

39. Savard (1967:265).

40. Bourget was such a powerful figure in Quebec history that he even appears in the pages of the classic novel of French Canada, Hugh MacLennan's *Two Solitudes*. MacLennan's character Athanase Tallard is walking along St. James Street in Montreal toward the Basilica,

> a good street to bless, considering the number of financiers who passed to work on it, the number of prostitutes who accosted you on it, the hundreds of people, each with his own secret little sins, who walked it every day. It needed the blessing of all the saints and of Bishop Bourget besides, who stood there near the pavement, also in bronze. An iron-willed man, an ecclesiastical prince—they said he had confronted even the paper Legate with his unbreakable will. (1986[1945]:221)

41. Handelman 1985.

42. Willner (1984:14–15).

43. See Lindholm (1990).

44. G. Stewart (1974:143, 144, 145).

45. Mathias and Varesano (1978:308).

46. Ibid., 306, 307, 308, 307.

47. Chiniquy (1900:128).

48. Ibid., 129.

49. Willner (1984:154–56).

50. M. Weber (1978:1114).

51. Worsley 1968; Chiniquy (1900:126).

52. Della Cava (1970:30–31, 62, 62, 65).

53. Willner (1984:91).

54. Della Cava (1970:129).

55. M. Weber (1947:371).

56. Chiniquy (1900:190).

57. Wallis (1982a:117).

58. Mol (1983:42).

59. Hall (1989:110).

60. Johnson 1979.

61. Hall (1989:231, 232).

62. Johnson (1979:322).

63. Mol (1983:42).

64. Bailey (1988:8–9).

65. See Baer (1978); Rambo (1982); P. R. Turner (1979).

66. Burke (1992:89).

67. Peacock (1988:95).

68. Ibid., 97, 94. On narratives, see Abu-Lughod (1993); Gottschalk, Kluckhohn, and Angell (1947); Langness (1965); Ochs and Capps (1996); Watson and Watson-Franke (1985).

69. Linde 1993.

70. Ewick and Silbey (1995:200).

71. Chiniquy (1886:82, 66).

72. Ibid., 386, 387.

73. Ibid., 401, ch. 40.

74. Ibid., 450, 454.

75. Patterson and Monroe (1998:316).

76. Chiniquy (1886:818).

77. Morin (1900:3).

78. Chiniquy (1900:250).

79. Welter 1987.

80. Chiniquy (1900:179, 180).

81. Ibid., 497.

82. Mol (1983:43).

83. B. R. Wilson (1975:26–27).

84. Mol (1983:43).

85. Bailey (1988:ix).

4. From First to Second Generation: Demography, Economy, and Society of the French Canadian Immigrants, 1860–1900

1. *Boston Journal*, 5-21-1860.

2. The town of St. Mary was located in what was originally called Beaver Township. I use Beaverville instead of St. Mary or Beaver in this chapter because it conforms to US Census labels from 1860 forward.

3. Swierenga 1989.

4. Kennedy 1864; Morehouse 1928.

5. Individuals were defined as French Canadian if they were born in Canada and had a French name, if either of their parents was born in Canada, or, especially in the case of younger individuals, in the 1900 manuscripts if a linkage (made by the author) could establish French Canadian heritage. Anglicization of names was not common, but where it was found, a linkage to a previous census usually established certainty of French Canadian heritage. Some anglicizations were phonic—Larreau became Larrow—but most were literal translations. Thus, the Greenwoods were originally the Boisverts, some Hickorys previously Desnoyers, and some with the family name Roi adopted King.

6. Gjerde 1985.

7. Kamphoefner 1987; Modell 1971; Ostergren 1988; Swierenga 1985.

8. Standard methodological practices, including surname identification and the order of listing, were followed to make inferences about relationships within households. For further discussion, see Easterlin, Alter, and Condren (1978); Graham (1983); and Laslett (1975). In some frontier regions, sex ratios were quite different, indicating a different pattern of settlement. Coombs (1993) finds a high proportion of young males in the population of central Wisconsin in the 1880s. However, he notes that the Canadians (undoubtedly, both French and English) had a normal age and sex distribution, suggesting a familial migration pattern to that region as well.

9. Little 1989, 1991.

10. Information on this family also comes from obituaries for members of this family published in the *St. Anne Record.*

11. Hopkins 1975.

12. Hopkins (1975) notes a number of overlapping kinship links within the Regnier family. I address this issue more specifically later in the chapter.

13. According to the Regnier genealogy, Isaac moved to the Ghent area in Minnesota with a group of fifty Canadian farmers. They bought more than four thousand acres of railroad land and possibly nonrailroad land, as well. Regnier acquired an entire section. A Catholic parish with a French-speaking priest was already established since the area had been settled earlier by Flemish Belgians (Hopkins [1975]).

14. *St. Anne Record*, 11-23-1906, 2-24-1911.

15. In an August 9, 1856, letter to Bishop Bourget, Chiniquy claimed that ten thousand French Canadians were with him and that the largest numbers came from elsewhere in the United States, Maine, Michigan, and New York. He enlivened this particular item of correspondence with dramatic tales of endurance sustained

by families who were desperate to join him (AAM). If the figure of ten thousand is accurate, Chiniquy is more than likely including families of French Canadians in Bourbonnais and Chicago, as well as in other part of Iroquois County. However, as noted earlier, Chiniquy was prone to exaggerate his figures. That the majority came from other parts of the United States is most certainly a misrepresentation Chiniquy made, no doubt, to counter critics who accused him of stimulating new emigration from Quebec.

16. Gates 1931a.

17. M. B. Bogue 1959.

18. Twelve French Canadian households in 1860 were headed by women—half of them listed no occupation, a third described themselves as farmers, one as a teacher, and one as a laundress.

19. A. Bogue (1963:56).

20. Of course, there is always the possibility of residence in another township or county.

21. Kamphoefner 1987; Gjerde 1985.

22. D. A. McQuillan (1978:66), 1990, 1993. There was a second but less substantial migration stream to Minnesota, which is where Peter Spink went when he left Iroquois County. Departures were occasionally reported in the local newspapers. For example, the *Kankakee Gazette* of March 11, 1886, reports that Joe Brule had departed for Currie, Minnesota, to take over a blacksmith shop, and the French Canadians who went to Minnesota are described as "men of substance" who paid cash. For further discussion, see Holmquist (1981).

23. *Kankakee Gazette*, 3-25-1869.

24. M. B. Bogue (1959:173).

25. D. A. McQuillan (1975:143); (1993:125); 1990, 1993.

26. Ibid., (1993:125).

27. Gordon 1964. See also McCaa (1993); Pagnini and Morgan (1990).

28. G. A. Ross 1989; Salamon (1980:295).

29. *St. Anne Record*, 10-25-1928.

30. Piddington 1965, 1976.

31. Lamaire 1973.

32. Piddington 1965; Miner 1939.

33. Gates 1941.

34. Gross 1996.

35. Bogue 1959.

36. *Kankakee Gazette*, 8-25-1881.

37. Establishing the religious affiliation of individuals is challenging and not fully complete. It comes from a variety of parish lists and membership rolls and other references, including newspaper obituaries, county atlases, and cemetery records.

38. Guignard 1976.

39. Hartford 1990.

40. Gjerde 1985.

41. Session minutes, March 1893, First Presbyterian Church of St. Anne. Curiously, Chiniquy's rather elaborate house was burned to the ground in 1893.

42. Hareven (1980:348).

43. Winters (1990:87).

44. The optimism was premature and overblown. The wheel-and-rim factory was forced into bankruptcy in 1911 and then briefly revived the following year. In the spring of 1922, the tile plant experienced labor troubles.

45. *St. Anne Record*, 11-10-1905.

46. Ibid., 12-25-1908.

47. Ibid., 7-5-1907.

48. Conzen 1980, 1985; Gross 1996; Ostergren 1981.

49. Friedberger 1983; Salamon 1980, 1992.

50. *St. Anne Record*, 7-6-1906.

51. Conzen (1985:269).

52. Garigue (1960:195).

53. *St. Anne Record*, 2-4-1910.

54. Amsbary (1904:34).

55. Qtd. in Vicero (1968:362). Elphege Daignault, a leader among the New England Franco-Americans, wrote in 1925: "The parish is for us the supreme mechanism for religious and national preservation. The parish constitutes the economy of our resistance to Protestantism and denationalization. It is the fortress of our race" (qtd. in Anctil [1980:20]). The emphasis on remaining Catholic, combined with characteristically large families, made French Canadians (or Franco-Americans) in New England one of the prime targets for nativists of the latter nineteenth century. See Vicero (1968).

56. Bouvier 1964, 1965; Charbonneau 1979; Henripin 1957; Miner 1967; Tepperman 1974; Truesdell 1943.

57. Early 1982; Hartford 1990.

58. French 1976; Hareven and Vinovskis 1978; Wilcox and Golden 1982.

59. Bouvier 1964, 1981; Guignard 1976.

60. Hareven and Vinovskis 1978. Elsewhere, Hareven argues that such low educational and occupational aspirations among French Canadians were an intentional choice.

> The choice was not blind traditionalism, but a reflection of what they most wanted (once they had decided to remain in the United States at all) from the American economic system. . . . The immigrants accepted low-paying textile jobs with only slight opportunities for upward mobility . . . because the factory's rapid labor turnover and its willingness to hire on the recommendation of trusted employees permitted families to support a close kinship network that extended back to Quebec. (1980:352)

61. Guignard (1976:75).

62. For a counterargument about these comparisons to the Chinese, which date back to the nineteenth century, and to matters of naturalization, see Anctil (1981a, 1981b). See also M. P. Richard (2008).

63. Qtd. in Coombs (1993:275).

64. Vinovskis 1984.

65. Bouvier (1965:152).

66. Ibid., 1968.

67. Bash 1955; Blumin 1975; Fliess 1988; Guest 1982b, 1990; Stern 1983; Tolnay, Graham, and Guest 1982.

68. Yasuba 1962; Easterlin, Alter, and Condren 1978; Laidig, Schutjer, and Stokes 1981; Schapiro 1982.

69. Vinovskis (1984) offers several important criticisms of the land-availability theory as an explanation of declining fertility.

70. Marshall 1950.

71. Gadbois 1987; Gutmann 1990; Gutmann and Fliess 1993.

72. Coale and Watkins 1986.

73. Frejka and Westoff 2008; Hayford and Morgan 2008; Janssen and Houser 1981; K. McQuillan 2004; Mosher and Hendenshot 1984; Ryder and Westhoff 1971; Westoff and Jones 1979; Williams and Zimmer 1990.

74. Leasure 1982; D. S. Smith 1987.

75. Amsbary (1904:30).

76. Bill 101 declares French the official language of Quebec and has had a direct impact on education, public signage, and use of language at work and in government communications.

77. Parker 1983; Susan Semenak, 1984, For Franco-Americans, It's Now or Never, *Kankakee Gazette*, January 9: B4.

78. Parker 1983.

79. Kankakee and Iroquois Counties, Federal Manuscript Census.

80. *Kankakee Gazette*, 9-5-1872, 9-21-1876.

81. Anctil notes a similar emphasis in New England where "the professed theory of 'Qui perd sa langue, perd sa foi' (Who loses his language loses his faith) became the ideological foundation of Franco-American *survivance*." He also observes that in Quebec as well, it was as if "a linguistic barrier between their parishioners and the Protestant masses was an extra safeguard against apostacy and loose morals" (1980:176).

82. Kamphoefner 1987.

83. Chartier 1996; LeBlanc 1988; Roby 2004.

84. Christiano 1987.

85. *Kankakee Gazette*, 10-15-1868.

86. Ibid., 7-24-1869.

87. *St. Anne Record*, 1-7-1901.

88. Personal communication.

89. Cormier 1958.

90. *St. Anne Record*, 3-12-1915.

91. Gans 1997.

5. Disputes and Social Boundaries

1. Avruch defines a dispute as "the social activation, the coming-into-visibility, of a conflict. It occurs when at least one party goes public in the conflict—brings it to the attention of others in the group or community or decides to act on it" (1996:241).

2. Colson (1995:66); Merry (1990:6).

3. Merry (1990:1).

4. Nelson 1981.

5. Basch (1999:3).

6. Merry (1990:175).

7. Engel 1984.

8. Some research does suggest that local disputes were just as common in nineteenth-century European communities. See, for example, M. Silverman (1989, 1995) on Ireland in the mid-nineteenth century.

9. Salyer 1995.

10. Friedman (1985:445). See also Hicks (1949).
11. CCR, 50-3708.
12. CCR, 50-3704.
13. CCR, 204-4376.
14. CCR, 50-3697.
15. CCR, 240-5650.
16. CCR, 61-6898.
17. CCR, 53-11797.
18. CCR, 251-3596.
19. Prude 1985; Hahn 1985.
20. CCR, 7-12501.
21. CCR, 9-12608.
22. CCR, 26-7091.
23. CCR, 9-3911. Daniels, in his study of two other Illinois counties between 1870 and 1960, finds that most cases were handled by uncontested judgments for the plaintiff on the civil side and guilty pleas in criminal dockets. Sizable proportions of filings dropped out without judgment on the merits. The exceptions were when a case went to trial or hearing (1985:392).
24. CCR, 18-9437; 26-9507.
25. CCR, 18-7752.
26. CCR, 4-4744.
27. CCR, 61-7736.
28. CCR, 74-9903.
29. Engel (1984), in a study of court cases in a rural Illinois county during the late 1970s, finds that the majority of contract litigation involved debts to businesses for goods and services. Why suits for personal injury were minimal is a question that he explores.
30. CCR, 26-4391.
31. CCR, 239-10290; 239-10382.
32. CCR, 53-231; 56-A16; 51-1595.
33. CCR, 61-394.
34. CCR, 62-1082.
35. CCR, 273-976; 273-976.
36. CCR, 30-232; 7-411; 62-781.
37. CCR, 95-2143; 110-2808.
38. CCR, 57-7634.
39. CCR, 18-8793.

40. CCR, 57-8304; 26-9712.

41. CCR, 260-6799.

42. CCR, 237-23; 237-16.

43. CCR, 4-4351.

44. Conservatorship, box 12, Probate, CCR, 257-30.

45. Ibid.

46. CCR, 19-2596. In her analysis of divorce cases in Los Angeles in the late nineteenth century, May found that "most problems and the most common vile behavior cited as grounds for divorce, stemmed from drink. Furthermore, in California, habitual intemperance was also legal grounds for divorce and was common in the 1880s." (1980:30). Daniels (1985) notes that in the latter nineteenth century in two Illinois counties he studied, offenses against prevailing morals—gambling, liquor, vice—dominated the courts. These declined over time as property and public-safety offenses increased.

47. O'Neill 1967; May (1980:2).

48. Basch 1999; Phillips 1988.

49. CCR, 9-11169.

50. CCR, 9-11393; 9-12079.

51. CCR, 9-12441.

52. CCR, 30-2403.

53. CCR, 273-3690.

54. CCR, 61-4450; 61-4970.

55. CCR, 257-25.

56. CCR, 51-1799.

57. *Kankakee Gazette*, 10-21-1898.

58. Family lore, private collection. A letter in family papers of Miggie Bedard, a descendant of Virginia Chiniquy, who was descended from Charles Chiniquy's brother Achilles, says that Lizzie Marcotte, who could not speak English, discovered the bodies. She was at the home on the night of the murder although she lived as a tenant on one of Chiniquy's farms three miles northwest of town. She said when she arose at 6:30, she noticed some things awry. She went out of the house through the kitchen and noticed that the outside door, usually fastened with a butcher knife in the jamb, was open. When she returned from her outing, she knocked on the door of Mr. and Mrs. Chiniquy. When there was no answer, she called the eldest son, Duff, and they entered the room to find the bodies.

59. *Kankakee Gazette*, 10-23-1898.

60. Ibid., 10-23-1898.

61. Kankakee County Bicentennial Commission, *Saga of St. Anne.*

62. *St. Anne Record*, 8-17-1939.

63. *Kankakee Daily Journal*, 1968; 9-1969.

64. See Brodkin (1998); Guglielmo (2003); Ignatiev (1995); Jacobson (1998); and Roediger (2005) on whiteness. See McGreevy (1996) for a discussion of the how white ethnic Catholics in Chicago dealt with race issues throughout the twentieth century. He argues that Catholicism, through ethnic churches, reinforced American segregation.

65. Laurent 1959. See also Daniels (1985).

66. Daniels (1985:406).

67. Gjerde (1997:19).

68. See Mach (1993) for elaboration of this point.

69. Engel 1984.

70. Taylor 1983.

71. M. H. Ross 1993.

6. The Miracles of St. Anne: The Historical Origins and Meaning of a Religious Pilgrimage

1. Some scholars of pilgrimage have adopted an approach similar to the one used here. See McKevitt (1991) and Eade (1991). See Dubisch (1995) for a brief review of these alternative approaches.

2. V. Turner 1973; Turner and Turner 1978.

3. Father Beaudoin to Bishop Bourget, 10-17-1871, AAM-CDF.

4. Father Letellier, notations, March 1883, archives, St. Anne Parish Church.

5. Ibid.

6. Most of the contributors were pastors of varying ethnic backgrounds, including Italian, Polish, and other Canadians. In addition, a house-to-house collection in Chicago raised $3,000.

7. Achilles was given a funeral in the Catholic Church on February 9, 1882. He was sixty-seven. His wife, Luce Fraser, died on April 23, 1883, at age sixty-two.

8. The devotion to Ste. Anne is strong among Breton fishermen, and the most famous shrine is located at Auray, France. Ste. Anne is perceived as an intercessor to both Mary ("May Mary look down with tender solicitude upon him who loves and serves her mother") and Jesus ("I pray thee to present me to thy Grandson, Jesus, so that being offered by thee I may be agreeable in His sight" (Gravel 1946:15). For more general discussion of pilgrimage sites in Canada, see Rinschede (1992).

9. F. B. Thornton 1954.

10. Rinschede 1992.

11. At the same time, other relics were sent to St. John's in New York City and to Ste. Anne-de-Beaupré in Quebec.

12. P. W. Williams 1980.

13. Crutches and other religious paraphernalia and votive offerings are also housed in this side chapel.

14. Preston 1992.

15. In the *St. Anne Record* of July 27, 1906, the name is given as Lucille Shaw.

16. *St. Anne Record*, 7-27-1906.

17. Ibid., 8-2-1907.

18. Ibid., 7-30-1909, 7-29-1910, 7-28-1911, 8-2-1912.

19. Ibid., 7-13-1922, 7-23-1925, 7-12-1928, 8-2-1928, 8-1-1929.

20. Ibid., 7-27-1939.

21. Rinschede 1990, 1994; Bax 1995.

22. Turner and Turner 1982.

23. Kurtz (1982:195).

24. Bax 1983, 1985, 1990, 1991, 1995.

25. Kselman and Avella 1986; Christian 1984.

26. Although the point is debatable, the strong political implications of something like Necedah, as described by Kselman and Avella, may explain why it did not persist, just as the absence of such implications may partly explain why the feast of Ste. Anne has endured. Also the miracles at Necedah were a short-lived and mostly local or regional event, while the 1850s schism in St. Anne received widespread national attention.

27. McLoughlin 1978.

28. Dolan 1985; Mullin 1996; Taves 1986.

29. Dolan 1978.

30. Neville (1987) describes open-air preaching as an important part of America Protestant ritual, as well.

31. Sinclair 1992.

32. Warner (1957:104).

33. Swiderski 1986; Morinis (1992:5).

34. Kselman 1989.There are, however, increasing examples in late twentieth-century America of lay-initiated cults or pilgrimages based on miracles that occur, for example, with images of the saints, Christ, or the Virgin Mary. On Good Friday 1989, a crucifix suspended over the altar of Holy Trinity Croatian

Catholic Church in Ambridge, Pennsylvania, closed its eyes, and within weeks of the event, thousands of visitors visited the church (Prorock 1997). A weeping image of St. Irene at St. Irene Chrysoalantou Greek Orthodox Church in Astoria, Queens, began to draw crowds in 1990 (Mireya Navarro, 1990, Saint's Weeping Portrait Draws Many, *New York Times*, November 5).

35. Anthropologists have noted a similar process among late twentieth-century outmigrants from areas of rural Europe who time their summer holidays to coincide with the celebration of the patron saint's feast day in their native villages (Brettell 1983; Kenna 1977, 1992). Neville (1987) has argued that for Protestants, going home to one's kin in the context of a family reunion is a form of pilgrimage.

36. Preston 1990.

37. Faiers and Prorock 1990.

38. Rivard (1906:659).

39. Herberg 1955.

40. Pope (1989:31).

41. As noted in earlier chapters, families were split apart by the schism. Protestants had Catholic relatives, and vice versa. Another indication of these efforts to come together is a reference in the *St. Anne Record* for July 14, 1921. A special ceremony was held on June 30 in connection with the unveiling of a bronze bust of Chiniquy in the Presbyterian Church. According to the story in the newspaper, "Protestants and Catholics sat side by side and one was no more devout than the other to pay him every honor due. Several former pastors returned including Reverend Giroux who had been his bodyguard and who called Chiniquy 'one of the greatest, if not the greatest, religious reformers since Calvin and Luther.'"

42. Chagnon (1976:27).

43. Falassi (1987:4).

44. Van der Leeuw (1961:331).

45. See Brandes (1988); E. Cohen (1992); Crain (1997); Cruces and Diaz de Rodo (1992); Eade (1992); Jackowski and Smith (1992); Kenna (1992), Rinschede (1992); Vukonic (1992). Of course, this connection is not limited to the Catholic world. See, for example, Hudman and Jackson (1992). Nolan and Nolan (1992) outline not only a variety of motives for religious tourism but also differences among pilgrimage shrines from those that are almost strictly devotional centers, to those that combine historic, artistic, and scenic pleasures, to those where the religious festivals are a principal attraction for onlookers.

46. V. Turner 1969, 1974, 1982; Firth 1973.

47. Firth (1973:177).

48. Abner Cohen 1976; Esman 1982; J. C. Mitchell 1956.

49. Dunnigan 1981; Galt 1973; Geertz 1957; T. Mitchell 1990.

50. Errington 1987.

51. Morinis (1992:29). For debate on communitas, see Bilu (1988); Morinis (1984); Murphy (1994); Sallnow (1981, 1987). There is also debate about the concepts of antistructure and liminality (S. Greenfield 1990; D. Weber 1995).

52. Eade 1992.

53. Kankakee County Bicentennial Commission (1976:149).

Conclusion

1. Stephen R. Kelley, 2013, Bonjour, America! *New York Times*, July 24, p. A23.

2. Rosaldo (1973:1003).

3. Frenette, Rivard, and St-Hilaire (2012:1).

4. I am grateful to one anonymous reviewer of this manuscript for drawing my attention to Rosaldo's observation and urging emphasis of this broader point of comparison between French Canadians and Chicanos.

5. The significance of this process of replenishment has garnered theoretical attention recently. See Jiménez (2010).

6. Ramirez (2006:271).

7. Brault (1986:70–73); Roby 1996c.

8. Roby and Frenette (2012:123; my emphasis).

9. Lamarre (2003:160). Roby describes the relationship between the priest and his people in even stronger terms. The priest was the leader of the people,

> capable of defending the interests of their compatriots, of reclaiming their rights, of baptizing them, and of defending the institutional framework centered on the parish. As for the ordinary people, they were expected to submit gracefully to the directions of their pastors, show themselves generous in the construction of churches, send their children to French school, support the press and the mutual societies of the French Canadians. They were expected to make their homes sanctuaries for the French language, region and traditions. (2006:162)

10. Lamarre 2003.

11. Guignard 1976.

12. Hartford 1990.

13. Lamarre (2003:159).

14. LeBlanc 1988.

15. Alba and Nee 2003.

16. Margolis (1995:29). On transnationalism, see Glick Schiller, Basch, and Blanc Szanton (1992:ix). See also Basch, Glick Schiller, and Szanton Blanc (1994). Foner (1997) questions whether transnationalism is a new process.

17. Portes and Zhou 1993; Zhou 1997a, 1997b. The literature on the second generation of post-1965 immigrants has grown significantly in recent years. See, for example, Foner (2009); Kasinitz, Mollenkopf, and Waters (2004); Portes and Rumbaut (2001); Rumbaut and Portes (2001); Zhou (1997b).

18. Alba and Nee (1997:849).

19. Ibid., 863.

20. Conzen (1990:305).

21. Conzen 1990; Williams, Johnson, and Carranza 1980.

22. Conzen (1990:322).

23. Wimmer (2009:250); (2008b:970).

24. M. P. Richard 2008.

25. Roby (2004:334; original emphasis).

26. Evans-Pritchard (1963:177).

27. Souvenir Program Booklet (1950:17).

28. Kankakee County Bicentennial Commission (1976:13).

29. See Brettell (1993) for a more complete analysis of this incident. I draw from this essay in my comments here.

30. Minister to author, September 1986, author's collection.

31. See Lougheed (2008).

32. Noel (1990:206–7).

33. Chick Publications is the subject of a couple of articles in *Christianity Today* in 1981 (see Metz [1981] and Anonymous [1981]). According to Metz (1981:52), Chick Publications at the time sold Bible tract comic books in thousands of bookstores. These attack the occult, the theory of evolution, and all branches of Christianity except fundamentalism. The rabid anti-Catholicism of many of these publications led the Christian Booksellers' Group to expel the publishing house from membership.

34. Alamo 1993.

35. Zeldin (1970:17).

Bibliography

Aberbach, David. 1996. Charisma in Politics, Religion, and the Media. New York: New York University Press.

Abramson, Harold J. 1971. Ethnic Diversity within Catholicism: A Comparative Analysis of Contemporary and Historical Religion. *Journal of Social History* 4(4):359–388.

———. 1973. Ethnic Diversity in Catholic America. New York: John Wiley and Sons.

———. 1979. Migrants and Cultural Diversity: On Ethnicity and Religion in Society. *Social Compass* 26:5–29.

———. 1980. Assimilation and Pluralism Theories. *In* Stephan Thernstrom, Ann Orlov, and Oscar Handlin, eds., Harvard Encyclopedia of American Ethnic Groups. Pp. 150–160. Cambridge, MA: Harvard University Press.

Abu-Lughod, Lila. 1993. Writing Women's Worlds: Bedouin Stories. Berkeley: University of California Press.

Ahlberg, Sture. 1986. Messianic Movements: A Comparative Analysis of the Sabbatians, the People's Temple, and the Unification Church. Stockholm: Almquist and Wiskell International.

Alamo, Tony. The Pope's Secrets. 1993. Tony and Susan Alamo Christian Foundation. http://alamoministries.com/content/english/Antichrist/PopesSecrets.pdf.

Alba, Richard, and Victor Nee. 1997. Rethinking Assimilation Theory for a New Era of Immigration. *International Migration Review* 31:826–874.

———. 2003. Remaking the American Mainstream: Assimilation and Contemporary Immigration. Cambridge, MA: Harvard University Press.

Alexander, Jon. 1983. American Personal Religious Accounts, 1600–1980: Toward an Inner History of American Faith. New York: Edwin Mellen Press.

Allain, Cecil. 1970. The Allain Family Tree. TS. Kankakee County Historical Society.

Ammerman, Nancy. 1987. Schism: An Overview. *In* Mircea Eliade, ed., Encyclopedia of Religion, vol. 13. Pp. 99–102. New York: Macmillan.

Amsbary, Wallace Bruce. 1904. The Ballads of Bourbonnais. Indianapolis: Bobbs-Merrill.

Anbinder, Tyler. 1992. Nativism and Slavery: The Northern Know Nothings and the Politics of the 1850s. New York: Oxford University Press.

Anctil, Pierre. 1980. Aspects of Class Ideology in a New England Ethnic Minority: The Franco-Americans of Woonsocket, Rhode Island, 1865–1929. Ann Arbor: University Microfilms International.

———. 1981a. Chinese of the Eastern States. *Recherches Sociographiques* 22:125–131.

———. 1981b. L'Identité de l'Immigrant Québecois en Nouvelle-Angleterre: Le Rapport Wright de 1882 [The identity of the Quebec immigrant in New England: The Wright Report of 1882]. *Recherches Sociographiques* 22:331–359.

———. 1993. The Franco-Americans of New England. *In* Louder and Waddell 1993, pp. 33–52.

Anderson, Benedict. 1990. Language and Power: Exploring Political Cultures in Indonesia. Ithaca: Cornell University Press.

Anderson, Russell H. 1929. Agriculture in Illinois during the Civil War Period, 1850–1870. Unpublished dissertation, University of Illinois.

Andreas, Alfred T. 1884–1886. History of Chicago. 3 vols. Chicago: A. T. Andreas.

Anonymous. 1883. Atlas of Kankakee Co. Illinois. Chicago: J. H. Beers.

———. 1893a. Portrait and Biographical Record of Iroquois County. Chicago: Lake.

———. 1893b. Portrait and Biographical Record of Kankakee County. Chicago: Lake.

———. 1900. History of the Catholic Church in Illinois in the XIXth Century. N.p.

———. 1925. The Chinese of the Eastern States. Manchester: L'Avenir National.

———. 1981. Booksellers' Group May Expel Chick. *Christianity Today*, October 23, p. 62.

Archdeacon, Thomas. 1985. Problems and Possibilities in the Study of American Immigration and Ethnic History. *International Migration Review* 19(1):112–135.

Archdiocese of Montreal. Archives. Catholic Church of Montreal, Canada.

Archives de Séminaire de Quebec, Quebec City, Canada.

Arnot, William. 1861. The Life and Labours of the Reverend Father Chiniquy. Glasgow: Religious Tract and Book Society of Scotland.

Asad, Talal. 1986. Medieval Heresy: An Anthropological View. *Social History* 11:345–362.

Audouard, Olympe. 1869. Le Far-West. Paris: E. Dentu.

Avruch, Kevin. 1996. Conflict Resolution. *In* D. Levinson and M. Ember, eds., Encyclopedia of Cultural Anthropology, vol. 1. Pp. 241–245. American Reference. New York: Henry Holt.

Baer, Hans A. 1978. A Field Perspective on Religious Conversion: The Levites of Utah. *Review of Religious Research* 19:279–294.

Bail, Christopher. 2008. The Configuration of Symbolic Boundaries against Immigrants in Europe. *American Sociological Review* 73(1):37–59.

Bailey, F. G. 1988. Humbuggery and Manipulation: The Art of Leadership. Ithaca: Cornell University Press.

Baird, Reverend D. 1860. The French Canadian Mission in Illinois. Cincinnati: Historical and Philosophical Society of Ohio.

Banks, Marcus. 1996. Ethnicity: Anthropological Constructions. New York: Routledge.

Barnes, Douglas. 1978. Charisma and Religious Leadership: An Historical Analysis. *Journal for the Scientific Study of Religion* 17:1–18.

Barrett, John Francis. 1958. Pastor Chiniquy, Illinois Apostate. Mundelein, IL: St. Mary of the Lake Seminary.

Barth, Fredrik. 1969. Ethnic Groups and Boundaries: The Social Organization of Culture Difference. Boston: Little, Brown.

Basch, Linda, Nina Glick Schiller, and Christina Szanton Blanc. 1994. Nations Unbound: Transnational Projects, Postcolonial Predicaments and Deterritorialized National States. London: Gordon and Breach Science.

Basch, Norma. 1999. Framing American Divorce: From the Revolutionary Generation to the Victorians. Berkeley: University of California Press.

Bash, Wendall. 1955. Differential Fertility in Madison County, New York, 1865. *Milbank Memorial Fund Quarterly* 33:161–186.

Bax, Mart. 1983. "Us" Catholics and "Them" Catholics in Dutch Brabant: The Dialectics of a Religious Factional Process. *Anthropological Quarterly* 56: 167–178.

———. 1985. Popular Devotions, Power and Religious Regimes in Catholic Dutch Brabant. *Ethnology* 24:215–227.

———. 1990. The Madonna of Medjugorje: Religious Rivalry and the Formation of a Devotional Movement in Yugoslavia. *Anthropological Quarterly* 62:122–145.

———. 1991. Marian Apparitions in Medjugorje: Rivaling Religious Regimes and State Formation in Yugoslavia. *In* Eric R. Wolf, ed., Religious Regimes and State Formation: Perspectives from European Ethnology. Pp. 29–54. Albany: State University of New York Press.

———. 1995. Medjugorje: Religion, Politics and Violence in Rural Bosnia. Amsterdam: VU Uitgeverij.

Beals, Ralph. 1952. Acculturation. *In* Alfred L. Kroeber, ed., Anthropology Today. Pp. 621–641. Chicago: University of Chicago Press.

Beckwith, H. W. 1880. History of Iroquois County. Chicago: H. H. Hill.

Beecher, Lyman. 1835. A Plea for the West. Cincinnati: Truman and Smith.

Berard, Z. P. 1923. Historical Sketch of the Parish of St. Anne and Its Noted Shrine. St. Anne, IL: St Anne Record.

Berger, Robert. 1963. Charisma and Religious Innovation: The Social Location of Israelite Prophecy. *American Sociological Review* 28:940–950.

Berton, Pierre. 1976. The Zeal of Charles Chiniquy. *In* My Country: The Remarkable Past. Pp. 138–154. Toronto: McClelland and Stewart.

Billington, Raymond A. 1938. The Protestant Crusade, 1800–1860: A Study of the Origins of Nativism. New York: Macmillan.

———. 1954. The Origins of Nativism in the United States, 1800–1844. New York: Arno Press.

Bilu, Yoram. 1988. The Inner Limits of Communitas: A Covert Dimension of Pilgrimage Experience. *Ethos* 16:302–325.

Blumin, Stuart. 1975. Rip Van Winkle's Grandchildren: Family and Household in the Hudson River Valley, 1800–1850. *Journal of Urban History* 1:293–315.

Bodnar, John. 1985. The Transplanted: A History of Immigrants in Urban America. Bloomington: Indiana University Press.

Bogue, Allan. 1963. From Prairie to Corn Belt: Farming on the Illinois and Iowa Prairies in the Nineteenth Century. Chicago: University of Chicago Press.

Bogue, Mary Beattie. 1959. Patterns from the Sod: Land Use and Tenure in the Grand Prairie, 1850–1900. Springfield: Illinois State Historical Library.

Boissevain, Jeremy, ed. 1992. Revitalizing European Rituals. London: Routledge.

Boon, James A. 1982. Other Tribes, Other Scribes. Cambridge: Cambridge University Press.

Bouvier, Leon. 1964. La Stratification Sociale du Groupe Ethnique Canadien Français aux États Unis [The social stratification of the French Canadian ethnic group in the United States]. *Recherches Sociologiques* 5:371–379.

———. 1965. A Genealogical Approach to the Study of French-Canadian Fertility 1650–1950. *Sociological Analysis* 26:148–156.

———. 1968. The Spacing of Births among French-Canadian Families: An Historical Approach. *Canadian Review of Sociology and Anthropology* 5:17–26.

———. 1981. The French-Canadians of New England. *In* Joan Rollins, ed., Hidden Minorities: The Persistence of Ethnicity in American Life. Pp. 75–99. Lanham: University Press of America.

Brandes, Stanley. 1988. Power and Persuasion: Fiestas and Social Control in Rural Mexico. Philadelphia: University of Pennsylvania Press.

Brault, Gérard. 1986. The French Canadian Heritage in New England. Hanover: University Press of New England.

Breton, Raymond, and Pierre Savard. 1982. The Quebec and Acadian Diaspora in North America. Toronto: Multicultural History Society of Ontario.

Brettell, Caroline B. 1983. Emigração, a Igreja, e a Festa Religiosa do Norte de Portugal: Estudo de um Caso [Emigration, the church, and the religious festival in the north of Portugal: A Case Study]. *Estudos Contemporâneos* 5:175–204.

———. 1985. From Catholics to Presbyterians: French-Canadian Immigrants in Central Illinois. American Presbyterians. *Journal of Presbyterian History* 63:285–298.

———. 1993. Whose History Is It? Selection and Representation in the Creation of a Text. *In* Brettell, ed., When They Read What We Write: The Politics of Ethnography. Pp. 93–106. Westport: Bergin and Garvey/Greenwood.

Brodkin, Karen. 1998. How Jews Became White Folks and What That Says about Race in America. Brunswick: Rutgers University Press.

Brown, Karen McCarthy. 1991. Mama Lola: A Vodou Priestess in Brooklyn. Berkeley: University of California Press.

Bruce, Steve. 1983. Social Change and Collective Behavior: The Revival in Eighteenth Century Ross-shire. *British Journal of Sociology* 34:554–572.

———. 1986. Authority and Fission: The Protestants' Divisions. *British Journal of Sociology* 36:592–603.

Bruner, Edward. 1986. Ethnography as Narrative. *In* Victor W. Turner and Edward M. Bruner, eds., The Anthropology of Experience. Pp. 139–158. Urbana: University of Illinois Press.

Bun, Chan Kwok, and Tong Chee Kiong. 1993. Rethinking Assimilation and Ethnicity: The Chinese in Thailand. *International Migration Review* 27:140–168.

Burke, Kathryn L., and Merlin Brindarhoff. 1981. Capturing Charisma: Notes on an Elusive Concept. *Journal for the Scientific Study of Religion* 20:274–284.

Burke, Peter. 1987. The Historical Anthropology of Early Modern Europe. Cambridge: Cambridge University Press.

———. 1992. History and Social Theory. Ithaca: Cornell University Press.

Burroughs, Burt. 1923. Legends and Tales of Home on the Kankakee. Chicago: Regan.

Bynum, Caroline Walker. 1992. Women's Stories, Women's Symbols: A Critique of Victor Turner's Theory of Liminality. *In* Bynum, ed., Fragmentation and Redemption: Essays on Gender and the Human Body in Medieval Religion. Pp. 27–51. New York: Zone Books.

Cain, Maureen, and Kalman Kulcsar. 1982. Thinking Disputes: An Essay on the Origins of the Dispute Industry. *Law and Society Review* 16:375–402.

Caird, James. 1859. Prairie Farming in America. London: Longman, Brown, Green.

Campbell, Charles B. 1906. Bourbonnais; or the Early French Settlements in Kankakee County. *Transactions of the Illinois State Historical Society* 11:65–72.

Campbell, John. 1898. History of French Canadian Protestantism. *Presbyterian Record* 23(1):5–13.

Canada. 1849. Pour S'enquerir des Causes et de l'Importance de l' Émigration qui a Lieu Tous les Ans du Bas Canada Vers les États Unis [To inquire into the causes and importance of emigration that occurs every year from Lower Canada to the United States]. Montreal: Rapport du Comité Special de l'Assemblée Legislative Nommé.

Caplan, Pat. 1995. Introduction: Anthropology and the Study of Disputes. *In* Caplan, ed., Understanding Disputes: The Politics of Argument. Pp. 1–10. Oxford: Berg.

Carey, Patrick. 1978. The Laity's Understanding of the Trustee System, 1785–1855. *Catholic Historical Review* 64:357–376.

Carrière, G. 1955. Une Mission Tragique aux Illinois [A tragic mission in Illinois]. *Revue d'Histoire de l'Amérique Française* 8:518–555.

Chagnon, Pauline Elva. 1976. Recollections of a Pioneer's Granddaughter. Kankakee: Kankakee County Historical Society Bicentennial.

Charbonneau, Hubert. 1979. Les Régimes de Fécondité Naturelle en Amérique du Nord: bilan et analyses des observations [Regimes of natural fertility in North America: Assessment and analyses of observations]. *In* Henri Leridon and Jane Menken, eds., Fécondité Naturelle. Pp. 441–491. Liège: Ordina.

Chartier, Armand B. 1991. L'Histoire des Franco-Américains de la Nouvelle-Angleterre [History of the Franco-Americans of New England]. Sillery: Editions du Septentrion.

———. 1996. The Spiritual and Intellectual Foundations of the Schooling of Franco-Americans. *In* Quintal 1996, pp. 233–266.

Chiniquy, Charles. 1857. Persecution aux Illinois de l'Abbé Chiniquy [Persecution in Illinois of Father Chiniquy]. Montreal: l'Avenir.

———. 1874. The Priest, the Woman, and the Confessional. London: W. T. Gibson.

———. 1884. President's Lincoln's Assassination Traced Directly to the Doors of Rome. Cincinnati: R. W. Mercer.

———. 1886. Fifty Years in the Church of Rome. Chicago: Fleming H. Revell.

———. 1900. Forty Years in the Church of Christ. Chicago: Fleming H. Revell.

Christian, William A., Jr. 1984. Religious Apparitions and the Cold War in Southern Europe. *In* Eric R. Wolf, ed., Religion, Power and Protest in Local Communities: The Northern Shore of the Mediterranean. Pp. 239–266. New York: Mouton.

Christiano, Kevin. 1987. Religious Diversity and Social Change: American Cities 1890–1906. Cambridge: Cambridge University Press.

Coale, Ansley J., and Susan Cotts Watkins. 1986. The Decline of Fertility in Europe. Princeton: Princeton University Press.

Cohen, Abner. 1974. Introduction. *In* Cohen, ed., Urban Ethnicity. Pp. ix–xxiv. London: Tavistock.

———. 1976. Two Dimensional Man: An Essay on the Anthropology of Power and Symbolism in Complex Society. Berkeley: University of California Press.

Cohen, Anthony. 1986. Of Symbols and Boundaries, or Does Ertie's Great Coat Hold the Key? *In* Cohen, ed., Symbolizing Boundaries: Identity and Diversity in British Cultures. Pp. 1–19. Manchester: Manchester University Press.

———. 1987. Whalsay: Symbol, Segment, and Boundary in a Shetland Community. Manchester: Manchester University Press.

Cohen, Erik. 1992. Pilgrimage and Tourism: Convergence and Divergence. *In* Morinis 1992, pp. 47–61.

Cohen, Ronald. 1978. Ethnicity: Problem and Focus in Anthropology. *Annual Review of Anthropology* 7:379–403.

Cole, Arthur. 1919. The Era of the Civil War, 1848–1870. Springfield: Illinois Centennial Commission.

Colson, Elisabeth. 1995. The Contentiousness of Disputes." *In* Pat Caplan, ed., Understanding Disputes: The Politics of Argument. Pp. 65–82. Oxford: Berg.

Conzen, Kathleen Neils. 1976. Immigrant Milwaukee, 1836–1860: Accommodation and Community in a Frontier Society. Cambridge, MA: Harvard University Press.

———. 1980. Historical Approaches to the Study of Rural Ethnic Communities. *In* Luebke 1980, pp. 9–13.

———. 1985. Peasant Pioneers: Generational Succession among German Farmers in Frontier Minnesota. *In* Hahn and Prude 1985, pp. 259–292.

———. 1990. Immigrants in Nineteenth-Century Agricultural History. *In* Lou Ferleger, ed., Agriculture and National Development: Views on the Nineteenth Century. Pp. 303–342. Ames: Iowa State University Press.

Conzen, Kathleen Neils, David A. Gerber, Ewa Morawska, George E. Pozzetta, and Rudolph J. Vecoli. 1992. The Invention of Ethnicity: A Perspective from the U.S.A. *Journal of American Ethnic History* 12:3–41.

Coombs, Jan. 1993. Frontier Patterns of Marriage, Family, and Ethnicity: Central Wisconsin in the 1880s. *Journal of Family History* 18:265–282.

Cormier, Louis-Philippe. 1958. La Presse Française de l'Illinois [The French press of Illinois]. *Revue d'Histoire de l'Amérique Française* 11:361–391.

Cottle, Simon. 2008. Social Drama in a Mediatized World: The Racist Murder of Stephen Lawrence. *In* Graham St. John, ed., Victor Turner and Contemporary Cultural Performance. Pp. 109–124. New York: Bergahn Books.

Crain, Mary. 1997. The Remaking of an Andalusian Pilgrimage Tradition: Debates Regarding Visual (Re)presentation and the Meanings of "Locality" in a Global Era. *In* Akhil Gupta and James Ferguson, eds., Culture, Power, Place: Explorations in Critical Anthropology. Pp. 291–311. Durham: Duke University Press.

Cruces, Francisco, and Angel Diaz de Rodo. 1992. Public Celebrations in a Spanish Valley. Boissevain 1992, pp. 62–79. \

Csordas, Thomas J. 1997. Language, Charisma, and Creativity: The Ritual Life of a Religious Movement. Berkeley: University of California Press.

Daniels, Stephen. 1985. Continuity and Change in Patterns of Case Handling: A Case Study of Two Rural Communities. *Law and Society Review* 19:381–420.

Dawley, Alan. 1976. Class and Community: The Industrial Revolution in Lynn. Cambridge, MA: Harvard University Press.

Della Cava, Ralph. 1970. Miracle at Joaseiro. New York: Columbia University Press.

Demers, J. H. 1947. Historie de Sainte Rose. Montreal: N.p.

DeVos, George A., and Lois Romanucci-Ross, eds. 1982. Ethnic Identity: Cultural Continuities and Change. Chicago: University of Chicago Press.

Dexter, Robert. 1924. Fifty-Fifty Americans. *World's Work*, August.

Dolan, Jay. 1975. The Immigrant Church. Baltimore: Johns Hopkins University Press.

———. 1978. Catholic Revivalism: The American Experience, 1830–1900. South Bend: University of Notre Dame Press.

———. 1985. The American Catholic Experience. Garden City: Doubleday.

Doty, Stewart. 1985. The First Franco-American: New England Life Histories from the Federal Writers' Project, 1938–39. Orono: University of Maine Press.

Dubisch, Jill. 1995. In a Different Place: Pilgrimage, Gender and Politics at a Greek Island Shrine. Princeton: Princeton University Press.

Ducharme, Jacques. 1943. The Shadows of the Trees: The Story of French-Canadians in New England. New York: Harper.

Duclos, R. P. 1913. Histoire du Protestantisme Français au Canada et aux États Unis [History of French Protestantism in Canada and the United States]. Montréal: Librarie Évangelique.

Dumont, Fernand, and Guy Rocher. 1964. An Introduction to the Sociology of French Canada. *In* Marcel Rioux and Yves Martin, eds., French Canadian Society. Pp. 178–200. Toronto: McClelland and Stewart.

Dunnigan, Timothy. 1981. Ritual and Interethnic Competition: Indito versus Blanco in Mountain Pima Easter Ceremonies. *In* Gilbert Kushner, ed., Persistent Peoples: Cultural Enclaves in Perspective. Pp. 132–150. Tucson: University of Arizona Press.

Eade, John. 1991. Order and Power at Lourdes: Lay Helpers and the Organization of a Pilgrimage Shrine. *In* Eade and Sallnow 1991, pp. 51–76.

———. 1992. Pilgrimage and Tourism at Lourdes, France. *Annals of Tourism Research* 19:18–32.

Eade, John, and Michael J. Sallnow, eds. 1991. Contesting the Sacred: The Anthropology of Christian Pilgrimage. London: Routledge.

Early, Frances. 1982. The Rise and Fall of Felix Albert: Some Reflections on the Aspirations of Habitants Immigrants to Lowell, Massachusetts, in the Late Nineteenth-Century. *In* Breton and Savard 1982, pp. 25–38.

Easterlin, Richard, George Alter, and Gretchen Condren. 1978. Farm and Farm Families in Old and New Areas: The Northern States in 1860. *In* Tamara Hareven and Maris Vinovskis, eds., Family and Population in Nineteenth Century America. Pp. 22–84. New York: Academic Press.

Eatwell, Roger. 2006. The Concept and Theory of Charismatic Leadership. *Totalitarian Movements and Political Religions* 7:141–156.

Ekberg, Carol J. 2000. French Roots in the Illinois Country: The Mississippi Frontier in Colonial Times. Urbana: University of Illinois Press.

Engel, David. 1984. The Oven Bird's Song: Insiders, Outsiders, and Personal Injuries in an American Community. *Law and Society Review* 18:551–582.

Eriksen, Thomas Hyland. 1991. The Cultural Contexts of Ethnic Differences. *Man* 26:127–144.

———. 2002. Ethnicity and Nationalism: Anthropological Perspectives. 2nd edition. London: Pluto Press.

Errington, Frederick. 1987. Reflexivity Deflected: The Festival of Nations as an American Cultural Performance. *American Ethnologist* 14:654–667.

Esman, Marjorie R. 1982. Festivals, Change, and Unity: The Celebration of Ethnic Identity among Louisiana Cajuns. *Anthropological Quarterly* 54:199–210.

Evans-Pritchard, E. E. 1963. Social Anthropology and Other Essays. New York: Free Press.

Ewick, Patricia, and Susan S. Silbey. 1995. Subversive Stories and Hegemonic Tales: Toward a Sociology of Narrative. *Law and Society Review* 29:197–226.

Faiers, Gregory E., and Carolyn V. Prorok. 1990. Pilgrimage to a "National" American Shrine: "Our Lady of Consolation" in Carey, Ohio. *Geographia Religionum* 5:137–147.

Faires, Nora. 1981. Ethnicity in Evolution: The German Community in Pittsburgh and Allegheny City, Pennsylvania, 1845–1885. Ann Arbor: University Microfilms International.

Falassi, Alessandro. 1987. Festival: Definitions and Morphology. *In* Falassi, ed., Time Out of Time. Pp. 1–12. Albuquerque: University of New Mexico Press.

Fenton, Steve. 2003. Ethnicity. Cambridge: Polity Press.

Ferguson, William. 1856. America by River and Rail; or, Notes by the Way on the New World and Its People. London: Nisbet.

Firth, Raymond. 1973. Symbols: Public and Private. London: Allen and Unwin.

Fliess, Kenneth H. 1988. Fertility, Nuptiality, and Family Limitation among the Wends of Serbin, Texas, 1854–1920. *Journal of Family History* 13:251–263.

Foner, Nancy. 1997. What's New about Transnationalism? New York Immigrants Today and at the Turn of the Century. *Diaspora* 6(3):355–375.

———. 2009. Across Generations: Immigrant Families in America. New York: New York University Press.

Forsey, Martin. 2006. Producing Cosmos? The Explanatory Power of Social Drama for School Reform. *Ethnography and Education* 1:285–300.

Fox, Cynthia A. 1995. On Maintaining a Francophone Identity in Cohoes, NY. *French Review* 69:264–274.

Frejka, Thomas, and Charles Westoff. 2008. Religion, Religiousness, and Fertility in the U.S. and in Europe. *European Journal of Population* 24:5–31.

French, Laurence. 1976. The Franco-American Working Class Family. *In* Charles H. Mindel and Robert W. Habenstein, eds., Ethnic Families in America. Pp. 323–346. New York: Elsevier North-Holland.

Frenette, Yves, Étienne Rivard, and Marc St-Hilaire. 2012. La Francophonie Nord-Américaine [North American francophony]. Québec: Presses de l'Université Laval.

Friedberger, Mark. 1983. The Farm Family and the Inheritance Process: Evidence from the Corn Belt, 1870–1950. *Agricultural History* 57:1–13.

Friedman, Lawrence M. 1985. A History of American Law. 2nd edition. New York: Simon and Schuster.

Fuoss, Kirk. 1995. "Community" Contested, Imagined, and Performed: Cultural Performance, Contestation and Community in an Organized-Labor Social Drama. *Text and Performance Quarterly* 15:79–98.

Gadbois, D. 1987. Fertility in Fredericksburg. *In* Myron P. Gutmann and Ken H. Fliess, eds., Fredericksburg, Texas: Reconstructing an Historical Community. Pp. 79–92. Austin: University of Texas.

Galt, Anthony. 1973. Carnival on the Island of Pantelleria: Ritualized Community Solidarity in an Atomistic Society. *Ethnology* 12:325–340.

———. 1991. Far From the Church Bells; Settlement and Society in an Apulian Town. Cambridge: Cambridge University Press.

Gans, Herbert J. 1997. Toward a Reconciliation of "Assimilation" and "Pluralism": The Interplay of Acculturation and Ethnic Retention. *International Migration Review* 31:875–892.

Garigue, Philippe. 1960. The French Canadian Family. *In* Mason Wade, ed., Canadian Dualism. Pp. 181–200. Toronto: University of Toronto Press.

———. 1964. Change and Continuity in Rural French Canada. *In* Marcel Rioux and Yves Martin, eds., French Canadian Society. Pp. 123–177. Toronto: McClelland and Stewart.

Garraghar, Gilbert. 1921. The Catholic Church in Chicago. Chicago: Loyola University Press.

Gates, Paul. 1931a. The Disposal of the Public Domain in Illinois, 1848–1856. *Journal of Economic and Business History* 3:216–240.

———. 1931b. The Land Policy of the Illinois Central Railroad, 1851–1870. *Journal of Economic and Business History* 3:554–573.

———. 1941. Land Policy and Tenancy in the Prairie States. *Journal of Economic History* 1(1):60–82.

———. 1945. Frontier Landlords and Pioneer Tenants. Ithaca: Cornell University Press.

Geertz, Clifford. 1957. Ritual and Social Change: A Javanese Example. *American Anthropologist* 59:32–54.

George, Joseph, Jr. 1976. The Lincoln Writings of C. P. T. Chiniquy. *Journal of the Illinois State Historical Society* 69:17–34.

Gerber, David A. 1982. Modernity in the Service of Tradition: Catholic Lay Trustees at Buffalo's St. Louis Church and the Transformation of European Communal Traditions, 1829–1855. *Journal of Social History* 15:655–684.

Gerhard, Fred. Illinois as It Is. Chicago: Keen and Lee.

Giddens, Anthony. 1979. Central Problems in Social Theory: Action, Structure, and Contradiction in Social Analysis. Berkeley: University of California Press.

Giguère, Madeleine. 1982. The Franco-Americans: Occupational Profiles. *In* Breton and Savard 1982, pp. 65–76.

———. 1996. New England's Francophone Population Based upon the 1990 Census. *In* Quintal 1996, pp. 567–594.

Gjerde, Jon. 1985. From Peasants to Farmers: The Migration from Balestrand, Norway, to the Upper Midwest. Cambridge: Cambridge University Press.

———. 1986. Conflict and Community: A Case Study of the Immigrant Church in the United States. *Journal of Social History* 19:681–697.

———. 1997. The Minds of the West: Ethnocultural Evolution in the Rural Middle West, 1830–1917. Chapel Hill: University of North Carolina Press.

Gleason, Philip. 1983. Identifying Identity: A Semantic History. *Journal of American History* 69:910–931.

Glenapp, William E. 1985. Nativism and the Creation of a Republican Majority in the North before the Civil War. *Journal of American History* 72:529–559.

Glick Schiller, Nina, Linda Basch, and Christina Blanc-Szanton, eds. 1992. Towards a Transnational Perspective on Migration: Race, Class, Ethnicity, and Nationalism Reconsidered. New York: New York Academy of Science.

Gordon, Milton. 1964. Assimilation in American Life. New York: Oxford University Press.

Gottshalk, Louis, Clyde Kluckhohn, and Robert Angell. 1947. The Use of Personal Documents in History, Anthropology, and Sociology. New York: Social Science Research Council.

Graham, James Q., Jr. 1983. Family and Fertility in Rural Ohio: Wood County Ohio in 1860. *Journal of Family History* 8:262–278.

Gravel, L. P. 1946. Novena in Honor of St. Anne. New York: Sentinel Press.

Greenfeld, Liah. 1985. Reflections on Two Charismas. *British Journal of Sociology* 36:117–132.

Greenfield, Sidney. 1990. Turner and Anti-Turner in the Image of Christian Pilgrimage in Brazil. *Anthropology of Consciousness* 1:1–8.

Greenslade, S. L. 1953. Schism in the Early Church. London: SCM Press.

Greer, Allan. 1985. Peasant, Lord, and Merchant: Rural Society in Three Quebec Parishes 1740–1840. Toronto: University of Toronto Press.

Gross, Stephen John. 1996. Handing Down the Farm: Values, Strategies, and Outcomes in Inheritance Practices among Rural German Americans. *Journal of Family History* 21:192–217.

Guest, Avery M. 1982a. Own-Child Estimates of U.S. White Fertility, 1886–1899. *Historical Methods* 15:127–138.

———. 1982b. Fertility Variation among the U.S. Foreign Stock Population in 1900. *International Migration Review* 16:577–594.

———. 1990. What Can We Learn about Fertility Transitions from the New York State Census of 1865. *Journal of Family History* 15:49–69.

Guglielmo, Thomas A. 2003. White on Arrival: Italians, Race, Color and Power in Chicago, 1890–1945. Oxford: Oxford University Press.

Guignard, Michael J. 1976. Ethnic Survival in a New England Mill Town: The Franco-Americans of Biddeford, Maine. Ph.D. dissertation, Department of History, Syracuse University.

———. 1996a. The Corporation Sole Controversy. *In* Quintal 1996, pp. 195–200.

———. 1996b. The Franco-Americans of Biddeford, Maine. *In* Quintal 1996, pp. 122–144.

Gutmann, Myron P. 1990. Denomination and Fertility Decline: The Catholics and Protestants of Gillespie County, Texas. *Continuity and Change* 5:391–416.

Gutmann, Myron P., and Kenneth H. Fliess. 1993. The Determinants of Early Fertility Decline in Texas. *Demography* 30:463–457.

Hahn, Steven. 1985. The "Unmaking" of the Southern Yeomanry: The Transformation of the Georgia Upcountry, 1860–1890. *In* Hahn and Prude 1985, pp. 179–204.

Hahn, Steven, and Jonathan Prude, eds. 1985. The Countryside in the Age of Capitalist Transformation: Essays in the Social History of Rural America. Chapel Hill: University of North Carolina Press.

Hall, John R. 1989. Gone from the Promised Land: Jonestown in American Cultural History. New Brunswick: Transaction Books.

Hamon, Edmond. 1891. Les Canadiens-Français de la Nouvelle-Angleterre [The French Canadians of New England]. Québec: Hardy.

Handelman, Don. 1985. Charisma, Liminality, and Symbolic Types. *In* Eric Cohen, Moshe Lissak, and Uri Almagor, eds., Comparative Social Dynamics: Essays in Honor of S. N. Eisenstadt. Pp. 346–359. Boulder: Westview.

Handler, Richard. 1988. Nationalism and the Politics of Culture in Quebec. Madison: University of Wisconsin Press.

Handlin, Oscar. 1941. Boston Immigrants: A Study of Acculturation. Cambridge, MA: Harvard University Press.

Hareven, Tamara K. 1980. Family Patterns. *In* Stephen Thernstrom, ed., Harvard Encyclopedia of American Ethnic Groups. Pp. 345–354. Cambridge: Belknap Press.

———. 1982. Family Time and Industrial Time. Cambridge: Cambridge University Press.

Hareven, Tamara K., and Maris A. Vinovskis. 1978. Patterns of Childbearing in Late Nineteenth-Century America: The Determinants of Marital Fertility in Five Massachusetts Towns in 1880. *In* Hareven and Vinovskis, eds., Family and Population in Nineteenth-Century America. Pp. 85–125. Princeton: Princeton University Press.

Harney, Robert. 1982. Preface. *In* Breton and Savard 1982, pp. vii–xi.

Hartford, William F. 1990. Working People of Holyoke: Class and Ethnicity in a Massachusetts Mill Town, 1850–1960. New Brunswick: Rutgers University Press.

Hastings, Sally O. 2001. Social Drama as a Site for the Communal Construction and Management of Asian Indian "Stranger" Identity. *Research on Language and Social Interaction* 34:309–335.

Havard, Gilles, and Cécil Vidal. 2003. Histoire de l'Amérique Française [History of French America]. Paris: Éditions Flammarion.

Hayford, Sarah R., and S. Phillip Morgan. 2008. Religiosity and Fertility in the United States; the Role of Fertility Intentions. *Social Forces* 86:1163–1188.

Hayne, David. 1982. Emigration and Colonization: Twin Themes in Nineteenth-Century French Canadian Literature. *In* Breton and Savard 1982, pp. 11–22.

Henripin, Jacques. 1954. La Population Canadienne au Début de XVIIIe Siècle [The Canadian population at the beginning of the eighteenth century]. Paris: INED.

———. 1957. From Acceptance of Nature to Control: The Demography of French Canada since the Seventeenth Century. *Canadian Journal of Economics and Political Science* 23:10–19.

———. 1972. Trends and Factors of Fertility in Canada. Ottawa: Statistics Canada.

Herberg, Will. 1955. Protestant-Catholic-Jew. Garden City: Doubleday.

Hicks, John. 1949. The Legacy of Populism in the Western Middle West. *Agricultural History* 23:225–239.

Higham, John. 1982. Current Trends in the Study of Ethnicity in the United States. *Journal of American Ethnic History* 2(1):5–15.

Holmquist, June D., ed. 1981. They Chose Minnesota: A Survey of the States Ethnic Groups. Minneapolis: Minneapolis Historical Society.

Holt, Michael F. 1973. The Politics of Impatience: The Origins of Know Nothingism. *Journal of American History* 60:309–331.

Hopkins, Martin Keith. 1975. Regnier Families in North America. Atchison: Privately printed.

Horobin, J. W. 1957. Adjustment and Assimilation. *Sociological Review* 5:230–254.

Houde, Mary J., and Jack Klasey. 1968. Of the People: A Popular History of Kankakee County. Kankakee: Kankakee County Board of Supervisors.

Hudman, Lloyd E., and Richard H. Jackson. 1992. Mormon Pilgrimage and Tourism. *Annals of Tourism Research* 19:107–121.

Hughes, Everett. 1943. French Canada in Transition. Chicago: University of Chicago Press.

Hughes, John, and John Breckenridge. 1867. A Discussion of the Question Is the Roman Catholic Religion Inimical to Civil or Religious Liberty and of the Question Is the Presbyterian Religion Inimical to Civil or Religious Liberty. Baltimore: John Murphy.

Ignatiev, Noel. 1995. How the Irish Became White. New York: Routledge.

Illinois Central Railroad Company. 1856. Illinois Central Railroad Company Offers for Sale. New York: John W. Amerman.

Iroquois County Historical Society. 1985. Iroquois County History. Watseka: Iroquois County Historical Society.

Jackowski, Antoni, and Valene Smith. 1992. Polish Pilgrim Tourists. *Annals of Tourism Research* 19:92–106.

Jacobson, Matthew Fry. 1998. Whiteness of a Different Color: European Immigrants and the Alchemy of Race. Cambridge, MA: Harvard University Press.

Janssen, Susan, and Robert M. Houser. 1981. Religion, Socialization, and Fertility. *Demography* 18:511–528.

Jensen, Richard. 1971. The Winning of the Midwest: Social and Political Conflict, 1888–1896. Chicago: University of Chicago Press.

Jiménez, Tomás. 2010. Replenished Ethnicity: Mexican Americans, Immigration, and Identity. Berkeley: University of California Press.

Johnson, Doyle Paul. 1979. Dilemmas of Charismatic Leadership: The Case of the People's Temple. *Sociological Analysis* 40:315–323.

Kamphoefner, Walter. 1987. The Westfalians: From Germany to Missouri. Princeton: Princeton University Press.

Kankakee County Bicentennial Commission. 1976. The Saga of St. Anne. Mimeographed booklet.

Kantowicz, Edward R. 1982. A Fragment of French Canada on the Illinois Prairies. *Journal of the Illinois State Historical Society* 75:263–276.

Kasinitz, Philip, John Mollenkopf, Mary Waters, and Jennifer Holdaway. 2008. Inheriting the City: The Children of Immigrants Come of Age. Cambridge, MA: Harvard University Press.

Kasinitz, Philip, John H. Mollenkopf, and Mary C. Waters. 2004. Becoming New Yorkers: Ethnographies of the New Second Generation. New York: Russell Sage Foundation.

Kemper, Steven. 1991. The Presence of the Past: Chronicles, Politics, and Culture in Sinhala Life. Ithaca: Cornell University Press.

Kenna, Margaret E. 1977. Greek Urban Migrants and Their Rural Patron Saint. *Ethnic Studies* 1:14–23.

———. 1992. Mattresses and Migrants: A Patron Saint's Festival on a Small Greek Island over Two Centuries. *In* Boissevain 1992, pp. 155–172.

Kennedy, Joseph C. G. 1864. Compilation of the Population of the United States in 1860. Washington, DC: GPO.

Klasey, Jack, ed. 1976. Grand Prairie. Kankakee County Educational Service Region.

Knobel, Dale T. 1996. "America for the Americans": The Nativist Movement in the United States. New York: Twayne.

Kobrin, Frances E., and Calvin Goldscheider. 1978. The Ethnic Factor in Family Structure and Mobility. Cambridge, MA: Ballinger.

Kselman, Thomas. 1989. Comment. Religious Devotions: Roman Catholic Pilgrimage in North America. Social Science History Association, Washington, DC, November 17–20.

Kselman, Thomas A., and Steven Avella. 1986. Marian Piety and the Cold War in the United States. *Catholic Historical Review* 72:403–424.

Kurokawa, Minako, ed. 1970. Minority Responses. New York: Random House.

Kurtz, Donald. 1982. The Virgin of Guadalupe and the Politics of Becoming Human. *Journal of Anthropological Research* 38:194–210.

La Comité Permanent de la Survivance Française en Amérique [The permanent committee of French survival in America]. 1945. La Vocation de la Race Française en Amérique du Nord [The vocation of the French race in North America]. Québec.

Laidig, G. L., W. W. Schutjer, and C. S. Stokes. 1981. Agricultural Variation and Human Fertility in Antebellum Pennsylvania. *Journal of Family History* 6:195–204.

Lamaire, Nicole. 1973. Kinship and Inheritance Patterns in a French Newfoundland Village. *In* Gerald Gold and M. A. Tremblay, eds., Communities and Culture in French Canada. Toronto: Holt, Rinehart, and Winston.

Lamarre, Jean. 2003. The French Canadians of Michigan: Their Contribution to the Development of the Saginaw Valley and the Keweenam Peninsula, 1840–1914. Detroit: Wayne State University Press.

Langness, L. L. 1965. The Life History in Anthropological Science. New York: Holt, Rinehart, and Winston.

Laslett, Barbara. 1975. Household Structure on an American Frontier: Los Angeles, California, in 1850. *American Journal of Sociology* 81:109–127.

Laurent, Francis W. 1959. The Business of a Trial Court. Madison: University of Wisconsin Press.

Laverdure, Paul. 1987. Charles Chiniquy: The Making of an Anti-Catholic Crusader. *CCHA, Historical Studies* 54:39–56.

Lavoie, Yolande. 1972. L'Émigration des Canadiens aux États-Unis avant 1930: Mesure du Phénomène [Emigration of Canadians to the United States before 1930: Measurement of the phenomenon]. Montréal: Presses Universitaires.

———. 1979. L'Émigration des Québécois aux États-Unis de 1840 à 1930 [Emigration of Quebecois to the United States from 1840 to 1930]. Québec: Éditeur Official du Québec.

Leasure, J. William. 1982. La Baisse de la Fécondité aux États-Unis de 1800 à 1860 [The decline in fertility in the United States from 1800 to 1860]. *Population* 37:607–622.

LeBlanc, Robert. 1988. A French-Canadian Education and the Persistence of La Franco-Americanie. *Journal of Cultural Geography* 8(2):49–64.

Legried, Ann M., and David Ward. 1982. Religious Schism and the Development of Rural Immigrant Communities: Norwegian Lutherans in Western Wisconsin. *Upper Midwest History* 2:13–29.

Levine, Bruce. 2001. Conservatism, Nativism and Slavery: Thomas R. Whitney and the Origins of the Know Nothing Party. *Journal of American History* 88:455–488.

Lieberson, Stanley. 1963. Ethnic Patterns in American Cities. New York: Free Press.

Lighthall, Anne Dean. Papers. Department of Rare Books and Special Collections, McGill University Libraries, Quebec.

Lincoln, Bruce. 1989. Discourse and the Construction of Society. Oxford: Oxford University Press.

Linde, Charlotte. 1993. Life Stories: The Creation of Coherence. New York: Oxford University Press.

Lindholm, Charles. 1990. Charisma. Oxford: Basil Blackwell.

Little, Jack I. 1989. Nationalism, Capitalism, and Colonization in Nineteenth-Century Quebec: The Upper St. Francis District. Montreal: McGill-Queens University Press.

———. 1991. Crofters and Habitants: Settler Society, Economy, and Culture in a Quebec Township, 1848–1881. Montreal: McGill-Queen's University Press.

———. 1992. Ethnicity, Family Structure, and Seasonal Labor Strategies on Quebec's Appalachian Frontier, 1852–1881. *Journal of Family History* 17:289–302.

———. 2012. L'Établissement des Canadiens Français dans les Cantons de L'Est avant 1861 [The establishment of French Canadians in the eastern townships before 1861]. *In* Frenette, Rivard, and St.-Hilaire 2012, pp. 89–94.

Lottinville, Armand J. 1942. The Lottinville Family. Washington, DC: Murray and Heister.

Louder, Dean R., and Eric Waddell, eds. 1983. Du Continent Perdue à l'Archipel Retrouvé: Le Québec et l'Amérique Français [From a lost continent to a rediscovered archipelago: Quebec and French America]. Québec: Presses de l'Université Laval.

———. 1993. French America: Mobility, Identity and Minority Experience across the Continent. Baton Rouge: Louisiana State University Press.

———. 2008. Franco-Amérique. Sillery: Septentrion.

Louder, Dean R., Christian Morissonneau, and Eric Waddell. 1993. Introduction. *In* Louder and Waddell 1993, pp. 1–14.

Lougheed, Richard. 2008. The Controversial Conversion of Charles Chiniquy. Toronto: Clements Academic.

Luebke, Frederick C., ed. 1980. Ethnicity on the Great Plains. Lincoln: University of Nebraska Press.

Mach, Zdzislaw. 1993. Symbols, Conflict, and Identity: Essays in Political Anthropology. Albany: State University of New York Press.

MacKinnon, Mary, and Daniel Parent. 2005. Resisting the Melting Pot: The Long-Term Impact of Maintaining Identity for Franco-Americans in New England. CIRPEE Working Paper, No. 05–17. http://papers.ssrn.com/sol3/papers.cfm?abstract_id=739627, accessed April 2013.

MacLennan, Hugh. 1986[1945]. Two Solitudes. Toronto: Macmillan Paperbacks.

Margolis, Maxine. 1995. Transnationalism and Popular Culture: The Case of Brazilian Immigrants in the United States. *Journal of Popular Culture* 29:29–41.

Marshall, Douglas G. 1950. The Decline in Farm Family Fertility and Its Relationship to Nationality and Religious Background. *Rural Sociology* 20:42–49.

Mathias, Elizabeth, and Angelamaria Varesano. 1978. The Dynamics of Religious Reactivation: A Study of a Charismatic Missionary to Southern Italians in the United States. *Ethnicity* 5:301–310.

May, Elaine Tyler. 1980. Great Expectations: Marriage and Divorce in Post-Victorian America. Chicago: University of Chicago Press.

Maynes, Mary Jo. 1992. Autobiography and Class Formation in Nineteenth-Century Europe. *Social Science History* 16(3):517–537.

Maynes, Mary Jo, Jennifer L. Pierce, and Barbara Laslett. 2008. Telling Stories: The Use of Personal Narratives in the Social Sciences and History. Ithaca: Cornell University Press.

McCaa, Robert. 1993. Ethnic Intermarriage and Gender in New York City. *Journal of Interdisciplinary History* 24:207–231.

McCormick Theological Seminary. Chicago Presbytery, Chicago.

McDonald, Maryon. 1989. "We Are Not French!" Language, Culture, and Identity in Brittany. London: Routledge.

McFarland, Daniel A. 2004. Resistance as a Social Drama: A Study of Change-Oriented Encounters. *American Journal of Sociology* 109:1249–1318.

McGreevy, John T. 1996. Parish Boundaries: The Catholic Encounter with Race in the Twentieth-Century Urban North. Chicago: University of Chicago Press.

McKevitt, Christopher. 1991. San Giovanni Rotondo and the Shrine of Padre Pio. *In* Eade and Sallnow 1991, pp. 77–97.

McLoughlin, William. 1978. Revivals, Awakenings, and Reform: An Essay on Religion and Social Change in America, 1607–1977. Chicago: University of Chicago Press.

McQuillan, D. Aidan. 1975. Adaptation of Three Immigrant Groups to Farming in Central Kansas, 1875–1925. Unpublished Ph.D. dissertation, Department of Geography, University of Wisconsin.

———. 1978. "Farm Size and Work Ethic: Measuring the Success of Immigrant Farmers on the American Grasslands, 1875–1925. *Journal of Historical Geography* 4:57–76.

———. 1990. Prevailing over Time: Ethnic Adjustment on the Kansas Prairies, 1875–1925. Lincoln: University of Nebraska Press.

———. 1993. French Canadian Communities in the Upper Midwest during the Nineteenth Century. *In* Louder and Waddell 1993, pp. 117–142.

McQuillan, Kevin. 2004. When Does Religion Influence Fertility? *Population and Development Review* 30:25–56.

Meier, Norma. 1980a. St. John the Baptist Catholic Church, Record, Book One, 1856–1879. Transcription and compilation. Owensboro: McDowell.

Merry, Sally Engle. 1990. Getting Justice and Getting Even: Legal Consciousness among Working-Class Americans. Chicago: University of Chicago Press.

Metz, Gary. 1981. Jack Chick's Anti-Catholic Alberto Comic Book Is Exposed as a Fraud. *Christianity Today*, March 13, pp. 50–53.

Miller, Kerby A. 1990. Class, Culture, and Immigrant Group Identity in the United States: The Case of Irish-American Ethnicity. *In* Yans-McLaughlin 1990, pp. 96–129.

Miller, Randall M., and Thomas D. Marzik, eds. 1977. Immigrants and Religion in Urban America. Philadelphia: Temple University Press.

Miner, Horace. 1939[1967]. St. Denis: A French Canadian Parish. Chicago: University of Chicago Press.

Mitchell, J. Clyde. 1956. The Kalela Dance. Manchester: Manchester University Press.

Mitchell, Timothy. 1990. Passional Culture: Emotion, Religion, and Society in Southern Spain. Philadelphia: University of Pennsylvania Press.

Modell, John. 1971. Family and Fertility on the Indiana Frontier, 1820. *American Quarterly* 23:615–634.

Mol, Hans J. 1976. Identity and the Sacred: A Sketch for a New Social-Scientific Theory of Religion: New York: Free Press.

———. 1983. Meaning and Place: An Introduction to the Social Scientific Study of Religion. New York: Pilgrim Press.

Morehouse, Francis. 1928. Canadian Migration in the Forties. *Canadian Historical Review* 9(4):309–329.

Morin, Joseph L. 1900. Prefatory Note. *In* Chiniquy 1900, 3–4.

Morinis, Alan. 1984. Pilgrimage in the Hindu Tradition. Delhi: Oxford University Press.

———, ed. 1992. Sacred Journeys: The Anthropology of Pilgrimage. Westport: Greenwood Press.

Morowska, Ewa. 1990. The Sociology and Historiography of Immigration. *In* Yans-McLaughlin 1990, pp. 187–238.

Mosher, William, and Gerry Hendenshot. 1984. Religion and Fertility: A Replication. *Demography* 21:185–191.

Mullin, Robert Bruce. 1996. Miracles and the Modern Religious Imagination. New Haven: Yale University Press.

Munch, Peter A. 1979. Authority and Freedom: Controversy in Norwegian-American Congregations. *Norwegian-American Studies* 28:3–34.

Murphy, Michael Dean. 1994. Class, Community, and Costume in an Andalusian Pilgrimage. *Anthropological Quarterly* 67:49–61.

Nader, Laura. 1980. Little Injustices: Laura Nader Looks at the Law. Odyssey Series. Watertown, MA: Documentary Educational Resources.

Nash, Manning. 1989. The Cauldron of Ethnicity. Chicago: University of Chicago Press.

Nelson, William E. 1981. Dispute and Conflict Resolution in Plymouth County, Massachusetts 1725–1825. Chapel Hill: University of North Carolina Press.

Neville, Gwen Kennedy. 1987. Rituals of Reunion in American Protestant Culture. Oxford: Oxford University Press.

Nida, E. A. 1958. The Relationship of Social Structure to the Problem of Evangelism in Latin America. *Practical Anthropology* 5:101–123.

Niebuhr, H. Richard. 1929. The Social Sources of Denominationalism. New York: Henry Holt.

Niehaus, Juliet Anne. 1984. Ethnic Formation and Transformation: The German-Catholics of Dubois County, Indiana 1838–1979. Ann Arbor: University Microfilms International.

Noel, Jan. 1990. Dry Patriotism: The Chiniquy Crusade. *Canadian Historical Review* 71:189–207.

Nolan, Mary Lee, and Sidney Nolan. 1992. Religious Sites as Tourism Attractions in Europe. *Annals of Tourism Research* 19:68–78.

Ochs, Elinor, and Lisa Capps. 1996. Narrating the Self. *Annual Review of Anthropology* 25:19–43.

Okamoto, Diane G. 2006. Institutional Panethnicity: Boundary Formation in Asian-American Organizing. *Social Forces* 85:1–25.

O'Neill, William L. 1967. Divorce in the Progressive Era. New Haven: Yale University Press.

Orsi, Robert A. 1985. The Madonna of 115th Street: Faith and Community in Italian Harlem, 1880–1950. New Haven: Yale University Press.

Ortner, Sherry. 1984. Theory in Anthropology since the Sixties. *Comparative Studies in Society and History* 26:128–166.

———. 1999. Thick Resistance: Death and the Cultural Construction of Agency in Himalayan Mountaineering. *In* Ortner, ed., The Fate of Culture: Geertz and Beyond. Pp. 136–163. Berkeley: University of California Press.

Ostergren, Robert C. 1981. Land and Family in Rural Immigrant Communities. *Annals of the Association of American Geographers* 71:400–411.

———. 1988. A Community Transplanted: The Trans-Atlantic Experience of Swedish Immigrant Settlement in the Upper Midwest, 1835–1915. Madison: University of Wisconsin Press.

Ouellet, Fernand. 1980. Economic and Social History of Quebec, 1760–1850. Ottawa: Institute of Canadian Studies, Carleton University.

Pagnini, Deanna, and S. Philip Morgan. 1990. Intermarriage and Social Distance among U.S. Immigrants at the Turn of the Century. *American Journal of Sociology* 96:405–432.

Paquin, Elzear. 1893. La Colonie Canadien-Français de Chicago [The French-Canadian colony of Chicago]. Chicago: Price.

Park, Robert E. 1930. Social Assimilation. *In* Edwin R. Seligman and Alvin Johnson, eds., Encyclopedia of Social Sciences, vol. 2. Pp. 281. New York: Macmillan.

Parker, James Hill. 1983. Ethnic Identity: The Case of French Americans. Washington, DC: University Press of America.

Patterson, Molly, and Kristen Renwick Monroe. 1998. Narrative in Political Science. *Annual Review of Political Science* 1:315–331.

Peacock, James L. 1988. Religion and Life History: An Exploration in Cultural Psychology. *In* Edward Bruner, ed., Text, Play and Story: The Construction and Reconstruction of Self and Society. Pp. 94–116. Prospect Heights: Waveland Press.

Pechilis, Karen. 1992. To Pilgrimage It. *Journal of Ritual Studies* 6:59–91.

Peel, J. D. Y. 1995. For Who Hath Despised the Day of Small Things? Missionary Narratives and Historical Anthropology. *Comparative Studies in Society and History* 37:581–607.

Phillips, Roderick. 1988. Putting Asunder: A History of Divorce in Western Society. Cambridge: Cambridge University Press.

Piddington, Ralph. 1965. The Kinship Network among French Canadians. *In* Piddington, ed., Kinship and Geographical Mobility. Pp. 145–165. Leiden: E. J. Brill.

———. 1976. A Study of French Canadian Kinship. *In* K. Ishwaran, ed., The Canadian Family. Pp. 555–579. Toronto: Holt, Rinehart, and Winston.

Pope, Barbara Corrado. 1989. Emile Zola's Lourdes: Land of Healing and Rupture. *Literature and Medicine* 8:22–35.

Portes, Alejandro, and Ruben Rumbaut. 2001. Legacies: The Story of the Immigrant Second Generation. Berkeley: University of California Press.

Portes, Alejandro, and Min Zhou. 1993. The New Second Generation; Segmented Assimilation and Its Variants among Post-1965 Immigrant Youth. *Annals of the American Academy of Political and Social Science* 530:74–98.

Potts, John. 2009. A History of Charisma. New York: Palgrave-Macmillan.

Preston, James J. 1990. The Rediscovery of America: Pilgrimage in the Promised Land. *Geographia Religionum* 5:15–26.

———. 1992. Spiritual Magnetism: An Organizing Principle for the Study of Pilgrimage. *In* Morinis 1992, pp. 31–46.

Price, W. J. 1959. Aux Origines d'un Schisme [At the origins of a schism]. *Revue d'Histoire de l'Amérique Française* 12:517–534.

———. 1960. Aux Origines d'un Schisme [At the origins of a schism]. *Revue d'Histoire de l'Amérique Française* 13:45–78.

Prorock, Carolyn V. 1997. Becoming a Place of Pilgrimage: An Eliadean Interpretation of the Miracle at Ambridge, Pennsylvania. *In* Robert H. Stoddard and Alan Morinis, eds., Sacred Places, Sacred Spaces: The Geography of Pilgrimages. Pp. 117–130. Baton Rouge: Louisiana State University.

Prude, Jonathan. 1985. Town-Factory Conflicts in Antebellum Rural Massachusetts. *In* Hahn and Prude 1985, pp. 71–102.

Quintal, Claire, ed. 1996. Steeples and Smokestacks: A Collection of Essays on the Franco-American Experience in New England. Worcester: Institut Français, Assumption College.

Rambo, Lewis R. 1982. Current Research on Religious Conversion. *Religious Studies Review* 8:146–159.

Rameau de Saint-Père, E. 1859. La France aux Colonies: études sur le développement de la race française hors de l'Europe [France in the colonies: Studies of the development of the French race outside Europe]. Paris: A. Jouby.

Ramirez, Bruno. 2001. Crossing the 49th Parallel: Migration from Canada to the United States, 1900–1930. Ithaca: Cornell University Press.

———. 2006. Migrants Canadiens-français dan l'Espace Nord-Américain 1830–1930: Une Synthèse Critique [French-Canadian migrants in North American space: A critical synthesis]. *In* Wien, Vidal, and Frenette 2006, pp. 267–281.

Redfield, Robert, Ralph Linton, and Melville Herskovits. 1936. Memorandum for the Study of Acculturation. *American Anthropologist* 38:149–152.

Reina, Ruben, and Norman B. Schwartz. 1974. The Structural Context of Religious Conversion in Peten, Guatemala: Status, Community, and Multicommunity. *American Ethnologist* 1:157–191.

Rice, John G. 1977. The Role of Culture and Community in Frontier Prairie Farming. *Journal of Historical Geography* 3:155–175.

Richard, Adrian. 1975. The Village: A Story of Bourbonnais. Bourbonnais: Centennial Committee of the Village of Bourbonnais.

Richard, Mark Paul. 2008. Loyal but French: The Negotiation of Identity by French-Canadian Descendants in the United States: East Lansing: Michigan State University.

———. 2009. "This Is Not a Catholic Nation": The Ku Klux Klan Confronts Franco-Americans in Maine. *New England Quarterly* 82:285–303.

Riessman, Catherine Kohler. 1993. Narrative Analysis. Newbury Park: Sage.

Rinschede, Gisbert. 1990. Catholic Pilgrimage Places in the United States. *Geographia Religionum* 5:63–135.

———. 1992. Forms of Religious Tourism. *Annals of Tourism Research* 19:51–67.

———. 1994. Catholic Pilgrimage Centers in Quebec, Canada. *Geographia Religionum* 8:169–192.

Ritter, W. Stuart. 1970. The Lewiston Model Neighborhood Area: A Comprehensive Community Planning Survey. Lewiston: Lewiston Model City Committee.

Rivard, E. L. 1906. Bourbonnais. *In* Newton Bateman, Paul Selby, William Kenaga, and George Letourneau, eds., Historical Encyclopedia of Illinois and a History of Kankakee County. Pp. 656–658. Chicago: Middle West.

Roberts, Simon. 1983. The Study of Dispute: Anthropological Perspectives. *In* John Bossy, ed., Disputes and Settlements: Law and Human Relations in the West. Pp. 1–24. Cambridge: Cambridge University Press.

Roby, Yves. 1996a. The Economic Evolution of Quebec and the Emigrant (1850–1929). I*n* Quintal 1996, pp. 7–19.

———. 1996b. From Franco-Americans to Americans of French-Canadian Origin or Franco-Americanism, Past and Present. *In* Quintal 1996, pp. 609–625.

———. 1996c. Franco-Americans and the Catholic Hierarchy. *In* Quintal 1996, pp. 201–206.

———. 2004. The Franco-Americans of New England: Dreams and Realities. Montreal: McGill-Queen's University Press.

———. 2006. Les Franco-Américains de la Nouvelle-Angleterre: un regard sur les sources imprimées d'avant 1930 [The Franco-Americans of New England: An examination of printed sources before 1930]. *In* Wien, Vidal and Frenette 2006, pp. 157–173.

———. 2012. La Paroisse et la Survivance [The Parish and survivance]. *In* Frenette, Rivard, and St.-Hilaire 2012, pp. 185–193.

Roby, Yves, and Yves Frenette. 2012. L'Émigration Canadienne-Française vers la Nouvelle-Angleterre, 1840–1930 [French-Canadian Emigration to New England, 1840–1930]. *In* Frenette, Rivard, and St.-Hilaire 2012, pp. 123–132.

Roediger, David K. 2005. Working toward Whiteness: How America's Immigrants Became White. New York: Basic Books.

Roney, John B. 1996. The Inside of History: Jean Henri Merle d'Aubigné and Romantic Historiography. Westport: Greenwood Press.

Rosaldo, Renato. 1973. Review of Chicanos: Social and Psychological Perspectives by Nathanial Wagner and Marsha Haug. *American Anthropologist* 75:1003–1004.

———. 1993. Culture and Truth: The Remaking of Social Analysis. Boston: Beacon Press.

Ross, G. Alexander. 1989. Delaying the Fertility Decline: German Women in Saginaw County, Michigan, 1850–1880. *Journal of Family History* 14:157–170.

Ross, Marc Howard. 1993. The Culture of Conflict: Interpretations and Interests in Comparative Perspective. New Haven: Yale University Press.

Royce, Anya Peterson. 1982. Ethnic Identity: Strategies of Diversity. Bloomington: Indiana University Press.

Rumbaut, Ruben, and Alejandro Portes, eds. Ethnicities: Children of Immigrants in America. Berkeley: University of California Press.

Ryder, Norman B., and Charles F. Westoff. 1971. Reproduction in the United States. Princeton: Princeton University Press.

St. James Episcopal Cathedral. Archives. Chicago.

St. John, Graham, ed. 2008. Victor Turner and Contemporary Cultural Performance. New York: Bergahn Books.

Salamon, Sonya. 1980. Ethnic Differences in Farm Family Land Transfers. *Rural Sociology* 45:290–308.

———. 1992. Prairie Patrimony: Family, Farming, and Community in the Midwest. Chapel Hill: University of North Carolina Press.

Sallnow, Michael J. 1981. Communitas Reconsidered: The Society of an Andean Pilgrimage. *Man* 16:163–182.

———. 1987. Pilgrims of the Andes: Regional Cults in Cuzco. Washington, DC: Smithsonian Institution Press.

Salvador, Mari Lyn. 1987. Food for the Holy Ghost: Ritual Exchange in Azorean Festivals. *In* Alessandro Falassi, ed., Time Out of Time: Essays on the Festival. Pp. 244–260. Albuquerque: University of New Mexico Press.

Salyer, Lucy E. 1995. Laws Harsh as Tigers: Chinese Immigrants and the Shaping of Modern Immigration Law. Chapel Hill: University of North Carolina Press.

Sandburg, Carl. 1926. Abraham Lincoln—The Prairie Years. New York: Harcourt and Brace.

Sanders, John. 1974. Beauty and Charisma. *Comparative Studies in Society and History* 16:182–186.

Savage, James P., Jr. 1964. Do-It-Yourself Books for Illinois Immigrants. *Journal of the Illinois State Historical Society* 57:30–48.

Savard, Pierre. 1967. La Vie du Clergé Québécois au XIX Siècle [The life of Quebec clergy in the nineteenth century]. *Recherches Sociographiques* 8:259–273.

Schapiro, Morton O. 1982. Land Availability and Fertility in the United States, 1760–1870. *Journal of Economic History* 42:577–600.

Schemerhorn, R. A. 1970. Comparative Ethnic Relations. New York: Random House.

Schneider, Jo Anne. 1990. Defining Boundaries, Creating Contacts: Puerto Rican and Polish Presentation of Group Identity through Ethnic Parades. *Journal of Ethnic Studies* 18:33–57.

Schweitzer, Arthur. 1974. Theory and Political Charisma. *Comparative Studies in Society and History* 16:150–181.

Sewell, William H., Jr. 1992. Introduction: Narratives and Social Identities. *Social Science History* 16:479–488.

Shea, John Gilmary. 1892. A History of the Catholic Church. New York: John G. Shea.

Sherman, Edwin A. 1893. The Engineer Corps of Hell; or Rome's Sappers and Miners: Containing the Tactics of the "Militia of the Pope," of the Secret Manual of the Jesuits. Internet Archive. http://www.archive.org/stream/engineercorpsofhoosher/engineercorpsofhoosher_djvu.txt.

Shils, Edward. 1965. Charisma, Order, and Status. *American Sociological Review* 30:199–213.

Sider, Gerald. 1986. Culture and Class in Anthropology and History: A Newfoundland Illustration. Cambridge: Cambridge University Press.

Silverman, Marilyn. 1989. A Laboring Man's Daughter: Constructing "Respectability" in South Kilkenny. *In* Chris Curtin and Thomas M. Wilson, eds.,

Ireland from Below: Social Change and Local Communities, Pp. 109–127. Galway: Galway University Press.

———. 1995. The "Inhabitants" v. the "Sovereign": A Historical Ethnography of the Making of the "Middle Class" in an Irish Corporate Borough, 1840–41. *In* Pat Caplan, ed., Understanding Disputes: The Politics of Argument. Pp. 111-136. Oxford: Berg.

Silverman, Marilyn, and P. H. Gulliver. 1992. Approaching the Past: Historical Anthropology through Irish Case Studies. New York: Columbia University Press.

Silverman, Sydel. 1979. On the Uses of History in Anthropology: The Palio of Siena. *American Ethnologist* 6:413–436.

———. 1986. Anthropology and History: Understanding the Boundaries. *Historical Methods* 19:123–126.

Sinclair, Karen. 1992. Mission to Waitangi: A Maori Pilgrimage. *In* Morinis 1992, pp. 233–256.

Smith, Daniel Scott. 1987. Early Fertility Decline in America: A Problem in Family History. *Journal of Family History* 12:73–84.

Smith, Jonathan Z. 1982. Imagining Religion: From Babylon to Jonestown. Chicago: University of Chicago Press.

Smith, Sydney F. 1908. Pastor Chiniquy: An Examination of His *Fifty Years in the Church of Rome*. London. Catholic Truth Society. https://archive.org/details/pastorchiniquyex00smit.

Smith, Timothy L. 1980[1957]. Revivalism and Social Reform: American Protestantism on the Eve of the Civil War. Baltimore: Johns Hopkins University Press.

Social Science Research Council. 1954. Acculturation: An Exploratory Formulation. *American Anthropologist* 56:973–1002.

Sorrell, Richard. 1981. The Survivance of French Canadians in New England 1865–1930: History, Geography, and Demography as Destiny. *Ethnic and Racial Studies* 4:91–109.

Souvenir Program Booklet of the St. Anne Community Centennial, 1950. The Heritage of St. Anne, St Anne, IL.

Stahl, Ann Brower. 2001. Making History in Banda: Anthropological Visions of Africa's Past. Cambridge: Cambridge University Press.

Staples, Moses W. 1859. Report of the Committee at Kankakee, Illinois on the French Colony at St. Anne under the Ministry of Reverend C. Chiniquy Made to the Committee at New York in December 1859. American and Foreign Christian Union.

Starr, June, and Jane F. Collier. 1989. History and Power in the Study of Law: New Directions in Legal Anthropology. Ithaca: Cornell University Press.

Steinmetz, George. 1992. Reflections on the Role of Social Narratives in Working-Class Formation: Narrative Theory in the Social Sciences. *Social Science History* 16:489–516.

Stern, Mark. 1983. Differential Fertility in Rural Erie County, New York, 1855. *Journal of Social History* 16:49–63.

Stewart, Doty C. 1995. How Many Frenchmen Does It Take to . . . ? *Thought and Action* 11:85–104.

Stewart, Gordon. 1974. Charisma and Integration: An Eighteenth-Century North American Case. *Comparative Studies in Society and History* 16:138–149.

Stritch, Alfred G. 1944. Trusteeism in the Old Northwest, 1800–1850. *Canadian Historical Review* 30:155–164.

Stutje, Jan Willem, ed. 2012a. Charismatic Leadership and Social Movements: The Revolutionary Power of Ordinary Men and Women. Oxford: Bergahn Books.

———. 2012b. Introduction; Historiographical and Theoretical Aspects of Weber's Concept of Charismatic Leadership. *In* Stutje, ed., Charismatic Leadership and Social Movements: The Revolutionary Power of Ordinary Men and Women. Pp. 1–20. Oxford: Bergahn Books.

Swiderski, Richard. 1986. Voices: An Anthropologist's Dialogue with an Italian-American Festival. London, Ontario: Center for Social and Humanistic Studies.

Swierenga, Robert. 1977. Ethnicity in Historical Perspective. *Social Science* 52:31–44.

———. 1981. A Denominational Schism from a Behavioral Perspective: The 1857 Dutch Reformed Separation. *Reformed Review* 34:172–185.

———, ed. 1985. The Dutch in America: Immigration, Settlement, and Cultural Change. New Brunswick: Rutgers University Press.

———. 1989. The Settlement of the Old Northwest: Ethnic Pluralism in a Featureless Plain. *Journal of the Early Republic* 9:73–105.

Tambiah, Stanley J. 1984. The Buddhist Saints of the Forest and the Cult of Amulets. Cambridge: Cambridge University Press.

Tassé, Joseph. 1874. Les Canadiens de l'Ouest [The Canadians of the West]. *Revue Canadienne* 11:467–474.

Taves, Ann. 1986. The Household of Faith: Roman Catholic Devotions in Mid-Nineteenth-Century America. Notre Dame: University of Notre Dame Press.

Taylor, Lawrence. 1983. Dutchmen on the Bay: The Ethnohistory of a Contractual Community. Philadelphia: University of Pennsylvania Press.

Tentler, Leslie Woodcock. 1983. Who Is the Church? Conflict in a Polish Immigrant Parish in Late Nineteenth-Century Detroit. *Comparative Studies in Society and History* 25:247–258.

Tepperman, Lorne. 1974. Ethnic Variations in Marriage and Fertility: Canada 1871. *Canadian Review of Sociology and Anthropology* 11:324–343.

Teske, Raymond H. C., Jr., and Bardin H. Nelson. Acculturation and Assimilation: A Clarification. *American Ethnologist* 1:351–367.

Tétu, Henri. 1898. Histoire des Familles Tétu, Bonenfant, Dionne, et Perrault [History of the families of Tetu, Benenfant, Dionne, and Perrault]. Quebec: Dussault and Proulx.

Thernstrom, Stephen. 1967. Urbanization, Migration, and Social Mobility in Late Nineteenth-Century America. *In* Barton J. Bernstein, ed., Towards a New Past: Dissenting Essays in American History. Pp. 158–175. New York: Vintage Books.

Thompson, Joseph. 1920. The Archdiocese of Chicago. Des Plaines: St. Mary's Training School Press.

Thornton, Frances B. 1954. Catholic Shrines in the United States and Canada. New York: Wilfrid Funk.

Thornton, W. Philip. 1984. Resocialization: Roman Catholics Becoming Protestants in Colombia, South America. *Anthropological Quarterly* 57:28–37.

Tilly, Charles. 1990. Transplanted Networks. *In* Yans-McLaughlin 1990, pp. 79–95.

Titiev, Mischa. 1960. A Fresh Approach to the Problem of Magic and Religion. *Southwestern Journal of Anthropology* 16:292–298.

Tolnay, Stewart E., Stephen N. Graham, and Avery M. Guest. 1982. Own-Child Estimates of U.S. White Fertility, 1886–1899. *Historical Methods* 15:127–138.

Trexler, Richard C. 1985. Persons in Groups: Social Behavior as Identity Formation in Medieval and Renaissance Europe. Vol. 36. Binghamton: Medieval and Renaissance Texts and Studies.

Trudel, Marcel. 1955. Chiniquy. Trois-Rivières: Éditions du Bien Public.

Truesdell, L. E. 1943. The Canadian Born in the United States. Toronto: Ryerson Press.

Tucker, Robert. 1968. The Theory of Charismatic Leadership. *Daedalus* 97:731–756.

Turner, Paul R. 1979. Religious Conversion and Community Development. *Journal for the Scientific Study of Religion* 18:252–260.

Turner, Victor. 1957. Schism and Continuity in an African Society. Manchester: Manchester University Press.

———. 1969. The Ritual Process. Chicago: Aldine.

———. 1973. The Center Out There: Pilgrim's Goal. *History of Religions* 12:191–230.

———. 1974. Dramas, Fields, and Metaphors: Symbolic Action in Human Society. Ithaca: Cornell University Press.

———. 1981. Social Dramas and Stories about Them. *In* W. J. T. Mitchell, ed., On Narrative. Pp. 137–164. Chicago: University of Chicago Press.

———. 1982. From Ritual to Theatre: The Human Seriousness of Play. New York: Performing Arts Journal.

———. 1986. Dewey, Dilthey, and Drama: An Essay in the Anthropology of Experience. *In* Turner and Edward M. Bruner, eds., The Anthropology of Experience. Pp. 33–44. Urbana: University of Illinois Press.

Turner, Victor, and Edith Turner. 1978. Image and Pilgrimage in Christian Culture: Anthropological Perspectives. New York: Columbia University Press.

———. 1982. Religious Celebrations. *In* V. Turner, ed., Celebration: Studies in Festivity and Ritual. Pp. 201–219. Washington, DC: Smithsonian Institution Press.

Underwood, Kenneth Wilson. 1957. Protestant and Catholic: Religious and Social Interaction in an Industrial Community. Boston: Beacon Press.

U.S. Census Office. 1853. The Seventh Census of the United States: 1850. Washington, DC: Robert Armstrong.

U.S. Federal Manuscript Census. 1860. Kankakee and Iroquois Counties.

Van der Leeuw, Gerardus. 1961. Religion in Essence and Manifestation. New York: Harper and Row.

Verrips, Jojeda. 1973. The Preacher and the Farmers: The Church as a Political Arena in a Dutch Community. *American Anthropologist* 75:852–867.

Vicero, Ralph Dominic. 1968. Immigration of French Canadians to New England, 1840–1900: A Geographic Analysis. Unpublished Ph.D. dissertation, Department of Geography, University of Wisconsin.

Vidal, Cécile. 2006. Le Pays des Illinois, six village français au Coeur de l'Amérique du Nord, 1699–1765 [Illinois country, six French villages at the heart of North America, 1699–1765]. *In* Wien, Vidal, and Frenette 2006, pp. 125–138.

———. 2012. Le Pays des Illinois, 1673–1818 [Illinois country, 1673–1818]. *In* Frenette, Rivard, and St.-Hilaire 2012, pp. 51–58.

Vincent, Joan. 1974. The Structuring of Ethnicity. *Human Organization* 33:375–379.

Vinovskis, Maris A. 1984. Historical Perspectives on Rural Development and Human Fertility in Nineteenth-Century America. *In* Wayne A. Schutjer and C. Shannon Stokes, eds., Rural Development and Human Fertility. Pp. 777–796. New York: Macmillan.

Vukonic, Boris. 1992. Medjugorje's Religion and Tourism Connection. *Annals of Tourism Research* 19:79–91.

Wade, Mason. 1950. The French Parish and Survivance in Nineteenth-Century New England. *Catholic Historical Review* 36:136–189.

———. 1968[1955]. The French Canadians, 1760–1967. Toronto: Macmillan.

Wallis, Roy. 1979. Salvation and Protest: Studies of Social and Religious Movements. New York: St. Martin's Press.

———. 1982a. Charisma, Commitment and Control in a New Religious Movement. *In* Wallis 1982b, pp. 73–140.

———. 1982b. Millennialism and Charisma. Belfast: Queen's University Press.

Wallman, Sandra. 1986. Ethnicity and the Boundary Process in Context. *In* John Rex and David Mason, eds., Theories of Race and Ethnic Relations. Pp. 226–245. Cambridge: Cambridge University Press.

Wallot, Jean-Pierre. 1971. Religion and French-Canadian Mores in the Early Nineteenth Century. *Canadian Historical Review* 52:51–91.

Warner, W. Lloyd. 1957. The Living and the Dead: The Study of the Symbolic Life of Americans. New Haven: Yale University Press.

———. 1963. Yankee City. Abridged ed. New Haven: Yale University Press.

Watson, Lawrence C., and Maria Barbara Watson-Franke. 1985. Interpreting Life Histories: An Anthropological Inquiry. New Brunswick: Rutgers University Press.

Weber, Donald. 1995. From Limen to Border: A Meditation on the Legacy of Victor Turner for American Cultural Studies. *American Quarterly* 47:525–536.

Weber, Max. 1947. The Theory of Social and Economic Organization. New York: Free Press.

———. 1978. Economy and Society. Berkeley: University of California Press.

Weil, François. 1989. Les Franco-Américains 1860–1980. Paris: Belin.

Welter, Barbara. 1987. From Maria Monk to Paul Blanshard: A Century of Protestant Anti-Catholicism. *In* Robert N. Bellah and Frederick E. Greenspahn, eds., Uncivil Religion: Interreligious Hostility in America. Pp. 43–71. New York: Crossroad.

Westoff, Charles F., and Elise F. Jones. 1979. The End of "Catholic" Fertility. *Demography* 16(2):209–217.

Wien, Thomas, Cécile Vidal, and Yves Frenette, eds. 2006. De Québec à L'Amérique Française: Histoire et Mémoire [From Quebec to French America: History and memory]. Québec: Presses de l'Université Laval.

Wierzbicki, Z. T. 1979. The Polish Schism in the United States. *Polish Sociological Bulletin* 4:47–56.

Wilcox, Jerry, and Hilda Golden. 1982. Prolific Immigrants and Dwindling Natives? Fertility Patterns in Western Massachusetts, 1850–1880. *Journal of Family History* 7:265–288.

Willems, Emilio. 1967. Followers of the New Faith: Culture Change and the Rise of Protestantism in Brazil and Chile. Nashville: Vanderbilt University Press.

Williams, J. Allen, David R. Johnson, and Miguel A. Carranza. 1980. Ethnic Assimilation and Pluralism in Nebraska. *In* Luebke 1980, pp. 210–229.

Williams, Linda B., and Basil G. Zimmer. 1990. The Changing Influence of Religion on U.S. Fertility: Evidence from Rhode Island. *Demography* 27:475–481.

Williams, Peter W. 1980. Popular Religion in America: Symbolic Change and the Modernization Process in Historical Perspective. Urbana: University of Illinois Press.

Willner, Ann Ruth. 1984. The Spellbinders: Charismatic Political Leadership. New Haven: Yale University Press.

Willner, Ann Ruth, and Dorothy Willner. 1965. The Rise and Role of Charismatic Leaders. *Annals of the American Academy of Political and Social Sciences* 358:77–88.

Wilson, Bryan R. 1975. The Noble Savages: The Primitive Origins of Charisma and Its Contemporary Survival. Berkeley: University of California Press.

Wilson, John. 1971. The Sociology of Schism. *In* Michael Hill, ed., A Sociological Yearbook of Religion in Britain, vol. 4. Pp. 1–20. London: SCM Press.

Wimmer, Andreas. 2007a. Ethnic and Racial Boundaries. *In* George Ritzer, ed., Blackwell Encyclopaedia of Sociology. Pp. 345–347. Oxford: Blackwell.

———. 2007b. How (Not) to Think about Ethnicity in Immigrant Societies: A Boundary-Making Perspective. ESRC Center on Migration, Policy and Society, Working Paper No 44. University of Oxford.

———. 2008a. Elementary Strategies of Ethnic Boundary Making. *Ethnic and Racial Studies* 31:1025–1055.

———. 2008b. The Making and Unmaking of Ethnic Boundaries: A Multi-Level Process Theory. *American Journal of Sociology* 113:970–1022.

———. 2009. Herder's Heritage and the Boundary-Making Approach: Studying Ethnicity in Immigrant Societies. *Sociological Theory* 27:244–270.

Winters, Donald L. 1990. The Economics of Midwestern Agriculture, 1865–1900. *In* Lou Ferleger, ed., Agriculture and National Development: Views on the Nineteenth Century. Pp. 75–96. Ames: Iowa State University Press.

Wirth, Louis. 1945. The Problem of Minority Groups. *In* Ralph Linton, ed., The Science of Man in the World Crisis. Pp. 347–372. New York: Columbia University Press.

Woodruff, S. A., Jr. 1950. A History of the Presbyterian Church in St. Anne, Illinois. Booklet. St. Anne Centennial Church Service, St. Anne, IL.

Worsley, Peter. 1968. The Trumpet Shall Sound: A Study of "Cargo" Cults in Melanesia. New York: Schocken Books.

Wright, Carroll D. 1881. 12th Annual Report of the Bureau of Statistics of Labor. Boston: Rand Avery.

———. 1882. The Canadian French in New England. Boston: Rand, Avery.

Yans-McLaughlin, Virginia, ed. 1990. Immigration Reconsidered: History, Sociology, and Politics. New York: Oxford University Press.

Yasuba, Yasukichi. 1962. Birth Rates of the White Population in the United States, 1800–1860. Baltimore: Johns Hopkins University Press.

Zeldin, Theodore. 1970. Conflicts in French Society: Anticlericalism, Education, and Morals in the Nineteenth Century. London: Allen and Unwin.

Zhou, Min 1997a. Segmented Assimilation; Issues, Controversies, and Recent Research on the New Second Generation. *International Migration Review* 31:975–1008.

———. 1997b. Growing Up American: The Challenge Confronting Immigrant Children and Children of Immigrants. *Annual Review of Sociology* 23:63–95.

Zunz, Olivier. 1985a. The Synthesis of Social Change: Reflections on American Social History. *In* Zunz, ed., Reliving the Past: The Worlds of Social History. Pp. 53–114. Chapel Hill: University of North Carolina Press.

———. 1985b. American History and the Changing Meaning of Assimilation. *American Journal of Ethnic History* 4:53–73.

Index

Italicized page numbers indicate figures, and an italicized *t* after a page number refers to a table.

CAROLINE B. BRETTELL is a University Distinguished Professor of Anthropology and the Ruth Collins Altshuler Director of the Dedman College Interdisciplinary Institute at Southern Methodist University. Her most recent books are *Civic Engagements: The Citizenship Practices of Indian and Vietnamese Immigrants* (coauthored with Deborah Reed-Danahay) and *Anthropological Conversations: Talking Culture across Disciplines.*